PSYCHOLOGY AND SELFHOOD IN THE SEGREGATED SOUTH

PSYCHOLOGY AND SELFHOOD
IN THE SEGREGATED SOUTH

ANNE C. ROSE

THE UNIVERSITY OF

NORTH CAROLINA PRESS

Chapel Hill

Designed by Courtney Leigh Baker and set in Whitman and
New Century Schoolbook by Tseng Information Systems, Inc.
Manufactured in the United States of America

The paper in this book meets the guidelines
for permanence and durability of the Committee
on Production Guidelines for Book Longevity
of the Council on Library Resources.

The University of North Carolina Press has been a
member of the Green Press Initiative since 2003.

Library of Congress Cataloging-in-Publication Data
Rose, Anne C., 1950–
Psychology and selfhood in the segregated South /
Anne C. Rose. — 1st ed.
p. cm.
Includes bibliographical references and index.
ISBN 978-0-8078-3281-3 (cloth : alk. paper)
1. Self—Southern States—History. 2. Identity
(Psychology)—Southern States—History. 3. Segregation—
Southern States—History. 4. Psychology (Study and
teaching)—Southern States—History. I. Title.
BF697.R654 2009
155.20975′09041—dc22
2008050483

13 12 11 10 09   5 4 3 2 1

FOR SCOTT AND JOHANNA,

AND ESPECIALLY

FOR DOLORES (1934–2008),

MY SHINING

LIGHT OF GOODNESS

CONTENTS

Acknowledgments | XI |

Introduction THE PURSUIT OF SELFHOOD
IN THE SEGREGATED SOUTH | 1 |

| 1 | HOW SOUTHERNERS THOUGHT ABOUT THE MIND
AND ITS ILLS BEFORE PSYCHOLOGY | 17 |

| 2 | THE PROMISE OF THE CHILD AND
THE LIMITS OF PROGRESS | 51 |

| 3 | THE TROUBLED PERSONALITIES
OF THE SOUTH | 87 |

| 4 | IN THE SOUTHERN BORDERLAND
OF MIND AND SOUL | 117 |

| 5 | THE SHORT LIFE OF SOUTHERN PSYCHOLOGY | 152 |

Epilogue THE SCIENCES OF THE SELF AS AN
INSTRUMENT OF SOUTHERN SELF-KNOWLEDGE | 185 |

Notes | 189 |

Index | 287 |

ILLUSTRATIONS

African American psychiatrists

at the Veterans Administration hospital,

Tuskegee, Alabama | 18 |

Jackson Davis of the General Education Board | 52 |

Hands of an African and ape compared | 64 |

Girls learning homemaking | 68–69 |

Charles S. Johnson of Fisk University | 96 |

Ernst Borinski and Tougaloo College

students | 128–29 |

ACKNOWLEDGMENTS

My father was born in the hills of northwest Georgia just before World War I. I am not sure exactly where. As a little girl growing up in New Jersey, I knew almost nothing about him or the place he came from. This book is the result of my curiosity. I could not have acquired understanding of an unfamiliar subject without the generosity of many people.

More often than not, archivists expressed skepticism that they had materials pertaining to the history of the psychological sciences in the South. Once we talked a little more, however, they not only brought me the boxes I had come for but also suggested additional pieces beyond what I imagined. On the ground level, they enriched my research. I heartily thank the staffs of the special collections departments of libraries connected with these institutions and especially the individuals whose names appear in parentheses: Appalachian State University (Hal Keiner); University of Arkansas (Anne Prichard); Atlanta University Center (Karen L. Jefferson and Cathy Lynn Mundale); Clark University (Mott Linn); Library of Congress; Cornell University; Duke University Medical Center (Jessica J. Roseberry); Emory University (Virginia J. H. Cain); Fisk University (Beth M. Howse and Vanessa Smith); University of Georgia; Howard University (Joellen ElBashir); Loyola University, New Orleans (Art Carpenter); Meharry Medical College; Memphis–Shelby County Public Library and Information Center (Patricia M. La Pointe and G. Wayne Dowdy); Mississippi Department of Archives and History (Clinton I. Bagley and Clarence Hunter); University of North Carolina; U.S. National Archives and Record Administration,

Southeast Region (Suzanne Dewberry); Oral Roberts University (Mark E. Roberts); Randolph-Macon Woman's College (Ted Hostetler); Rockefeller Archive Center (Darwin H. Stapleton, Kenneth W. Rose, Mindy S. Gordon, and Camilla Harris); Tougaloo College (Minnie W. Watson); Tuskegee University (Cynthia Wilson); Vanderbilt University Medical Center (Mary H. Teloh and Randy Jones); University of Virginia Special Collections, Alderman Library, and Historical Collections, Health Sciences Library; and Yale University.

Factual questions can sometimes be more difficult to resolve than interpretive issues. I am grateful to individuals who provided information that has enhanced the accuracy of my text: Sheila L. Darrow, Central State University, Wilberforce, Ohio; Lauren Gluckman, Library of the Penn State Dickinson School of Law, University Park; Marilyn King and Gary McMillan, American Psychiatric Association; and Jocelyn Wilk, Columbia University Library.

My travel and writing received essential support from the American Philosophical Society, National Endowment for the Humanities, Rockefeller Archive Center, and Penn State University (Department of History and Institute for the Arts and Humanities). Sally McMurry and Gregg Roeber, as successive heads of Penn State's Department of History, were attentive to my research and sustained it in tangible and intangible ways.

I have been greatly privileged to speak personally with men and women who contributed to the establishment of psychological knowledge in the South. They graciously shared their memories with me, and they went out of their way to provide documents that I could not otherwise have acquired. Their enthusiasm for my work has been sustaining, and I thank them sincerely: Rives Chalmers, M.D., Nancy Cox, Ross Cox, M.D., the late Richard E. Felder, M.D., and Patrick T. Malone, M.D., all of the Atlanta Psychiatric Clinic; Robert Coles, M.D., of Harvard Medical School; and the late Vivian (Mrs. Bingham) Dai and Meiling Dai. Trudier Harris of the University of North Carolina kindly met with me to discuss her recollections of growing up in Alabama. The late Annie Laurie Peeler, president of the Lillian E. Smith Foundation Inc., responded to a simple request from me with a long letter explaining the interest of Lillian Smith and Smith's brother Frank A. Smith in mental health. I thank the Smith Foundation for permission to quote from the Lillian E. Smith Papers.

Fellow scholars have provided encouragement, research leads, and challenging questions. I am deeply indebted to old and new friends. Robert Abzug, George Baca, Bruce Clayton, Lawrence J. Friedman, Lewis Perry, and Nan Woodruff lent support at early stages. David Edwin Harrell Jr. and Anthea D. Butler gave expert advice on Pentecostal sources, and Gabrael St. Clair shared her insights on the psychologist Frederick Payne Watts. Mike Milligan contributed his knowledge of Howard W. Odum, and Adam Rose supplied information on the economics of southern health care. Susan E. Myers-Shirk generously lent her unpublished work on pastoral counseling. Carol Reardon prepared me for the intricacies and rewards of interviewing. Laura Knoppers organized a discussion forum at Penn State, where Lori Ginzberg and Dan Letwin raised issues that stayed with me throughout my research. Gabrielle Spiegel kindly arranged a presentation at the Johns Hopkins University History Seminar that sharpened my thinking about science, social science, culture, and regionalism. Among the participants, I especially thank Jane Dailey, Pier Larson, Dorothy Ross, Mary Ryan, and Bertram Wyatt-Brown. William H. Tucker helped me to understand my material from the viewpoint of a psychologist. He showed me how psychologists would interpret my argument and what themes they would consider essential. I am very grateful for his interest, knowledge, and friendship.

By far this book owes its deepest scholarly debts to Bertram Wyatt-Brown and Johanna Shields. Bert maintained his enthusiasm through many bumps in the road and played just about every conceivable role along the way. He promoted the project in multiple venues, knew when to pose difficult questions and when to hold back, and, along with his wife, Anne, hosted a dinner in my honor that he cooked himself. Johanna Shields read and reread every word of the manuscript with the critical eye of a first-rate scholar and lifelong Alabamian. Whenever I thought I had discovered the true South, she was there to listen and offer reflections.

What I learned from my teachers remains the foundation of the way I interpret history. Clarity, breadth, and ethical concern have shaped the work of David Brion Davis, the late Sydney E. Ahlstrom, and the late Robert Elias. I hope my writing also represents these values.

Penn State colleagues and students have contributed a healthy mix of empathy, information, and skepticism. Gary Cross, Amy Greenberg, Philip Jenkins, Tony Kaye, and Cathy Wanner came forward with characteristic soundness and helpfulness at a moment of crisis. The late Bill Petersen was always good for some mailroom humor that brightened my day. Doug Putchat, Patrick Wallace, and Jeremy Garskof masterfully completed research and editorial tasks. I often try out my ideas in class, and the responses of my students, positive or negative, are consistently eye opening. I am privileged to interact with college students who are curious, sincere, and probing.

ProCopy in State College is my home away from home. I thank its efficient and friendly staff.

Chuck Grench of the University of North Carolina Press has gone many extra miles on my behalf. I thank him for his commitment. I also acknowledge a debt of thanks to Anna Laura Bennett, Paul Betz, Katy O'Brien, David Perry, the external readers for UNC Press, and the press's Board of Governors.

Friends and family have listened, worried, helped out, and celebrated, as the occasion required. Billy and Susan Harris, Diane Lichtman, Rick Melintz, Amy Paulson, Diane Flanel Piniaris, and Claudia Jaker Zimmer, all steadfast friends, are truly my personal anchors. My uncle and aunt, Douglas and the late Miriam King, have been the source of family memories as well as exemplars of healthful living—enjoying square dancing, gardening, and sailing in coastal Maryland well into their eighties and nineties. My children, Ellie and Jon, have become adults of insight and caring, and I could wish for no more. They are in all truth my greatest joy. I am thrilled to have a person as fine as Colin join our family as Ellie's husband. Everyone who knows me sees right away that the human beings in my life compete with the canines. Nothing pleases my hounds, Katie and Winston, so much as having me at home at my computer, and they are such perfect company that I forget they don't talk (yet). George the Frog, now eighteen years old, has happily witnessed the end of another book.

Dear friends Scott Lenhart, Johanna Shields, and the late Dolores Dungee define intelligence and compassion by their everyday behavior. I have been the recipient of their many kindnesses, and they are my models of decency. Naming them in my dedication is a small token of my esteem and gratitude.

INTRODUCTION **THE PURSUIT OF SELFHOOD**

IN THE SEGREGATED SOUTH

The sciences of the mind arguably served Western culture in the twentieth century as the chosen means of self-knowledge. Inquiries into human
nature stretching back to the Bible, filled with insights about motivation
and behavior, bore a kinship to modern psychology, and beginning with
the Enlightenment, philosophical debates about cognition and scientific
investigations of racial temperaments offered secular terms for reflection
about identity as well. These enduring conversations converged around
1900 in a fascination with the self, newly conceived. This person was individualized and indeterminate. Not wholly fixed by a God-given or racial
nature, every human being seemed to possess an elusive subjectivity affected by circumstances. In their own ways, the era's medical psychiatry,
experimental psychology, and psychotherapy acknowledged a malleable
personality.[1]

Early optimism that the psyche might be explained and repaired by
means of these premises, and society restored in the process, has faded.
The thought that we might adjust our social environments to secure private well-being seems almost quaint. Nonetheless, the psychological disciplines as we know them began precisely with excited attention to a self
in flux and in context, and the passing of this mood was no simple matter of scientific progress. Social outcomes tested psychological ideas, and
in America, the struggle between the new mental sciences and regional
mores was unusually tangled in the segregated South.

The rise of the scientific study of selfhood and the establishment of legal segregation were nearly simultaneous, and their relationship was both natural and problematic. "From about 1888 to 1895 a wave of laboratory-founding swept over America," recalled one historian of experimental psychology, at the same time that massive humanistic works such as William James's *Principles of Psychology* (1890) and G. Stanley Hall's *Adolescence* (1904) appeared in print.[2] In 1896 *Plessy v. Ferguson* gave federal sanction to the separation of the races in public places. It is easier to grasp the conflict between psychology's expansive temper and segregation's restrictions than to discern the pair's subtler kinship. Although psychological ideas have been adapted to serve many political masters, the early American field celebrated individual development in a flexible environment. On the surface, segregation struck a similar note by endorsing the races' autonomy. Yet the deeper aim of Jim Crow was the preservation of mastery and subordination. Hopes for growth and self-fulfillment, as presented by psychologists, posed a cultural threat in a society that made the races unequal.

Psychology and segregation shared a taste for civility, however, and their predilection for quiet social adjustment situates them in the same historical period. Just when well-educated Americans were beginning to turn away from the sweeping canvas of evolutionary struggles to explore the mind's hidden mechanisms, the nation's elites endorsed racial policies based more on law and manners than on politics and physical force. Indeed, segregation worked in large measure psychologically: statutes defined identities, but socialization was the means of ensuring compliance.[3] The awareness of personality common to psychologists and segregationists does not mean that there was complicity between them. It does make them inhabitants of a single culture, who could and most likely would communicate, as well as clash.

The South was the principal American site of encounter between early psychological ideas and a customary inequality of the races so central to the region's identity that its prescriptions long defined social behavior. Roughly 90 percent of African Americans in 1900 lived in the former slave states, and even after decades of black exodus, more than half reside there now.[4] These statistics help establish the South as an essential place for an investigation of how the psychological sciences responded to racial identities and injustices. Our suspicion of cultural essentialism and embrace of a global perspective, however, make the subject of personality in one region seem little more than a footnote in a provincial tale.

The truth is sadly otherwise: this is everyone's history. Precisely because segregation cannot be separated from southernness and the South was never isolated, how the self was discussed there in a repressive era is no marginal matter. The American South is indeed a complex geographic subculture, and its tragic experience, honor code, and religious conservatism are traits in addition to its racial arrangements that are said to distinguish it. We are fascinated by the region because it includes more than Jim Crow.[5]

Similarly, southern commentary on racial matters has always been part of national and international debates about race and racism. "An interesting aspect of this phase of anti-Negro thought," wrote I. A. Newby in 1965, referring to belief in racial dispositions attributed to biology, "was its acceptance by persons who were little interested in the Negro or what racists called 'the Negro problem,' and even less interested in the popular extremism which that problem generated."[6] Whether conceived as an endowment of nature or culture, racial identity as an analytical category has commanded the Western imagination. If day-to-day interracial contact had little to do with ideas, the South might not be a promising focus for a study of science and race. Yet it seems unwise to suppose that lifelong intimacy with racial mores made reflection on human nature any less compelling. This thought recommends my subject: what became of a reform-minded psychological idiom in a society immured in racial injustice, and what happened to its people as a result. From this angle, the South's social intricacy and worldwide connections are not liabilities but instead tools to unravel troubling events. Had southerners spoken in a single voice or repelled unfamiliar ideas — had regional identity been less fuzzy — there would be no story worth telling.

This book examines the consequences of the psychological idea of an indeterminate self for the American South between the ratification of racial segregation by *Plessy* and the slow dismantling of social separation in the two decades after *Brown v. Board of Education* in 1954. It is a history of a specific time and place, and although science, race, and region are all my themes, the principal goal is to explain regional experience. I argue that segregation was responsible for blocking the development of psychological commentary on racial relations articulated by southerners and responsive to southern culture. In place of the scientific ideal of dispassionate investigation, fear, anger, and distaste stirred by segregation shaped southern discussions of the psyche. Only with great caution did moderates of both races working in psychological fields openly explore their theories' social implications. Many southern black intellectuals, in contrast, quickly saw how valuable an assertion of environmental determinism was for racial reform; those who went north to escape Jim Crow themselves, however, recast the problem of segregation as a generalized racism. Northern philanthropists and researchers brought psychological information southward for many decades, but it was racial reactionaries seeking a conservative haven who were most likely to stay. Although southern universities gradually made commitments to psychological research and teaching, and increasing numbers of patients had access to therapy, public conversations among scientists about the mind in the South, and particularly about the states of mind of contemporary southerners in a racially troubled region, were muffled, abstracted, or strident. Nor was the failure strictly intellectual. In the absence of clear thinking and plain speaking about regional matters, racial inequity continued to affect professional opportunities in the psychological fields and access to mental health care. Americans like to believe that science improves society, but psychological experts in the South stumbled when it came to self-knowledge. Because they declined to analyze region, their work was limited by its problems.

Some readers will object that my charge of evasiveness in southern psychology during segregation mistakes the character of science. General laws are the goal of systematic inquiry, one may argue, and early American social science was especially determined to match natural science's objectivity.[7] The scope and significance of the *Brown* decision in particular depended on research indicating that racial separation anywhere causes minority children to feel inferior.[8] So, too, the medical successes of psychotherapy rely on the application of principles to individual cases.

The truth in all these points obscures the fact that science is also empirical. In the period I study, American social science eagerly cast "society as the patient," the title of an article in 1936 in one professional journal.[9] Southerners equipped with psychological knowledge backed away from this mission when the subject bordered on racial mores. The evidence I offer suggests that it was emotionally easier and socially safer for southern professionals to theorize about racial psychology than to analyze local con ditions. Their use of abstraction did not mean that they had no practical interests, and their detached style much resembled the wider American scientific habit of seeking to influence public policy by presenting research as broadly truthful. In the South, however, concern with the authority of science worked side by side with the unspeakable difficulties of segregation to restrain regional analysis.

Some of the roots of our current scholarly commonplace that racial categories are culturally constructed lie in this southern penchant for indirection. We speak generally about racial identities, as if self-image may be separated from its historical origins and reform consists of enlightenment. Yet racial behavior is only artificial so far as all culture is humanly made, and race relations in America have been entwined in southern history especially tragically. Skimming over regional entanglement risks simplification.

The disinclination to speak concretely about southern racial behavior in an earlier period was by no means the handiwork of southerners only. The South deeply disturbed Americans of the segregation era. It was "the nation's problem child number one," declared the Princeton psychologist Hadley Cantril in 1941, because it suffered "retarded cultural development."[10] Outsiders' zealous forays into the South to work a cure alternated with widespread distaste for the region and its consequent neglect. I wish to explore American forgetfulness about region, using the historical case of the migration of psychological ideas about personhood, to better apprehend the cultural influence of place and of the South in particular.

To say that intellectuals who otherwise thought long and hard about the development of identity skirted the implications of segregation does not mean that an appreciation of subjectivity failed to take root in the South at all. Over and over, even the most provocative southern views of selfhood circled the subject of racial mores with studied caution. Nonetheless, attentiveness to the latest theories was a necessary precondition of professional reluctance.

A sense of the plasticity of the individual psyche entered the South after 1900 through such activities as school reform, settlement work, veteran care, legal debates, and religious revivalism. These informal routes of intellectual transmission were unusually important because provincialism as a mind-set restrained southern science. The impression of educated northerners and southerners alike that the South was a scientific outpost meant that no person of ambition could be expected to sacrifice his career for the sake of southern development. Pride or shame, as the case might be, contributed to slow growth. Only 5 southern universities had experimental psychology laboratories in 1929, out of 117 institutions included in a national survey, and the northern specialty training of virtually all southern practitioners of the mental sciences at the time confirms the weakness of professionalism at home. Teachers, social workers, sociologists, and faith healers clearly helped circulate ideas in the South about how people behave and why. White teachers at a Mississippi workshop in 1937 observed their instructor encourage a student's self-confidence in spelling by giving "her simple sentences until she had had success several times," and Tougaloo College made Clifford Beers's classic story of his mental illness, *A Mind That Found Itself*, recommended reading for black teachers a decade later.[11]

My interpretation centers on examples of psychological interest that reveal how awareness of selfhood figured in public life. Although my strategy includes analyzing professionals in their social contexts, I have not written an institutional history of southern mental hospitals or a disciplinary survey of the psychological specialties in the southern academy.[12] This emphasis on work in the field follows the mood of the psychology of self-culture. No longer did mental disease preoccupy theorists. Whether an investigator pictured identity as a stream of consciousness, product of maturation, or series of behaviors, the interest was normal human nature. On-site observation and psychological tests were preferred methods to assess subjects as close as possible to their everyday circumstances.[13] The southern professionals I highlight examined ordinary pursuits such as learning, communicating, and healing, all the while, though, skirting the personal consequences of racial segregation.

Indeed, to proceed as if progress in the mental sciences were equivalent to hospital reform or scholarly achievement reinforces a false contrast between an enlightened North and a retrograde South. Concentrating on leading men helps make the new view of identity more concrete, but an emphasis on professionalism also dangerously leads toward the half-truth that southern science was simply backward. At a time when disciplinary boundaries were still permeable, philosophers, sociologists, and psychiatrists were prominent among early architects of psychological thinking of an environmental slant, and the best known were not native southerners:

William James, G. Stanley Hall, and John Dewey, all grounded in philosophy; Franz Boas, Robert Park, and W. E. B. Du Bois, social scientists; and Adolf Meyer and William Alanson White, medical doctors. Of these men only Du Bois, the first African American to complete a doctorate at Harvard, was compelled to accept a southern job, at Atlanta University in 1897. The presumption that a black scholar belonged at a black college, more often than not located in the South, made his migration almost predestined. By the same token, southern-born white men who left a mark on psychological study before World War I, including James Mark Baldwin, John B. Watson, and W. I. Thomas, never returned to the South to work after their graduate training.[14] The North was the place of opportunity.

To be sure, the Southern Society for Philosophy and Psychology, begun in 1904, was the first regional association devoted to investigation of the mind, and its priority might restore the South's image as a pioneering site. A mood of exile dominated its inception, however. The brainchild of a Yale-educated philosopher teaching in Alabama, the organization elected either one of the famous expatriates, Baldwin or Watson, president for half of the first decade, and meetings were held as often in mid-Atlantic cities as in southern states. Since slave times, southern declarations of sectional pride contained notes of doubt about the vitality of the region's high culture, and this self-condemning habit might well have led educated southerners now to seize on the uneven geography of psychological scholarship as the whole truth.[15] But in other ways as important to twentieth-century mental science, the South resembled the rest of the country.

Americans faced limited options for therapy in an atmosphere deeply marked by utopian hopes for cures for many decades after G. Stanley Hall earned the nation's first doctorate in psychology at Harvard in 1878. Although reformers were inclined to present the South's state-run asylums as unusually horrific, care was scarce nearly everywhere. *But for the Grace of God* was the desperate title of a memoir of Georgia's Milledgeville State Hospital around 1950, when only one full-time psychiatrist served the 10,000 patients who made it "the world's largest insane asylum."[16] Data collected in the mid-1930s located four-fifths of public psychiatric clinics for children in just five northern states, however, and not one in a community with a population smaller than 150,000. Wealth was clearly as decisive as region for patients seeking treatment. Le Roy Percy of Birmingham, an attorney, traveled northward to the Phipps Psychiatric Clinic in Baltimore in search of relief before taking his life with a shotgun at home in 1929.[17] But anyone then living outside a few American cities would similarly travel and pay for private treatment.

Nor was fervency restricted to the proverbial Bible Belt. Authors eager to spread respect for psychological knowledge found consumers ready for a new gospel. Clifford Beers's 1907 account of his recovery from suicidal depression was in its form a conversion narrative. Likening his mood change from despair to "elation" to being "born again," he saw his campaign to prevent mental illness as "an obligation placed upon me by God."[18] Although his mental hygiene movement, centered in New York, was a serious effort to detect emotional problems early in childhood, his own story was pure revival, drawing readers through forty-one printings of *A Mind That Found Itself* by the early 1980s. Across the nation, fascination with mental science's redemptive potential outran practical solutions for the mentally ill.

Racial assumptions insisting on the natural inequalities of biological groups were also articulated more precisely as science outside the South. This evolutionary view attributed fixed intelligence and temperaments to visually distinguishable peoples. It long served as the dominant psychology across the nineteenth-century West and survived, even flourished, in the hands of an intellectual minority at a time when most scholars were being persuaded of the self's flexibility. I. A. Newby again states the irony that "no anti-Negro work ever enjoyed the success of *The Passing of the Great Race*," the grand exposition of the laws of global racial competition issued by Madison Grant in New York in 1916.[19] Scrappy southern polemics, in other words, fell short of more polished efforts at science.

A simple tabulation of a cluster of articles on the mental endowment of the races in scientific journals before World War I indicates that even numerically these studies were not mainly southern. Among researchers who assessed physical variables such as brain size and mixed-race descent, one did his work at Johns Hopkins University, four at St. Elizabeth's Hospital in the District of Columbia, and the last in the Milledgeville hospital. Having access to black patients was as crucial as a southern location to the argument that the races had unequal capacities. The authors' professional mobility confirms the wide acceptance of racial analysis as good science well into the century. Robert Bennett Bean, who measured brains at Johns Hopkins, became chair of the Department of Anatomy at the University of

Virginia in 1916, just one year before E. M. Green, who speculated about psychosis in the black patients at Milledgeville, become superintendent of Pennsylvania's State Hospital for the Insane.[20]

I argue, however, that advocates of innate racial differences, particularly in the aftermath of the *Brown* decision, embraced the South as a special refuge. In the face of mounting faith in individual potential across Western culture, a vocal cadre of dissenting scholars transformed the old theory of racial biology into an updated psychology of intelligence, and they headed south to teach. What was once a scientific orthodoxy became an outsider's critique, and the catalyst was that northern social behavior could deviate from inherited racial conceptions.

In 1917, for example, near the end of a long career at Clark University, G. Stanley Hall advised an incoming student from Arkansas, Francis C. Sumner, an African American, to give up his plan to study in Germany, because "if you make your study of psychology a practical matter you can be of greatest service to your own people." The white truism that the black mind had a limited capacity and modest needs informed this discouraging remark. Nonetheless, Sumner earned his doctorate at Clark in 1920, becoming the first black American to achieve a Ph.D. in psychology, and he wrote his dissertation on psychoanalysis.[21] In contrast to Sumner's success at Clark, the University of Georgia awarded its first doctorate in the field to a black student in 1974. Its Department of Psychology had the first laboratory in the Deep South, founded in 1907, and a Cornell-trained scholar born in upstate New York was chair for thirty-five years beginning in 1916.[22] In 1959 a white man achieved the first doctorate awarded in psychology. Segregation made the difference in these regional histories of black scholarship, and although it is noteworthy that Georgia's premier public university accepted no black students until 1961, unequal access was not the sole characteristic of Jim Crow that skewed southern responses to new thinking about identity.

It was the psychological mind-set of segregation that most affected how southerners heard developmental ideas about personhood. Segregation was less a mandate for racial separation than a system of interaction, and its "unspoken etiquette," to borrow wording from Melton McLaurin, daily sustained feelings of superiority or inferiority and prescribed behaviors of command or obedience.[23] Although the roots of these interracial dynamics lay in slavery, twentieth-century customs, backed by law, repeated lessons of pride and shame. In a society where both races were now said to be free, manners silently exposing the lie of democratic professions added a burden of untruthfulness to obligation. It was normative, for example, for a black person to step aside for whites in a crowded place, to go to the back door of a white home, and to be called a diminutive like "uncle" or "auntie" instead of "Mr." or "Mrs." You knew you were seriously ill if black family or friends advised you to consult a white doctor. Once at the office, you sat in the Negro waiting room until all the white patients had been seen. Even where there was an inch of breathing space, awareness of race hovered over the smallest decision. In a private car, whites and blacks of the opposite sex almost never rode together in the front seat, although an older black woman well known to a young driver's white family on occasion sat next to him.[24]

Members of both races, whether lowly or famous, generally observed these rules for fear of gossip, ostracism, or violence. Our scholarly inclination to depict historical figures as deliberate actors is tested by the spectacle of modern people routinely submitting to expectations that defied true civility. Free agents might be expected to comprehend psychological theories of constructed individuality, but these southerners, white and black, commonly permitted themselves to be restrained by prescription and the emotions that customary practices provoked. Because I offer a historical study of a vexed encounter between a particular science and society, it is worthwhile to pause to examine the mentality of Jim Crow. Memoirs are especially useful to "tell about the South," to borrow the title of Fred Hobson's book, which echoes William Faulkner in turn. Combining disclosure and concealment, intimacy and posturing, solitary confession and cultural resonance, reminiscences have suited "the southern rage to explain" in a way that the precision of the mental sciences could not match.[25] Literary recollection blends truth telling with apology and a tacit plea for compassion, and southerners have revealed themselves in the medium, to an extent.[26]

At segregation's psychological center was the emotional intimacy of the races. When Walter White noted the "sex-obsession" of the white South in his exposé of lynching, *Rope and Faggot* (1929), he implied that miscegenation bore symbolic weight for the tangle of racial relations overall. Self-doubt was the soul-eroding message conveyed to black southerners by demeaning contacts with whites. "It was difficult, virtually impossible, to combine manhood and blackness under one skin in the days of my youth," recalled Benjamin Mays, the longtime president of Morehouse College, in 1971.[27]

Mastery, though, involved its own pressures. Stunned by his own revulsion when his lips touched the saliva left by a black friend named Bobo on a needle used to inflate a basketball, Melton McLaurin, as a teenager in North Carolina after World War II, discovered how crucial self-control was to whiteness. Because he kept "Bobo from guessing that his actions had destroyed my emotional composure," "I had preserved my status as superior."[28] Uncertainty about the thoughts of subordinates could be as wearying as the need to command. Although segregation promised social clarity, its reliance on authority and fear instead elicited reserve. As "the simple, honest, 'old-time Negro'" grew rarer after 1900, yielding sometimes to new assertiveness but more often to caution, "many whites," writes the historian Lawrence Friedman, "were desperately concerned with the same essential question — how to restore contact and communication with blacks." So deep, apparently, was the wish of Howard Odum, the North Carolina sociologist, to feel that he knew his black neighbors that he cast much of *Rainbow round My Shoulder* (1928) in the first-person voice of a fictional wanderer, "Black Ulysses." First the social scientist reports that "impulse and circumstances rather than planning and judgment [are] the guiding forces" of blacks; then we hear confirmation from Ulysses: "I was pretty smart an' lazy, too," "havin' lot o' fun, drinking lot a liquor."[29] Odum's use of literary license to speak for blacks revealed not only his sore need for reassurance but the psychological irony of racial interdependence. Segregation forced blacks to rely on whites for basic rights, but whites needed blacks for self-esteem and a feeling of safety.

Although the logic behind a culture often eludes its members, southerners of both races were aware of the edifice of segregation and trained their children to conform. Childrearing deliberately ingrained emotional habits. Psychiatrists in the 1960s observed behavior that recent legislation could not easily transform. In the opinion of black clinicians William Grier and Price Cobbs, the "heritage of slavery" forced a black mother to relinquish her son's love. Although her restriction of "his masculine assertiveness" to fit him for "his subordinate place" served his survival, restraint incurred an emotional price: "Black men develop considerable hostility toward black women as the inhibiting instruments of an oppressive system." The

Harvard psychiatrist Robert Coles, observing Deep South children of both races during the early days of school desegregation, similarly glimpsed "parental injunctions." Young white students "from segregationist homes, urged by their mothers to keep good distance from the one or two colored children among them," could be seen, in Coles's hopeful estimate of their psychic openness, "forgetful of these ideas and pleas in the abandon of play."[30] Not only race but also factors such as class, location, and time affected southern parenting, and psychological professionals held various theories about the effects of home life on behavior.[31] Yet in all their forms, the emotional postures of segregation were not learned anew from circumstances by each generation but instead were passed down through families seeking to equip their children for this social world.

In the midst of their training, young southerners nonetheless awoke to the realities of race with the jolt of a thunderclap. Southern memoirs situated racial issues at crises in the establishment of personal autonomy. For white writers like Harry Crews, born in rural Georgia in 1935, awareness of the race of black playmates shattered childhood idylls. In his "almost hermetically sealed" region, where blacks and whites worked together in the fields cultivating tobacco, Crews learned at age five from an aunt how to speak of a prosperous black farmer. "You don't say 'Mr. Jones,'" she corrected; "you say 'nigger Jones.'" Because "we were all dutiful children," Crews remembered, the little boy repeated, "nigger Jones," realizing for the first time that his best friend, Willalee, also belonged to the alien race.[32]

Black authors, in contrast, do not recall ever feeling innocence, and resistance, not loss, anchored selfhood for them. But race was as strongly entwined with their maturation. Benjamin Mays began a long life testing racial restraints when he defied his father as a teenager. Sadly embodying white wishes in his subservient manner and lowly ambitions, Hezekiah Mays ordered his son home from college in South Carolina in 1914 to help with the planting. Benjamin refused: "So the break with my father came and it was final."[33] At issue were the men's conflicting responses to Jim Crow, and Benjamin staked his manhood on rebellion. The trauma of severing childhood ties may always be part of growing up. But in the South, the strained race relations of segregation singularly informed this painful passage.

Alongside southerners' sharp awareness of race, commentators have time and again noted a regional propensity to dreaminess. There was a "conspiracy against reality in favor of romance," wrote W. J. Cash in 1941. He listed a string of causes for detachment in *The Mind of the South*, including the sensuous landscape, dull country living, Celtic ethnicity, and black temperament.[34] Other writers linked disengagement to the difficulty of facing the truth about race. Among rural black youths studied by Charles S. Johnson, the impossible conflict between increasing education and static opportunity pushed many to "retreat helplessly into the shadowy security of a make-believe world." As the teenagers imagined what it would be like either to be white or to move north, they sacrificed progress, Johnson implied, where they were. Among whites, moral misgivings about "the fundamental inequity in their society" led them "to avoid guilt by deluding themselves" about the nature of segregation, in the view of Melton Mc-Laurin.[35]

However the race problem might inspire fictions, southerners seemed more comfortable with indirect expression than stark facts. William Alexander Percy made race the centerpiece of this lesson in *Lanterns on the Levee* (1941). Because "good manners spring from well-wishing," making them a kind of story, "they are fundamental as truth," Percy began, "and much more useful." His servant, however, unmasked him. "I was in the shower, not a position of dignity at best, and Ford strolled in, leaned against the door of the bathroom, in a relaxed pose of the Marble Faun, and observed dreamily: 'You ain't nothing but a little old fat man.'" Soon "we parted," that is to say, Percy fired him, and the reader is left to decipher Percy's reason for including the embarrassing anecdote.[36] If one valid reading is that Ford, as the racial outsider, literally told the naked truth, then the episode pleads the value of maintaining appearances.

We are now so used to the psychotherapeutic truism that evasion is a sign of repression that we expect to find explosive emotion hidden behind southerners' imaginative habits. Rarely restrained by the possibility that the elaborate rituals of segregation were just social rules, observers over the decades have searched out the South's underlying passions. "Closer to nature, closer to the heat of the night, closer to the passion of hot summer nights" were the words one southern psychiatrist chose to describe his region in recent years, echoing the suspicion of an earlier generation of northern scholars that miscegenation was segregation's secret foundation.[37]

Southern violence, however, has drawn more comment than has illicit love. Once the nation's principal site of dueling, an instrument of retribution between equals, the South in the twentieth century became the place Americans associated with white lynching of black victims. By the 1960s, a decade when public disorder seemed rampant in America, historians and social scientists vigorously debated whether violence remained a peculiarly southern trait.[38] However much mythmaking has embellished the South's passions, expressions of feeling have been personal and interracial in form. The public record shows southerners reaching across racial lines with desire or rage directed at individuals. There was nothing impersonal about the torture of lynching victims, for example, a spectacle to which parents saw fit to bring children. Southern emotion does not have to be judged excessive to say that the elaborate proprieties of segregation normally contained and channeled the powerful feelings evoked by the system's own burdens and insults.

I use the troublesome terms "southerners" and "the South" to denote a people and a place marked by experiential familiarity with full legal and institutional inequality of the races. Many attributes of the region's inhabitants other than racial awareness profoundly affected how they reacted to the thought that the self is a fragile product: feelings about illness and death, children and education, poverty and privilege, and sinfulness and mercy. I hope I do not neglect these qualities. I include examples that require comment on internal southern divisions along lines of geography, class, and gender, as well as race. I do not mean to ignore southern variety.

It was segregation that marked the broad South as provincial during the first half of the twentieth century, however, and it was provincialism as an outlook that guaranteed that southerners acquired psychological information and then limited its applications. So often did southerners declare, "I'm agin it," a "defense mechanism" against the unfamiliar in the opinion of Alabamian Clarence Cason in 1935, that even tolerance of new trends in science there might seem a wonder.[39] Yet feelings of disadvantage oddly drove forward the migration of intelligence instead. Southern white intellectuals were especially anxious to appear up to date, black thinkers looked northward to escape cultural isolation, and northern scholars jumped at the chance to test their theories on their neighbors' deformities. Psychology's promise of individual progress through scientific intervention reached the South because of a gnarled interdependence between parts of the nation. Segregation, however, restrained discussion of the message so hopefully acquired.

The outcome of the exchange contributed to the end of an era in psychological science as well as in southern society. The close identification of the *Brown* ruling with the assurance that environment shapes identity exposed the now-aging psychology of nurture to skepticism when American racial problems did not yield easily to resolution after 1954. A new biology of racial intelligence, forged in the shadow of a notion of self that now bore the stamp of liberal science by its connection with *Brown*, became the intellectual hallmark of racial conservatism, acquiring credibility by its surface resemblance to the rising field of genetics.

The South was the location of some of these developments and the subject of others. But on the whole, southerners active in the psychological disciplines did not become leading voices in midcentury debates about the disposition of racial issues in human societies, and opportunities for the treatment of mental illness still lagged in the region at the close of formal desegregation in the early 1970s. More deeply, by the time legal segregation finally ended, very few southerners who devoted their careers in the psychological sciences to the personalities of human beings had asked forthrightly about the implications of their ideas for racial inequity. They did not find an assured professional voice for the ethical dilemma. My question is why the once-dominant American psychology of personhood did not better serve the South. To answer, I begin with how southerners thought about mental wellness and derangement as a lens for popular assumptions about selfhood before psychological specialists and information began to refashion traditional knowledge.

| 1 | HOW SOUTHERNERS THOUGHT

ABOUT THE MIND AND ITS ILLS

BEFORE PSYCHOLOGY

Veterans Administration Hospital no. 91, opened in 1923 on land sold to the government by Tuskegee Institute in Tuskegee, Alabama, was the first American facility where black psychiatrists cared for black mental patients. Nearly 400,000 African American soldiers had served in World War I, and about half of the more than 350 patients in residence at the hospital by mid-1924 were "suffering," according to an official report, "with nervous and mental diseases."[1] There was no discussion of mental illness, however, during the turmoil of the hospital's earliest days.

On the night of July 3, 1923, "a parade of the Ku Klux Klan," counted by one newspaper as 700 men, "wended its way in sixty-seven automobiles through the grounds of Tuskegee Institute and disappeared without further demonstration."[2] At issue was the hospital's proposed use of black staff. For months Robert Russa Moton, Booker T. Washington's successor as principal of Tuskegee, had battled the claim of officials at Veterans Administration (VA) that "there is not a sufficient number of colored personnel" to fill the hospital's needs, and he had won. "These people have a right to prove their ability to be of service among themselves," wrote President Warren Harding to Alabama's governor on May 1. Even then, federal policy could not dispel local white opposition, settle backroom politicking over the choice of black leadership, or recruit black professionals with civil service qualifications who were willing to work in the rural South. The appointment of Dr. Joseph H. Ward of Indianapolis in July 1924 as the

Toussaint T. Tildon, M. O. Davis, and George C. Branche, among the earliest African
American psychiatrists in the South, at the Veterans Administration hospital, Tuskegee,
Alabama, as they appeared in *Souvenir Program: Dedication Exercises, Recreation Building*,
1927. Courtesy of Tuskegee University Archives, Tuskegee University, Tuskegee, Alabama.

hospital's first black medical director finally slowed contention that, at its
height, engulfed the National Association for the Advancement of Colored
People (NAACP), the all-black National Medical Association, and admirers
and critics of both races who sent Moton their opinions about black ability,
autonomy, and resistance.[3]

From the perspective of mental science, the furor was most noteworthy
for its silences. The needs, treatment, and physical presence of the patients
in Tuskegee received almost no notice. The politics of race, and specifically whether blacks would be allowed to demonstrate expertise and exert
power, eclipsed attention to mental illness. White newspapers did not stir

fears that a colony of abnormal blacks threatened public safety, and the black press did not herald the effort of Solomon Fuller of Boston, the nation's first black psychiatrist, to teach his specialty quickly to a handful of doctors en route to Tuskegee. Although the VA aired the opinion that syphilis often caused black dementia, a diagnosis that stopped veterans' benefits, the public otherwise heard little about the origins of the patients' disorders. Scant concern for rehabilitation meant that a "basement room [that] is too small, has no seats and is poorly lighted and ventilated" was the first recreation area.[4] In sum, the opening of the Tuskegee hospital was a medical landmark because it was a serious response to black mental illness, but the details of pathology and treatment were not newsworthy. Moton typically defined the issue as black authority and saw the solution as political. The election of "1928 is not so far away," he wrote in 1927 to Frank T. Hines, director of the VA and a man with known partisan ambitions, "and if you have any wishes in the matter if you will indicate to us, then we will in turn touch every possible source we can render to your service."[5]

The invisibility of patients in this saga was a sign that Americans were still largely unaccustomed to thinking about personality as malleable and mental illness as potentially responsive to specialized care. Even Tuskegee's black doctors spoke in private memos of psychiatric conditions as if they were equivalent to other diseases and of mental patients as merely ill. This apparent lack of interest in mental dynamics does not mean that the controversy was unaffected by assumptions about the races. The existence of a fixed "negro character," as a professor at the University of Mississippi phrased it in 1914, remained an American commonplace, and IQ tests given to military recruits during the war ostensibly confirmed the superior native intelligence of white soldiers using up-to-date psychological instruments.[6] Many whites who read about the turmoil at Tuskegee would have denied that black patients were curable and that black doctors were capable. In this way, belief in racial natures inherited from nineteenth-century science may well have quietly shaped current events.

Victorian biology was just one tool for explaining the mind before the advent of a psychology of selfhood, however, and in the South long-held feelings about mental derangement deeply affected how southerners of both races conceived of personality. The South did not ignore the mind and its problems before acquiring psychology, and in fact did quite the opposite. Mental illness must be nearly universal, and its presence forces a society to make decisions about norms and deviance. Inner states inimical to personal peace and social disharmonies intertwined with private torments are given different names, but every culture draws some line between normal and abnormal behavior. As interest in subjectivity grew in the South, new ideas encountered established responses to mental wellness and distress. Christianity, conjure, folk cures, and medical institutions, including public asylums and private sanitariums, had offered southerners psychic healing. Both races felt the influence of these mores, and because illness can upset social routines, a black southerner at times stepped in to treat a white acquaintance during a medical crisis. Philosophically, the conflict between southern traditionalism and the new science was profound: psychology recast mental illness, once felt to signify a breach in the cosmic order, as personal dislocation. Slowly, however, and in spite of such logical tension, southerners began to think of individual minds as treatable entities.

Three themes lay the groundwork here for my interpretation of how the South reacted to a psychology of personal development: traditions of care for the mentally ill in communities, strategies of self-therapy devised by troubled individuals, and routes of cultural migration by which psychological innovations reached the South. The words "before psychology" in the chapter's title connote an early time to an extent, but the phrase also refers to social settings where psychological treatment was unavailable and to a mind-set that was resistant to medical science. The absence of psychology could be as much a cultural as a temporal condition.

Community Therapies

More than one contemporary southerner remembers how the neighborhood of his or her childhood tolerated the presence of its mentally ill. Although it was said in Wade, North Carolina, around 1950 that Sam McNeil killed a man before spending time in a black asylum, he seemed "a harmless and rather likable member of the community" to Melton McLaurin, then a white teenager. "The state of one's sanity—or lack thereof" prompted "folk expression," writes Trudier Harris of Tuscaloosa's African Americans. "Her bread ain't done" and "She out of her tree" formed verbal bridges to troubled people typically kept at home by black families, not sent to institutions.[7] Without romanticizing the acceptance of abnormal residents by southern towns, where they sometimes suffered from family shame, deep poverty, and social violence in special ways, the authors highlight grassroots traditions for coping with the psyche. The good-natured naming of Harris's memory is a sign that answers might not be medical or even material but instead emotional or spiritual. Everyone knew about Sam, McLaurin implies: psychological distress was a matter of public knowledge and concern. Both writers note that asylums were segregated, meaning unequal and white-controlled. Although it is not surprising that racial norms shaped responses to mental illness, the similarity of attitudes toward psychic disorder across the color line may be. In these intimate and conflicted communities, bounded in their inhabitants' imaginations by invisible forces, psychological deviance seemed part of an inevitable order.

Christianity of a kind tightly focused on personality was a nearly universal source of answers about afflictions, including mental illness, for southerners. Calvinist Protestantism hammered away at private habits like wearing makeup and jewelry in a mood "so compulsive, so without humor," wrote Lillian Smith in disgust in the 1940s, that it ignored social sores such as segregation and poverty.[8] In this world, sin was the origin of illness. "If the baby born next door was a queer, still brat which would plainly never be right in the head," W. J. Cash told readers of *The Mind of the South* in 1941, the child and other misfortunes were "direct visitations from the hand of God, inexplicable, or explicable only on the hypothesis of sin, and to be borne without complaint."[9] Although the same theology held out promises of grace and repentance, southerners had a hard time escaping feelings of fatalism and guilt when it came to illness. This sense of resignation found expression in an indifference to medical treatment that frustrated reformers. Helen Witmer, a sociologist at Smith College in the 1930s who advocated a national network of outpatient psychiatric clinics for children, reached the same conclusion as Cash: many parents saw a troubled child as God-given punishment for their sins, making consulting a psychiatrist "a confession of failure." Her state-by-state survey of existing facilities across the country forced Witmer to reflect on the strength of old-time religion in the American hinterland. Nowhere outside a major city was there a full-time psychiatric center for children in 1935, in part, she believed, because potential patients would not come.[10] According to the South's own commentators, the region seemed unusually marked by self-blame and submission to God-given hardship.

The logic of evangelicalism did offer God's forgiveness as a cure and prayer as a means, however, and southerners turned warmly to faith as "an antidote, a palliative, an escape," observed Hortense Powdermaker following her anthropological fieldwork in the Mississippi Delta in the mid-1930s. She watched Pentecostals of both races pray with abandon over the sick at annual late-summer revivals.[11] Erskine Caldwell, reflecting much later on his father's career in Georgia as a Presbyterian minister, confirmed prayer's emotional power. No "humanitarian project" ever made a man "known as a beloved pastor." The honor came solely "by visiting members to pray for them in their own homes."[12] Yet prayer, so crucial, was an oddly inert therapy, because the words were a mere conduit for God's will. The "faith healer" who treated Harry Crews during a mysterious paralysis never touched the boy's deformed legs, explaining, "Them is the Lord's laigs an He's seed them laigs and He's laid His hand on them laigs and He knows, so it don't bother me none that I ain't seed'm." Recovery "mought be today, or it mought be tomorrow. Whatever it is God will allow."[13]

Spiritual submission did not keep Christianity from anchoring hope, to the point that early physicians treated it jealously as a rival. Scientific training encouraged doctors to see pious emotion as a cause of mental aberration. The belief of some black patients that "they are prophets and possess divine power" was a typical delusion of the race, in the view of one psychiatrist at the Government Hospital for the Insane in Washington, D.C., in 1914. Even in 1952, as a postwar surge of faith swept the nation, a psychologist at Georgia's Milledgeville State Hospital wrote in his diary that patients "are not allowed to have a Bible" because "reading it excites" them. "A preaching patient will disturb a whole ward." The therapist's irritation inadvertently revealed how instinctively southerners coped with pain by taking their troubles to the Lord.[14]

Psychiatrists more openly censured conjure, the belief that illness was the result of a spell. Most likely they felt free to condemn folk culture because it lacked Christianity's respectability and seemed a product of the black mind, although southern whites consulted hoodoo doctors as well. The black patient's susceptibility to "fear of the supernatural, the suspicions of his fellows and the necessity of guarding at all times against bad luck and the machinations of enemies" made the race more prone than whites to psychosis, concluded E. M. Green at the Milledgeville hospital in 1914.[15] A contemporary complained that families of sufferers took them to "fake doctors for the removal of this 'spell.'"[16]

Ethnographers were more willing to see that witchcraft had an inner logic that addressed mental illness. Fieldwork in Africa in the 1930s led E. E. Evans-Pritchard, the British anthropologist, to respect the psychological cast of "the Zande mind." A misfortune worked by conjure was "a psychic act," usually born of a grudge, that impelled the victim to perform rites to uncover the perpetrator. Sickness was the most common reason for suspecting malevolence, and because a neighbor's hard feelings were typically the cause, a cure might combine medicine with payment or vengeance.[17]

In 1931 Zora Neale Hurston explained conjure's transatlantic migration in an issue of the *Journal of American Folk-Lore* devoted to "Hoodoo in America." "Your broken-spirited daughter" was the name chosen by a suppliant who sought a remedy from a conjurer for "words of bitter regret" in her family, and, like this case, the problems presented were often emotional: neglect by children, abandonment by a lover, or cruelty from friends. The diagnosis in hoodoo was not spiritual or psychological but interpersonal. Conjure served intimate settings where relationships had gone wrong. Not surprisingly, use of Christian objects in America supplemented folk medicines and amulets. One hoodoo doctor told a petitioner to hang a horseshoe and a picture of Jesus on her door, and another practitioner had Hurston read the book of Job during the writer's investigative apprenticeship, because "all hold that the Bible is the greatest conjure book in the world."[18] As a healing art, conjure eclectically treated psychic pain.

This blending of medical, religious, and occult remedies was not unique to the traditional South. In early modern England, clergymen commonly used their learning to serve their parishioners as doctors, and most of them believed that witchcraft might be complicit in illness.[19] Biracialism distinguished the American variant, however, and although customs of African origin dominated this largely fugitive network, white southerners inherited a European lore of spirit possession that must have made conjure seem familiar. One consequence during slavery was that owners sometimes visited slave conjurers in search of healing, and they recorded folk cures in their prescription books.[20]

The practice represented a modest reversal of racial authority that Charles W. Chesnutt, the African American author, captured in tales collected as *The Conjure Woman* in 1899. Writing at a crucial moment in the implementation of Jim Crow laws, Chesnutt worried that by depicting the animistic vision of hoodoo, favored by the popularity of regional fiction, he would reinforce a stereotype of black primitivism. The stories themselves were faithful to the magical conceits and psychological realism of conjure. Set in slavery, they followed the ministry of Aunt Peggy, the conjure woman, who transforms "po Sandy" into a tree to keep him from being sold away from his wife and makes "Sis' Becky's pickaninny" a bird to enable the child to visit his mother on a distant plantation.[21]

It was in the narrative framework, however, that Chesnutt quietly upset racial mores in a way consistent with healing customs. In layer upon layer of storytelling, we first hear about the tales from an Ohio businessman who moves to North Carolina for the sake of his wife, Annie, who suffers from "a settled melancholy" also described as "depression."[22] There, the doctor visits, but it is Uncle Julius, the black coachman, who lifts her spirits by chronicling Aunt Peggy's supernatural remedies. His medical success does not revolutionize the racial order. Parallels in the fiction evoke the tragedy of black submission: Annie's vague neurasthenia contrasts with the slaves' sharp sadness, and the South, a place where Yankees find healing emotion, is also a site of bondage. Yet as if by magic, Uncle Julius thrives as a physician of the psyche precisely because, as a storyteller, he commands hoodoo's lore.[23] His prestige as a healer was true to the prescientific culture still meaningful in the South when Chesnutt wrote at the turn of the twentieth century.

Whether southerners conceived the metaphysics of illness in Christian or pagan terms, or both, the belief that the mind is subject to forces transcending personal and even physical realms was central to their heritage. The psychological sciences, focused on individuals as discrete entities, would erode this sensibility though not erase it. Yet day-to-day care of mental problems was hardly an abstract enterprise in southern communities, and most basically it was the work of families. The age-old equation of solitude and disorder in Western culture must have encouraged the hope that sanity, if lost, might best be restored among kin. "Men and women without households were vagrant and pariah," writes Michael MacDonald about Renaissance England, and by this logic a wandering reason might likewise be anchored by family bonds.[24] In the traditional American South, families who could not articulate why nearness to loved ones might be therapeutic still kept their abnormal members at home out of love, duty, shame, ignorance of institutional alternatives, or, if informed, fear of them. Their instinct dovetailed with the view of family obligation held by public authorities. In an ironic twist, one distressed woman in the 1820s spent years roaming the South Carolina countryside, often naked, because the county government believed her family should step in.[25] Home care depended in practice on willing relatives.

In a white culture that revered family honor, mental illness in fact presented kinfolk with conflicting impulses to protect, hide, or even reject an unhappy relative, as did these South Carolinians. Although all illness is a disturbing breach of nature, psychic dysfunction uniquely threatens human norms by its adjuncts of self-alienation and social deviance. The instinct to wish it away was strong among people who prized a good family name. The suicide in 1950 of John Gould Fletcher, a leading Arkansas author, elicited flat-out denial from one acquaintance who sent condolences. "I do not believe he took his own life," she told Fletcher's widow, in defiance of the coroner's ruling. "It seems to me a great pity people are free to say such things when he cannot defend himself."[26]

The stigma she associated with suicide caused households to be guarded generally about their emotional troubles. *Lanterns on the Levee*, William Alexander Percy's 1941 memoir of the Mississippi Delta, was so psychologically informed and personally candid that we might expect truthfulness throughout. Dropping names like Freud and Jung and laying bare his boyish love for his "divinely café-au-lait" teenage nurse, Percy ended with a confessional flourish: "Of all the people I have loved, wisely and unwisely, deeply and passionately, I have loved no one so much as myself. . . . I have no regrets. I am not contrite. I am grateful."[27] Yet he spoke tersely of family tragedy, the suicide followed by the drowning death of cousins, a husband and wife, that made him, an aging bachelor, the surrogate parent of their three sons. "My favorite cousin, Le Roy Percy, died two months before Mother's death, and his brave and beautiful wife, Mattie Sue Phinizy, two years after Father's."[28] That was all. Mental illness so jeopardized the pride of southern families that coping could consume their energies, but in the utmost privacy if possible.

Anxiety about intrusion among black families dealing with mental illness grew from a different motive: fear of intervention by white officials or even victimization by lynch mobs preying on the weak.[29] But whatever reason pushed kinfolk inward, one consequence was that household members were the primary doctors. Home treatments for all kinds of illness led field-workers from Meharry Medical College in Nashville, where generations of black doctors trained, to bemoan "self-medication" among rural blacks in the 1930s. "Narcotics and stimulants," including tobacco, alcohol, and patent products, were what the authors meant by self-cures, and they were gratified that the number in their sample that habitually took a drug without doctor's orders fell from 85 to 20 percent between 1932 and 1936 because of the health education they provided.[30] The line between lay and professional medicine was indistinct, however, and doctors were not blameless if families showed poor judgment. When a marshal near Tulsa in the 1910s confronted E. H. Abington, an Arkansas-born physician, about the alcoholic content of the doctor's patent formula, To-Ho-Ya, Abington confessed that the secret ingredient was a diarrheic, though, facing punishment, he may not have been truthful. His employment of traveling "entertainers" of both races to hawk his remedy across the western South helps explain why families dosed themselves with such products.[31]

Many of the medicines were anesthetic because they were mood altering, and even if the initial ailment was physical, medication might lead to dependency. Even Coca-Cola, the universal southern beverage marketed from Atlanta, included coca leaves in its formula until just after 1900, making it akin to cocaine and suggesting how casual modest use of stimulants was. But alcohol left the most visible trail. Memoirs most commonly picture white men drinking to cope, and rehabilitative institutions grew in response to excesses. A sanitarium that was designated "Wallace (Alcoholic)" appeared on a list of Memphis hospitals, for example, in 1935. Dosing at home, however, remained the norm. Within months of a suicide attempt and hospitalization in 1945, John Gould Fletcher wrote in his diary, "I get drunk—having nothing better to do. Condition desperate." Shortly before his self-inflicted death five years later, a shopping list in Fletcher's pocket diary placed alcohol among household necessities: "eggs, bacon, grapefruit—canned, liquor."[32]

Who in the family decided which of these medications to give? At a time of few effective treatments, illness brought thoughts of death fearfully close, and a crisis could disturb customary household authority by favoring someone with occult gifts. There was a reason in 1940 for the mother of young Harry Crews to treat his earache with the hair of "Auntie," born in slavery: the wooly tuft, his mother explained, kept his ear welloiled and warm. But as his fever rose and led to weeks of paralysis, it was Auntie, unopposed by the white family, who at night "would sit up with me sometimes for hours, talking in her old, soft, mother's voice of a world I had never heard anybody else even hint at."[33] The charism the boy felt in Auntie was one instance of the superior psychological insight of "these old black matriarchs," Lillian Smith reflected in 1949. They "knew secrets of child rearing and secrets of sanity that our psychiatrists have been learning the hard way for the past sixty years through research, and that white mothers still know too little about."[34] Natural instinct, the same trait that southern whites normally cited to mark blacks as inferior, seemed a special grace when it came to affliction, particularly to troubles of the mind and heart.[35] Although welcoming a servant's emotional presence most likely did not give her control of medical care, she might gain domestic power in health matters.

The same folk culture that prized these mystic feelings during sickness deepened the reluctance of white families to consult doctors. For both races, fatalistic thoughts linking illness with death brought with them an odd combination of superstitious fear and stoic resignation. Southerners viewed hospitals as places to die, forcing doctors quite often to perform surgery in homes. E. H. Abington performed a cataract operation in the house of an Arkansas woman who refused to go elsewhere.[36] This phobia of medical science could yield suddenly to acceptance of death. The grandfather of Harry Crews saw a doctor only twice in his life, for his army physical during World War I and for lung cancer at age eighty-three, for which he declined treatment. For this old man, death was less a foe than an intimate.[37] Poverty, rural isolation, and, for blacks, worry that black doctors were poorly trained and white ones unsympathetic were social facts that also limited use of physicians. So long as professional medicine seemed either practically out of reach, symbolic of desperation, or irrelevant to one's fate, families avoided it.[38]

The tenacity of this aversion to doctors is even clearer in light of how integrated into southern communities physicians really were. At least in towns, where most who served the countryside lived, they were familiar figures who would come to your home, if families overcame their own resistance. Humble backgrounds could form bridges to their patients. Charles Victor Roman apprenticed with an "old root-doctor" in rural Tennessee in the 1880s before he began the education that made him a professor at Meharry Medical College in Nashville. Although he spoke later only about their "herb-gathering," he most likely learned something of hoodoo, too, because many who prescribed "roots," the generic term for folk cures, were also conjurers and hence called "two headed doctors."[39] Casual contacts with doctors were common as well. The strictly part-time practice of many physicians, who needed a reliable income in addition to medicine, meant that they socialized with fellow townsmen in their other careers. E. H. Abington also worked as a farmer, druggist, and banker in communities along the Arkansas-Oklahoma border.

Any psychological advice of a medical kind that the average family received came from the local doctor, and because southern medical schools taught almost nothing about psychiatry until the late 1920s, instinct was a physician's main resource. The results were as variable as human nature. Abington, still an unashamed segregationist in 1955 when he published his memoir, *Back Roads and Bicarbonate*, could not have respected blacks if he treated patients across the color line, as most white doctors did. Resentful of any person of color who moved to his "lily-white district," he dismissed *Brown v. Board of Education* with the aphorism, "You can't mix oil and water." There was natural compassion, in contrast, in the gesture of another white country doctor who closed the eyes of a dead child with two nickels of his own because the family had no money.[40] This sensitivity was Carl Whitaker's model in the late 1940s when he insisted that all Emory University medical students both get and give psychotherapy as part of their training. He envisioned psychiatry as a tool for every "practicing physician" who stood in a lineage descending from the "medicine man" to "the priest class" and old-fashioned doctor, as he and his coauthor Thomas Malone explained in *The Roots of Psychotherapy* (1953). Their view recalled a southern past in which necessity made ordinary doctors into psychologists.[41]

Mental institutions had begun to dot the southern landscape in 1773, however, when Virginia opened the region's first asylum in Williamsburg, and by 1900 individual southern states supported one or a few public hospitals. On one level this impersonal care seems an anomaly among people given to prayer, home cures, and family doctors. Nineteenth-century asylum reformers and resident physicians in fact revered science as the ideal source of a hospital's medical knowledge and patient regimen, and twentieth-century experts persisted in efforts to make these largely custodial institutions live up to enlightened standards. Frank Luton, Vanderbilt School of Medicine's first psychiatrist, produced a balanced report on Tennessee's three state-sponsored asylums in 1938, in which he described them as a cross between well-managed hospitals and chambers of horrors, with patients idling on wooden benches, "dark and ugly" seclusion rooms, and "*urine soaked*" concrete floors. He stopped short of endorsing eugenic sterilization of selected patients, a drastic expression of the impulse to curb nature by science favored by some southern colleagues employed by asylums. Luton nonetheless displayed typical professionalism by presenting mental institutions as objects of public concern distant from life outside their walls.[42]

Fellow southerners did not share his detachment. As Luton's survey noted, the gates of Central State Hospital, only seven miles from Nashville on Murfreesboro Pike, were open every day except Sunday, and this accessibility was symbolic of how southern custom long handled the space between communities and institutions for the insane. A connection between them did not always signal tolerance, because the age-old discomfort with mental aberration might inspire cruel curiosity. Women patients at the South Carolina Lunatic Asylum in 1855 complained that they were "gazed at as if they were rare specimens of wild beasts" by visitors permitted to tour the grounds near Columbia.[43] Clearly guarding their own sense of self by making others a spectacle, these observers remained emotionally engaged with the inmates, albeit through feelings of fear. Melton McLaurin tells a more positive story. When his grandmother spent twelve years in North Carolina's state asylum at Raleigh beginning around 1930, her sister lived there, too, to care for her.[44] Despite the fervent wish of asylum administrators for rationality and system, local mores worked as a countervailing force. Whether southerners viewed patients with superstitious distaste, family loyalty, or neighborly regard, they approached these sites in ways attuned to tradition.

If their behavior in effect domesticated large institutions, smaller clinics that treated mental illness fit even more readily into southern cities and towns. Although old practices of housing the indigent insane in jails or in homes as boarders at public expense had all but disappeared by 1900, new kinds of short-term and outpatient care kept sufferers visible in localities. Proximity did not necessarily mean acceptance. The organization of the Memphis city directory of 1901 reflected the time-worn view of illness as a moral judgment. Under "Hospitals, Asylums, Etc.," we find "Crofford's Sanitarium for the Disease [sic] of Women" alongside residences for unwed mothers, orphanages, and the "Poor and Insane Asylum." Crofford's was one of a growing number of rest homes offering cures for the nervousness associated with women. A similar Memphis facility, Gartly-Ramsay Hospital, later specializing in psychiatry, advertised itself in 1910 as "convenient to cars."[45] Although close to the families and friends of patients, private clinics accommodated people who were not only emotionally troubled but, in light of the city directory's organization, socially troubling. In contrast, Atlanta's Neighborhood Union, a medical project serving the city's black population beginning in the 1910s, seemed bent on avoiding moralizing. Its records used concrete terms to describe the activities of black doctors and nurses who used space in churches and schools to examine patients, including psychiatric cases.[46] To the extent that the Neighborhood Union's staff refrained from moralistic language, the agency's clinical papers departed from a tradition fraught with emotion about illnesses affecting character. Southern communities took care of inhabitants afflicted with mental disorders, but they also disdained them.

The tiny number of southerners who attended the region's colleges studied the mind in a way that reinforced a distinction between its normal functioning and disease and yet taught their obligation to sufferers as well. Across the transatlantic world, psychological investigation in higher education began as a branch of nineteenth-century philosophy, and the intellectual alliance traditionally made the object of analysis man's God-given nature. Austin Southwick Edwards tried to make psychology scientific at the University of Georgia after his arrival there during World War I, but he could also sound like an old-fashioned philosopher, a tone that aligned him with southern academic norms. In 1920, as bold readers in the urban North keenly sampled Freud's theories on sexuality and the unconscious, "the contents of consciousness" was Edwards's subject in *The Fundamental Principles of Learning and Study*. His advice that good students need strong habits of connecting ideas harked back to John Stuart Mill and so-called British associationism, and his faith in introspection as the method of scholastic progress echoed Wilhelm Wundt, his teacher, and more distantly, the Cartesian tradition. The intellectual mastery he predicted was, at its root, a form of character building: "Feeling Habits and Moral Education" was one chapter's title.[47] Edwards's goal to improve individuals using psychological principles linked him with new trends. Yet his premise that reflection explains a normative consciousness made him a cousin to philosophers. The mind explored in early southern philosophy classrooms was less like a brain than a soul.

Most southerners well into the twentieth century had little or no contact with either professional medicine or higher education, however. The South remained "a feudal land," in John Egerton's words. In 1930 only one southerner in a thousand graduated from college, in stark contrast to the one-third of high school graduates who went to college from "Middletown," the midwestern city studied in the 1920s by sociologists Robert and Helen Lynd.[48] Academic habits of mind had little dislodged southern custom. Country people on the move, as many were, carried with them the age-old belief that madness bespoke a bedeviled universe. The existence of disturbance in nature, whether thought to originate in sin or human malevolence, was taken for granted, and when illness affected the mind, its incidence was at once fearsome and familiar. Families and neighborhoods cared for distracted members as a sober and inevitable duty. Science had not yet inspired widespread faith that disease might be cured.

Although early southerners shared this mood with other traditional peoples, the region's racial order distinguished its experience of mental disturbance. Mark Twain revealed his southern roots when he paired Huck Finn's feeling "lonesome" at the sound of "a dog crying about somebody that was going to die" with Jim's trying to wrest prophecy from his hairball.[49] Both whites and blacks accepted enchantment of a kind that considered insanity a visitation. The white assumption that people of color were more primitive could enhance black authority in situations of psychic distress. Making T.P., overseen by Dilsey, Benjy's keeper in *The Sound and the Fury*, William Faulkner not only followed southern custom but put characters together who possessed insight that defied reason.[50] Here abnormality showed its capacity to disrupt society as well as the mind.

What would distinguish psychological science from southern folk culture was not its sophistication so much as a conviction that the individual mind was susceptible to deliberate manipulation. Whereas mental troubles once linked the sufferer with the motions of the cosmos, psychotherapy focused in depth on unique personalities. Yet there was nothing easy or automatic about adopting psychological theories or treatments, either for the region or for a person, and for many years southerners dealt with private difficulties on their own.

Self-Treatment

It may be that mental illness is inherently lonely. "I think that John was lonesome all his life," reflected the widow of John Gould Fletcher after his suicide in 1950. Lillian Smith, whose productivity obscured how closely she managed her feelings, wrote a few years later, "I know thousands of people; but that is a lonely kind of knowing."[51] The discomfort of a mind out of step with surrounding norms may have been exaggerated in historical southern communities. There, the same logic that explained the suffering of broken souls passed judgment on their deviance, and local authorities and families mixed the care they gave with distaste and shame. Practical difficulties—scarce doctors, rural isolation, and poverty, all exacerbated by racial inequity—were probably less instrumental than public opinion in making a person in turmoil feel alone.

Some who were beset by inner demons, however, turned necessity into opportunity by undertaking their own treatment. "Five years ago I was a complete neurasthenic," W. J. Cash wrote proudly from Charlotte, North Carolina, on a questionnaire for his New York publisher around 1940, "but I have since largely cured myself."[52] His autonomy was a matter of attitude as much as medical fact. Doctors had addressed his mood disorder, and Cash was knowledgeable about psychiatry by the standards of the day. It was his reluctance to turn himself over to doctors and their theories that made him every bit as traditional as his neighbors. Although perhaps everyone resists admission of illness and its threat to the self, there was a type of southerner who adhered doggedly to personal strategies for preserving psychological balance. Despite feelings of solitude, these people were a natural part of a society that hung back from medical science.

The sketches that follow consider four southerners in chronological order who had access to the best psychological care then available but who preferred to remain their own doctors. Between the 1920s and 1950s, W. J. Cash, John Gould Fletcher, Lillian Smith, and Robert Burgette Johnson made less use of therapies than they could have. Whether their reserve was a symptom of their troubles or more assistance would have helped them, I cannot say. It seems clear, however, that their choices belonged to a culture that was at least as uncomfortable with psychological treatment as with mental illness.

Suicide typically casts a shadow over the victim's life in the eyes of survivors, framing each event as a step toward self-destruction. Yet no one could have been more aware of the psychopathology of Wilbur Joseph Cash (1900–1941) than Cash himself, who ended his life soon after the successful publication of *The Mind of the South*. How compulsively Cash shared embarrassing personal details suggests that self-revelation must have been psychologically useful. To his publisher he confessed "my incorrigible habit of expecting the worst." To a magazine editor he explained "my usual fear of being led into taking over other men's notions." To a reporter he admitted that fame made him unable "to do anything save guzzle beer and go to bed."[53] Because not one of these correspondents was a close friend, Cash's deprecating self-analysis seems inappropriate, although less so than the medical history he included in public documents. He had not been able to work as a journalist, he noted in a 1932 application for a Guggenheim Fellowship, because his "hyper-thyroidism" led to "nervous erethism." He repeated the diagnosis when he reapplied in 1940, reporting that "the illness was mainly neurasthenic rather than physical" and at times produced a paralyzing "defeatism." On the author's questionnaire for his publisher, he admitted that he was "constantly depressed" at the thought of being "hopelessly lazy."[54] It must have eased Cash's social awkwardness to open communication by mentioning his worst traits, thereby turning potential critics into intimates by means of a common secret. The habit not only drew attention to his personality but reminded everyone that he, too, saw his deficiencies and controlled them. Allaying his distress by weaving anxieties into casual conversation, Cash may have believed that he worked his own cure.

You would never know by listening to Cash that he ever saw a doctor. In contrast to his free-flowing commentary on his states of mind, his references to medicine were vague and laconic and conveyed deference mixed with distaste. In his first Guggenheim application, he presented himself as a good patient who, "on the advice of my physician," once went home to rest in "my native village" and later "enter[ed] a hospital, where I remained for several months." The only other note on treatment in his personal papers was indirect: his fiancée spent "two years in a tuberculosis sanitarium," he told an acquaintance in 1938, some of it in a "ward, the rest of whose inhabitants were what we so bravely call white trash."[55] Perhaps unpleasant memories of his own hospitalization translated into this snobbish social judgment.

Even if Cash, like his peers, was suspended between awe and fear of medical expertise, the clinical attention he received was uncommon. As a college-educated man who lived mostly in urban Charlotte, he had the sense and means in 1932 to follow his doctor's orders and consult a specialist at Johns Hopkins University Hospital, where he was x-rayed for a suspected brain tumor. Although only a handful of southerners could have entered a first-class facility, recollections of Cash focus on the deficiency of his medical care. In the 1960s his Charlotte doctor "stated flatly that had Cash been in the hands of the right psychiatrist," reported Cash's first biographer, "he would have survived into ripe old age."[56] True, there was no psychiatrist at all in Charlotte, but Cash's regimen of vitamins, rest, and travel was in line with the current treatment of nervous debility, and he may have declined psychotherapy at Johns Hopkins, an institution shaped by Adolf Meyer, the noted psychiatrist. The impulse of relatives and friends of a suicide victim to blame themselves obscures how gingerly Cash sought professional answers. By the time of his death, he and his doctor were drinking buddies in Charlotte, sharing an interest in the mind. Both may have felt comfortable with their neighborly relation, but its effect was further to derail any search for a medical cure.[57]

Like members of literate elites throughout history, Cash had the luxury of gaining personal insight by reading and writing, and he used his talent for self-protection. "As a consequence of illness, I have acquired a considerable knowledge of abnormal psychology and human anatomy and physiology," he told his publisher, and although he most often mentioned Sigmund Freud, he also cited John B. Watson, a South Carolina–born Baptist like himself. Watson had been anxious to leave his native region and religion in 1900 when he entered the University of Chicago; when Cash named him in print in 1933, Watson was near the height of his popularity as a crusading behaviorist and dogmatic materialist. Cash, the unmarried adult son of evangelical parents, may have been as intrigued by Watson's rebelliousness as by his ideas on habit formation.[58]

Indeed, Cash's eclectic psychological studies remained dilettantish in the sense that he showed no interest in endorsing any theory of personality. His life's work, however, was a psychograph of the South, and the region he sketched was his own character writ large. From the time of Cash's submission of "The Mind of the South" to H. L. Mencken's *American Mercury* in 1929 to his publication of the book of the same title the year of his death, he gave the typical southerner two main traits: "a magnificent incapacity for the real" and "an intensely individualistic mind."[59] This was the impression Cash created when, living at home with his parents in the 1930s, he "frequented the benches around the courthouse square," in one biographer's words, or "would sip beer at a local hangout" with friends until shyness made him "noiseless in a crowd."[60] Yet it was the activity of writing itself that most closely matched the dreamy solipsism Cash described, and although he often complained that he was "horribly stuck" or filled with "depression and dislike" of the work, the book was more truly his therapy. His evolving sense of himself safely informed a sense of his people, and vice versa. Cash believed that he discerned "the ancient mind of the South," and whether he discovered the region's folk soul or not, his cure for his mental instability—private reflection with books and pen—was a time-tested remedy.[61]

Why Cash hung himself in a hotel room in Mexico City within months of his marriage has never been settled, but lack of insight into his dependence on his habitual strategies of self-care at least opened the way. The man who kept himself afloat by talking about his neuroses was now far from home and, worse, supposed to be blissful. Cash and his fiancée, Mary, had agreed in 1938 to delay their marriage until he finished his book, but when "the approaching 'happy' wedding ceremony had us both gloomy and sunk," she recalled, they eloped on a whim on Christmas Eve 1940.[62] Dark notes continued amid professions of contentment. He was "going through the settling down process," Cash reported in a letter, "a not altogether easy one for a man who has been a bachelor for 39 years." Mary later confirmed his trying "bachelor's adjustment."[63] Cash had traded his gloomy routines, in step with the measured expectations for life in the traditional South, for a conventional dream of happiness. During his last days, when he imagined himself stalked by Nazi agents, it was as if his familiar psychic pain took a menacing external shape in a country that he and Mary had entered as a "writers' paradise."[64] Without his comforting self-therapies in the forms of his neighbors and manuscript, Cash was defenseless.

John Gould Fletcher (1886–1950) of Little Rock, Arkansas, remembered mainly as a poet, had far more contact with psychiatry than did Cash, but he never deviated from his belief that his mental crises were acute illnesses from which he emerged, as he said of one episode, "completely cured."[65] The gap between his casual approach to treatment and real trauma suggests a simplistic idea of the psyche. Lifelong depression, two suicide attempts, and four hospitalizations for mental breakdowns between 1926 and 1945 did not lead Fletcher to the conclusion that he had an ongoing problem. Without a developmental view of personality, he saw periods of medical care as times of rest and recovery. Although it might have made sense in 1926 to follow up two weeks in an English clinic with "a quiet holiday" in Cornwall, in his biographer's phrase, Fletcher's inclination in late 1944 to substitute travel for therapy after an overdose of sleeping pills reflected his coolness to psychiatry. A bed was open in a Memphis psychiatric hospital, his wife told friends less than two weeks after Fletcher tried to end his life, "but John feels so much better, he said when he goes to Memphis he wants to go to have a good time." They would go "just for a vacation."[66]

As it turned out, Fletcher relapsed and spent most of the winter at the facility, where he was treated with electric shock, and over the decades doctors also prescribed psychotropic drugs including Luminal, "gold treatments," and medicines identified in his diary only as shots. Although there were terrible moments, like the night in 1934 when he arrived at a hospital at ten o'clock and still at four o'clock the next morning was "screaming for his sister," the nurse wrote, "almost uncontrollable," Fletcher never gave up a strictly somatic model of mental illness. "I utterly collapsed," he said of one hospitalization in his 1937 autobiography, and when he came home, "I was cured."[67]

To be sure, psychiatry has always acknowledged the physiology of emotional disorders. It was Fletcher's inability to imagine that his dichotomy of sickness and health might be too rudimentary because personality is complex that set him apart from the new science. Nor was he shortsighted only about his own case. When his wife collapsed in July 1945, not long after he came home from Memphis, he unquestioningly recorded the doctor's diagnosis in his diary as "colitis — a secondary infection caused by . . . [illegible] germ," never wondering if her illness might relate to her repeated requests that spring for a marital separation or to her feeling, whispered to friends, that his hospitalization was "a cure for me."[68] Despite wartime discussions in the press of the psychology of combat fatigue, Fletcher could not conceive of a psychosomatic illness.[69]

His one-dimensional view of the mind makes his reading of Freud surprising, yet his study of psychoanalysis was serious. "Sigmund Freud dies at midnight," he wrote in his diary in September 1939. Ten years later he wrote in his diary again that Freud "pictured himself as the Moses that would redeem his race from its neuroticism." Once out of the ghetto, Jews "became neurotic as they realized that their culture only flourished sporadically in a civilization, orbit not theirs." Whether Fletcher first read Freud for self-help or to hear the ideas of an influential man, he became focused on Freud's Jewishness and seemed unable to separate the thinker from stereotypes. "Old Jew with mouth full of gold teeth — shylock obsession," he observed on a transatlantic voyage in 1926, and this feeling remained his subtext when he began his journal entry in 1949, "There is something peculiarly Jewish about psychoanalysis."[70] We may wonder if Fletcher hung onto a crude medical psychology because the Jewish connections of psychoanalysis made it unacceptable to him. As a contributing author to I'll Take My Stand (1930), Fletcher took the side of Southern Agrarianism against modernism, a philosophy sometimes blamed on the Jews.[71] For whatever motive, Fletcher studied Freud and rejected him. He managed his illness with his own view of nervous disease.

Around the first of the year 1946, Fletcher dreamed of "gasping choking" to "death by water," echoing a tarot prophecy.[72] He drowned himself in a pond near his home four years later. He had continued to seek treatment by getting shots and visiting therapeutic baths, as well as doctoring himself with alcohol and cigarettes, once five packs a day.[73] He seems in his heart to have given up on medicine, however, as he rephrased his mental problems as religious ones in his diary. Although psychology itself took an existential turn after the war, Fletcher read no new works but became locked in a classic debate with the devil recognizable to any southern preacher and congregation. "Our Father who art in heaven — but unless thou art also on earth, there is now no heaven," he began a parodic Lord's Prayer in 1945.

"Hallowed be thy name—but there have been many names of God, and all have been hallowed by man. We cannot hallow any name, we who live at the bitter end of time." At four o'clock one morning in 1948, he scribbled down a more hopeful "creed": "*We are led towards God*" and "*must each find it [truth] for ourselves.*"[74] Fascinated the same year by Thomas Merton's story of his conversion to Catholicism, *The Seven Storey Mountain*, Fletcher had only a fragile confidence in spiritual transformation. "The convert today is nearly always, the desperate person," he observed, "the person no longer in control of himself." He still wished to believe there is a "full purpose of God in relation to ourselves," though it be hidden, because life without faith "leads, or should lead, to suicide." Yet as Nietzsche's judgment of Christianity as a "confession of weakness" tugged on Fletcher, his logic left him little protection.[75]

Although it is idle to wonder if the range of psychological theories then current might have saved Fletcher, it is clear that he barely opened this door. A leading intellectual, he was as wary as his neighbors of the latest science, avoiding hospitals except in crisis, seeking God for shelter, and resigning himself to apparent fate. Throughout, the experiential core of his illness may have resembled this diary entry: "Once again, life begins to get intolerable. . . . Am in tears because of my struggle with deep depression."[76] There are perhaps as many ways to understand his emotion as there are cultures, however, and in his day Fletcher's choice of words from simple medicine and piety was notably conservative.

For Lillian Smith (1897–1966) of Georgia, the challenge is to disentangle her knowledge of psychology, friendships with psychiatrists, and reputation as a neurotic from her private emotional needs. Ralph McGill, editor of the *Atlanta Constitution*, was on the mark when he reviewed her *Killers of the Dream* (1949) as "an attempt to depict the problem of race in the South in terms of psychiatric fears, guilts and complexes."[77] Smith's correspondence stated even more clinically that "segregation is an ancient, psychological mechanism"—"a form of cultural schizophrenia"—used universally when people "want to shut themselves away from problems which they fear and do not feel they have the strength to solve." If "a southerner is the only person who can encourage other southerners," her logic made Smith the region's therapist, a thought seconded by Karl Menninger, the Kansas psychiatrist, when he praised her as "a keen physician."[78]

McGill, however, turned Smith's psychological talk into a polemical weapon. "Miss Smith" was a "zealot" who made her case "so emotionally" that her "own psychological agony cries from her words." If the charge of derangement was not enough, he added sectional disloyalty and sacrilege: she recruited "that good Viennese, Freud," to cite alongside "Christ" for a "distorted" result. McGill's rhetoric stirred anxieties about insanity and psychiatry in his readers in order to defend segregation against her uncompromising attack, and his partisan intent makes me cautious about asking a similar question about Smith's state of mind. Yet in the years following the publication of her book, Smith had every reason to lose her mental balance and seek professional help: six recurrences of cancer beginning in 1953, plus the deliberate burning of her house and papers in 1955 by local teenagers who judged her a radical integrationist.[79] When she instead maintained outward poise, she showed that she shared some of McGill's distrust of psychiatry. Enthusiastic about psychology as a social cure, she stoically faced her own trials.

There was a mental cost to Smith's cancer. When she expressed dismay in 1955 at the redundancy of a "For Whites Only" sign over a drinking fountain at an all-white clinic, she placed herself in a grim picture. "There we sit: malignant human beings," all "facing their dread disease" and "levelled down pretty low by this cancer business."[80] In this light the reserve in her friendship with Lawrence Kubie, the New York–based psychoanalyst, is noteworthy. An expert on the psychology of creativity as well as a stalwart liberal on race, Kubie contacted "My dear Miss Smith" as soon as he reviewed *Killers of the Dream*, "my favorite" of her works, he repeated in 1961. They corresponded stiffly as "Dear Lawrence Kubie" and "Dear Lillian Smith" until 1954, when the "privilege" of using "Lillian" made him "feel heartwarmed and close."[81] Although they met whenever she visited New York, it was a sign of their bond that he traveled to her home in rural Georgia, a long flight and then several hours' drive from Atlanta, shortly before her death.[82]

Through all, Smith never said how she felt about her cancers, and Kubie never asked. In 1955 he arranged cancer treatment in New York and showed his esteem for her when he thanked the specialist for being candid with his friend. Truthfulness was not then the norm in women's care. To Lillian, however, he simply repeated his colleague's praise of "what good control you have," and he returned to her psychic strength the next year when he called her "one of the glorious exceptions" to the "neurotic distortion" commonplace in gifted people.[83] Both of them implicitly set a high bar for a treatable emotional problem, despite their commitment to therapy. When one of Smith's friends abandoned psychoanalysis, she mourned, "Oh, this turning away from help. . . . I do not quite understand why we fear so much what exists inside us." Yet in her relationship with "Larry dear," her lament remained an abstraction.[84] There was no expression of fear of suffering, relief at remission, or sorrow at impending loss.

Smith was most genuine when she was angry, and her disdain of William Faulkner offers a glimpse of the intolerance of abnormality that drove her own self-restraint. In her mind their quarrel was about which South, aberrant or healthy, would prevail. Faulkner's fiction exuded "the aroma of illness," she complained to Kubie in 1957, and soon she wrote furiously to Paul Tillich that the novelist's latest book was "a diabolical travesty, a blasphemous piece of writing." "Faulkner does not know what 'ultimate things' are" and had no wish to learn. The world will imagine all southerners to be Snopeses, the family Faulkner used to probe amoral emotion, she told another acquaintance; "here is our Nobel prize winner thinking with the mob."[85] Jealousy underwrote her criticism in part. "No Pulitzer prize as you know," she reminded a reporter around 1964, suspiciously repeating her indifference to acclaim when she added, "I'd remember if it were the Nobel prize; but these little awards don't amount to much." Yet she was also sincerely repulsed by Faulkner's disregard of the "moral imperative," a quality that should impel writers who "have felt the edge of ugliness" to bear witness to "the beauty that lies on the other side of the edge."[86]

For all her reading of the psychoanalysts, Smith remained squeamish about human perversion. She expected psychology to redeem without pausing too long to unmask. Like a preacher confronting sin, needing to be just intimate enough with the enemy to be repelled, she held herself to a higher standard. In this she followed her parents, prosperous Methodists. Neither of them revealed feelings. "Her private world we rarely entered," she recalled of her mother. When her father learned of "the death of his beloved favorite son, he gathered his children together, knelt down, and in a steady voice which contained no hint of his shattered heart, loyally repeated, 'God is our refuge and strength, a very present help in trouble.'"[87] In their generation, evil seemed to force a choice: embrace degeneracy with the lust of willful damnation, as did Faulkner's characters, or utterly resist it at a high emotional cost. In her behavior Smith remained a born-again southerner.

Suicide can be a person's most self-revealing act, and although Smith once oddly raised the subject, it would have been contrary to her character to expose herself, whatever her despondency. Feeling insulted after a television interview, she told Kubie about liberal southern writers who had taken their own lives. "People have hoped I would; well—I don't know," she concluded, ending defiantly, "Guess I'm too curious about what will happen next here on earth!"[88] For someone who said she spent fifteen years "reading Sigmund Freud, Ferenczi, Rank, Jung, Adler, Menninger, and reading them carefully again and again," Smith's guarded nature is at the very least surprising.[89] Talking about the self, and particularly the identity of her region, seemed to substitute for talking about herself, an indulgence not permitted by her heritage.

Reticence also shaped the experience of Robert Burgette Johnson (1922–65), the second child of Charles S. Johnson, the sociologist and first black president of Fisk University. Family pride was a determining force in responses to Bobby's "depressions," the term used by his father's biographer, and in the Johnsons' wish to protect both their good name and Bobby, they repeated the practice of generations of southerners who tried to resolve their difficulties in private.[90] Looking back, Bobby understood that growing up as the son of a black leader under segregation was like living in a fishbowl, and when he went to Cornell as a graduate student in the 1950s, he felt "great relief that whatever I did would reflect on me," he wrote home, "but not on the family back in Nashville."[91]

He had enough problems to make gossip a burden—failing to gain admission to his father's alma mater, the University of Chicago, in the late 1940s and then drinking, getting divorced, and making slow progress at Cornell—and he habitually saw his failings through others' eyes. "I know I was a big disappointment to the family," he apologized to his mother in 1947.[92] If we read between the lines of Bobby's letters, it seems his parents kept up pressure to be careful of appearances. He learned to fight for his self-esteem against their worries about impressions. "The central issue," he lectured them in 1954, "is your having enough faith and respect for my common sense not to get alarmed every time someone sees a boogeyman under the bed." But he also grasped that the family rule for dealing with troubles was to bring them home. In what sounds like a ritual of contrition, he vowed, as a thirty-two-year-old man, that "my salvation rests in myself and in whatever product I have been able to make from the excellent background that you gave."[93] If family respectability was part of the problem, it also dictated the solution, as the Johnsons tried to work their own cure.

Psychology helped Bobby in a limited way if measured by his family's familiarity with the new field. He received "therapy," says Charles Johnson's biographer, although there is no mention of treatment in private papers.[94] At least some contact with professionals might be expected in light of his father's pioneering use of current mental science in his sociological fieldwork. As Charles Johnson built up Fisk's social sciences in the 1930s, he admired the interpersonal psychiatry of Harry Stack Sullivan, who became a friend, and he launched the argument that segregation harms the development of black children. Bobby, also a sociologist, knew less about psychological ideas. Although references to his "internal conflict" and a "psychological quirk" punctuated his letters, he noted in 1955 that psychiatrists collaborating with him on a community project were "as naïve about community, action, and desegregation as I was about psychiatry."[95]

For the father even more than the son, there was a gap between theory and self-insight, and although anyone who studies abnormality must hope that professional knowledge will never be needed at home, the distance between Charles Johnson's expertise and his parenting seems rooted in racial pressures. The father his children knew was a public man absorbed in protecting his race. "I've been keeping up with you through the papers," Bobby wrote from Cornell, and the news showed him his father's importance. "I've always been impressed by Daddy's ability to forsee [sic] and anticipate trends in research," he wrote, adding a list of examples.[96] Bobby's instinct to approach his father as a professional was based on a habit cultivated by the parent. As president of Fisk in 1952, Charles Johnson had his secretary compose a common letter to his scattered children, and even before his appointment, he let efficiency dictate family communication when he sent an identical text, containing career advice, to his two older sons.[97] It takes no genius to guess why Bobby revered his father's ambition. Segregation made Charles Johnson's work an all-consuming calling that supplied the main, if not the only, bridge to Bobby. In a family devoted to obligation and reputation, psychological theories and therapies remained for the most part adjuncts of career.

Bobby's consultations with his parents by mail did not resolve his on-going loneliness. The black community of Elmira, New York, the subject of his dissertation research, was "stand-offish," and Philadelphia, the site of his first job, was "impersonal & cold" and left him "lonely and moon-ing."[98] He seemed to take his solitude with him, and although his family was truly his anchor, their support could not make him feel connected. Like Cash, Fletcher, and Smith, Bobby Johnson developed a technique of self-care, in his case behaving repeatedly like the prodigal son. All four had an exceptional acquaintance with psychology for their time and place, but they remained personally loyal to old remedies of self-restraint, family management, neighborly gossip, and, in extremity, self-destruction. Their willingness to endure psychic struggle stands in contrast to the growing scientific optimism about diagnosis and cure. Although each had a role in bringing new ideas to the region, the difference between what they said and how they lived is a reminder of how slowly southerners changed. But innovations did come south, along narrow paths before wider roads.

Early Migrations

Whether one believes that modern mental science began in Leipzig with Wilhelm Wundt, Vienna with Sigmund Freud, or Cambridge with William James, the field did not originate in the American South, and the move-ment of people and ideas across regional borders was the means by which psychology took root there. Before World War II, southern conditions dis-couraged the in-migration of professionals, and particularly doctors, the experts who might be expected to spread psychological precepts. "Post-bellum South Carolina," writes one scholar, "was not a fertile field for physicians, because many people were too poor to afford their services," and similar poverty elsewhere deterred southerners from entering medi-cal practice, prompted established doctors to leave, and dissuaded north-erners from resettling in the South.[99] Segregation was an added disincen-tive for black physicians. In 1961, when Lloyd C. Elam, born in Arkansas, agreed to move from Chicago to Nashville to begin a psychiatry program at Meharry Medical College, "it was not yet popular for a black family with origins in the South to return there," he recalled.[100]

To fill out a grim picture, duress often figured in the decisions of profes-sionals who did pursue southern careers. The South's segregated colleges and hospitals long offered the principal opportunities for northern-trained African Americans, and the refugee intellectuals who fled totalitarian states beginning in the 1930s took southern jobs mainly when other positions were not open. Yet if all these circumstances make the early practice of southern mental science seem a forced exercise for the disadvantaged, the South was in truth less a wasteland than a frontier. Anyone schooled in psychiatry or psychology might make a difference there because so few were knowledgeable, and in these small circles, personal acquaintance influenced the transmission of ideas to an unusual degree.

It was the wealthy who went north in pursuit of cures and there met professionals who followed their patients back home. In one case, the quest for health in the extended Percy family, scattered across Alabama, Mississippi, and Tennessee, drew a leading psychiatrist to the South. Four Percys entered private Baltimore psychiatric clinics between 1911 and 1932.[101] The family's inclination to trust psychiatry enough to journey northward grew from its members' medical habits. Their preference for holistic cures tacitly recognized the role of mood in health and led Camille Percy, who had heart disease, to sanitariums in Michigan and New York in the early 1920s for treatments focused on diet, bathing, and rest. Because family members often went along, it seems the Percys tried to adapt medicine to southern ways. Thus when Camille was too ill to go north in 1928, her husband took her and a nurse to a Gulf Coast hotel, where he hoped to find "quail shooting" for himself, he telegraphed the owner, and "if so will bring dog."[102]

The Percys' impulse to blur the line between treatment and domesticity introduced Harry Stack Sullivan (1892–1949) to the South. Born in upstate New York, Sullivan most likely met the family as a young psychiatrist in Baltimore, consulted for the depression of Le Roy Percy of Birmingham in 1925. Seven years later Sullivan traveled to Greenville, Mississippi, to counsel Le Roy's sons after their mother's accidental death, and in seven more years he was back in Greenville, again the Percys' guest, at work on a scholarly project. Sullivan did fieldwork for "Memorandum of a Psychiatric Reconnaissance," his appendix to Charles S. Johnson's *Growing Up in the Black Belt* (1941), at the request of academic friends. It may well have been his Mississippi connections that inclined him to accept the task of interviewing black teenagers.[103]

The Percys did not personally invite George Gartly and R. C. Ramsay to Memphis, but the family's northern medical travels do suggest why these

Canadian-born male nurses opened a fifteen-bed clinic there in 1909, which by the 1950s was a psychiatric hospital. "My wife some years ago was at Battle Creek and took the treatment," wrote Camille's husband to the Battle Creek Sanitarium in 1928.[104] This was where Gartly and Ramsay learned nursing, and although Camille's stay probably postdated their student days, it is a fair guess that the facility had a steady stream of southern clients whom the young men hoped to serve closer to home. The Percys did not mention that the Battle Creek clinic was the pioneering institution for holistic health founded by Seventh-Day Adventists in the 1860s. The family's practical wish for healing evidently bypassed the Adventist theology that guided the religious group's natural therapies. For Gartly and Ramsay, though, the South may also have represented mission territory, if they were Adventists themselves.[105]

As a river city, Memphis was reasonably accepting of outsiders. The deep southern roots of one longtime neurosurgeon, whose grandfather fought for the Confederacy, received proud mention in the doctor's obituary, but the press also praised the cosmopolitanism of a local psychiatrist, born in Vienna in 1899 and most likely Jewish by heritage, by calling him a "medical Marco Polo."[106] Although Gartly soon began studying medicine at what became the University of Tennessee College of Medicine, the men's nursing background produced therapies that were sensitive to the mutual influences of environment, body, and mind. In 1910 "Gartly & Ramsay Hospital" advertised its specialty as "Physiological Therapeutics" in the Memphis city directory, including "Hydrotherapy, Electricity, Massage, Manual Swedish Movements, Physical Culture, and carefully regulated dietary."[107] The eclectic treatments may have appealed to patients disturbed by a mix of somatic and psychological ills, making it logical that this "was one of the first hospitals in Memphis to receive mental patients," in a newspaper's words, and to devote itself later to psychiatry only. It was the hospital's first certified psychiatrist who treated John Gould Fletcher in 1944, and drinking problems led William Faulkner to seek help at Gartly-Ramsay in the 1950s.[108] As patients of means began to come from a distance, the hospital gained a national reputation. Yet its origins apparently lay in the interpersonal contacts of turn-of-the-century southerners who went north for medical care.

Education was another compelling object that sent southerners northward, and the knowledge they gained and friends they made predictably had consequences back home. In the early days, students rarely planned to specialize in any one of the emerging psychological fields. Not only did they know little about them, but paths of study were also unclear. Various theorists who pictured personality as individuated and dynamic could be found almost anywhere in a virtual maze of humanistic, social scientific, and medical disciplines. In a typical story, John B. Watson left South Carolina in 1900 thinking that his doctorate at the University of Chicago would be in philosophy, but he finished in psychology under James Rowland Angell.[109] Before long, advanced students more readily fixed on a vocation in psychiatry or psychology as a career goal. Frank Luton and Merrill Moore, who earned M.D. degrees at Vanderbilt School of Medicine in 1927 and 1928, respectively, were among the school's first graduates to become psychiatrists. Their acquaintance was a small bridge for the southward movement of psychological concerns.

Of the two, Luton (1898–1979) was the good soldier. He trained for three years as an intern at Johns Hopkins under Adolf Meyer, whose self-styled "psycho-biology" began with the premise that the patient's mind develops in real interaction with concrete experience. Luton then joined the Vanderbilt faculty and took up bread-and-butter tasks like reforming state-run asylums.[110] Moore (1903–57), by contrast an iconoclast, settled in Boston after studying at Harvard but never severed home ties. "I was running toward maturity," an obituary quoted him as saying, "not running away from anything."[111] Poetry was one passion that kept him connected with the South. An author of more than 50,000 sonnets and a psychiatrist to poets including Robert Frost, Moore had belonged to the Fugitive circle of writers at Vanderbilt in the early 1920s. In 1956 he joined Donald Davidson, John Crowe Ransom, Robert Penn Warren, and other onetime Fugitive poets in Nashville for a reunion.[112]

Although Tennesseans might find Moore's long-distance ocean swimming odd and his decision to will his body to Harvard Medical School even odder, he kept up a collegial relationship with Luton. Moore arranged to stain and photograph "brain sections" that Luton sent to Boston in 1932. The same year, Moore wrote that he and his wife were attending lectures by Hanns Sachs, the noted Freudian, and during the war he sent Luton information about Anna Freud's work in England with refugee children.[113] These contacts gain significance if we note that Luton was the first licensed psychiatrist in Tennessee. Presumably he sent the tissue samples because they could not be adequately analyzed locally, and although reports on the Freudians were unsolicited, they were news in a place where psychoanalysis was little known.

Moore also worked to resettle refugees from Nazism in his native region. A Methodist, he was also a philo-Semite. Late in life he fondly recalled "two hook face women," German-born Jews, who sold him notebooks in their Nashville drugstore when he was a boy. Even if this memory seems contrived, Sidney Hirsch, who was certainly Jewish, and Milton Starr, who probably was, were close friends of Moore during his Vanderbilt years.[114] The real catalyst for Moore's placement work, however, was Hanns Sachs. Sachs, who fled Vienna, leaving family behind, psychoanalyzed Moore in Boston from 1934 to 1938 as part of Moore's analytic training. Clearly infatuated, Moore showered Sachs with gratitude, lining up a stenographer, securing library privileges, contacting publishers, introducing him to local psychiatrists, and even inviting him to see Disney's *Snow White* with his family. Moore's feeling for Sachs underscored the enormity of Nazism. "The European situation is incredible," he told Sachs days before the German invasion of Poland. "Only one acquainted with the deep forces in the human mind can appreciate the significance of what has happened."[115]

The result was furious activity to recruit southern friends to help refugee scholars. Moore urged Dr. Israel Newman at Augusta State Hospital to issue a work affidavit for a possible immigrant, and Starr, now a Nashville businessman, promised to fund Sachs's publications. Moore hoped the South would offer not only employment but healing. "There is something about the South," he reflected in a letter to Sachs, who was vacationing in South Carolina with the Starrs: "warm climate, warm people, that type of friendliness that is refreshing," so different from the "apathy, depressiveness, hostility and the kind of hard bitten accomplishments that people seek for here."[116] What gain for southern psychiatry grew out of Moore's efforts is a matter of speculation. But at the very least, Sachs gave psychoanalytic lectures about creativity in 1938 at North Carolina's Black Mountain College, an experimental haven for intellectuals, and in the background, southerners heard about the real-life traumas of European psychiatrists.[117]

American racism was also responsible for the international flavor of early southern psychiatry. Before World War II, prejudice set most foreign-born professionals of color on a single path: specialty training in the North followed by a job in the South. In notable cases, the Rockefeller Foundation helped Rafael Hernandez (1897–1976), Ernest Y. Williams (1900–1990), and Bingham Dai (1899–1996) — natives of Puerto Rico, the British West Indies, and China, respectively — to get advanced instruction in psychiatry around 1930. White Americans' habit of classifying people in one of two racial categories contributed to their subsequent placement at Jim Crow schools. Hernandez "is a mixture of Spanish and Negro blood," wrote a Rockefeller official in New York in 1938 to a dean at Columbia, although there is no evidence for this conclusion except his Puerto Rican origin. The racial inference does explain the administrator's "surprise" that Hernandez passed the "Psychiatry Board," making him a certified specialist, as well as the sarcasm of the man's comment that "he holds the impressive title of Professor of Anatomy, Neurology, and Psychiatry" at Meharry Medical College.[118]

Dai moved across the color line from Fisk to Duke in 1943, but the other men struggled on for achievement. Williams sold real estate part-time to help support Howard University's psychiatry program, and Hernandez, nearly sixty, faced insulting inquiries from the state of Alabama about the legitimacy of his internship, completed twenty-five years earlier, when he took a post at Tuskegee veterans' hospital in 1955.[119] The tenuous quality of all three careers should not overshadow their contributions to southern psychiatry. Almost single-handedly, Hernandez and Williams represented psychiatry for years at the country's only African American medical schools, and Dai was one of the first figures in the nation to introduce Asian theories and therapies into psychological care.[120] White disregard of nonwhite talent led to its concentration in the South, where, surviving prejudice, scholars of color served the region.

All the pressures and opportunities associated with the pursuit of health, schooling, and work opened the South to the influence of psychological innovation. But as one might expect, it is harder to penetrate the motives of the migrants than to chart their paths. Anyone's movement across cultural boundaries is likely to stir a combination of nostalgia and expectancy that complicates self-expression, and in the case of the South, additional factors, most notably race, could all but silence reflection. Charles Prud-homme, who in 1956 became the first African American certified by the American Psychoanalytic Association, cast a veil in his memoir over his time as associate medical officer of the Tuskegee hospital. Although he had been assured by the friend who hired him that "I would like it at Tuskegee," he quickly closed, "In 1943, after about four and a half years in Tuskegee, I returned to Washington and Howard."[121] There is nothing about being a black psychiatrist in the rural South, except that he left.

So did at least one of the Boston psychiatrists trained hastily in 1923 for the newly opened hospital, perhaps anticipating the difficulties of those who stayed. After serving for two decades as a psychiatrist, Toussaint Til-don became the institution's superintendent in 1946, and it was part of his job to supply examining rooms, equipment, and hot lunches on days when the black men recruited as test subjects for the government's decades-long syphilis experiment came there for checkups. Tildon was "very cooperative and sympathetic," reported a doctor employed by the U.S. Public Health Service in 1948. But it seems fair to wonder how Tildon faced the tensions among his roles as a psychiatrist, a civil servant, and a black man him-self.[122]

No matter how instrumental migratory professionals were in laying foundations for southern mental science, their influence was slow to reach beyond the South's leading colleges and hospitals, most often found in cities. The psychological medicine they practiced conveyed the message that the mind can be explained and controlled, but the prevailing southern view was less scientific. Most southerners did not assess individual behavior systematically unless it was deranged, and because they saw aberration in metaphysical terms as the fruit of sin or malfeasance, their instinct was to accept its necessity. Mental illness was as natural in a haunted cosmos as it was frightening, and families and communities coped with the afflicted as an obligation. Even the region's intellectuals who were intrigued by psychological concepts tried to live by simple fortitude themselves.

In time, a new sense of personality began to emerge. Because the South's schools were few and poor by national standards, it might seem unlikely that an appreciation of human potential for self-correction would take root through education. The magnitude of southern need for instruction at every level drew northern philanthropy in like proportion, however, and as schools grew up at many, if not every, crossroads, an interest in child development accompanying educational reform began to spread. Children, then, were a catalyst for turning southern thoughts about the psyche from a mood of brooding over the mind's defects to hopes for its health. But from the first, segregation left its mark on the educational crusade.

| 2 | THE PROMISE OF THE CHILD

AND THE LIMITS OF PROGRESS

Jackson Davis was a true believer in the educational reforms that carried up-to-date psychological ideas southward in a dramatic way. In 1947, shortly before his death, Davis repeated the principles that shaped his thirty-two-year career as a southern agent for the General Education Board (GEB), an arm of the Rockefeller Foundation. Visiting an Alabama school, he described the "philosophy motivating the projects": first, "the school is the best single agency for developing social and economic changes," and second, "permanent changes will come through the proper direction of children."[1] Children were all but absent in early southern discussions of personality, which focused in their rudimentary way on derangement, and so Davis's optimism about the child's plasticity might seem a northern view. Testimony after Davis's death, however, emphasized his southernness. "He knew Southern education and educators intimately," wrote a former coworker, and President Benjamin Mays of Morehouse College titled his memorial "He, Too, Was Southern."[2]

Born in Virginia in 1882, Davis first traversed the region in a buggy as a county school superintendent. He needed extra gas rations for his car during World War II because he was so often on the road. Everywhere he seemed comfortable with fellow southerners. Not only did he sit down with girls at a "canning party" in 1911, but he recorded in his diary how they steamed the tomatoes. Although he was white, he ate with blacks, remembering with pleasure a lunch at a "colored teachers' meeting" of

Jackson Davis of the General Education Board, perhaps at his office in Burkeville, Virginia. Courtesy of Jackson Davis Papers, Special Collections Library, University of Virginia Library, Charlottesville.

"parker house rolls, veal croquettes, apple fritters, coffee and cream puffs."[3] Straddling the racial worlds of segregation even in an official capacity required firm purpose, as did serving a northern philanthropy aiming to aid southern schools. A religious man, Davis saw his work as a calling, but he had also studied around 1900 at Teachers College of Columbia University and absorbed its scientific vision of childrearing.[4] That southerners posthumously celebrated his influence was a sign that his faith in child nurture had taken hold. Across the South, children anchored a new sense of the psyche as complex, comprehensible, and susceptible to guidance.

The implications were radical. Psychological ideas that endorsed child nurture in a managed environment sharpened awareness of the personhood of children across the color line. Science made every child an object of value. In the long run, there were southerners who turned excitement about children's potential into an argument for equal rights, and yet others, disconcerted by the same changes, who defended racially separate education with renewed determination. In the heyday of southern school reform before World War II, my focus here, strenuous activity overshadowed precise arguments for either side. Some whites repeated long-standing doubts about black children, however, as soon as upgraded segregated schools began to appear.[5]

Reforms in the professional training of southern psychiatrists and psychologists between the wars produced even more mixed results, both practically and morally. Often the same leaders, northern and southern, who warmed to the cause of normal children allowed racism to shape the expansion of the South's psychological teaching in other settings. In Nashville, white skepticism about black intelligence restrained the growth of psychiatry as a field at the city's medical schools. Sponsors could not imagine black specialists curing black mental patients. In Durham, North Carolina, Duke University hired the British-born psychologist William McDougall, known for his racial conservatism, to establish its psychology program. Eager to move southward to a welcoming region, McDougall lent the stature of his science to the racial status quo.

All three cases show how a psychology attentive to selfhood grew in the South as part of a near revolution in education. The region's schools were so poor that they were inevitably improved. Meharry Medical College "may be compared in standing with the medical school maintained by mission boards at Tsi-nan-fu in North China," lamented one visitor from the GEB in 1934.[6] The social uses of psychological ideas in the region, however, were more varied. For every time that mental science challenged racial segregation, psychology elsewhere adapted to prejudice.

The Discovery of the Southern Child

The Progressive movement in American education at the turn of the twentieth century celebrated children as the subject of instruction, schools as the place, and psychology as the method. Although the reformers were not racially blind, the new thinking stressed the plasticity of students in an adjustable environment. Southerners could not deny that their schools needed attention, because the region had virtually no public systems before Reconstruction, and, once these began, jobs often served as political spoils. Leaders in the southern field indeed seemed eager to reform. When George Peabody College in Nashville proposed a new curriculum to train high school teachers in 1925, psychology was a core first-year subject, along with English, history, and biology. Nearby at Fisk University, where most undergraduates became teachers, administrators purchased basic books in educational psychology for the new library three years later.[7] Although titles of additional sources that Fisk hoped to buy went on for pages, much American school psychology in fact grew from a single intellectual stem. William James supervised the first American doctorate in psychology, completed by G. Stanley Hall at Harvard, and Hall later mentored John Dewey at Johns Hopkins. In a case of the student's honing the teacher's ideas, it was Hall who first focused on children.[8]

The persuasiveness of Hall's pioneering essay, "The Contents of Children's Minds" (1883), lay in its modesty.[9] Skirting theoretical battles, Hall (1844–1924) explained how Boston kindergarten teachers questioned three pupils at a time in a coatroom to find out what the children thought, hoping to thereby improve their own teaching. The implications of the experiment were profound: children were great storehouses of ideas, some shocking and all in flux. Americans had not tried to systematize childrearing before they acquired the habit of developmental thinking in the nineteenth century. Once childhood seemed the point of individual origin, an expert like Hall might recruit science for analysis and guidance.

He courted readers of all opinions by muffling controversy. On matters of faith, he repeated what the children said about right and wrong without judging their answers against denominational doctrines, and the more outrageous their beliefs—that God is "*blue*" or "God *kills* people or *beats them with a cane*" in hell—the calmer his reassurance that falsehoods "will be shed [by the child] with its milk-teeth when more solid mental pabulum can be digested."[10] His evolutionary ideas, too, might have disturbed pious people had he not aired them quietly. Professing caution about "the evolutionary dictum that the child's mental development should repeat that of the race," Hall went on to say that children learn better in the countryside where they retrace "the experiences of primitive man."[11] He was just as equivocal about racial science. At a time when it was fashionable to call every social group a race with a character fixed by heredity, he merely recorded the differing responses of his "Irish" and "American" subjects and noted that "what is within and what is without" both shape "the child's soul."[12] Hall is not typically seen as a philosophical pragmatist, but he clearly kept company with them, and here he rejected theorizing in favor of concreteness in a way akin to James and Dewey. Most basically, he asked every teacher to reconsider the child: "Alas for the teacher who does not learn more from his children than he can ever hope to teach them!" He rightly added that his work had "great importance for anthropology and psychology."[13]

Although the simplicity of the notion of the child's potential helped Hall gain a wide audience, his distaste for dogmatism also drew a variety of students to Clark University in Worcester, Massachusetts, where he became the first president in 1888. Coming from the South, Howard Odum of Georgia and Francis Sumner of Arkansas wrote dissertations under Hall in the early years of the new century. The two men could hardly have been more dissimilar. Odum endorsed segregation until his death in 1954; Sumner so bluntly denounced racism as a graduate student in the local press that he was forced to recant.[14] Their identical bonds with Hall suggest the adaptability of his core concept of child development. Yet in the South, the message of growth still faced obstacles erected by racial dogma, religious conservatism, and poverty.

The comparative claims of nature and nurture that Hall passed over with good-humored moderation belonged to a debate intertwined with the Jim Crow system. Even if Hall wished to circumvent a sterile conflict by offering a practical plan instead, he must have known that popular racial ideas cast doubt on psychologically informed schooling. Why raise hopes about children if race predetermines accomplishment? It was not only cruel, one heard said, but also imprudent to encourage black expectations.

Hall was all the more vulnerable because belief in a racial hierarchy set by nature was not a peculiarly southern mind-set but a commonplace in nineteenth-century Western culture. When psychiatrists worldwide who encountered patients of color entered the discussion, they produced a clinical literature that seemed to confirm innate racial differences. Whether a doctor in Washington, D.C., in 1891 explained that blacks were "naturally timid, suspicious and emotional" or a Calcutta psychoanalyst observed in 1924 that women "of a superior racial type" have "the strongest attraction for individuals belonging to a racially more primitive type," the premise was that race underwrites personality.[15] Hall and like-minded educational psychologists obliquely challenged this view by stressing the child's capacity to change. One southern critic predictably snarled back in 1914 that "Northern friends of the negro" risked causing "friction" with their educational plans.[16] But there was enough moderate opinion among southerners to strike an intellectual compromise. Odum, for one, urged in a second doctoral dissertation at Columbia University in 1910 that social harmony required educating children according to their unequal racial capacities.[17] Embracing the Progressive faith that education is socially essential, Odum devised a racial rule that allowed the project of overhauling southern schools, safely segregated, to proceed.

In the same way, the South's Calvinist Protestantism, forbidding soil for rational childrearing, modestly allied itself with reform. The predominance of the nearly 100 Baptist students at Meharry Medical College in the mid-1930s, almost double the number of Methodists (the next-largest religious group), was typical of the region, and Baptist adherence to adult conversion and baptism classed children among sinners.[18] Child-centered schooling was surely contrary to strict Calvinist doctrines and discipline.

Religious practice was friendlier to children, however, and these habits favored compromise with the new science of childhood. Churchgoing was so much a family matter that children felt welcome. "We go to church regularly every Sunday," a black teenager told a sociological field-worker from Fisk in the 1930s. "The whole family belongs." An Alabama girl in the same study conveyed her mixed feelings of marginality and attachment: "I never joined the church yet, but I pray."[19] No Calvinist would neglect the moral instruction of children, even if the inevitability that the child would err was equally clear, and this attention to behavior produced an affinity between pious lessons and the personality goals of developmental psychology. It served "mental health," Mississippi teachers learned at a workshop in 1948, for children to acquire a sense of "fair play, honesty, kindness, and other character traits" through membership in clubs.[20] Although evangelical Christians would not mistake moral virtues for God's saving grace, neither did they resist educators far more confident about human freedom than they were. Intellectual conflict, though real, was muted, and forward-looking southerners comfortably blended learning and faith. "I took advantage of the meeting of the Baptist Association" nearby, reported the principal of a South Carolina summer school for teachers in 1918, "and secured Prof. BF. [sic] Hubert of the State College, who addressed the large gathering of families and teachers on vital subjects along agricultural lines."[21]

Poverty, manifested in small part in inadequate schools, may have seemed an even more intractable barrier to hopes for children than race or theology. Although neither the South's underdevelopment in 1900 nor its inattention to schooling was a simple matter of economics, the physical conditions of learning were profoundly discouraging. Studies by reformers, such as a health survey of black students in one Mississippi county during the school year 1943–44, tended to focus on the worst cases, but the facts were indeed sobering. The twenty-five pupils enrolled at Peter's Rock met in a church lit by a kerosene lamp and served by a surface privy; they had no source of drinking water. The five-room building at Jonestown, accommodating more than 300 students, was magnificent by contrast, with electricity, a pump, and two pit privies. Yet only half of the children who attended the first school and one-third of the second school's total were present on the day of the health examination. Illness, insufficient clothing, rural distances, farm labor, and the indifference of families most likely kept the others at home.[22]

Against this background, pride in the acquisition of chairs, desks, and blackboards, expressed in a South Carolina newsletter for black teachers in 1937, makes sense, as does the aspiration of one county supervisor to add "libraries, dictionaries, flags, et cetera."[23] Progress did not close the distance, however, between the most and least equipped schools. At a model school operated by the University of Mississippi at Oxford in 1936, white elementary students had materials to make baskets, costumes, masks, and "individual dictionaries of words needed in writing stories." Here the organizers' psychological goals, such as cultivating "creative self-expression" and the habit "of doing one's best," seemed attainable.[24] But elsewhere southerners' sense of their poverty injected skepticism into discussions of child development. When a onetime Mississippi teacher and state legislator observed in a letter in 1940 to the state school superintendent "that Mississippi is a poor state," she not only explained but justified deficient black public education.[25] The truth was, however, that many of the region's schools were so threadbare as to make optimism about children seem fanciful.

Yet schooling was the centerpiece of a massive plan for southern revitalization launched by northern philanthropists at the turn of the century and supported by progress-minded southerners such as Jackson Davis. The GEB, the wealthiest of the foundations devoted mainly to southern work, alone spent $325 million by the time its funds were exhausted in the 1960s. The South offered surprisingly little resistance to the Yankee incursion. "Executive Says Northerners Would Educate Negroes out of Their Station, Which South Knows Best," read a *New York Herald* headline in 1901, referring to sharp words from Georgia's governor.[26] Although northern benevolence clearly stirred defensive emotions connected with the twin white southern pieties of sectional liberty and racial hierarchy, state legislatures and school administrators in the South were soon working side by side with the philanthropists.[27]

The triumph was the result of the northerners' conservative notion of progress, in large part sincere but also designed to win over southern white leaders. The campaign in its way was psychological. Some clippings collected by the Southern Education Board (SEB), predecessor of the GEB, self-righteously bemoaned new Jim Crow laws effecting "Disenfranchisement of Negroes," in the words of the *Chicago Tribune* in 1901. Yet the SEB also saved an article called "Negroes Down South and Up North," which judged the "South a Better Place for Negroes," from another Chicago publication.[28] Worries about black migration most likely helped sustain northern benevolence. Although no single motive actuated all participants in this far-flung movement, white men, northern and southern, seemed to recognize in each other a common wish for nationwide economic growth with a minimum of social turmoil. Education, focused on individuals and tolerant of their inequalities, was an ideal tool to enhance the productivity and stability of communities at once.[29]

Over the decades following the founding of the GEB in 1902, southern educators and their northern supporters fell into now-familiar habits of sponsored development: southerners wrote letters detailing their needs, administrators devised guidelines for funding, and traveling agents became mediators. Foundations tended to specialize, so that the Rosenwald Fund built schoolhouses and libraries, the Jeanes Fund sent black supervising teachers to country districts, and the GEB underwrote teacher training in colleges and workshops. State governments made matching contributions at the philanthropies' request, and New Deal agencies cosponsored programs during the Depression. Although contemporaries warmed to the visionary quality of donating "Millions of Dollars for South's Schools," as one headline declared, the project was also driven by arrogance. The foundations expected money, management skill, and social science to work a regional miracle.[30]

The foundations' grand ambitions in fact threatened to deflect attention from schoolchildren and to overwhelm curiosity about the psychology of learning with a sociological agenda. Although making schools the hubs of communities was a commonplace goal of Progressive educators, students could lose out if teachers had too many tasks. The risk that zeal for learning might make rudimentary subjects seem unworthy of notice was clear in John Dewey's *Democracy and Education* (1916). Praising "the power to learn from experience" as a state of mind, Dewey (1859–1952) called education a "Necessity of Life" and a "Social Function" in chapter titles, but he said little about actual schools.[31] More practically, the same eagerness for lifelong growth pervaded the rural education movement, which produced a literature most likely familiar to reformers concerned with the South. "The decay of rural civilization can be prevented only by maintaining a physically and mentally vigorous people on the farms," explained *Progressive Trends in Rural Education* in 1926, a task that "must ultimately find its solution in education." The school was not just a place for children but also a "community center," continued the author, a professor at a Massachusetts normal school. There lectures and classes for adults would be an "attractive" alternative to "the pool hall, the dance, 'auto-parties,' 'movies.'"[32]

Southerners in touch with the latest pedagogy seemed excited by the social potential of the school. "'Improved Instruction in Every School' / Has been approved as the golden rule," began one stanza of a poem by a South Carolina Jeanes teacher, who concluded, "Also, 'Oconee County Must Glow and Grow / And each will help to make it so.'" A North Carolina county welfare official wrote in 1921, "At night the farm agt and I have given slides and lectures" in schoolhouses, in response to a survey question, "[What has] your group . . . tried to do to *bring the School Work and Community closer together?*" Elsewhere in the state, schools hosted free medical clinics and "Parent-Teacher clubs."[33]

Yet small staffs and distrust of innovation kept other districts focused on basics. "As a group, we can not report," began one respondent, because she was "an individual worker," and another said that his county was "not in sympathy with the idea of welfare work."[34] In places where penury or traditionalism restricted the services offered at schools, children did not necessarily receive better care. Scarce resources could hamper their progress just as much as an overtaxed teacher could. But the all-too-evident needs of southern schoolchildren generally forced philanthropies to begin with elementary tasks. In South Carolina alone, the Rosenwald Fund constructed 500 schoolhouses by the late 1940s, and Jeanes teachers, vowing "to make classrooms attractive," coaxed communities to improve buildings with paint, "trees, shrubs and flowers."[35] Sadly, poverty helped protect children as the center of interest.

Southern race relations, in contrast, required fewer adjustments of northern plans. Segregation was never in question. Although star theorists of education like Hall and Dewey said little about race, the philanthropies entered the field with a clear purpose to aid black schools. "Let the Darkey Work at a Trade or Hoe Cotton," crowed a North Carolina newspaper in 1901, to which Julian Hawthorne, a leading voice of northern reform, compliantly replied, "The almost unanimous answer" to black schooling is that it should be "industrial education." Hawthorne sweetened the negotiation by proposing simultaneous improvement of white schools.[36]

Behind the scenes, the philanthropies pleaded respectfully for small concessions for black students. The GEB's New York office told a professor at a Mississippi black college in 1914 that it never initiated discussion of the appointment of a state supervisor for black public schools, as the correspondent had asked. But exactly one year later, the governor-elect of Mississippi petitioned the GEB to fund the position; almost surely there were words off the record. In South Carolina, the GEB soon heard a complaint from the state school superintendent that the foundation was causing him "bitter personal and official antagonism." But Jackson Davis went right on interviewing candidates for the post of black school supervisor in private, recommending a man whose "attitude toward race is sane." "He recognizes that relations are steadily improving and that, as a matter of justice and economic well being, more must be done for the education of the Colored children, but that it is a matter of growth, calling for wise and tactful plans on the part of school men." Like many deals transacted in the shadow of politics, Davis conceded that his choice "was not an ideal man" but "as good a man as we could get for the work in South Carolina."[37] Yet moderation may be said to have helped black children in the long run. In 1932 a Mississippi official talked to the GEB about hiring "a well trained Negro woman as a Director of Teacher Training for Negro schools." Although

Florence Alexander still answered to a white man, her graduate work at Columbia University, as well as her race, was an asset to her teachers and their pupils.[38]

In this way, the foundations' businesslike style set in motion modest forces of change. Psychological knowledge advanced, and here and there segregation retreated a few steps. When seventy-seven black rural elementary teachers told organizers of a Mississippi health workshop in 1948 that they rated lectures delivered on child psychology second only to talks on venereal disease, they showed a professionalism unimaginable the year of Alexander's appointment, when three-fifths of the state's black instructors had not finished high school.[39] The GEB's first stated purpose on a list of ten, "To promote education within the United States of America without distinction of race, sex, or creed," made no promise to seek racial equality.[40] Keen on collecting data, the foundation could have found few statistics in 1900 indicating parity in the skills of white and black children, and it worked only selectively to close the gap. Universal literacy, the keystone of reform, should not be underestimated as an objective, when Virginia alone had 130,000 children who were illiterate in 1914, nearly twice as many of them black as white.[41] But the GEB seemed otherwise disinclined to confront inequities. In neighboring cases in 1942, administrators said no to a request from the North Carolina College for Negroes for a pilot project to improve its students' health, although the school had no doctor, nurse, or infirmary, but yes to a nutrition clinic for white children staffed by professionals at the Woman's College of the University of North Carolina. Nearly three years later, after the GEB grew dissatisfied with the white experiment, its officers in effect transferred the funds to the black school, although they still paid only for a nutritionist and a nurse.[42] The transaction perfectly reflected not only the philanthropy's comfort with racial separation and hierarchy but also its pragmatism. Its guiding racial attitudes were clear yet at the same time undogmatic and susceptible to modification.

The foundation in fact experienced some of its most frustrating moments when it tried to apply psychological theories to its southern activities. The movement's initial premise was simple: personalities grow well in a wholesome environment. When Jackson Davis described one of the "colored schools" he visited in 1911 as "painted inside—good blackboards—slate—well-lighted, windows washed, floor clean," he measured by this standard.[43] Psychological science did not stand still, however, and the GEB sponsored primary research in the hope that it would have practical value.

The specialization and abstraction of researchers proved disappointing to the sponsors. One report described academic infighting at a 1934 conference of child psychiatrists at Princeton, where "different theoretical viewpoints were expressed to justify the difference in emphasis preferred by each individual." Gestalt psychologists who met the next year to discuss personality at the foundation's expense used arcane terms like "radix" and spoke in generalities. "Learning is to change movement so that it is better for you" was one thought recorded in the transcript.[44] Hosting conferences was at least inexpensive compared with funding the infant behavior laboratory at Yale founded by Arnold Gesell, a student of Hall. After fourteen years of support, Gesell was "greatly distressed" in 1938 to learn that he would receive only $75,000 from the GEB over the next five years. Though conceding his claim that he had "amassed voluminous data," the foundation saw "little change in Gesell's general attitude or concepts" and sensed that "he lacks insight."[45]

Southern colleges successfully petitioned for research money as well, although northern sponsors seemed to begin with fewer expectations for pathbreaking work. When the GEB purchased a one-time orphanage in Atlanta for Spelman College in 1936 to house its "child development research program," publications were not the goal. A home-office memo described the facility as "a laboratory and training center for students" and a source of advice on "the needs of Negro families" for parents of the nursery school children.[46] As these northern biases connected with region and race exacerbated the difficulty of applying theory to life, the child psychology that came south was always one step removed from the cutting edge.

The rudimentary nature of this science, however, most likely helped it to catch on. By the 1930s casual use of psychological language was becoming commonplace in southern schooling. "As a whole the class lacks confidence in themselves," observed the director of a white school in 1937. Black teachers at Hampton Institute the previous summer learned that they should undertake "study of each individual child before deciding upon the accomplishments of the child."[47] Health education in particular spread awareness of emotional needs. The philanthropies favored health lessons from the beginning, not only because policy makers judged southern hygiene poor but because they believed the region's schoolchildren, especially black ones, had limited intelligence. Jackson Davis heard Virginia educators say in 1911 that "literature [was] too complex for negroes" and their "work must be simple." "Stressed health work" was the solution he noted in his diary.[48]

Southern children of both races in fact studied health texts that devoted more and more space to mental outlook as a component of wellness. The 1917 edition of *Primer of Sanitation* valued attitude to the extent that it meant a commitment to cleanliness. "*Sanity* and *sanitation* mean the same in their origin," and "to practice sanitation is to act sanely and sensibly." "The Mystery and Majesty of the Mind" was the title of an entire chapter, in contrast, in *Health for Body and Mind* in 1936. Students read that when the brain, "nature's masterpiece," succumbs to illness, "mental pain may be . . . as serious in its aftereffects as physical pain," making treatment essential. "If one finds that he is unable to see any sunshine in life, he ought to talk things over with a parent or some other adult — a physician or a clergyman, for example."[49] Your feelings matter, the text said unmistakably to child and adult readers alike.

Other schoolbooks about human nature put racial differences closer to the center of discussion. Although the philanthropies flooded the South with advice, some educators spoke with a different inflection. Robert Bennett Bean, long recognized as an expert on brain anatomy at the University of Virginia, was nearly sixty in 1932 when he published his short book *The Races of Man*. Brain evolution reached a "climax in the White Race," Bean wrote, and "the psychic activities of the Black Race are a careless, jolly vivacity, emotions and passions of short duration, and a strong and somewhat irrational egoism." The volume's numerous photographs suggest that Bean designed it for student use, and his nearly exclusive choice of pictures of aboriginal Africans to represent the black race drove home the lesson that black character was primitive and fixed. Two hands set side by side in one image over the caption "THE HAND OF AN ADULT BANTU NEGRO AND THE HAND OF A GORILLA" affirmed evolutionary theory and black bestiality at once. When Bean thanked New York field-workers for the photograph, he underlined his cosmopolitanism and the authority of his science.[50]

Whereas official records establish the familiarity of southern teachers with *Primer of Sanitation* and *Health for Body and Mind*, it is unclear which

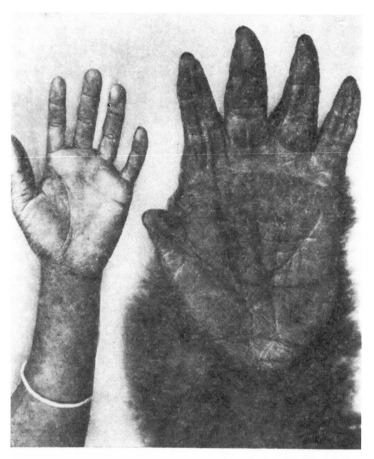

Fig. 13—THE HAND OF AN ADULT BANTU
NEGRO AND THE HAND OF A GORILLA

Hands of an African and ape compared in an illustration from the textbook *The Races of Man* (1932), by Professor Robert Bennett Bean of the University of Virginia.

schools assigned Bean's text, issued in New York. He was not the only southern educator, in any case, to contrast the minds of the races. Joseph Peterson and Lyle Lanier of Nashville, respected professors of psychology, reported "an enormous and reliable superiority of whites over negroes in all four intelligence tests" they administered in the 1920s.[51] In effect Peterson and Lanier translated Bean's crude Darwinian analysis into reputable psychology, all the while preserving the older man's conviction that the races are unequal by nature. To ask how much these southerners dissented from the Progressive mood, however, yields various answers. All leaned further than many peers toward nature in the argument with nurture, but race was a general concern of all white educators. Even these men, moreover, jumped on the bandwagon of child development.

Although public schools were most affected by excitement about children's possibilities, other southern sites unconnected with northern sponsors show the sentiment's wide reach. Summer camps served families who could pay, and their directors, attentive to professional currents, gave thought to the campers' psychological health. The 1938 brochure for Camp John Hope for black children in Macon County, Georgia, promised "a well rounded program which will contribute toward health, character, and personality development of youth." Fun was the immediate object: the camp offered a range of activities from swimming to tennis to pageants. But its codirector, Frankie V. Adams, a professor at the Atlanta School of Social Work with a master's degree in education from New York University, was serious about her stated goal of providing guidance to boys and girls. When she added that "citizenship, religious, and moral growth will be emphasized," her tone was more spiritual than scientific, a balance that was true not only to her own convictions but, she may have inferred, to the principles of parents she wished to reach.[52] In the South an easy link of sacred and secular was not unusual. However she described her expectations, though, Adams surely knew how crucial self-discovery in a safe atmosphere was for black children.

Psychology more thoroughly infused Lillian Smith's Laurel Falls Camp in the north Georgia hills. The therapeutic idiom used by the parents underscores how eager privileged whites were for child guidance. One mother called her eight-year-old "only baby," Barbara Ann, "a complex little personality" in a four-page typed letter to Smith before the summer season in 1944. "I have long since given up being an amateur psychologist," began another parent, who went on to take the "blame for most of Collin's emotionalism." "She is bossy but not very imaginative—and no sense of humor at all that we can discern," the writer confessed.[53]

Smith elicited this detailed frankness. When she took over the camp from her father in 1925, she disliked its "authoritarianism." "I was engrossed with changing the camp; I was reading Freud, systematically, at this time, and other psychoanalysts; and other psychologists," she recalled. Although the preface to the parents' questionnaire of the 1940s asked for each girl's "good qualities," "we can help her more if we also know something of her little problems, her weaknesses, her 'failures,'" Smith coaxed. Counselors were told to note campers who were "gifted," "sympathetic," or given to "temper displays," and the staff kept logs. Barbara Ann, for one, was observed at camp to be just as "spoiled and babyish" as her mother predicted, but, the log showed, "she can also be charming."[54] Despite escalating rhetoric in the South about the personalities of schoolchildren, psychotherapy for young people was rare at this time, and Smith appeared to answer campers' families' wish for assistance.

If the worries about their daughters' traits among these well-off parents seem paltry, they gain importance as a force behind the furor over school desegregation in the years after the *Brown* decision. The conviction that your child, white or black, had the potential to succeed through enlightened schooling infused southern education with emotion, and the decades-long investigations of children as learners were the source of this faith. Just as they hoped, the foundations detected broad changes in opinion. A 1949 report submitted to the GEB recalled a time when "Negro schools were tolerated, but not encouraged" in South Carolina: "This opposition was based on the belief that the more educated the Negro was, the greater the possibility that he would stir up trouble in the community." Social tranquility, in contrast, was the expected outcome by the 1930s. A Mississippi lawyer by then felt "no doubt that education acts upon the Negroes as it does upon everybody else and has a tendency to decrease their criminal tendencies."[55]

These testimonies in the GEB files no doubt favored views that southern compilers believed northern officials wanted to hear. The northern agencies plotted their work from the start, however, as a closely managed campaign. Unacceptable southern ideas were politely ignored. During World War II, Howard Odum, now the South's leading sociologist, asked

for funds "to promote interracial understanding" by developing "an elementary school reader about both races in the southern people developed
so as to give the Negro proper interpretation and place." "Books play a
very small part in race prob.," a private GEB memo responded dismissively,
as if to say that the home office judged Odum's social vision excessively
cautious.[56] Progress and realism, in contrast—the philanthropy's own
values—were keynotes of a 1944 pledge to the GEB from Virginia authorities "that the Negroes of this State should be given educational opportunities equal in every way to those provided for white students."[57] Without
shame, the foundations set out to mold the South using money to achieve
compliance. For southerners of both races, learning to see children's minds
as susceptible to training guided by science was an intellectual price to be
paid for better schools.

The long-term result resembled the therapeutic mind-set later dismissed by some social critics. Psychology so insists on adjusting the individual to circumstances, according to this argument, that the self becomes
the false object of reform efforts better directed at problems of social structure. Perhaps some southern educators in foundation-sponsored programs
were lulled into this kind of psychological myopia. Organizers did keep
curricula narrow. A summer class for "selected Negro leaders in elementary education" offered in 1950 by the University of Arkansas was titled
"Child Study and Mental Health." White teachers at a similar gathering
in North Carolina after the war received a handout declaring that the
"Teacher Should Be Able to Recognize Mental Hygiene Problems" and list-
ing "withdrawing" or "domineering," being "depressed" or "over-excitable,"
and showing "abnormal sex interests" as typical disorders.[58] Segregation
gave these simple lessons unstated racial implications, however, that most
likely were not wholly lost on participants. Although the races remained
scrupulously separated in public schools, ideas about child psychology presented to black and white teachers were indistinguishable. Racial inequities in education were very real, but the region's educational psychology
tacitly recognized that a child was a child.

This quiet egalitarianism grew from a new appreciation of children.
Southerners came to value the child's personality in the process of improving their schools. Whereas black teachers studied English and arithmetic
in South Carolina during the summer of 1918 to improve their own skills,
later workshops turned from content to methods of instruction as dictated

Girls belonging to a Canning Club sponsored by the General Education Board, Cumberland County, Virginia, early twentieth century. Courtesy of Jackson Davis Papers, Special Collections Library, University of Virginia Library, Charlottesville.

by the needs of the learner.[59] Parents were similarly energized by their children's promise. "They care for their horses, they care for their dollars; / They care for their lodgers, their fancy fine collars," lamented a Virginia song titled "Why Parents Don't Visit the School" in 1914: "But little do we think they care for their scholars, / Because they don't visit the school." By contrast, parent interest led to better pupil attendance by the 1930s, and a South Carolina Jeanes teacher confirmed, "Fathers and mothers are glad to assist in every way in order that their children may have better minds and bodies."[60]

Jackson Davis took pleasure in illustrating progress in education with nearly 6,000 photographs taken during his career. He believed that lecturing with slides, such as one picturing barefoot children surrounded by walls covered with writing in the absence of blackboards, stirred "human inter-

est" in school reform. Other photographs showed neatly dressed schoolchildren furnished with the right implements to complete their tasks. In these, philanthropic assistance seemed to visibly enhance cleanliness, industriousness, and self-respect. Only rarely in Davis's candid shots did a student look up from her work to face the camera, as did one elegant young black woman in a group of five girls peeling produce for canning. Her pose challenges the viewer to take note of her individuality, much as the campaign for southern schooling brought the potential of the region's children to light.[61]

A Psychiatric Backwater

Although treatment of mental illness can be slow and discouraging, one might expect southerners growing more comfortable with child psychol-

ogy also to be hopeful about curing adults. The psychological ideas inform-
ing the work of the northern foundations assumed that the mind can be
understood with common sense and the environment adjusted to nurture
development. Scientific study of human nature would aid comprehension
and reform. The same philanthropies took a keen interest in medicine and
funded new campuses in Nashville, for example, for the Vanderbilt University School of Medicine and Meharry Medical College in the 1920s.[62]
Yet southern psychiatrists were restrained, if not somber, about mental
health. As a young professor just back at Vanderbilt in 1933 from a psychiatry internship in Baltimore, Frank Luton told his students, "There are
patients we can do nothing with." He repeated, "I have to accept the fact
that there are patients that I can't help" to a class in 1938, the same year
a Kentucky colleague wondered in a letter to Luton whether "we ought
to stress therapy a little more" at an upcoming meeting of the Southern
Medical Association's Section on Neurology and Psychiatry. "It is my feeling that because therapy is so called most of us have a tendency to duck it
and some even scoff at those particularly interested in it as being idealists
and sentimentalists and that sort of thing."[63]

If these remarks convey a welcome realism next to the educators' zeal,
they also testify to the fragile life of psychiatry as a medical specialty in
the South before World War II. The field's sophistication was its stum-
bling block. Requiring highly trained professionals and well-equipped
hospitals, psychiatry did not advance easily in a region wary of medical
science. Nor did whites seem able to imagine that a black doctor might
master psychiatry or a black patient recover. In crude terms, it was more
palatable for white sponsors to construct a rural schoolhouse and send
the teacher to summer school than to arrange the internships, supply the
hospital beds, and negotiate the interracial cooperation needed to build
up psychiatry. Convinced that common schooling could be redemptive,
the northern foundations had little compelling motive to push for better
treatment of the mentally ill. For decades, southern psychiatrists, their
patients, and the idea that serious mental problems may be untangled remained peripheral to regional interests. Not surprisingly, psychiatry practiced by and for African Americans lagged behind what was available to
white southerners.

From the 1910s to the 1940s, Nashville was the hub of medical reform selected by northern philanthropy. Vanderbilt's School of Medicine was to be the region's flagship. "The Rockefeller Foundation has had and continues to have an interest in the influence of this school in the South," the organization confirmed in 1934, to the tune of $15 million in gifts "for its medical school and hospital" since 1920. A few miles away, Meharry Medical College was nearly the sole school in the country educating black men and women of southern origin to be doctors, dentists, pharmacists, and nurses. Arguing that the health of the races was interdependent and yet separate care essential, a 1910 survey by the Carnegie Foundation concluded, "Make-believe in the matter of negro medical schools is therefore intolerable." Five southern black medical colleges quickly closed, as northern funding now favored Howard University in Washington, drawing mostly northern students, and Meharry.[64] The proximity of Vanderbilt and Meharry promised to make Nashville a showcase for high-quality segregated medicine. The foundations' preference for improving society through education perhaps also recommended the city. Nashville demonstrated a commitment to higher education. Fisk University and Tennessee Agricultural and Industrial College, black institutions, and Peabody College, a white school, all trained teachers, and Scarritt College for Christian Workers, also white, shifted its emphasis over the years from missions to social work.[65]

There was no instruction in psychiatry in Nashville before 1930, but university administrators sought to develop the specialty, and the donors responded. The dean of medicine at Vanderbilt explained to a Rockefeller visitor in 1933 that "25–40% of the patients at Vanderbilt have some psychiatric difficulties," and foundation officers at a meeting in New York the next year heard that "the teaching and practice in mental diseases in the south of the United States are deplorable."[66] The philanthropies addressed the deficiency by means of their own specialty, education. Not only would general practitioners made proficient in psychiatry spread their knowledge through the region, but state-supported asylums might be bypassed, thereby avoiding potential conflicts with politicians and the institutions' doctors.[67] The absence of accommodations for mental patients at the Vanderbilt and Meharry hospitals did hamper instruction in psychiatry. Nor did Nashville City Hospital, serving mainly the poor, have psychiatric beds. On the outskirts of town, Central State Hospital for the mentally ill doubled its population between the world wars, making the patient-doctor ratio in 1938 more than 500 to 1, and here medical students of both races got their clinical experience.[68] As a southern city, Nashville might have taught medical students as much about psychiatry outside the walls of the institution as within. The specialty first faced its own difficulties, however, connected with religion, race, and social class.

Whereas psychology and Christianity blended in southern classrooms when teachers approached personality development as a matter of moral growth, there was friction from the start between religion and medicine. Both of Nashville's medical schools were formally Methodist until Andrew Carnegie forced Tennessee's bishops to relinquish control of Vanderbilt's program in 1913 as a condition of his gift. Although the church sued and lost, the philanthropies continued to eye southern piety suspiciously. Alan Gregg, architect of the Rockefeller Foundation's nationwide efforts for medical education and a doctor himself, felt at home playing golf in 1931 with Vanderbilt's dean of medicine, but less cozy in his "hotel 'with a radio in every room' and a lugubrious and fanatical choice of hymns for Sunday music."[69] This discomfort could have practical consequences. Scarritt College's ineligibility for GEB funds was unfair, its president claimed in 1941, because "the College has suffered by reason of the word 'Christian' in its title."[70] Individuals who were a short step removed from these conversations took polar positions in the ever-simmering debate between science and faith. Lawrence K. Frank, lately of Rockefeller's New York office, was zealous for science in 1936 when he wrote about "the etiology of the sickness of our society" and described social recovery as a "manageable problem." Although Allen Tate similarly saw a "radical division" between reason and contemplation, he defended the soul, warning that "the scientific mind always plays havoc with the spiritual life" unless enlisted in its cause. A leading Southern Agrarian, Tate was teaching English at Vanderbilt when he published his thoughts in *I'll Take My Stand*.[71]

These theoretical differences did not visibly affect medical policy in Nashville. Yet science seemed precariously superimposed on old-fashioned religion in the clinic and classroom. As Vanderbilt's only full-time professor of psychiatry during the 1930s, Frank Luton delivered a range of lectures on psychobiology, psychopathology, child psychology, and therapy. On the ward, however, he inquired of a patient, "Is your soul saved?" "Try to be," was the reply. "Ever talk to the Lord? . . . Told one time you talked to him." "Not ever as know of," the man said first, then qualified his thought, "Nothing talk about here, yes at home." Perhaps teasing out the person's delusions rather than asking real questions, Luton, an active Presbyterian, was familiar with religious experience.[72] But his work offered little common ground between the classification of mental disorders and problems of salvation.

Even so, Luton recognized that moral restraint could impede treatment. Childhood warnings about masturbation led some patients to "see it as a great sin," Luton explained to his students, and in general "the lack of sex knowledge that people get is almost unbelievable." Ignorance about the body might be compounded by guilt about being ill. One patient was aware of "her own shame of having mental trouble," and self-blame held others back from consulting a doctor. "Psychiatrist [sic] have a bad name," one man told Luton; "wouldn't go to you but something is wrong with my mind."[73] Even if distrust of self and science was not altogether rooted in Christian conservatism, the link was likely in the South.

Was the tiny budget for psychiatry at Meharry similarly related to its president's missionary background? When John Mullowney retired from the position after nearly two decades in 1938, the college's lowest-paid faculty position was its lecturer in psychiatry, who made $300 a year. At one point during his presidency, Mullowney also held the title "professor of applied psychology and professional efficiency," although he had no formal training beyond a correspondence course in 1916. The "Bureau of Human Betterment" had promised to prepare him in ten lessons by mail "to specialize in mental healing." Meharry still had a strong Methodist bloc on its board of trustees in the 1930s, and Mullowney had served the church in China. Perhaps piety was one reason that psychiatry lagged at the college.[74]

Racism was far more instrumental, however, and although there is no shortage of evidence that Mullowney, who was white, was prejudiced, one man was a minor obstacle in a society structured to preserve black subservience. The GEB knew of Mullowney's bias. The president "distinctly shows race prejudice," reported a former black colleague in 1933, a view confirmed by the white evaluator sent by the foundation to investigate. "He clearly regards the Negroes as an inferior race . . . and he has set definite limits to what should be given them . . . as evidenced by his fixed ideas concerning the library, research, and advanced instruction."[75] Psychiatry from this perspective was a wasteful extravagance. "Knowing Negro Psychology to be what it is" was Mullowney's casual opening to a Methodist official in 1934.[76] The black mind was different, and he had mastered it.

His attitude was not out of line with the assumptions of other whites involved in Nashville medicine. The dean of Vanderbilt's medical school asked Alan Gregg for more hospital beds for "colored patients" because they "afford the very best type of material for teaching purposes." The GEB supervisor who voiced "surprise" in 1938 that Rafael Hernandez, Meharry's lone psychiatry instructor, earned board certification in the specialty went on to note that Hernandez "has had little or no opportunity to gain adequate knowledge of psychiatry." Hernandez had in fact completed residencies in neurology and psychiatry in New York at Columbia University's Presbyterian Hospital, supported by a Rosenwald Fellowship.[77] Yet the official's snap judgment was a self-fulfilling prophecy as a rule. Whites convinced that the black psyche was inferior neglected the race's psychiatric training and care.

Seen from this angle, the vast difference between whites' acceptance of psychology for black children and resistance to psychiatry for adults grew from their sense that mental problems and medical solutions were too complex for the race. Elementary teachers might coax all schoolchildren forward, but the thought of black specialists treating intricate personalities was another matter. Psychiatric training for Meharry students limped along as a result. During the 1940s and 1950s, Hernandez periodically came and went in pursuit of opportunities elsewhere, and when he was gone, Luton sometimes supervised a ten-hour practicum for black students at Central State Hospital. But, already overtaxed, he taught only the first session himself.[78]

Although segregation approved such noblesse oblige, it impeded more than token racial cooperation. A Scarritt College professor teaching a course at Fisk, physically adjacent to Meharry, spent two hours a day on buses and street cars in 1943 to cover less than five miles between her home school and the class. The difficulty of travel was a measure of social distance, seen again when representatives of Meharry, Fisk, and Tennessee Agricultural and Industrial converged to greet President Roosevelt in 1934. Fisk's white president praised the schools in official remarks as "a center for Negro education scarcely equalled in the country," and Mullowney recalled warmly a few days later "how appropriate it was for Dr Hale, the president of the Negro institution, to be flanked on either side by the white presidents of the other two Negro institutions as we marched up the driveway preceding the great parade."[79] But the truth was that separation of the city's medical programs, based on an awareness of race as acute as Mullowney's, all but guaranteed Meharry's neglect of psychiatry. Sporadic contact with Vanderbilt could not counterbalance white feelings of dismission and apprehension about black thoughts and emotions.

In the late 1940s, the medical school at Vanderbilt was "bankrupt," and Meharry was negotiating a move to St. Louis. The professed reason for both was "Community Failure," as one headline read, and although the similarity of the diagnoses makes the rhetoric seem like breast-beating aired to spur donations, local interest in medicine was meager. Public funds from the city and county provided less than 2 percent of contributions to Meharry between the world wars, a newspaper reported; 85 percent came "from foundations."[80] Sometimes the color line alone blocked support from white citizens for black medical care. "We are neither white or black," explained Mullowney's successor at Meharry, also a white man, in his letter of resignation in 1943. His family was ever "on the fence" in a racial no-man's-land without "community relationships and close friendships."[81] Because the rich were nearly always white and the poor often black, distaste for poverty reinforced white indifference. Although Meharry's hospital did a public service by admitting "indigent Negro patients," well-off whites would have imagined the task an unpleasant one. If blacks themselves felt a "lack of confidence in Meharry" that kept them away, as a report said, then whites must have pictured its wards as squalid. Meharry's graduates around the country loyally donated roughly half a million dollars to the college by 1947, not enough, however, to offset the inaction of the powerful.[82]

Members of the local elites were exactly whom Frank Luton cultivated, in contrast, during the postwar crisis. Perhaps "the hostility that now exists toward Vanderbilt," to use Luton's words, originated in its indebtedness to northern capital. Confident that "work and publicity and possibly professional public relations" would convert Nashville's leaders, Luton became his own fund-raiser for psychiatry.[83] Using a technique in 1946 that he later perfected, he sponsored a visiting doctor who "impressed the women of the town with his attitudes about child psychiatry." A men's club then agreed to "sponsor the movement for the acquisition of funds" for a child guidance clinic. By 1957 the out-of-town guest was a celebrity, Dr. William

Menninger of Topeka, who lobbied the Tennessee legislature on behalf of mental health.[84] Once it became clear to Luton that hard work and expertise would not win the community, he tried presenting young patients as socially appealing and psychiatrists as glamorous to stir empathy in high places.

This outreach was simply a new strategy to cope with the ongoing problem of civic leaders' lack of interest in the mentally ill, however, and Luton's career, along with Hernandez's, bore marks of accumulated handicaps rooted in religion, race, and now social class. The irony was that Luton's success as a public servant was the result of his specialty's weakness at Vanderbilt and how continuously he had to toil to keep it going. Nearly fifty years old at the end of World War II, he was the only full professor on a staff of three psychiatrists, who, lacking their own department, taught rudimentary mental science to the medical school's undergraduates. He offered two classes to medical students and supervised their clinical work in three locations in 1946–47, as well as giving three courses to nurses and one to social workers. Although he also served on city and state committees and routinely saw patients at three hospitals, he had to report that year to his chair in the Department of Medicine that he had no publications. Under the heading "Research Activities," he explained, "None except in a minor capacity as a consultant to the surgical psychiatric study now going on in the Department of Surgery." Two years before, he described his research as "Mental Hygiene"; his only project, a study begun in 1935 to introduce child psychiatry to a rural county, was never completed.[85]

When his dean announced a "radical departure" for the medical school in 1949 based on the principle of the "inseparability of research and education," Luton had the seniority to be an effective spokesman but too many duties to launch a research agenda.[86] As if on a treadmill, he worked in the 1950s to rebuild psychiatric professionalism by recruiting Tennessee specialists for a society to replace a group that "disintegrated," he told a friend, "during the War." Nor did his retirement from Vanderbilt in 1964 slow his public activities, which earned him the post of Tennessee's commissioner of mental health in 1969. Few people then would have known how much Luton's civic-mindedness owed to his early isolation. Having started part-time at Vanderbilt in 1931 at a modest salary, he did not feel secure enough in 1938 to take his family on vacation because he was also "thinking of building a house."[87] Luton became good at taking on too much in the cause of psychiatry because his field had little recognition.

He does not seem to have been acquainted with Rafael Hernandez, although Hernandez, just a year older than Luton, similarly struggled to represent psychiatry at Meharry. Segregated wards at the public hospitals where both doctors practiced perhaps meant they rarely crossed paths. Hernandez was as harried as Luton, in any case, by his schedule. When he returned to Meharry in 1930 after his advanced study in New York, he taught anatomy, neuroanatomy, histology, and embryology, as well as psychiatry. He sensed, however, that his job was a dead end. Pursuing college degrees like a man possessed, he seemed driven at once by innate curiosity and a hope to find a career door unobstructed by racism. In this mood he earned a B.S. from Tennessee Agricultural and Industrial College and a law degree from Kent College of Law in 1940 while also teaching. Yet it was the military that offered a fresh path. Having enlisted as a major in the Army Medical Corps at the war's outset, he later practiced at four veterans' hospitals. An executive order in 1948 desegregated all VA facilities, over protest from the American Psychiatric Association, and here Hernandez could elude segregated medicine. His name never left Meharry's catalogue for long, though, and he retired from the college in 1967 as director of its hospital's outpatient care.[88]

Hernandez's professional history signaled how hard it was for a man of color under Jim Crow to succeed as a professor of psychiatry. A talented musician, he must have found solace in his avocations, playing cornet, trumpet, and piano, as well as composing. "A quiet, introspective, unassuming person," his daughter reflected in the 1980s, "Rafael Hernandez left a legacy for practicing psychiatrists which encompassed a job well-done, a patient well-cared for, and a life well-lived."[89] What he achieved was won against the odds.

In a small way, psychiatry at least established itself between the world wars as an influence in Nashville medicine, which is more than can be said for its place in rural health care nearby. At the same time that country schoolteachers were learning that they should nurture their pupils' psychological wellness, it was clear to doctors, foundations, and government that "there still remains a large proportion of the population untouched," in Frank Luton's words, by knowledge of mental disorders. When the philanthropies willingly fielded pilot projects outside Nashville in the 1930s, the work was limited in scope. Child development, by then a theme of proved popularity, was the focus of all three rural studies with a psychological component conducted by local colleges. In two analyses of black youth, there was no mention of mental illness. *Rural Negro Health* (1937) reported fieldwork in health education conducted by a Meharry professor of public health, and *Growing Up in the Black Belt* (1941) by Fisk University's Charles Johnson described sociological variables shaping personality. Only Luton's "mental health demonstration" in Williamson County took a medical approach to the emotional problems of rural children.[90]

The effort sank under the magnitude of the task. Most immediately seeking to add child guidance clinics to public health care, Luton drafted a proposal for the Rockefeller Foundation in 1935 that he admitted was "rather broad." He was right to say that "to improve the health of the total population"—his stated "object"—he needed to study whites and blacks in the city hub as well as the hinterland, along with elements of infrastructure such as government and schools. Ten years was his projected time frame for the research. Although Luton hired first-class staff, including a psychiatrist from Boston so "beloved" by his rural Tennessee town that its Rotary Club made him president, the work was suspended in 1942.[91] Even on the outskirts of Nashville, arguably the medical capital of the South at the time, the average person's options for psychiatric care remained a bed in an urban hospital or the public asylum.

Luton may have written with a sense of personal failure in a report for the state in 1951 that there was "no separate accommodation for psychotic children" at Central State Hospital, "where occasionally children are admitted for observation because there is no other place for them."[92] His plan for outpatient assessment of children had aimed not only to catch problems early but to avoid random mixing of curable and incurable cases. The public had to be made hopeful about recovery to seek treatment, yet state-funded facilities remained forbidding places visited only in desperation.

This new survey of mental health care in the Nashville area, the first account of institutions since his massive review for the state in 1938, did note improvements. Vanderbilt hospital now had beds reserved for psychiatric patients, operated an outpatient clinic about ten hours a week, and made a psychiatrist available to the college students on Thursdays. Although the earlier scarcity of psychiatrists meant that hospitals of the

1930s relied on easy-to-administer medications like Metrozol and Luminal, there was talk therapy after the war. By then Luton had instructed medical students for years about the need to "sit for hours or days and talk," and his enthusiasm for interpreting "the stream of talk" may have helped turn local practice toward conversation.[93] Even so, "psychotherapy for the psychoneurotic is inadequate because of the limited staff," Luton reported of Thayer veterans' hospital, and necessity may have similarly driven the use of "electric shock therapy . . . given to outpatients" at Riverside Hospital "for the colored." Innovative at first glance, shock treatment was likely cheaper than therapeutic sessions. Nor was there any question that black care lagged behind white treatment. Under the heading "Hubbard Hospital Psychiatric Service," the site connected with Meharry, Luton noted, "No facilities at present."[94]

As early as 1931, the year Luton began teaching at Vanderbilt, the GEB had doubts about whether the medical school would energize southern health care as hoped. A foundation memorandum reported that a GEB visitor judged Nashville City Hospital "one of the worst general hospitals he has seen in the U.S.," and the report continued cynically, "It is premature to discuss the influence of Vanderbilt on medicine in the South when there is scarcely any evidence that the institution has as yet materially affected the service in its one supplementary teaching hospital." As damning was its lack of reputation. The official "scarcely ever heard the name Vanderbilt mentioned in medical discussions in Alabama during his visits there, whereas Johns Hopkins and Tulane are referred to frequently as the most important medical centers within reach."[95] Although the GEB, along with its parent Rockefeller Foundation, continued funding Vanderbilt to build up its star status, the advantages of Nashville as a medical hub—professional schools, hospitals, and colleges for both races—did not revolutionize psychiatry as a specialty even locally.

No other southern city offered as promising a configuration of institutions as Nashville if the goal was biracial medical reform. "The negro needs good schools rather than many schools," declared the 1910 Carnegie report on black medical training, and the five Jim Crow colleges it ruled unfit—in Raleigh, Louisville, Knoxville, Memphis, and New Orleans—soon closed.[96] Nearly every black doctor of southern origins until the middle of the century went to Nashville for his education.

In the white world, growing numbers of physicians between the wars offered psychiatric treatment typically to affluent patients in the South's largest cities. Commercial centers seemed friendliest to the idea of mental cure. "Memphis in Front Rank as Hospital and Clinic Center," tooted a booster-spirited headline in a local newspaper in 1933. Patrons were loyal to the city's sanitariums, and some owner-psychiatrists also taught at the medical college of the University of Tennessee.[97] New Orleans had the South's only visible Freudians. Dr. Robert Coles of Harvard remembered that the New Orleans Psychoanalytic Society had more liberal ideas about therapeutic technique than did Boston psychoanalysts around 1960, and at least one doctor with Freudian leanings was publishing much earlier.[98] Atlanta was less cosmopolitan than the ports. One Emory medical student in the 1940s who became a psychiatrist recalled a lone professor in the field who taught classification of mental disorders but gave "the impression that nothing could be done psychiatrically."[99] Even where white psychiatry more readily took root, however, treatment of anyone except the well-to-do was unusual, and segregation added racial exclusion to the mix. Black patients were welcome at just two of the sixteen Memphis medical facilities that the white press so proudly described.[100] It is clear why the Rockefeller organization selected Nashville for its side-by-side experiments in white and black medicine, and why they expressed frustration at slow progress.

Obstacles to psychiatric program building in the South did not preclude advances in the care of seriously ill patients. Stray references to psychiatrists' private practices indicate that they spent many hours in contact with human problems. Luton used his own activities as a model in 1946 when he tried to recruit a navy doctor to the local veterans' hospital by promising "an office here at Vanderbilt and some chance for private practice."[101] His letters and lectures suggest his connection with patients. Still in training at Johns Hopkins in 1930, Luton thanked a former patient from Georgia for a gift of sugar cane and wondered if the man could "make some statements in regard to your ability to adjust, and as to the judgment of whether you have improved."[102] In Vanderbilt lectures, his tone conveyed experience when he coached medical students to "get the information [you need] without interfering with that rapport" with patients and particularly to avoid making anyone feel ashamed. This was what "we call the Art of Medicine."[103] As he taught on ward rounds, he spoke with a man suffering from "delirium" and left notes emphasizing profoundly mixed feelings. "Clearing up of mental picture, good prognosis to family and patient. Not fooled to [sic] much[. May] get well may have another episode and get worse."[104] Luton had none of the ebullience of the school reformers who were enthusiastic about child development but nearly as sharp a sense of the psyche's mutability. Called to discuss "sterilization of mental incompetents" in 1953 by a state official proud of his "part in passage of a sterilization law in my home State of Georgia," Luton left no record of sympathy with the proposal's genetic determinism except that he kept the meeting's handouts.[105] Hardly rosy, his psychiatry was nonetheless attuned to variations within and among personalities.

Whereas the schools' gospel of child wellness had wide appeal, however, the psychiatrist's understanding mainly fell on deaf ears. The sociology of southern medicine made wealthy whites the principal audience for the idea that psychiatry was not just caretaking but was instead a science of recovery. Private patients, charitable donors, and government officials all belonged to the same narrow social segment. In a typical story, 1935 obituaries of a Memphis psychiatrist noted that the public child guidance clinic the doctor promoted "was discontinued for lack of funds," but "he had a large private practice."[106] The psychology of the situation limited psychiatry as well. At least in modern times, it is hard to compete with the hopefulness inspired by children. Mentally ill adults, reminders of human frailty in southern communities, must have seemed an unpleasant subject by comparison. Trusting a teacher would have come more naturally than trusting a doctor, too, for people who were fatalistic about medicine.

Race was the last factor. Whites who were positive about black children's elementary achievements might at the same time be negative about the complexity of deranged adults and the capability of black physicians. The strategy of the northern foundations for improving southern education and medicine was the same: to make schools instruments of progress that were respectful of social order. Yet almost predictably, the South's strenuous faith, widespread poverty, and color line gave school psychology and medical psychiatry very different receptions.

An Oxford Don in Durham

If the mental sciences came to serve segregation in Nashville because of the tenacity of racial tradition, psychological ideas honoring the color line were deliberately cultivated in Durham, North Carolina. Once again, innovations were imported, and educational reform was the instrument of change. William McDougall (1871–1938) was unusually cosmopolitan by any American standard. British-born, McDougall spent his last two decades in the United States and the years after 1927 at Duke University. "McDougall has come over," one American professor gossiped privately in 1921. "Whatever we may think of some of his work he is unquestionably a leading psychologist," the man equivocated in a mood increasingly shared by colleagues around the country. McDougall's views "mirrored the more conservative arguments in most of the contemporary issues of his day," one biographer clarifies, and the evidence is compelling: at a time when social scientists generally believed they could adjust environments to mold human nature, McDougall argued that instinct is powerful, racial inheritance fateful, eugenics essential, and telepathy possible.[107] This improbable mix of biological determinism and the chance of spiritual intervention did not make McDougall a simple traditionalist. Rather, only "real sciences" would avert "world chaos," he hammered away during his American sojourn.[108] An uncorrupted psychological theory was needed to restore natural hierarchy, and he had it.

McDougall was the most visible early psychologist to embrace the South specifically for what he took to be old-fashioned ways, and in the white academy the attraction was mutual. The anecdote circulated, Bruce Kuklick reports in his history of philosophical study at Harvard, where McDougall taught in the 1920s, "that he received a letter from the president of the newly constituted Duke University asking him to recommend a psychology chairman for Duke. McDougall replied, 'I accept.'"[109] Although repetition exaggerated the details, the hiring of McDougall flowed from a synergy between a white southern wish to guard tradition and an intellectual who was eager for a podium. Not all outsiders interested in the South were social moderates, nor were all white southerners willing to compromise. Especially after the *Brown* ruling in 1954 fanned contentious debate, a younger generation of psychologists moved southward to advocate the races' unequal intelligence. McDougall might well have disliked their style, but all had the same analysis of American regions, and in both eras, white southern conservatives thereby acquired updated psychological defenses.[110]

In contrast to the incoming professionals of the 1950s and 1960s, however, whom right-wing southerners welcomed as heroes in a national contest, McDougall was a cosmopolitan man in an obscure place. He remained nearly a visitor, but he still left a considerable professional mark. He arrived at the moment when James B. Duke, whose family made fortunes in the Carolinas in tobacco and hydroelectric power, endowed Trinity College in Durham so generously that its name and mission changed. As legend held, McDougall and William Preston Few, Trinity's president, concurred from the start that human beings have inborn natural and moral traits, although the men's affinity did not restrain McDougall from negotiating the highest salary of any Duke professor. The South appealed to him, he told Few, and he gushed in the print version of a 1931 British radio address that "the spacious tree-clad campus of many an American college and university is a place of great charm and beauty."[111]

McDougall nonetheless seemed to feel that the South was provincial. His rare published comments about the region were invariably dropped as asides, and bemused irony was unmistakable in a 1934 preface when he alluded to his "journey around the world" in 1926–27 as a trip "which, owing to unforeseen alteration of my course, terminated in North Carolina."[112] He considered leaving almost as soon as he arrived. In 1929 he told Few about a prospect for returning to Oxford; Duke retained him by compressing his teaching duties into one semester a year. He spent months at his newly purchased sixteenth-century English home. The attraction of the South as an idea for McDougall did not make him a southerner.

Nor did living there influence him deeply enough to change his psychological theory. McDougall was so defensive about being "an age too advanced for you" when he first wrote to Few that he mentioned twice that he was over fifty, and his scholarly maturity was most likely one reason that his established positions played out in the South without major revision.[113] Although neither aging nor recurrent illness slowed his daunting output of twelve books during his last decade, his experimental and theoretical efforts at Duke could have been predicted by anyone familiar with his career.

Always an advocate of controlled laboratory tests despite his own preference for general exposition, McDougall initiated two extended series of experiments: measurement of the inheritance of learned behavior in white rats, in hopes of reviving Lamarckian theory, and investigation of communication without clear biological foundation among humans, or "extra-sensory perception," the phrase soon devised by McDougall's protégé, J. B. Rhine. The inquiries were surprisingly similar. Both aimed to suggest the possibility of mental forces without simple physical correlates, both belonged to a controversial borderland in the psychological discipline, and both began for all practical purposes at Harvard. McDougall made one small bow to the reputed piety of his southern hosts. "Religion and the Sciences of Life" (1932) was one of his infrequent publications to appear first in the South, and its defiance of conventional science was forthright. Man is "a vehicle or channel through which the spiritual realm finds partial expression," a proposition he held provable by "the strictest methods of empirical science." Far more often choosing a publisher in New York or London, however, McDougall mainly used the South as a staging ground for international persuasion.[114]

The prominence of instinct, race, and tradition in McDougall's social psychology gave it a resemblance to white southern values. But like his experimentalism, his theorizing was little affected by his residence in the South. Before immigrating to Boston, McDougall's line of vision moved systematically from the individual personality in *Introduction to Social Psychology* (1908) to human history in *The Group Mind* (1920). Along the way, his belief in the determining influence of natural endowment, whether personal or racial, increased, at the same time that the drift of Western social science was in the other direction. His *Introduction to Social Psychology*, with its keen analysis of inborn instincts as mediators between sensation and action, sold 100,000 copies by the time he moved to Duke, but the simultaneous advance of culture as an explanatory variable among social scientists put McDougall on the defensive. His opponents' false psychology, encouraging faith in the potency of acquired habits, would not stop civilization's "downward plunge," he told a Boston audience in 1921. Once a society's complexity outpaced its people's native intelligence, and especially the vision of leaders, decline followed, unless the group achieved the "self-consciousness" to make progress "truly teleological."[115]

McDougall's theory of progress would have sounded like a philosophical rather than biological proposition were it not for his premises that each culture expressed its race's character and that able leaders were the natural superiors of their peers. He long advocated an elite-focused eugenics devoted to enhancing reproduction in prominent families. Nostalgia for a well-ordered world, sadly set on the road to destruction by technology in recent times, must have helped recommend the South to McDougall. Retreat was not the answer, however, without "a science of society," he declared before he left England, to guide restoration.[116]

A fully articulated psychological science taught in a professional fashion was precisely what Duke acquired from McDougall. His failure to produce original work in the South may well have mattered less than his professionalism. As the first chair of the psychology department, he hired faculty, launched courses, and established a laboratory, and the program awarded thirteen doctorates between 1929 and 1938, not far behind the fifteen completed at the South's then-star graduate institution in the field, Peabody College for Teachers in Nashville. Many psychologists found some of the Duke research questionable. Psychic mediumship was the subject of one early dissertation, and an internal revolt in 1934 by faculty members anxious about reputation forced Rhine's parapsychology experiments out of the department.[117] Nor did McDougall's social conservatism become the uncontested signature of Duke's mental sciences. In 1940, the year of Few's death, Richard S. Lyman arrived at Duke under the sponsorship of the Rockefeller Foundation to establish the Department of Neuropsychiatry in the School of Medicine. A native of Hartford, Lyman behaved like a latter-day abolitionist when he used the world crisis as a wedge to train black psychiatric aides at the all-white university. The initiative was too bold to last, but the project nonetheless reflected the mind-set Lyman brought to Durham. Through all these crosscurrents, however, McDougall's brain-child flourished. The Duke psychology department granted the most Ph.D. degrees of any southern program between 1939 and 1948.[118]

McDougall's brilliant restatement of neo-Darwinian ideas in psychological terms was as crucial to his success as his administrative skill. He professed to believe that his field was individualistic and instrumental, thereby making his psychology seem on the surface an agent of progress. In *The Group Mind*, composed during World War I, he dismissed the nineteenth-century scholarly habit of explaining a "normative" consciousness, as opposed to diverse psyches, as "unduly simplified and in fact misleading," and his work as a therapist to British soldiers lent authority to his argument for pluralism. This assertion that human nature is complex did not stop McDougall from plentifully using phrases like "racial mental qualities," however, in the same text. He also reinvented the concept of race statistically by means of the bell curve. "That races are endowed in different degrees with innate intellectual capacity is implied by the difference between the curves for whites and colored," he summarized army intelligence tests in *Is America Safe for Democracy?*[119]

New to America when the book appeared in 1921, McDougall seemed to learn from sharp criticism of the work not to compare particular races. He published nothing about African Americans while he lived in the South, and yet the centrality of race to his historical thinking gave segregation a theoretical umbrella, perhaps all the more useful for its generality. Even when he spoke grandly about science as his cause, it was clear that the discipline he believed redemptive was his own, "a science of the imponderables, in short, of human nature and its activities."[120] McDougall offered himself to southerners as the true standard-bearer for psychological knowledge.

In fact, he had competition in the interwar South from other opinions about psychological development that rode the same wave of educational improvement. It seems like comparing apples and oranges to place the intricate analysis of human destiny that McDougall anchored in a showcase department next to the simple notions of child development presented to southern public school teachers. Where to put the institutional stalemate of psychiatric training in Nashville in the picture is even more vexing. There were commonalities, though, among the initiatives. All advanced with southern education, involved outsiders to the South, and carried messages about racial identity. Segregation was the powerful mediator between each approach to the mind and southern society, and for many decades psychology had little visible effect on the racial inequities of the region. A psychological way of thinking about individual selfhood gradually spread among southerners, however, and its appeal depended on the presentation of mental science as a component mainly of education and not medicine. Psychiatric reform seemed restrained by overtones of disorder and fatalism, while child nurture and experimental psychology successfully stirred optimism about progress. Southern social psychology between the wars was similarly served by its appeal as a pragmatic social science.

| 3 | THE TROUBLED PERSONALITIES

OF THE SOUTH

The South came to symbolize America's problems beginning with denunciations of slavery during the age of Jackson. A century later, with the diagnosis much the same, social science appeared as a cure. When the resurrection of the Ku Klux Klan in the 1920s and the shock of the Great Depression focused national attention on the region's hatred and poverty, psychology offered explanations. Alongside academic studies, Clarence Cason, a professor of journalism at the University of Alabama, prepared a reflection on southernness for publication in 1935 that he called a "psychograph." Although he was old-fashioned enough also to label his sketch a "character," he chose terms like "inferiority complex" and "defense mechanisms" to convey the self-doubting habits of his home place.[1]

No one close to Cason realized how hazardous social analysis could be until it was too late. Just days before *90 Degrees in the Shade* appeared in print, Cason fatally shot himself in his office. He left no note, but his correspondence with the University of North Carolina Press reveals a man torn between the roles of critic and loyal son. He felt "disagreeably" about the publisher's blurb describing his "typical southern boyhood" surrounded by "velvet blossoms of magnolia trees" and placing him "in the romantic school of literature." His intent was rather to expose social problems and stimulate reform. Yet plain speaking was dangerous. "To me, there is no greater satisfaction than life in a quiet university community," and he wished "to guard against the chance that some inadvertent statement might give offense" to his board of trustees, already grumbling about him.[2] Within the adult writer was the little white boy the book remembered, who once witnessed the body of a lynching victim dragged into town and who later made friends on a train with the porter because "he and I were parts of the same civilization."[3] Caught between shame of the South and love of it, Cason underestimated the private emotions he exposed by probing regional psychology. Passion, however, just as much drove the public conversation about the South's personality in which he so briefly engaged.

Intellectuals between the wars examined the South in terms borrowed from three areas of interest in contemporary social science: mob behavior, personality formation, and folk culture. The work had a great deal in common. Because dynamic groups were the subjects of inquiry, writers managed to bypass the distracting nature-nurture issue promptly raised in the study of individuals. In this era of collective awareness, researchers typically worked in teams and aimed to influence public policy. New research sponsors joined the familiar northern foundations to put investigators in the field, including public commissions, university-based institutes, and the New York–based NAACP, founded in 1909. The goal of many analysts was to persuade the national government to act: a federal antilynching bill loomed contentiously behind mob studies, school desegregation became the objective of personality researchers, and New Deal support for disadvantaged American regions, especially the South, was the wish of white southern folk experts. From beginning to end, a social consciousness dominated the projects.

These varied inquiries explored southern psychology, but they also gave rise to scholarly habits that limited investigation of the region. Reports did convey the South's tragic tensions, sometimes in melodramatic terms. Lynch mobs gave vent to "primitive impulses to vengeance," said a black investigator, and a white scholar expected the same outcome when threats to folkways precipitated "violence and emotional debauch." Segregation daily subjected black youth, wrote a third observer, to "serious warping influences."[4]

A damaging evasiveness nonetheless pervaded southern social psychology as an academic enterprise. Black intellectuals, at risk under segregation along with other people of color, had to find safe ways to speak critically of the southern system. For the most successful, national acclaim offered a professional ticket out of the South, and in the process, their

racial analysis lost much of its regional orientation. In contrast, the social theory of Howard Odum celebrated regionalism, but it fell short on
the side of psychological precision. As Odum transformed the notion of
a folk stage of development, a commonplace in the social sciences, from
a descriptive category to a southern ideal, he outlined no clear view of
how the thoughts and emotions of his community might work. The reason
that some scholars preferred generalization and others were inclined to
understatement, I argue, was that it was dangerous, troubling, or both,
depending on who you were, to dwell on segregation. In the midst of much
discussion of the South, there were crucial omissions.

White Predators

When social scientists made southern lynch mobs their subject beginning
in the 1920s, they turned a timeworn image of whites as bearers of civilization on its head. The white race could be advanced only so long as the black
race seemed backward, and the crowds of white southerners that gathered
for ritual slayings appeared by most measures deficient in rationality and
virtue. Evolutionary biology had for decades presented racial hierarchy as
the natural state. As late as 1906, W. E. B. Du Bois could recruit no expert
to write for his survey, *The Health and Physique of the Negro American*, who
would clearly refute racist science by stressing the handicaps of nurture.
He fell back on a paper by a white doctor who at least denied that "the
Negro is inferior" by nature but who still held that "environment must
act upon something."[5] As long as racial identity seemed biologically fixed,
people of color remained primitive in the eyes of white scientists who described human history as a series of developmental stages. "Only 300 years
ago the negro ancestors of the race were naked dwellers on the west coast
of Africa," marveled a psychiatrist at a public hospital in 1914. Still close
to the "depths of savagery," the black psychotics she treated displayed the
"characteristics of children."[6]

Although the psychology of white people received scant attention in
racial surveys, whiteness was arguably their principal subject. "The dichotomy in white Southern thought between black savages and white
civilization" was symbiotic, explains the historian Lawrence Friedman.
Educated whites who repeated that blacks were brutes could believe in
their own "refinement, eminence, and civilization," no matter how badly

members of their race behaved.[7] But the avalanche of writings on lynching after World War I reversed the terms: now whites were primitives. The Ku Klux Klan, by its very nature "a thing of passion," releases "deeply rooted atavistic tendencies," observed Frank Tannenbaum, a recent graduate of Columbia University, in 1924. So stalwart a southerner as Howard Odum confessed that the mobs exhibited "unbelievable extremes of savagery . . . reminiscent of primitive orgy, maniacal frenzy, and holy combat."[8] Southern events account in part for the swell in attention to white lawlessness. The reorganized Klan first appeared in Georgia in 1915, and although the number of lynchings had decreased each decade after 1890, the crimes were now of "greatly aggravated brutality," reported Walter White of the NAACP in *Rope and Faggot* in 1929.[9]

Southern mobs also compelled notice, however, because they embodied the capacity for collective brutality of respectable people that repeatedly shocked twentieth-century whites during World War I. The mobs' torture and mutilation of victims, White believed, showed "the effect of the war—the lust for blood and cruelty which the war did not wholly satiate" and that found an outlet in "mob sadism." Two decades later, World War II made the Nazi Party seem analogous to lynch mobs in Hadley Cantril's *The Psychology of Social Movements* (1941), and Lillian Smith drew the same comparison when she called her fellow southerners "in a way more evil" than the Nazis because the gas chambers at least shortened suffering.[10] Yet even if worldwide atrocities contributed to American outrage over lynch mobs, their crimes, parading as justice, helped make the region into a symbol of civilized barbarity. White mobs were among the "darker phases of the South," the phrase Tannenbaum chose for his book title, and their deviance cast the white mind in an ominous light.[11]

For decades these mobs remained a magnet for changing fashions in psychological theory, to the point that it is a wonder southerners did not weary altogether of the academic field and reject even their fledgling science of child development. In the 1920s the Freudian craze in liberated social circles spilled over into mob studies as an emphasis on sexuality. The Klan's hysteria about black sexual predators "advertises sex" in a prudish region where whites had "a curious sensitiveness to matters of sex," Tannenbaum wrote.[12] The ritual hunt, mutilation, and murder offered respite from otherwise suffocating repression. When theorists of a later generation affirmed the healthy ego's autonomy of the id's impulses, Can-

tril, based at Princeton, reasoned that because racial prejudice in southern whites had become "part of the ego," lynching presented itself as a
"*solution*" to perceived threats to self-interest. For *Social Psychology* (1965),
Roger Brown borrowed game theory from his colleagues at postwar Massachusetts Institute of Technology and Harvard to explain mob decision
making.[13]

Behind all these analyses loomed Gustave Le Bon's *The Crowd* (1895),
judged by Brown to have "dominated the literature on the subject for several generations."[14] Produced in France at the close of a tempestuous century, the book described the crowd as "a single being" with a group psychology distinct from the minds of its members. Equally susceptible to
illusions and demagogues, mobs released a mass "unconsciousness [that]
is perhaps one of the secrets of their strength," although their force was
"only powerful for destruction," never social repair. A bourbon by instinct
as well as a brilliant sociologist, Le Bon imagined crowds forming "on the
ruins of so many ideas formerly considered beyond discussion, and to-day
decayed or decaying, of so many sources of authority that successive revolutions have destroyed."[15] Readers swayed by his pessimism would judge
crowd activity an indictment of a culture.

No wonder, then, that northern analysts most doggedly probed the
southern mobs' deviance, or that southern opponents of lynching downplayed the lynchers' psychology. To distant observers, lynching was the
simple outcome of the South's tedium and religious fanaticism. The
"Gopher Prairies of the West," familiar to every reader of Sinclair Lewis,
were "highly diverting when compared with the average small town in the
South," explained White, whose roots as a black man from Georgia, now
living in New York, gave his judgment added authority. He pictured lynchings as an entertainment sanctioned by a "vitriolic and ignorant ministry."
"A primitive religious background" forbade healthy amusements, Cantril
concurred. Lynching grew, Tannenbaum concluded, from such "starved
emotions."[16]

In the face of regional stereotyping, southern scholars understandably
skirted the mob's mind-set. Even the title of Arthur Raper's *The Tragedy
of Lynching* (1933) conveyed his wish to restore dignity to the subject.
"Tragedy" changed sporadic violence from a sign of psychic primitivism
into a noble flaw. Charged to conduct his research by the biracial Southern
Commission on the Study of Lynching based in Atlanta, Raper correlated

the incidence of lynchings in sample counties with data pertaining to such variables as income, crime, and education. His sociological approach, consistent with his recent doctoral work in the field at the University of North Carolina, kept quiet about the possibility of mass passion by focusing on social disadvantage. To the extent that he looked into the lyncher's mind, Raper retained an Enlightenment faith in reason, if supported by wealth. "Mobs and lynchings eventually can be eliminated," he brightly predicted, "if the irresponsive and irresponsible population elements can be raised into a more abundant economic and cultural life."[17] Yet the book's tacit dissent from mob psychology's predisposition to see men as beasts could not altogether dispel lynching's perversion. Repeated references to insanity seemed to betray Raper's sense of the crime's repugnance: the mental patient who joined a mob, the victims who were crazy, the need for better laws to manage the deranged.[18] These details about abnormality strained against his professed confidence in social engineering. Even so, Raper clearly avoided the preoccupation with emotion and the emotionalism of crowd studies that intimated that the white South was a culture of lynchers.

Raper's neglect of mob theory hinted at the impossible questions that writings on lynching pathology opened for southerners of both races. If the region was to develop a constructive social psychology, its premises could not begin with white savagery. During the NAACP's campaign for a federal antilynching law stretching from the 1920s to the 1940s, southern whites, even those repelled by lynching, struggled with the image of white hordes. Walter White tenaciously lobbied Congress as the NAACP's agent, aided by the press's instinct for sensational news. "Throng in Florida Awaits a Lynching" and "Eye Witness of Lynching Reveals Fiendish Torture" read typical headlines in New York newspapers in 1934, and on the whole public opinion awoke to the cause of ending vigilantism. Gallup polls at the beginning and end of 1937, the year in which proposed antilynching legislation made the most progress, reported that Americans of all regions except the South sustained or increased their support for a federal law. *Time* recognized that regional pride spurred the white South's resistance when the magazine compared the legislation's sponsors to "carpetbaggers." "That's what we are really defending: the privilege of setting him free ourselves," echoed William Faulkner's protagonist, the lawyer Gavin Stevens, in the novelist's reassuring myth of an abortive lynching, *Intruder in the Dust* (1948).[19]

Yet the invective of Senator Theodore Bilbo of Mississippi revealed a less respectable motive for opposition to reform: defense of the moral virtue of the white race, so assaulted by the conceptual tools of the newer psychology. Born in 1877, Bilbo summoned enduring ideas about black nature when he called Walter White "the Ethiopian" on the Senate floor. As provocatively as he could, Bilbo pictured White as a man "with a zeal and frenzy equal if not paramount to the lust and lasciviousness of the rape fiend in his diabolical effort to despoil the womanhood of the Caucasian race."[20] So long as blacks remained savages, even whites who formed lynch mobs were heroes, not barbarians. As the southern filibuster wore on for weeks, Ellison Smith, the senator from South Carolina nicknamed "Cotton Ed," one day mutely testified against psychology itself. As *Time* explained, he "relieved his feelings by grabbing *America's 60 Families*," with its talk of "subconscious feeling of guilt," and "slamming the book to the floor, stamping his big feet on it."[21] Both senators understood that segregation thrived on old-fashioned faith in unchanging racial temperaments. The chance that a circumstance, such as a lynching, could unpredictably distort personalities irrespective of color was a dangerous idea.

Although it seems safe to guess that every southern black scholar believed Le Bon's analysis was true for white mobs, not one produced a study centering on the theme of mass violence. Black academics did have a research role. Walter Chivers, professor of sociology and psychology at Morehouse College, helped Raper with *The Tragedy of Lynching*. Very likely Chivers recruited black field-workers to collect data, a necessary practice for white investigators. Yet even these fact finders encountered hostility in the countryside, and their experience is a reminder of the dangers black intellectuals faced.[22] They were well aware of their jeopardy. The NAACP hired White in 1918 in part because his light skin and blond hair let him mingle anonymously in lynching crowds, and in 1946 a reasonable fear impelled friends to follow a car carrying Thurgood Marshall, visiting Tennessee to argue a case for the same organization, after his arrest on false charges.[23]

In this atmosphere, it seems inevitable that the region's black social scientists spoke about racism in ways that did not require them to dwell on white perversion. At the same time, black victimization so dominated crowd studies that the approach offered them no direct path to an investigation of normal black life. Time and again northern white analysts of lynching distinguished the "southerner" and the "Negro" as fevered actor and pitiful object. As long as Tannenbaum wrote that "the South gives indications of being afraid of the negro" and Cantril described "the southerner who has this frame of reference toward the Negro," no black person was part of a South that by definition was white. Mob theory did not easily dislodge racial stereotypes. Tannenbaum talked unselfconsciously of "the weak-minded negro [who] becomes haunted by delusions, by an irresistible craving to exhibit his powers, to participate in the forbidden thing."[24] Whiteness, no matter how horrible, remained the core subject of lynching studies, and for reasons of self-protection and self-interest, southern black writers chose to stay clear.

No law mandating federal penalties for members of lynch mobs ever passed, and White, who devoted his career to the legislation, was increasingly isolated after 1940. Although a steady decline in the number of lynchings was a practical reason the campaign stalled, the psychological premises of the movement were also problematic. The thought that collective brutality might erupt without warning, like a primitive unconscious in ordinary citizens, made tragic sense in these decades. Yet to say that crowds were driven by a common mind fogged by emotion was nearly as static a view of psychology as the earlier, physiological descriptions of the races. Academic social scientists who explained the extreme stands and inner dynamics of mobs did not contest their essential irrationality. A good instrument to measure the ebb and flow of communal anger, crowd theory lacked psychological exactness, and its sweeping lens contributed to the impression that lynch mobs were representative of white southerners overall.

The effect was to further polarize the regions and races. Faulkner must have known that he evoked a conventional picture of a mob when he sketched "weathered still almost inattentive faces and the same faded clean cotton shirts and pants and dresses" of the crowd that "had already condemned" the accused, Lucas Beauchamp, and consented to "their complete relinquishment of individual identity into one." His counterargument was a counterimage: Lucas walking away a free man through a typical Saturday's "impenetrable mass of tops and hoods [of cars] moving in double line at a snail's crawl around the Square" where they gathered for sociability.[25] Provocative in fiction, analyses of crowds served the South less well as a social psychology.

Black Victims

At about the same time that public interest in antilynching laws was waning, Charles S. Johnson (1893–1956) of Fisk University spoke at the White House Conference on Children in a Democracy convened by Franklin Roosevelt in the spring of 1939. "We who have been working intimately with Negro children," his text read, witness "the frustrations, timidity, over compensations, anti-social activities, and what Gertrude Stein once referred to as 'nothingness.'" He must have been convinced of the phrase's value, because it appeared again in his *Growing Up in the Black Belt* (1941), this time backed up by the idea of "personality development." Defining personality "as the organization of the individual's habits and behavior patterns in adjustment to his environment," Johnson repeated the strenuously dynamic view of both person and setting so influential in the social sciences between the wars.[26]

In the South, scholarship on personality thrived on its kinship to child-centered schooling. The GEB funded a series of case studies of black youth issued by an advisory group, the American Youth Commission (AYC), in 1940 and 1941: Allison Davis and John Dollard's *Children of Bondage*, E. Franklin Frazier's *Negro Youth at the Crossways*, and Johnson's volume, all presenting southern material, and W. Lloyd Warner and his colleagues' *Color and Human Nature*, focused on Chicago. Every volume advertised the term "personality" in its subtitle or on the first page, and the use of biracial teams of investigators underscored the project's liberalism. Early on, personality theorists in the North were intrigued by the South, and their interest paved the way for the youth studies. From start to finish, however, it proved difficult to keep the region in focus, as race as a more inclusive variable stole attention from place.[27]

Although the related ideas of a common culture and individual personalities became widely popular beginning in the mid-1920s, the University of Chicago was the seedbed for the theoretical strand that most affected the South. "Nashville is the ancestral seat of many of Chicago's oldest Negro families," Johnson wrote privately with a twist of irony in 1929, and

Charles S. Johnson, Fisk University sociologist. Courtesy of Special Collections, John Hope and Aurelia Elizabeth Franklin Library, Fisk University, Nashville.

whatever the sociological truth of the cities' connection, an academic debt ran southward.[28] Robert Ezra Park (1864–1944), a sociologist, mentored a number of doctoral students who settled in the South, and Edward Sapir (1884–1939), an anthropologist, produced a thinner southern legacy but a crisper analysis of the interaction of psyche and culture with the help of his friend, Harry Stack Sullivan, the psychiatrist.

Park's unusual acquaintance with the South was the foundation of his intellectual influence there. A white man from Minnesota, he spent almost a decade at Tuskegee Institute as a publicist for Booker T. Washington at the turn of the century and another decade at Fisk University following his retirement from Chicago in 1936 teaching sociology alongside his former student, Charles Johnson. Park's admiration for Washington turned his attention from crowds, the subject of his doctoral dissertation in Germany, to race, and his contributions to sociology seemed products of his southern experience: the ideas that biracialism is a social system, that race relations progress through predictable stages, and that geographic location affects human interaction.

Park's age and training in a discipline with only a secondary interest in individual psychology made him slow to adopt the personality concept.

In 1918 he said clearly that "racial temperament . . . consists in a few elementary but distinctive characteristics, determined by physical organizations and transmitted biologically." Racial nature then "select[s] out of the mass of cultural materials" what suits "its needs at a particular period of its existence."[29] Although he used the terms of the day for "Personality and Cultural Conflict" in 1931, his instinct to keep biology in the picture shaped his essay "Mentality of Racial Hybrids" the same year. "The mulatto and the mixed blood," he observed, were "the product of a double inheritance, biological and cultural."[30] Park seemed a reluctant convert to the increasingly environmental perspective on character sweeping the social sciences. Nonetheless, his dedication to the sociology of race, commitment to black graduate students, and intimacy with segregation explain why four scholars he trained contributed to the book series: Johnson, Frazier, Dollard, and Robert L. Sutherland, the general editor.[31]

Sapir taught at the University of Chicago for only six years before moving to Yale in 1931, and Sullivan had no connection with the university at all. Yet their all-day meeting in 1926 in a Chicago hotel room, where Sapir sought out the visiting psychiatrist to speak about his grief at his wife's death, led to a scholarly collaboration with southern consequences. Sapir was already adding consideration of the unconscious mind to anthropology's discussions of culture, and Sullivan's interest in interpersonal relations was pushing him to rethink psychiatry's emphasis on disease physiology. They discovered in each other an adventurous attraction to interdisciplinary work, and Sapir, more the writer and teacher of the two, explained how psychologically complex individuals anchor culture. Dissatisfied with anthropology's usual focus on customs, he declared in 1932 that culture inheres "in the interaction of specific individuals and, on the subjective side, in the world of meanings which each one of these individuals may unconsciously abstract for himself from his participation in these interactions."[32] German-born and Jewish by background, Sapir began his career as a specialist in American Indian languages. Most likely it was his bold integration of theories in anthropology, psychiatry, and linguistics that caught the eye of officials of the Rockefeller Foundation, whose funding helped bring him to Yale as a Sterling Professor. His first task was to teach a yearlong seminar in 1932–33 for international scholars titled "The Impact of Culture on Personality."[33]

It was the seminar's failure that forged a connection between Sapir's version of personality theory and the American South. Even before the studies of black youth, the South served as a psychological laboratory, albeit by accident. The Rockefeller planners behind the Yale colloquium began with an international objective. Seminar members from around the world would distill an "inventory covering in a systematic fashion the aspects of culture which have a marked influence in the development of personalities," according to one foundation memorandum, and especially, in the words of another, try "to learn where the pressure upon the individual was heaviest." The "international understanding" they took home would combat totalitarian regimes.[34] Yet few of the participants from the many troubled parts of Europe and Asia could return to their native countries to work constructively at the program's end, and scholars in Sapir's circle at Yale, sensing the obstacles to international work, gradually turned their sights southward.[35] Before the seminar began, the Depression had called attention to the poverty of blacks as a group and the South as a region, and Hortense Powdermaker, a close colleague of Sapir at Yale, had launched comparative studies of black communities in Connecticut and Mississippi. Soon John Dollard, who followed Sapir as a protégé from Chicago to Yale, was also in Mississippi doing fieldwork.[36]

Caste and Class in a Southern Town (1937), Dollard's case study of Indianola, Mississippi, naively put psychology on trial. During the year he had spent in Europe recruiting social scientists for Sapir's seminar, Dollard (1900–1980) studied at the Berlin Psychoanalytic Institute, where Freud's friend, Hanns Sachs, was his analyst. Although his eventual choice of book title reflected his sociological training at Chicago, psychoanalysis informed his understanding of southerners. He supplemented conventional fieldwork with a modified "psychoanalytical interviewing method" for nine black subjects, thereby entering a minefield on the subjects of sex and race.[37]

Believing it "an untruth" to deny "a complex mental life to the Negro," Dollard encouraged each one's free associations during sessions of about four hours a week. His attention to dreams and sexuality, including miscegenation, were unsurprising for a Freudian. When he further examined the color line, an inevitable focus for a student of Park, he found segregation's psychopathology. Black violence, for example, was neither an expression of innate "savagery" nor "emotional instability" but a "human response to frustration" in a situation in which angry aggression, produced by restriction, could safely be turned only on one's peers. Turning to whites, he exposed their truisms about black character, such as the race's dishonesty, as "distortions and excuses" belonging to the "defensive beliefs of the white caste."[38] Dollard's local newspaper, the *New Haven (Conn.) Register*, captured the work's methodological and political punch when it declared that, for "the first time in science research," Dollard "has employed the principles of psychoanalysis on Negroes in the deep South in order to obtain information which lays bare rivalry between the colored and white man."[39] *Caste and Class in a Southern Town* told readers that segregation was not peaceful, that both races were psychologically damaged, and that psychoanalysis claimed the status of science.

Dollard said that his allergies kept him from passing judgment on the proverbial bad smell of blacks, and "Gulliver with Hay Fever," the review title chosen by Donald Davidson of Vanderbilt, summed up southern reaction to the book: Dollard was too absorbed in theorizing to let his senses show him the real South.[40] Even if critiquing his method was the way reviewers expressed unhappiness with his content, they were clearly uneasy with psychoanalysis used as social psychology. Whites and blacks agreed that the book's psychological reasoning was too abstract. Davidson, a leading Agrarian, complained that Dollard turned "a race problem" into "simply a problem in Human Relations," and W. E. B. Du Bois said the text "lacks the proper sociological background" for its "brilliant Psychoanalytical interpretation," a remark damning by excessive praise when it came from a sociologist. Lyle Lanier, the Vanderbilt psychologist, doubted the status of psychoanalysis as a truth-telling science. Freud's ideas were "almost entirely an affair of the clinic," based on "unobserved, and *unobservable* 'mechanisms.'"[41]

Although southern critics denounced Dollard in unison, they had opposing motives. E. Franklin Frazier was repelled by Dollard's neutral pose as a "scientist qua scientist": "Men are not satisfied merely to understand the nature of cancer." To the traditionalist Davidson, however, academicism blinded Dollard to how much "Southern solidarity on the race problem is still virtually unshaken."[42] The same obtuseness to southern facts that made Dollard too little a reformer for Frazier made him too liberal for Davidson. Dollard's intriguing blend of psychoanalysis and sociology launched his successful career at Yale. A note of congratulations on his "distinguished achievement" came from James R. Angell, the university's president, who was by training a psychologist.[43] In contrast, southern readers were unappreciative of theoretical cleverness that dwelled on their maladjustment.

The investigators of black young people learned restraint from the controversy. When Dollard himself returned south in 1939 to coauthor his volume *Children of Bondage* with the black anthropologist Allison Davis (1902–83), he downplayed psychoanalysis. Freud's "findings parallel those of behaviorism at many points," the new book explained tamely, "and anticipate them at others."[44] True to the temper of the GEB, the AYC's black youth books aimed to induce reform by being studiously inoffensive. Observers could see that psychology was the principal interest of the studies, but there would be no sweeping cultural diagnosis. Douglas Southall Freeman, editor of the *Richmond (Va.) News Leader*, called it an investigation "of the mind of Negro youth," and the *Washington Tribune* cited an AYC source saying the subject was "the inner feelings of the Negro boy and girl as they encounter problems of race." Predictably, an in-house report used the words "personality development."[45]

The hypothesis was that "the abnormal position occupied by the Negro in American life" caused "isolation, feelings of social inadequacy, inhibitions, conflicting ethics, limited social participation, frustration, etc." in children. Davis expressed hope in a prospectus for "wide dissemination" of the conclusions. Schools and social services would learn from the monographs, and there would be "popular brochures on the problem for use in adult education among Negro and white groups" and "poster exhibits for loan to schools, libraries, and other organizations."[46] Caution was nonetheless the mood from the start. "Since 90 per cent or more of Negro youth are forced either by law or custom or both to obtain their cultural improvement through segregated institutions," the steering committee stated in 1936 as a matter of fact, racial separation would "necessitate a specially administered program in most instances for Negro youth."[47] Expecting to demonstrate that segregation distorted personality, the organizers had no plan to confront it directly.

Assembling a biracial staff of social scientists was still a brave move for the time, although tasks were divided in a way that muted psychological speculation about the children. Johnson, Davis, and E. Franklin Frazier (1894–1962), principal authors of the southern studies, all earned doctorates in sociology or anthropology at the University of Chicago and held positions at premier Jim Crow colleges. White scholars with psychological training played secondary roles. Harry Stack Sullivan wrote one chapter each for Johnson's book on the Black Belt and Frazier's study of border-state cities, and Dollard advised Davis about interviews with adolescents in the urban Deep South. Perhaps disadvantaged children were worth only so much of the time of acclaimed white intellectuals, or the sponsors wished to avoid resistance to psychological theory of the kind that consumed Dollard, or they assumed that diagnosis of the psychic difficulties of black young people required little expertise. The research assignments, in any case, favored the social application of personality ideas of modest complexity.[48]

Every facet of the project had enough elasticity, however, both to fan creativity and cause contention, circumstances that made the books' reception uncertain. Monroe Work of Tuskegee Institute, serving as a consultant, pronounced the personality concept vague. The team "included in your study more than one approach to personality," he wrote, in part because child development "is a subject still to be studied rather than a tool" of accepted validity.[49] This imprecision in fact gave each author considerable space. Charles Johnson, supported by a huge staff of thirty-five field-workers, data analysts, and theorists, made *Growing Up in the Black Belt* the most eclectic of the texts. Examining eight rural counties with black majorities in five states, Johnson asked Hortense Powdermaker for advice on anthropological method, recruited Eli Marks of Fisk to devise psychological tests, and solicited Sullivan for psychiatric insight. His conclusion that children absorbed the defeatism of a "Negro community . . . built around the idea of adjustment to being a Negro" was predictable. But along the way he offered penetrating comments on the children's growth: that fantasy was a safety valve, that education was a fetish, and that protecting children from the hurt of demeaning customs was a driving motive in parents.[50]

Children of Bondage, by Davis and Dollard, in contrast, was anchored in life histories of eight teenagers in New Orleans and Natchez, Mississippi. It aimed for depth instead of breadth and mixed sociological interest in status-seeking with psychological attention to child nurture. Ultimately class became a matter of psychology, because "the chasm [between classes] is a behavioral one." Lower-class childrearing, indifferent to "taboos" enforced by prosperous blacks, limited mobility within the black "caste."[51]

The premise that class depended on personal habits might have been problematic for Frazier, called "a maverick neo-Marxist" in the 1960s. His impatience with Dollard's scientific detachment in *Caste and Class in a Southern Town* was an earlier sign that Frazier would not permit curiosity about the mind to obscure social structures in his *Negro Youth at the Crossways*. Notes on aggression, self-doubt, and desire for assimilation did not preclude analyses here of black advocacy groups and community leaders.[52] Intellectually, the series thrived on the ambiguity about what personality meant.

Practically, though, black scholars fell into disagreement about how to handle the volumes' diversity, at the same time the white sponsors clarified how restricted their ambitions were. Everyone verbalized high expectations. "Evidence of change in attitude," "Changes in practice of institutions and organizations," and "Effects of the project on the feelings of people" were optimistic category headings in a 1940 report for the GEB prepared by Robert Sutherland.[53] The problem was the literary means. Ira Reid of Atlanta University worried that the case studies represented "such voluminous material as to be of little value except to scholars." He favored collapsing them into "a single coordinated report of one, or at most two volumes."[54] Allison Davis, in contrast, believed that he and Dollard offered "a vivid and intimate presentation of the humanity of Negro children" using the case-study method. He, too, opposed "a scholarly format," but wanted each volume to have a "popular" style "to reach the great body of general white readers."[55]

Neither man was successful. In 1943 the cloth monographs were selling for $2.25 each, at the high end of publications available from the AYC, which offered one guide, *The Community and Its Young People*, for fifteen cents. The sponsors seemed not to fear white hostility so much as to be stuck in the rut of education reform. Although a GEB officer confirmed when the books were in production that "we want a popular format," he was "delighted" in 1940 to "find they are being used to considerable advantage in the special seminars and summer schools which I visited." Two lists, one consisting of names of state agents for southern black schools and the other of workshops for teachers of both races, all GEB sponsored, guided marketing.[56] Institutional reform in the meantime fell by the wayside. Two proposed pilot guidance clinics for black children, intended to translate the research into counseling, did not go forward. Nor did the federal government take action, despite the presence of Department of the Interior officials on the project's advisory board. Although one foundation agent was sure that "interest in the Negro study is so general among the leaders and institutions of the South," the main audiences for early spin-off talks were northern professors.[57]

Few men of either race connected with the studies would have been surprised or even disappointed when the South faded from view. A combination of choice and wrangling jeopardized the southernness of the research from the beginning. Race, not region, defined its goal. The premise that "minority racial status" had personal consequences was blind to geography, and Sutherland, a good publicist, emphasized the work's broad importance. As "world conditions are challenging the stability of our nation's democratic institutions, the peaceful solution of our own minority problem takes on a special urgency."[58] Rhetoric alone could not dictate exactly which areas to study, however, and although the black exodus from southern farms made decisions about cases genuinely problematic, the investigation's internal dynamics seemed to relentlessly deflect attention from the southern countryside. The northern academy exerted pressure on site selection and individual careers. Allison Davis included Natchez, for example, because he was already doing fieldwork there for his mentor at the University of Chicago, the anthropologist W. Lloyd Warner. Warner in turn managed to make black Chicago the subject of the final case study, *Color and Human Nature*, with himself as first author, and the book added to the overrepresentation in the series of a northward-moving urban population. Frazier, who had left Fisk for Howard in 1934, focused more on Washington, D.C., than Louisville, Kentucky.[59]

In all these decisions, the personal indignities of segregation for black scholars reinforced other reasons to investigate northern and border-state locations. When Davis took a job at the University of Chicago during World War II, Charles Johnson became the only researcher of the group still living in the South. Johnson was well aware of the demographic trend that made his book the sole inquiry into the lives of rural young people: 80 percent of black families lived on southern farms sixty years before, he reported, in contrast to 50 percent when he wrote.[60] Perhaps his massive research grew not simply from his anomalous task in the project but from his recognition that he was documenting a dying culture, even if a repressive one. Perhaps, too, he sensed that southern black social science as a genre might be equally evanescent.[61]

Although the self-consciously "psychological" argument of the *Brown* decision in 1954 strongly echoed the AYC book series's conclusion about personality, scholars located in the South who had ties to the original work exerted little influence on the ruling. This outcome might have been predicted in light of the uncertain southern focus of the case studies themselves. The northward shift of scholars and scholarship, however, was a gradual process. Note 11 of the Supreme Court opinion made reference to research to corroborate its logic that "separating the races is usually interpreted as denoting the inferiority of the Negro group" and that "a sense of inferiority affects the motivation of a child to learn."[62] The last line of the citation read as if stating the obvious: "And see generally Myrdal, An American Dilemma (1944)." The investigation of race relations coordinated for the Carnegie Foundation by Gunnar Myrdal, the Swedish economist, helped to refocus racial justice as a national problem. Many of the scholars who worked in the southern field during the 1930s, including Davis, Frazier, and Johnson, contributed to the volume.[63]

Southerners were far less visible a decade later. Of thirty-five social scientists who signed "The Effects of Segregation and the Consequences of Desegregation," a document accompanying the appellant's briefs to the Supreme Court in 1952, only one resided in the South: Bingham Dai, yet another former student of Robert Park who now taught at Duke. Charles S. Johnson seems to have added his name at a later date. Davis and Reid, also original signers, now held positions in the North. Most of the scholars were white, but not one lived in the South, and it is a fair guess that the large number from the urban Northeast, including thirteen from New York City, had little personal contact with the region.[64] Although the South soon felt the primary practical impact of the *Brown* doctrine, southern social scientists concerned with personality were no longer at the forefront of racial debate.

The strategic advantage to restating the problem of segregation as a general issue of prejudice obscures the element of distaste for the South behind the change. The preference of northern social psychologists for controlled experiments to measure racial awareness in children was in part simply a matter of regional style. Kenneth B. Clark (1914–2005), however, who pioneered racial personality testing in the late 1930s with his wife, Mamie Phipps Clark (1917–83), clearly disliked the South, his wife's native place.

Earning doctorates in psychology at Columbia University, the Clarks quickly gained a reputation for their evaluation of the attitudes of nursery school children in Washington, D.C., and New York. As a method, the technique replaced fieldwork in a region that for Kenneth epitomized black servility. Born in the Canal Zone and raised in Harlem, Clark embodied the assertive "new Negro." When he became the object of "racial insult" at the New York office of *Time* in 1939, he responded with a "letter of protest" to tell the editors that a black man "using a pen rather than a slop mop" would not let the offense pass. When his wife doubted her ability after the University of Minnesota denied her a scholarship, he roared back at her, "Statements of inferiority are out of the question." "Don't don't don't" he wrote all over his letter, reinforcing his advice: "For God's sake don't worry about that test you took for Minnesota." With the exception of the miserable year, 1941–42, he spent teaching at Hampton Institute in Virginia, separated from his wife at Columbia and their new daughter, he dismissed a string of possibilities at segregated colleges before beginning a long career at the City College of New York.[65]

Privately he battled his wife's southernness. A doctor's daughter from Arkansas, Mamie became "Katherine," her middle name, at his insistence during their courtship, and she seemed to accede to his willfulness when she professed in 1936, "I even like it [New York] better than Hot Springs and that's saying something for New York."[66] In his eyes "the sincerity and good sense of the two individuals" being married legitimized the couple's elopement just weeks before Mamie's graduation from Howard University in 1938. The importance of "traditions and rites" never occurred to him, he apologized to Mamie's father, a man left "hurt, disappointed, and bitter" by their deception.[67] Deference was simply not a word in Kenneth Clark's vocabulary, and his racial psychology operated without regard to custom in much the same mood.

It may be argued that personality research did not really turn its back on the South. Rather, it sank shallow roots there from the start. The AYC rightly identified the region as home to the American problem of segregation. The money, training, and even personnel for the books were mainly northern, however, and the project's impact on the practice of southern social science seemed superficial. At least southern black youth became the subject of systematic interest, one might respond, which is more than seemed true for white ones. The social scientists' public declaration in connection with *Brown* judged that segregation imposes "a distorted sense of social reality" on both races; next to the many volumes about black socialization, though, the process of white development remained "obscure."[68] Speculating that southern whites growing up experienced guilt, cynicism about ideals, and unwarranted pride, the signers wondered how these schoolchildren would respond to desegregation, but they did not ask openly why southern white scholars had collected so little data about the influence of segregation on young people of their own race. Perhaps the answer was obvious: in a population that neither wanted racial reform nor believed in the need for self-blame, there was little motive for critical self-analysis. Instead, the region's most prominent white social scientist, Howard Odum, celebrated the folk mind and mourned its endangerment.

The Mind of an Out-of-the-Way Place

The Depression had turned American attention to the South as a region long experienced in disadvantage, and some writings made its culture seem not so much distorted as unusually quaint. Established interests in the social sciences in primitive societies, social evolution, and immigration gave scholars concepts to describe premodern peoples. A historical orientation had once dominated ethnography, seen in works such as E. B. Tylor's *Primitive Culture* (1871) and L. H. Morgan's *Ancient Society* (1877), and the contrast between traditionalism and modernity informed the twentieth-century views of theorists including William Graham Sumner, W. I. Thomas, and Robert Redfield. Studies that recast southern provincialism as a sociological stage were able to borrow familiar terms. The South was a "feudal" land inhabited by "peasants" and regulated by "folkways."[69]

Howard Odum (1884–1954) of the University of North Carolina, who constructed a social science of regionalism after 1930 around respect for folk tradition, claimed a leading role. The racial conservatism of Odum's vision was close to the surface. The thought that generations-old habits determined behavior in closed settings could be made to serve segregation, and of all the social psychologies currently explaining the South, the notion of a folk mind seemed best suited to staunch regionalists devoted to white supremacy. Odum's vagueness about the workings of the folk psyche may well have enhanced his idea's utility as ideology. Looking too closely at the mental underpinnings of social oppression could not have been pleasant or politic for loyalists to regional precedent, especially as national opinion on race relations moved in more liberal directions before and during World War II. Black analysts who applied folk theory to southern society were far less squeamish than Odum about examining psychology. These were the same authors who elsewhere used the personality concept to show segregation's crippling effects, and they had no wish to preserve the South's racial integrity. The folk studies of the interwar South were subject to one or another imbalance, depending on the author's race: either a regional emphasis without psychological acuteness or attention to motivation with no love for regional tradition.

Odum's career-long use of folk analysis shows the flexibility of an approach suspicious of theory. The belief in nature's creativity that anchored folk study favored data collection and discouraged abstraction, and in this mood Odum published the texts of hundreds of spirituals from his dissertation in the *American Journal of Religious Psychology and Education* in 1909. The "social nature and unconscious ideals" of the "negro," he explained, "bubble out from his spontaneous social songs."[70] It was not until two decades later, however, when Odum was an acclaimed expert on education, race, and planning, that he placed the idea of folkways near the center of his research agenda. By the time he delivered his presidential address to the American Sociological Society in December 1930, the nation's economic crisis gave Odum an opportunity to push the discipline in a fresh direction. "Folk and Regional Conflict as a Field of Sociological Study," the speech's title, dressed up the presumed traditionalism of his home ground in scientific terms to make regional folk life an academic subject and a social ideal. Who in hard times produced by modern dislocations could altogether resist the appeal of a "folk society which was organic, natural, and material" and not wonder how to reclaim it?[71]

The next year Odum warned readers of the *Nation*, however, that southern folkways were threatened. "Lynchings, Fears, and Folkways" censored white mobs for their "lawless revolt," but the real culprit was criminal statute. So long as lynching was "a recognized custom," "the enforcement of law" against mob activity "by local or State forces would mean literally civil war in the community." Left alone, unpressured folkways would evolve through "education, publicity, civil appeal, and courageous leadership."[72] Worldwide exposure to totalitarianism reinforced Odum's critique of aggressive "stateways" in *Understanding Society* in 1947. Although he had to admit that Nazism venerated its nation's folk spirit, "Hitler's Germany was the perfect example of artificial society and super-technology" suppressing indigenous mores. With all of nature and history on their side, "*the folkways ultimately defeat the stateways*," Odum emphasized, or at least so he hoped.[73]

This celebration of instinctive living potentially made the study of psychological mechanisms irrelevant. If the folk behaved without reflection in response to their natural and human environments, dualisms of mind and body and of subjectivity and objectivity—centuries-old anchors of philosophical and later psychological thinking in Western culture—seemed inapplicable to them. Yet Odum did not ignore the possibility of a folk mind, citing a string of authorities, and the real question is why he paid lip service to mental science without stating a theory of his own. His most genuine debt was to *Folkways* (1906) by the Yale sociologist William Graham Sumner (1840–1910), a volume that Odum called "pioneering." As the nation's premier social Darwinist, Sumner began with the premise that human beings seek pleasure and avoid pain because we are like "other animals."[74] Settled customs—"folkways"—result from successful adaptation. Although Sumner might have choked at Odum's impulse to romanticize the southern folk, the men shared an elitism, explicit in Sumner's work and assumed in Odum's. "Thinking and understanding are too hard work" for the brutish "masses," Sumner judged, so their mores become harnessed to institutions devised by "leading men." Sumner's respect for the powerful emotions that made popular life "shallow, narrow-minded, and prejudiced" did not preclude rationality in the few.[75]

Perhaps Odum's belief in social hierarchy contributed to his repeated rejection of "the collective mind assumed by Wundt." By its title, *Elements of Folk Psychology* (1912) by the German scholar Wilhelm Wundt (1834–1920) would seem a perfect sourcebook for Odum. One problem was its equation of psychology with ideas. A cognitive psychologist and Hegelian, Wundt did little more than line up the values of successive societies that he believed produced human self-consciousness over time. Still, it was Wundt's challenge to individuality, not his narrow conception of mental processes, that bothered Odum. Much as the imagined harmonies of traditional places appealed to him, he resented the conformist pressures of the nation-state and advancing technology. Whether logical or not, individuality had to be a trait of Odum's folk mind.[76]

Yet no observations about personal motivation appear in his work, and if psychological astuteness seems too much to ask of a sociologist, it may be remembered that even Sumner had a rudimentary notion of drives. Instead, Odum continued to recruit theorists to explain aggregate behavior. The Gestalt school was a favorite because its members insisted that the meaning of any single motive, thought, or memory emerges only in its relationships. Defining culture as a "total Gestalt" in the 1940s, Odum praised "the realistic individually-socially equipped personality," although given the laboratory base and scientific aspirations of most Gestalt work, this social application bore only a distant kinship to the group's research.[77]

Psychology and Folk-Lore (1920) by R. R. Marett, an Oxford anthropologist, offered Odum the further idea, copied in *American Regionalism* (1938), that "survivals survive" if "they are the constantly renewed symptoms of that life of the folk which alone has the inherent power of surviving in the long run." A champion of the need of folk studies to investigate the mind, Marett dismissed scholarly "learning" as a method in favor of "human sympathy and common sense," advice that may have appealed to students of primitivism but gave them little guidance.[78] Even "Freud's 'cultural superego,'" finally, turned up in Odum's presidential speech of 1930. To make the point that modern societies have folkways, albeit in tension with "stateways," Odum referred to the analogous contest between elemental instincts and civilized restraint outlined in Freud's *Civilization and Its Discontents*, published the same year.[79] All this work dovetailed with Odum's view of how society functions, but the three perspectives left him with disparate explanations of mental activity, focused respectively on brain physiology, communal impulse, and sexuality. He neither tried to reconcile the positions nor stated a preference for one.

Ambitious to build up southern sociology, Odum relied on academic shortcuts, including liberally quoting from himself in successive publications and substituting mystifying phrases (black "extrawhiteman-organizational" habits) for patient analysis.[80] Perhaps haste also accounts for the stream of psychological references that stood in place of his own synthesis about the mind's operation. But Odum had been outspoken about black temperament as a young man, and he was less blunt about disposition later, when his beliefs became professionally questionable. "The Negro," he wrote with assurance in *Social and Mental Traits of the Negro* in 1910, has "little conception of the meaning of virtue, truth, honor, manhood, integrity" and is "shiftless, untidy, and indolent." These were among "the inner qualities of the Negro's nature."[81] Former colleagues who edited a posthumous collection of his writings in 1964 stated that "in the next twenty years science did an about-face on racial differences," but Odum "was apparently little disturbed by them [criticisms] . . . and he saw no reason for any formal 'repudiation' of the book."[82]

All the while, he continued to project in stories what could no longer easily pass as fact. His narrator described the "ramblin' minds" and "quick changing moods found in the Negroes" in *Rainbow round My Shoulder* (1928), the first volume of a trilogy about a wandering modern "Black Ulysses." Completed by *Wings on My Feet* (1929) and *Cold Blue Moon* (1931), the series self-consciously created a folklore to illustrate "folk background and folk urge, of picaresque tension, of regional culture and contacts." In the books, generalities about black character mixed as if naturally with sociology and fiction.[83] It would have been quite another thing to profess a simple belief in racial natures within the academy, however, and it is a fair guess that Odum found none of the other psychologies he tested as compelling. The result was that the mental dynamics behind folkways remained vague. Sometimes these customs seemed an expression of white interests. "We are afraid, and it makes us mad," Odum wrote in 1931 to explain the genesis of lynching in anxiety over the durability of white supremacy. Here "we" denoted whites. But in fact the Civil War paved the way for "the development of a folk society for both races," Odum had said.[84] For Odum, probing the mind-sets of the races in the traditional South without the neat premise of racial endowments might have felt like entering an intellectual morass.

No other scholar of the interwar years was so committed to folkways as a theory, but the isolationist mood of the era may have contributed to surging interest in American primitivism and especially the peculiarities of the South. Most investigators were more curious than Odum about folk psychology. Newbell N. Puckett and B. A. Botkin, white scholars located in the North, seemed charmed by southern usages, dismissive of their value, and yet intrigued by how customs came to be. They agreed that a kind of ambition or regard led "the backward folk . . . to imitate the more advanced," in Puckett's words. Blacks consequently adopted lore of European origin, and although "the superstitious state of mind" of the folk was "a-logical-mystical," Botkin said, the dominance of unreason was temporary. "As science advances, then, superstition recedes," he stated as a rule, and Puckett concurred, "These ancient beliefs of the Negro are rapidly disappearing under the influence of education and general racial advancement."[85]

Although Puckett quarreled with the African American "race pride" that produced embarrassment about "these mental cornerstones" of "group progress," it is easy to see why folk study made many black intellectuals uncomfortable.[86] Charles Johnson, for one, testily dismissed "the 'folk Negro'" of "familiar lore" and scholarship—the "simple, trusting servant, addicted to petty crimes and sexual looseness"—as a "stereotype."[87] Yet other African Americans resisted such skepticism. Zora Neale Hurston, who studied anthropology with Franz Boas and Ruth Benedict at Barnard College in the 1920s, did extensive southern fieldwork, although when she published her material as *Mules and Men* in 1935, some black reviewers predictably called the collection too "pastoral."[88] Hurston later criticized *Brown v. Board of Education* for implicitly devaluing black schools by the order to integrate, and it might seem that her enthusiasm for folklore years before had also set her outside the black mainstream. But E. Franklin Frazier's casual mention of "folkways and mores" in his *Negro Youth at the Crossways* may make us think again.[89] Why would a book devoted to the utilitarian "personality" concept acknowledge the force of collective behavior in terms so risky for black Americans?

The simple answer is that language devised to distinguish between savage and civilized societies remained current among social scientists, even though faith in humanity's steady progress had dimmed. Without making folk life an ideal, black researchers were led by their training to separate primitive from modern behavior. Besides, their analytical use of "folk" and "peasant" quietly refuted demeaning white applications of the same words. Just seven years before Charles Johnson censored the folk stereotype, he was on the other side of the fence in *Shadow of the Plantation* (1934), where he called rural southern blacks "an American type which can most nearly be described as 'folk'" and "the closest approach to an American peasantry." Among scholars nationally, this was not an original thought. Robert

Redfield, an anthropologist at the University of Chicago, labeled this population "our principal folk" in 1930. Johnson, though, produced an extended study of black life in "feudal" isolation that made the inhabitants of the countryside seem a backward-looking repository of "the surviving traditions of an earlier period."[90]

His commitment to the premise that this culture was archaic did not mean that he accepted the situation. Metaphors were telling. "The shell of the past hangs on," he observed at one point, and later, "The weight of generations of habit holds the Negro tenant to his rut."[91] Yet if Johnson shared none of Odum's nostalgia, his loyalty to an evolutionary framework merits further reflection, and the role of the sociologist W. I. Thomas (1863–1947) seems the key. Five volumes of *The Polish Peasant in Europe and America* (1918–20), coauthored by Thomas and Florian Znaniecki, appeared while Johnson was a graduate student at the University of Chicago, where Thomas taught until 1918. Thomas did not so much detect the hidden hand of the past on the present, like Sumner and Odum, as describe historical transformation. In the Polish case, "social disorganization" at home released peasants from the bonds of custom, set them adrift on a lonely passage, and regrouped them, now purposeful individuals, by "social reorganization" in America.[92]

Because Johnson's book did not discuss northward migration, his picture of black peasants seemed static next to Thomas's cycle. Nor did he develop Thomas's wealth of psychological assumptions. Not only did Thomas posit elemental human "wishes" for intimacy, control, and safety, but he borrowed the link between mind and environment from philosophical pragmatism, asserting that "every manifestation of conscious life . . . involves a tendency to action." Temperament, character, and life organization, in turn, were phases in the normal sequence of growth that moved individuals toward social adjustment and self-direction.[93] As Johnson worked on *Shadow of the Plantation*, he was also experimenting with the personality concept as a psychological theory, publishing an essay he titled "Negro Personality Changes in a Southern Community" in 1934 as well. Abandoning the peasant model for the rural black South after this book, he drifted away from Thomas's communal psychology.[94]

It was E. Franklin Frazier who applied folk theory to southern black life in a way that silently defied Howard Odum. He rejected Odum's view of a sacred tie between the South's home soil and its folkways. Rather, "force of circumstances," Frazier explained with understated irony, made slaves "take over, however imperfectly, the folkways of the American environment."[95] The statement appeared in *The Negro Family in the United States* (1939), the black masterwork based on the folk concept. Frazier faithfully applied Thomas's sweeping vision of peasant transformation to African American progress from slavery to urban migration. He could seem misty eyed about "the humanity of their simple folk background" when he described free blacks in the postbellum southern countryside, because he saw "the dissolution of the rural folkways" that lay ahead. Idiosyncrasies of rural families that were rooted in slavery, including high rates of illegitimacy, desertion, and female leadership, lost their "harmless character" in cities, now "divorced from the folkways of these simple peasants."[96] Drawn to the honesty and intimacy of the folkways, Frazier could not accept specific habits. Yet overall, his ambivalence about the "folk" stage of black history was conditioned by his certainty that it would end. This dramatically distinguished Frazier from Odum.

Part of the power of *The Negro Family* was its systematic historical analysis, derived from Thomas's logic, and Frazier similarly found the kernel of his book's psychology in *The Polish Peasant*. Thomas believed that sexuality was the normal means for satisfying a need for self-validating contacts, and Frazier made sex, in tension with authority, seem a driving social force. As Frazier described "sexual hunger" repeatedly released from the control of African taboos, slave masters, and black male family heads, Freud seemed an influence, as he had been for Thomas before. Echoes of *Civilization and Its Discontents* could be heard here. Although Frazier imagined "the authority of the father" to be the crux of stability, he no more rejected society's emotional substructure than did Freud. Slave families sprang from "spontaneous feelings of affection," originated mainly in mothers, and upwardly mobile "Black Puritans" were guilty of "an exaggerated valuation upon moral conduct . . . in opposition to the free and uncontrolled behavior in the larger Negro world."[97] Folk analysis allowed Frazier to make emotion an attribute of black racial health.

The Negro Family represented the apex of Frazier's focus on psychic processes behind southern folkways. This was the first study he published after moving from Fisk to Howard, and later monographs, including *Negro Youth at the Crossways* and *Black Bourgeoisie* (1955), were urban focused. Nonetheless, Frazier's attachment to black folkways as a symbol grew in proportion to his distance from the rural South. If it was foolish to think about perpetuating peasant culture, remembering it with respect was crucial. The urban black middle class showed "much confusion as to standards of behavior and beliefs" because "they reject the folk heritage," he wrote for *The Negro Church in America* (1964), published soon after his death.[98] Still believing that the future offered the self-determination needed to secure racial justice, Frazier found moral guidance in the past.

No less than other southern social science initiatives of the 1920s and 1930s, folk studies were connected with public policy, and yet perhaps no one would have expected *The Negro Family* to have the greatest impact in the long run. For decades Odum was the most earnest advocate. Donald Davidson stated the obvious in his essay "Howard Odum and the Sociological Proteus" when he wrote that "the North Carolina school" aimed to sell regionalism to the "Leviathan" state. Odum's team of scholars hoped in effect to put the South on the New Deal's map, with enough success in their eyes that Rupert Vance, for example, professed that his *Human Geography of the South* (1932) "exceeded the expectations" he set for its influence.[99] Odum's own defense of folkways sought to preserve segregation, however, and by the time he died in 1954, he must have realized that outside the South the message fell increasingly on deaf ears.[100]

Frazier, in contrast, did not live to see a dubious fame. As the Great Society worked to extend racial reform from civil rights to social welfare, Daniel Patrick Moynihan, as Lyndon Johnson's assistant secretary of labor, issued *The Negro Family: The Case for National Action* in 1965, better known as the Moynihan Report. With sixty-one footnotes, the paper's reputed reliance on Frazier may be overstated. Still, Moynihan's choice of title, praise of Frazier's book as a "classic study," and substantial quotations from the original all convey the report's indebtedness.[101] Concluding that "divorce, separation, and desertion, female family head, children in broken homes, and illegitimacy" characterized the urban black family, Moynihan labeled the result a "tangle of pathology," a phrase borrowed from Kenneth Clark.[102] Although the coherence of Frazier's analysis may have attracted Moynihan, then a young social scientist, he extracted a static, expedient diagnosis from a panoramic history for the purpose of social engineering. Social disorganization was no longer a natural phase of development but simply a problem, and the South and its folkways, the starting point for northern slum dwellers, was all but forgotten.

The potential of the folk model between the wars to elucidate a regional psychology remained similarly unfulfilled. Stepping back, it is easy to see what Odum meant. In the South's rural past, customs grew up that addressed elemental needs, bound the races together, and conditioned thinking, and these habits continued to inform the present, for better or worse. The terms of analysis risked overstating the primitivism of an area that, after all, was part of Western society. But the notion of folkways still had a lesson for American social science: history made elusive by lack of documentation stands behind modern cultures.

Even in the best of circumstances, the folk mind presents obstacles to interpretation, however, and Odum came to the task with inhibitions of his own. The variety of theories available to him about the motivations of premodern peoples suggests how much assumptions substitute for evidence that may be difficult, even impossible, to collect. He added a reluctance to examine the psychology of his subjects at all. Suppose whites were not gentlemanly but instead cruel, blacks were not submissive but angry, and one race were not clearly superior to the other? Conversely, black investigators who applied the folk image to their less educated peers took the chance of confirming stereotypes. Suppose fieldwork unearthed evidence for what whites thought they knew already, that the black race was backward? Although southerners seemed best positioned among American social scientists to study a disadvantaged rural population, racial politics restrained them.

From their nineteenth-century beginnings, the social sciences sought not only to understand society but also to identify problems and oversee solutions, and yet when social psychology entered the South, the impression of regional pathology left by research was enough to overwhelm optimism. "Is the inner life of the Negro utterly different from ours?" wondered William Alexander Percy in his plaintive memoir of the passing of white patriarchy, Lanterns on the Levee, in 1941. Although he judged the blacks among whom he lived to be "deeply alien and unknowable," the problem for the white South in these decades was precisely that scientific investigators were so busy answering Percy's question, to the neglect of corresponding scrutiny of how the thoughts and motives of white individuals were shaped by their race.[103]

The work proceeded along lines reminiscent of Reconstruction. Northern whites collaborated with southern black scholars on studies meant to influence government policies. No white southern social theorist waged so grand a counteroffensive as Howard Odum, as he struggled to frame race safely in the concept of region. Racism made social research a minefield of taboos. Black analysts could neither broach the subject of white violence nor dwell on their own race's deficiencies, and whites steered away fearfully from thoughts of the psychological causes and effects of segregation. Although culture shapes science in every society, here race relations made psychological discussion hazardous and, when conclusions touched nerves, fed distaste for the discipline. In our mind's eye we can see Cotton Ed Smith trampling the psychology book in the Senate. Yet his anger was a sign that southerners were hearing about the minds of their people, like it or not. As psychology across the nation took an existential turn after World War II, its practice in the South drew closer to a mainstay of southern tradition: religious experience.

| 4 | IN THE SOUTHERN BORDERLAND

OF MIND AND SOUL

Southern piety commanded attention no matter how practitioners of the mental sciences felt about religious belief. The region's
faith intruded, among other places, in postwar discussions of
the much-heralded new theory of the "anti-democratic personality." The literature alternatively labeled this individual "ethno-
centric," "prejudiced," and "authoritarian," and theorists devised questionnaires to identify the type in populations. The "F scale" measured a
predisposition for "fascism," and the test's name signaled the European
orientation of the émigré scholars who anchored the collective work, *The
Authoritarian Personality* (1950).[1] White southerners in the United States
were not their focus, and yet it seemed only a matter of time before researchers analyzed segregationists. Lack of self-insight, habitual stereotyping, and superstitious belief were traits associated with prejudice, all said
to grow from childrearing based on fear rather than love.[2] The authoritarian model could easily categorize the white South's attachment to good
manners, social order, and Christian faith as protofascist.

Instead, white southern bigots became the improbable heroes of a
campaign to resist European determinism. Theorists of authoritarianism
offered a grand view that all prejudices have a common origin in deficient
parenting, understood in more or less psychoanalytic terms. In a pragmatic spirit, American scholars disassembled the package, and some cited
the South as a counterexample. A small but steady stream of investigations
beginning in the 1950s demonstrated that white southerners scored higher

on the "N scale," the test of "anti-Negro" prejudice, than on allied measures of other forms of ethnocentrism. The disparate results raised questions about the elegant holism of the authoritarian idea and permitted startling optimism: simple racism acquired during normal socialization seemed comparatively fixable. White southerners were "*latent liberals*," said one researcher, not pathological cases crippled by interlocked prejudices.[3]

Piety in particular could be a source of hope in this American adaptation of authoritarian theory. Even native social scientists otherwise devoted to reason were willing to test the Europeans' reduction of spiritual beliefs to outward projections of a divided self. Inquiries into white southern authoritarianism debated the statistical correlation between churchgoing and racial liberalism, and when the relationship seemed close, the South's reputation as the nation's stronghold of religious faith came oddly to signify the region's progressivism.[4]

This unexpected twist in the American conversation about the authoritarian personality brings to light a more general truth about the alliance of psychology and religion in postwar America and especially in the South. Across the nation, science and faith seemed to enter into a new covenant of mutual tolerance. A therapist such as Carl Rogers and a theologian such as Paul Tillich both considered creating identity a matter of ultimate concern transcending rational understanding. Troubling memories of war and nearly utopian hopes for peace seemed equally to impel this existential turn in mental science.[5] In the South, a region typically identified by Americans with religious fervor, the conditions for a psychological renaissance seemed finally to have arrived.[6]

To an extent, the promise was beautifully fulfilled. The marriage of mind and soul liberated southerners working in the psychological disciplines from the sober mind-set of medicine and the racial questions of sociology. A psyche pictured as free from the restraints of the body and caste seemed marvelously susceptible to renewal. Human relocations during wartime increasingly opened the South to new therapies and faiths, and on the margins of the region's historical evangelical Protestantism, healers of a phenomenological bent drew on Asian philosophies, European existentialism, Judaism, Catholicism, Protestant liberalism, and Pentecostalism.

The result was an effervescence of healing experiments that resembled a religious revival. Southerners had long relied on transcendence as the answer to bodily disease and social injustice, and the postwar movement seemed nourished by ingrained spiritual habits. The emotionalism and evanescence characteristic of awakenings, however, also limited this one. Intellectual tensions between science and religion persisted because they were not systematically addressed. Lonely prophets, charismatic leaders, and spectacular mass events provided little solid foundation for institutional reform. A few brave souls who were equipped to blend psychology and ethics were moved to denounce segregation. But the varieties of faith healing largely bypassed racial inequality and so left it intact. Enthusiasm about the mind's capacity for recovery, although truly advancing mental science, curiously ignored the South as a place.

My discussion explores cases selected to display the range of philosophical orientations: three newcomers to the South who were members of ethnic minorities, a freewheeling group of psychiatrists in Atlanta, and Christian initiatives in mental health, most dramatically the grassroots Pentecostal healing revival that took off at the war's end. All these figures and movements had visible connections with the international postwar impulse to link psychology and metaphysics. Their stories reveal southern variants of a commonplace orientation.

A Southern Refuge

In the 1940s the white South remained so solidly populated by conservative Protestants of British stock that it is hard to picture what life was like there for Bingham Dai, born in China; Ernst Borinski, a German Jew; and Joseph Fichter, the Jesuit son of parents of German background. Yet from the viewpoint of professional psychology, it is more difficult to imagine how southern theory and its applications might have developed had they not come. Although all three acquired interdisciplinary training in the social sciences, only Dai (1899–1996) concentrated on psychotherapy. The interest in mental science of Borinski (1901–83) and Fichter (1908–94), both sociologists, was more modest. In each case, though, ethics unfamiliar in the South—whether Confucian, Jewish, or Catholic—informed the men's activities. The systems stressed obligation to neighbors as much as individual salvation.

The men were accidental southerners, socially speaking. Circumstances led them south, but all stayed, and they brought cosmopolitanism to the circles in which they traveled. Although Borinski told an interviewer who visited him in Jackson, Mississippi, in 1980, "I feel completely at home here," his comfort must have grown along with his transformation of the place.[7] All behaved as outsiders when they challenged segregation, and whether we account them naive or brave, their attention to race relations shows that existential psychology could become socially engaged. Despite Borinski's warmth about his adopted land, they remained solitary figures and, in that sense, resembled prophets who left a fragile legacy.

The life of Bingham Dai was turned upside down by war. Dai's dream was to introduce psychotherapy to his native China. Hired in 1935 by the psychiatrist Richard Lyman to teach psychoanalytic technique and preventive mental hygiene at Peiping (Beijing) Union Medical College, he soon sent his pregnant wife to the safety of her family in New York, where her Chinese-born parents had settled, in response to Japanese belligerence. In 1939, pretending to be Japanese, he himself escaped. Dai had well-placed friends in the United States, all with southern connections. He had been a graduate student of Robert Park at the University of Chicago beginning in 1929 and a participant in Edward Sapir's seminar on culture and personality at Yale, where he discovered psychoanalysis under the influence of John Dollard and Harry Stack Sullivan. The position Park now arranged for Dai at Fisk University, where Park had retired, seemed more than a stopgap. Its social scientists were "embarked on a research [sic] in race and cultural relations in situations in different parts of the world," Park assured him, and they were "eager" for "a young man representing different cultures" to compare segregation with "similar situations in other parts of the world."[8]

Dai's three years in Nashville were a mixed success. Although his commitment to desegregation began with his interviews of black youth at Fisk's "sociological clinic," he had never been in the South before. The campus, where the family lived, was like an elite ghetto, and the strain of the Dais' anomalous situation finally sent them back to New York. His wife, an artist, thrived there, but "as to myself," Dai explained to Lyman, now head of the new Department of Neuropsychiatry at Duke, his "official publicity work" for the Chinese government "cannot satisfy a mind that is interested in more fundamental problems than the events of the day."[9] Within months Lyman brought Dai to the School of Medicine in Durham. The atmosphere was electric. Wartime concern with soldiers' psychology had enabled Lyman to launch a controversial program to train black psychiatric workers at the white school. Still, Dai was the sole "professor of mental hygiene," with a Ph.D. for his credential, on a faculty of medical psychiatrists. His status freed him from routine teaching but made reappointment uncertain. On this margin, he may have found the medical school's "foreign fellows" program welcoming. Most of the international staff came from the British Isles, but there were eight Chinese fellows, including Dai, during the twenty years after the school's founding in 1930.[10] More privately, Dai's daughter, now turning six, entered a white elementary school. His employment by a white institution resolved some of the ambiguity about the family's racial classification under Jim Crow.

Ernst Borinski moved south more purposefully than Dai, at least so he recalled. He did not want to be a social scientist at "any established institution" but instead sought "an interesting teaching job," he said in 1980. He was in his mid-forties in 1947, when the American Missionary Association interviewed him in New York for Tougaloo College, and he later explained his qualifications as "experiences with people, experience of persecution, experience of army, experience of success and failure."[11] A Holocaust refugee, disinclined to recount painful memories, Borinski chose spare phrases to suggest a life radically disrupted by public events. He escaped Germany in 1938, three years after the Nuremberg Laws prevented him from continuing as a law professor at the University of Jena. After serving as a draftee in the U.S. Army, he talked his way into a master's program in sociology and education at the University of Chicago, unable to document his previous schooling.

Perhaps a wish to "liquidate my past" motivated Borinski's change of field. He nonetheless valued sociology as a "discipline to find explanations and solutions for the problems of the society in which he lives," in the words of a Tougaloo College student who later interviewed him.[12] His acquaintance with African Americans in the army and at Chicago helps account for why he approached a southern black college for work. Yet he did not fully anticipate the indeterminacy of his own racial status. "You must have gone out the wrong entrance," observed Tougaloo's black dean, who came to meet Borinski's train the day the new teacher arrived. Having left the station by the white door, Borinski had trouble finding his ride.[13] Being Jewish was a further complication. When he deplored segregation, a newspaper, he recalled, made "a great cry about a German-Jew coming to Mississippi and telling us good Christians what it meant to be a Christian."[14] The enforced social detachment Borinski encountered must have resembled the experience of the northern Congregationalists who established Tougaloo for the freedmen during Reconstruction. Nazism not only prepared him to endure the discomfort but gave it meaning.

Joseph Fichter seems the least exotic of the three men as a Jesuit in largely Catholic New Orleans. But his German background set him apart from the city's French Catholic tradition, his slim formal schooling deviated from the order's emphasis on scholarship, and his working-class hometown of Union City, New Jersey, populated by immigrant families, bore little resemblance to the South. Chance, combined with his religious vocation, brought him there. The Jesuits' southern province accepted candidates with modest Greek and Latin proficiency because of the area's small pool of applicants. A high school dropout and bricklayer when he decided on the priesthood in 1930, Fichter had no choice but to join the order in a place where its training included classical languages. Yet he had little interaction with southern society before his ordination in 1942. Jesuit discipline required permission from superiors for even such small freedoms as buying books, and, although effectively exiled from the urban Northeast, he poured out articles for Catholic magazines in the 1930s on industrial labor and unions, for him familiar subjects. The world crisis kept him physically in the South, after the order declined to send him to Belgium for study in 1937 because of "the extremely tense and serious situation" abroad.[15] Culturally, though, he remained an outsider.

It was not until Fichter went northward at the end of the war, first for summer courses at the University of North Carolina and then to Harvard for a doctorate in the Department of Social Relations, that he seemed ready to approach southern society. Social science had been his passion for some time. "I must ask you to postpone your special studies" in order to teach at Loyola University, wrote the Jesuit provincial of New Orleans in 1944. The class "may make the change of plans a little harder: It is religion." "You are a sociologist, but first of all you are a priest," he added, logic that required no explanation.[16] When Fichter returned once again to Loyola in 1947 with a Ph.D., he was eager to investigate the South from a Catholic standpoint.

The three incoming teachers found themselves at odds with the academic status quo. All had absorbed the interdisciplinary mind-set that dominated the northern academy, but their new institutions tended to pigeonhole mental science with either medicine or religion. Years of funding of southern schools by private foundations and government had only modestly dislodged an old-fashioned matter-spirit dualism in university teaching. In a collection of scientific papers edited by Richard Lyman in Beijing, Bingham Dai not only opposed "too much of a distinction between the mind and body" but criticized medical psychiatry's habit of seeing the patient "as an isolated individual" detached from his social milieu.[17] It is true that Duke recruited Lyman, known for his sympathy with sociological currents in mental health, to carve out a program in neuropsychiatry from its Department of Medicine. Dai remained a self-described "lay analyst" among doctors, however, who acquired a reputation, a later colleague observed, "as the only person on psychiatric grand rounds who would not talk about diagnosis."[18]

Moral concerns framed psychology, in contrast, at Loyola and Tougaloo. Even after Joseph Fichter became chair of Loyola's sociology department and champion of a social work program in the late 1940s, the school's core offering in psychology stayed in the philosophy department as half of a one-year sequence completed by "theodicy," justification of God's plan for humankind. In a course description unchanged since the 1930s, psychology included cell biology, epistemology, evolution, "origin of man," and "immortality of the soul."[19] When Fichter urged Loyola's president to support social science inspired by "Catholic social ideas," he meant recent church teachings on topics like family and labor, not abstractions that kept the college "intellectually still back in the last century."[20] Heartily in favor of an alliance of sociology and faith, Fichter was impatient with scholasticism's heavy hand.

Tougaloo felt so strongly about its spiritual mission in the years after Borinski's arrival that it changed its name to "Tougaloo Southern Christian College" for nearly a decade. In light of mandatory chapel attendance, dress restrictions, and supervised relations between the sexes in the 1920s, it is not surprising that an early psychology class promised to teach the student the "laws of the human mind" and to help in "guiding his own thought and action in accordance with these laws." A minister was still teaching psychology, along with philosophy and religion, at Tougaloo when Borinski arrived.[21] An unobservant Jew, Borinski fell comfortably into the habit of hosting Christmas and Easter socials for students, accompanied by his

"German-styled Refreshments."[22] He nonetheless envisioned social science as something more than a moral tool.

Fichter and Borinski quickly became anchors of struggling sociology departments, and they influenced psychology teaching on their campuses when they set out to reform the social sciences. Social psychology was one of the courses Fichter had added by 1949 to modernize sociology, along with classes on statistical methods, race relations, and regionalism. Borinski, who taught six courses in his field the same year, left Tougaloo's psychology program more to itself, although by the 1960s students could elect new classes in human development and mental health.[23] Dai escaped the time-consuming tasks connected with curriculum development because his main responsibility at Duke was to offer training analyses to medical residents. A bit older and more professionally established than the other men, he was poised to have his writing take off in the South.

Dai spoke truly in 1979 when he reflected, "I have learned from various schools of psychotherapy but am attached to none."[24] Scientifically, his thinking was neo-Freudian and unusually focused on ethnicity. During his training in the 1930s, he was psychoanalyzed by Harry Stack Sullivan and then Leon Saul of Chicago, an orthodox Freudian; once on his own, he relied on standard techniques of free association and analysis of dreams. Yet despite his wish to find points of entry into the unconscious mind, he was more optimistic than Freud about human self-control. Dai's frequent use of the words "ego" and "self" linked him with peers who thought consciousness could regulate irrationality. More positively, he believed children have a "spontaneity and adaptability" that healthful nurture should preserve, an idea he expressed in 1949 in, not surprisingly, the journal *Progressive Education*. He had relied earlier on the theories of William James and John Dewey for "The Growth of the Self," a graduate school essay submitted in 1932 to George Herbert Mead, the Chicago philosopher, and in later years he noted the likeness of this Western trust in natural gifts to Chinese philosophy.[25]

Dai's international perspective shaped his convictions as well as his ideas. This was a time when the practice of psychotherapy on nonwhite patients was not simply rare but questionable. He must have sensed a need to say clearly that "the black child also has a self" when he reported on his private interviews with young people at Fisk.[26] The same point was implicit in an account of his psychoanalysis of a man in Beijing in 1937 published in the journal *Psychiatry* during the war. But no matter how important it was for science to publicize nonwhite cases, Dai knew the ambiguity of turning these subjects into objects of scrutiny, because he himself had been used for an academic paper by Leon Saul on ethnicity and psychoanalysis. His identity appeared "in a very disguised form," Saul wrote with some embarrassment in 1938, and Dai would receive "a copy for your own censorship and comments."[27] Dai's vulnerability as an outsider was one source of his empathy for people of varied backgrounds.

His drive to integrate science and humanism also had personal roots. "My Initiation into the Social Sciences" was the title Dai gave to the capstone chapter of an autobiography required for Sapir's Yale seminar in 1932 that he structured as a search for values. Most of the foregoing pages were about religion. Sent as a boy to Christian schools after an uncle's conversion precipitated the family's embrace of the Western faith, Dai later eagerly entered St. Johns University in Shanghai, an Episcopal college, "to study this great religion and to discover its secrets."[28] He twice told an anecdote connected with his disillusionment, once in this narrative and again in a lecture around 1960: the bishop, who was also the school's president, ordered him off a bench in front of the prelate's residence because Dai was Chinese.[29]

Doubts about Christianity as practiced led Dai to investigate Hinduism, Buddhism, and Confucianism, and after he became a resident of the Bible Belt, he remained a critic of pious ethnocentrism. But whatever the means of enlightenment, the purpose was "personality education," as he told Sapir, based on the premise, quoting Mencius, a Confucian, that "only those who have developed their own potentialities to the fullest can understand Heaven or what their life mission is going to be."[30] As a teacher in China in the mid-1920s, Dai nurtured his students "along physical, intellectual and moral lines" through readings, discussions, and interviews. In Durham he still aimed to help individuals "grow, substantially undiverted, toward self realization," words borrowed from the German-born analyst Karen Horney. Science and philosophy were partners in a process that was both psychological and spiritual. Dai wished "to introduce science to China in a more natural and more effective way than has been attempted so far," the Yale statement concluded.[31] Frustrated in this plan, he became a psychotherapist in America, without losing sight of the deep questions that engaged him as a young man.

The existential tone of Dai's work linked him with Borinski and Fichter. Borinski was not at all pious, but life under the Nazis gave him an ethical imperative and the instincts of a fugitive to pursue it. "I learned out of my Jewish experience very much for my operation here in Mississippi," he recalled with characteristic vagueness, although the lessons can be inferred.[32] Equality was his goal when he took Tougaloo students for ice cream at a Jackson drugstore in 1947 and resisted the management's badgering until the business served them on the condition that they would then "get out of here right away." His Social Science Forum, eventually hosting speakers of national stature at campus discussions, reflected the social scientist's impulse to "build bridges between people." Because he had once lost basic rights, however, he also knew how to dissemble. As "an outsider" in Mississippi, "I played this game very carefully by often pretending I just don't know" about segregation, thereby testing its limits.[33] Distanced from Jewish orthodoxy, Borinski nonetheless followed his tradition by behaving ethically himself and seeking justice.

Fichter's far more explicit wish to integrate social science and Catholicism produced disappointment during the same years. Although his faith in both remained firm, he privately doubted their short-term alliance. He confirmed his intent "to put social science at the service of the Church" in a letter to his Jesuit superior in 1955, a month after he told an acquaintance, "I've been in the midst of this controversy on religion versus social science since 1951" because of his research.[34] That was the year the first of four projected volumes of *Southern Parish* appeared in print, only to be quickly suppressed by the church. Writing with almost visionary "belief that the reintegration of Western society, particularly on the American scene, can take place only through Christianity in the form of the Catholic Church," Fichter documented the gap between high principle and lax practice in a massive sociological survey of a New Orleans parish.[35] He envisioned reform, but others were simply embarrassed.

Even before the book controversy, Fichter's plan to host interracial meetings caused tension. Inspired to promote integration by Gordon Allport's Harvard seminar on prejudice, he received a letter marked "*Confidential*" in 1948 from Loyola's president saying it would be "more prudent not to invite Fa [*sic*] Howard," who was black, "to dinner at the present time." A nun at Xavier University, a black school, tried to make light of official caution when she quipped to Fichter that the two colleges might hold "an interracial tea at which both groups would eat cookies and sip punch standing."[36] Biracial gatherings eventually began, but by then Fichter was frustrated enough to decline an offer to be president of the American Catholic Sociological Society because Loyola "is a Jim Crow school." "Whatever institutional prestige accrues from the position should go to a non-segregated college." Fichter found Catholic teaching on brotherhood best expressed in the idea of the church as Jesus' "mystical body," the subject of a papal encyclical in 1943.[37] The conflicts of the postwar decade must have made it hard, however, to balance his loyalties to religion and science.

Psychology played a role at the intersection of ethics and social action for all three scholars. Unlike southern Protestants, whose emphasis on conversion made evangelicalism "a highly individualistic religion," in the words of a homegrown critic, Dai, Borinski, and Fichter came from traditions focused on how to behave toward fellow humans.[38] Their social science in turn was existential yet not abstract, as Confucianism, Judaism, and Catholicism positioned them to see, as Fichter wrote, "the logical connection between prayer, study and personal virtue, on the one hand, and action, cooperation, and social virtue, on the other."[39] Fichter himself was reserved toward psychology. Although Catholics, including clergy, had long studied the mind, the impulse of secular science to blur the line between brain and soul made the church wary of the psychological disciplines. Even so, Fichter published advice on raising unprejudiced children in his newsletter, the *Christian Impact*, in 1953 and soon brought a psychiatrist to Loyola to critique the "unscientific theory" of racial differences in intelligence.[40]

Borinski's Social Science Forums at Tougaloo made psychology a more regular theme. "The Psychology of Culture Changes and Culture Conflicts" and "Are We Normal or Insane[?]—Community and Institutional Responsibilities for Mentally Ill Citizens," both talks by professionals from the state mental hospital, were early topics, around 1950, and other speakers examined connections between psychology and race, education, and crime before the conversations slowed down in the 1970s. Because these experts mingled in the schedule with clergy, politicians, and a range of professors, the message to students was that mental science was a valuable intellectual and social tool.[41]

Dai's application of psychology to current issues was, in contrast, nation-

ally visible. He signed the social scientists' statement about the damaging effects of segregation on children that influenced the Supreme Court in *Brown*. He was the only supporter who lived in the South, where his isolation underscored his courage.[42] Although *Brown* revolutionized the South, however, Dai's personal legacy was less detectable. The many training analyses he conducted at Duke before his retirement in 1969 and then near his new home in the North Carolina mountains were so legendary that students called the process "Daianalysis." Yet in Durham he "restricted his involvement in departmental and administrative activities" and in "public life so as to prevent embarrassment to patients and former patients," re-

Ernst Borinski with Tougaloo College students in the Social Science Laboratory, 1960s. Courtesy of the Mississippi Department of Archives and History, Jackson, and Tougaloo College, Tougaloo, Mississippi.

called a colleague. Perhaps Dai preferred to be quietly influential because the method suited his personality. He was remembered as "gentle, kindly, soft-spoken, serious," and above all "contemplative."[43] The young man who set out to introduce psychological science to China must have been more ambitious, however. He began his life in the South as an exile. Free because he was out of his element, Dai was not well situated to carry out institutional change.

Borinski and Fichter were similarly marginal. Although Borinski seemed to savor the chance given him by fate to protest injustice, he lived alone for years on the Tougaloo campus, fitting neatly into neither of Jackson's racial categories. He recollected being asked to speak about desegregation at a nearby white college because "I was the closest to a black person they could get, not in terms of color but in terms of commitment and so on." Borinski was not the only Holocaust refugee to occupy this racial no-man's-land. Nineteen traditionally black colleges hired Jewish scholars uprooted by Nazism, but not all the schools were in the South, nor were all the professors social scientists. The cumulative effect on the practice of southern psychology would have been modest.[44] For Fichter, one effect of the *Southern Parish* controversy was that he seemed always on the run. Between 1953 and 1972, he held eleven visiting professorships as far away as Chile and for as long as his five years at Harvard. Gaining international prominence and local notoriety by the same stroke, he spent many of his productive years away from New Orleans, where eventually he retired.[45]

Yet even if the men were unable to put an enduring stamp on academic programs, protégés, or community reform, their encounter with the South brought their unique qualities into sharp focus. Their interdisciplinary scholarly habits and minority backgrounds opened the way for social tensions. But the southerners who heard them were challenged, and over the years Dai, Borinski, and Fichter gained respect in the region. In contrast to many earlier outsiders with liberal views who made brief contact with the southern mental sciences and then returned home, these three stayed. The incompleteness of their assimilation at least guaranteed sustained dialogue with southerners about the ethical dimension of social science.

Experiential Medicine in Atlanta

Psychiatry as practiced by the doctors who formed the Atlanta Psychiatric Clinic was a good deal more unconstrained by rationalism or, for that matter, any conventional religion. Authenticity, communication, and transformation were the means and goals of therapy. So bold were the doctors' methods that the experiment attracted national notice. At Emory School of Medicine, where the group began, a Rockefeller Foundation official described ward rounds in 1949 as "an exciting if somewhat bewildering experience." "No effort was made to obtain any history or unravel the dynamics of particular cases." The staff simply offered to listen or "sat in silence waiting for the patient to say something." Carl Whitaker (1912–95), chair of the psychiatry department, told the visitor in passing about his own "schizophrenic background," and the observer thought his temperament "enables him to participate in his patient's waking dreams" with, Whitaker claimed, "a high degree of therapeutic effect."[46] Had Whitaker seen the man's report, he might well have been pleased instead of insulted. Mental patients were cured not by diagnosis and physical treatment, he argued, but by immediate encounter with the therapist. In 1953, the year Whitaker and his Emory colleagues began their private clinic, they called the doctor-patient bond "an acultural, deeply affective therapeutic psychosis." In the 1960s they described therapy as "on-going experiencing" and a "feeling relationship."[47]

What name to give an approach stressing the higher realism of irrational communion was a puzzle. "Psychoanalytically oriented" was the earliest wording, presumably because of its emphasis on the therapeutic relationship, followed later by "phenomenological," tying the method to the philosophy of consciousness, and last, "experiential psychotherapy," the title of a coauthored article in 1963.[48] Two years later Whitaker left to take a job at the University of Wisconsin, however, and soon the office divided. "Everyone concerned seemed most alive and enthusiastic if a little bewildered," the foundation observer repeated in his memo of 1949, and arguably, it was precisely the associates' exuberance that gave their clinic the temporary brilliance of a shooting star.[49] Therapists eager to engage consciousness were less interested in nurturing institutional foundations, a tricky enterprise in any event in postwar Atlanta. Yet in its heyday, the practice courted personal transformation with all the intensity of a frontier revival.

Psychological care of American soldiers had lately brought mental health to the public's attention, and the professionals who gathered at Emory were part of the tide. The dislocations of wartime favored encounters among therapists in situations that elicited experimentation on patients who were not institutionalized. The need for speedy treatment pushed Carl Whitaker to introduce half-hour sessions led by two psychiatrists in Oak Ridge, Tennessee, where he cared for veterans. He also used bottle-feeding to induce rapid regression to an infantile stage imagined to hold the key to adult dysfunction. Whitaker may have found it easy to be innovative because he had little training in psychiatry. Originally a gynecologist from upstate New York, he worked with delinquent boys in Kentucky before moving to Oak Ridge in 1944. John Warkentin was his professional "mate" there, Whitaker said later, and like his partner, Warkentin had advanced degrees in both psychology and medicine from northern schools. Feeling "as if having children (i.e., patients) together gave us a kind of professional marriage," Whitaker brought Warkentin along to Atlanta in 1946.[50]

Thomas Malone (1919–2000) did not join them until 1949, but he resembled his predecessors in his rehabilitation of soldiers, interdisciplinary interests, and southward drift. Born in the coal-mining region of northeast Pennsylvania, Malone attended Duke on a football scholarship. In 1948, now with a Ph.D. in psychology from Duke and an academic position there, he published his research on group therapy for returning soldiers where "the social organization was democratic." The supervising therapists deliberately stood back and let solidarity and charismatic "patient leaders" do the work of emotional repair. Perhaps the experiment caught the interest of the Emory group, whose members by now were adopting nondirective methods as well. Once in Atlanta, Malone began a free medical education in exchange for teaching what he knew about psychotherapy.[51]

Two southerners, Rives Chalmers and Richard Felder, were influential in the same Emory circle. Both were doctors first exposed to psychiatry in the military. The navy offered Chalmers (b. 1918) instruction in psychiatry when he was stationed in the Pacific, and by happenstance he studied in Washington with Harry Stack Sullivan, now with a long history of southern ties, and Frieda Fromm-Reichmann. Felder (1918–2008) observed psychotherapy as an army captain at a base hospital in Germany.[52] Being from the South affected each man's decision to join Emory's psychiatry department in a different way. Chalmers, whose ancestors settled in post-Revolutionary Virginia, recalled seeing Atlanta as "the growing metropolis of the South." Although he had considered leaving the region, his marriage to a South Carolinian during the war made him more inclined to answer an inquiry from Whitaker in 1947.[53] Felder was firmly situated in Georgia, but he faced skepticism from his family about entering an unfamiliar field. Coming from Florida, a state with no medical school of its own, Felder became a successful internist after earning an M.D. degree at Emory in 1944. His gradual shift to psychiatry provoked incomprehension at home, a response heard more often in a part of the country where mental cure remained a novel idea.[54]

In practical terms, the Emory doctors found a common cause in the psychiatric training of medical students, albeit of an unconventional kind.

Because Atlanta was "a psychiatric desert," Whitaker told a correspondent in 1947, it was perfect for "pioneering" measures. "I am amazed at how fertile the soil is," he continued, though this hospitality had more vigorous grassroots sources than he saw.[55] It was true Georgia lacked services that Frank Luton had been fighting for in Tennessee, for example, since the early 1930s. In 1949 the development of the psychiatric wing and child guidance clinic of Atlanta's public hospital was still in progress. The state mental hospital at Milledgeville was notoriously overcrowded, and because "outpatient facilities are not widely available in Georgia," the Rockefeller officer noted, "most patients on return home have to work out their problems by themselves."[56]

The same surge of interest in mental health that prompted Emory to recruit the psychiatrists, however, offered them a promising climate. The Georgia Federation of Women's Clubs began lobbying for revision of commitment laws during the war. Soon the Georgia Association for Mental Health formed to crusade for awareness of mental illness, producing a high-pitched "religious fervor," a state official said in 1960.[57] These initiatives could be double edged: stirring public concern, they brought questionable answers. Under a 1937 law, Georgia was second only to North Carolina in the number of "mental defectives" sterilized in 1953. The women's clubs wanted to move black patients from Atlanta to the veterans' facility at Tuskegee, Alabama, in the late 1920s because "the congested quarters in the hospital renders it impossible to properly segregate the two races."[58] Clearly, there was an audience in Atlanta for new ideas about psychiatric care, but the Emory group had to make itself heard.

In writings stretching from the earliest days to the 1990s, the members identified psychic growth originating in the unconscious as the goal of therapy and the doctor's own transformation as the condition of the patient's cure. "It is the therapist's unconscious anxiety, the anxiety of being and becoming" that energizes the relationship, Felder and a coauthor wrote in 1991, echoing an emphasis on the "irrational component of the integrated therapist" by Whitaker and Warkentin a quarter century before.[59] Although Whitaker used plainer language in 1950 when he said a doctor must learn "to function more adequately as a person," consensus about the primacy of the caregiver explains the "radical character of the program" for Emory medical students.[60] Everyone, not just those interested in psychiatry as a specialty, participated in group therapy and later treated patients, first in a cluster of student-therapists and then one-on-one. The "conventional trappings and techniques of psychiatric education" were missing, observed Lawrence Kubie, the psychoanalyst, dispatched by the Rockefeller staff to investigate. There were "almost no didactic lectures; almost no formal noon clinics and case presentations; very little time spent fitting patients into crude nosological categories," because the purpose was not transmitting knowledge but nurturing self-awareness. Cheered by the refreshing chaos, Kubie likened his conversation with students to "a Christian Science experience meeting," though more "tough-minded, plain-spoken, and sincere."[61]

Why the project caused "considerable tension," as Whitaker confessed, is also clear. If the medical school's administrators expected to develop psychiatry as a separate field, the outcome instead was the infusion of psychotherapy into every branch of medicine. For Whitaker, that was the point. His "teaching program transcends the limited scope of the psychiatric department," he wrote proudly to the Rockefeller office. "The whole medical student-faculty community seems to become involved in a group process."[62] Although many students were won over, colleagues and parents rose to defend rationality, authority, and restraint. Some professors believed, Warkentin reflected later, that "group therapy might be anti-educational, since it emphasizes motivation and feeling, rather than logic and factual learning." In their own classes, they found students now "too uninhibited in their critical evaluation of medical teaching." Parents complained about their sons' "new thinking," as if self-revelation were shameful.[63] Whatever the psychiatrists were doing, in some eyes it was not medical science. Worse, they wanted everyone else on board.

It is not surprising that the doctors submitted orchestrated resignations to the medical school in 1955 to practice full-time at their clinic. Younger colleagues remembered the office as "a place where people were working themselves to death," and the group had reason to guess at the outset that its method, objectionable in the academy, would be popular outside it.[64] The reassuring message was that mental disease was not frightful but instead curable by trust and freedom. Throughout their years at Emory, the doctors had kept busy with local speaking engagements. Parent-Teacher Association meetings were the most frequent audiences, hearing talks that in one way or another advised families about how to raise "happy children," the title of a lecture in 1953. But organizations of nurses and dental hygienists, charitable societies, the Rotary Club, and the American Council of Jewish Women also invited the psychiatrists, and newspapers spread the word as well.[65] "Emory Doctors Test Love as a Cure for Insanity," a feature in the *Atlanta Journal and Constitution Magazine* in 1951, explained how Whitaker and Malone cured a schizophrenic patient by "deep parental love in a therapeutic sense." Warkentin counseled in the same pages that if we "learn to EXPRESS our feelings" in an "H-bomb-threatened world," we can "stay sane."[66]

Although the articles reduced experiential therapy to simple formulas, the publicity served the men's intention to be socially useful. *The Roots of Psychotherapy* (1953), by Whitaker and Malone, reproduced their medical school program in print by explaining psychotherapy to the "practicing physician, no matter what his specialty." Mental health information was too important to restrict to specialists, and the clinic's members continued to produce brief essays for general practitioners on treating psychosis, circulated by the Medical Association of Georgia, after they moved to private practice.[67] What the psychiatrists offered was more a message about human potential than a medical technique, and reception in the community was warmer than among professors of medicine.

Simple as their faith in self-expression sounded, however, the approach contained ambiguities that affected the clinic in the long run. Most surprising in light of the trouble at Emory was the wish to establish experiential therapy as a science. Looking back in a memoir, Whitaker singled out Alan Gregg, longtime director of medical research of the Rockefeller Foundation, as "somebody who has truly found himself."[68] For Whitaker, whose method resembled spontaneity, esteem of Gregg seems odd. In a distinguished lecture series at Yale in 1941, Gregg praised systematic investigation as a new instrument of medical progress, and although Whitaker might have agreed that the character of "the *man*" behind an experiment determines its value, the disregard of routine at Emory makes the men's friendship unexpected. Yet it was Gregg whom Whitaker contacted about funding in the late 1940s, and Whitaker must have been disappointed when Robert Morrison, delegated to observe by the Rockefeller office, advised against sponsorship. "Clinical research is always difficult and especially so in an atmosphere as unfinished and highly charged as this one."[69]

Continuing gestures of respect for science dispel the suspicion that Whitaker cultivated Gregg only for the money. *The Roots of Psychotherapy* presented itself as "a scientific formulation of the art of psychotherapy." Charts elucidating technical terms such as "anamnesis stage" and difficult concepts like "symbolization" conveyed the impression that therapy required specialized knowledge as well as empathy.[70] As doctors writing for doctors, the authors were not ready to throw off the profession's regard for precision. Their loyalties were also divided between rational and irrational sources of insight. Two articles by clinic members in the late 1950s explained, first, that a delusion may reveal true information and, second, that a fantasy shared by therapist and patient may yield understanding. These defenses of imagination appeared in scientific journals, however: the *Southern Medical Journal* and *Diseases of the Nervous System*.[71] Ultimately, Whitaker seemed to try to quiet the tension between unreason and reason by accepting a new academic position. In 1957 he counted himself among the "many of us who are not clearly research workers," as if he felt marginalized, and although he did not have to renounce the free spirit of experiential therapy when he went to Wisconsin, perhaps he welcomed its psychiatry department's scientific tone.[72] The intellectual structure of the academy may have eased the inherent dilemma of being a physician of the unconscious.

For at least one of the Atlanta group, Whitaker's departure helped lift the pressure to appear scientific. "Music of the Interview" was a reflection published in 1968 by Richard Felder, an accomplished pianist and organist. He explained that he and his patients played a piano in his office as the mood struck them. Adding tunes to conversation was a metaphor for the unfolding chords and pitches of emotional interaction, and for Felder, the musical trope stuck. He later subtitled a book about therapy *A Symphony of Selves*.[73] Felder's invention of wording true to his experience was perfectly suited to a movement that aspired to be always fresh. Kubie had been thrilled in 1949 to find none of "the dead wood of useless and elaborate case histories" that cluttered conventional wards.[74] But the doctors' enduring attachment to medicine suggests how hard it was to disregard their training.

Their treatment of families further illustrates how constrained a radical method was by respect for inherited language. Once the therapists stopped serving Emory's teaching hospitals and began seeing patients living at home, they met with entire families. Already convinced that mental health depends on relationships and experienced with group therapy, they were prepared to launch family sessions. Their thinking about families, however, remained surprisingly Freudian. Whitaker led a discussion about the origins of schizophrenia in the "oral period" at a professional conference the clinic hosted in 1955, and Malone moderated a dialogue on "countertransference," a psychoanalytic term he adapted to mean the doctor's emotional investment.[75]

To an extent, both men deliberately stretched old concepts. The writings on infancy of Melanie Klein, a revisionist of Freud but not a renegade, had influenced Whitaker. But when he interrupted a lengthy talk at his conference about breastfeeding to wonder if "all experiences at whatever age" contribute to psychosis, he injected doubt that the disease was a simple "intake problem." Malone's loose definition of a Freudian term evoked a louder outcry from the visitors. "I protest right off!" said one. "No, no!" added a second, and, chimed in a third, "Where did you get that idea?" Such dissension left the impression that the meeting was "confused and disorganized," as Whitaker described one panel, and a key source of conflict was how much the Atlanta therapists honored conventions of psychoanalysis that poorly matched their experimental temper.[76]

Had the group wished to become a school of thought, its members might have devised unique terms more systematically. But early and late, they professed to teach the universal qualities of good therapy, not a technique, and their style deliberately defied parochialism. Use of epigraphs from world literature in *The Roots of Psychotherapy* resembled Thomas Malone and his son's decision to quote Carl Jung, Gregory Bateson, Melville, Whitman, Yeats, and Emerson in a single page of *The Art of Intimacy* in 1987.[77] As writers, the doctors assembled great thoughts as if they wished to draw readers toward a realm where the truths of philosophy and science were identical.

This transcendental mood set the clinic in an awkward relationship to its community. The therapists' slim involvement in civil rights in Georgia perhaps goes without saying. The men's training as doctors did not emphasize sociological components of psychological problems, and private practice brought them in contact with patients who could pay. At times the print record reveals a startling disconnection from surrounding racial contention. Because participants at the 1955 conference used the words "black" and "white" simply to designate untreatable and treatable patients, someone connected with the dialogues' publication in Boston added a footnote to clarify that the usage was psychiatric, all the more sharply highlighting the meeting's silence on color.[78]

Inattention to racial issues does not mean that the men were prejudiced. Malone participated in a panel on "prejudice and world conflict" in 1951, alongside Benjamin Mays of Morehouse College, and Felder recalled that the clinic had at least one black family as patients in the mid-1960s. Rives Chalmers left the strongest record of all the men on civic reform, and many of his causes, including improving the state hospital, outpatient care, and sentencing laws, had to raise racial questions. Selected in 1953 by the Atlanta Chamber of Commerce as one of the young men "most likely to provide leadership in the metropolitan area several years hence," he counted Martin Luther King Sr. among his friends.[79] None of Chalmers's colleagues was similarly recognized, however, and the practice's dominant interest was nurturing human potential. Like America's romantic reformers in the past, the Atlanta therapists envisioned individual transformation of nearly mystic depth and kept their distance from local conflict.[80]

When they were in their element, however, they were masterful. Tensions in the approach faded when they spoke about patients. Testy exchanges during the schizophrenia conference were silenced by comments about their dogged experimentation with cases. Whitaker, Warkentin, and Malone explained that they tried housing psychotic patients in sanitariums, hotels, rented houses, or at home. They similarly tested a succession of therapeutic methods until they settled on multiple doctors for one patient and occasional family conferences.[81] If the doctors' emotional involvement in therapy was as intense as their attention to detail, their success must have been considerable.

Their own interrelationships resembled their bonds with patients, and deliberately so. Kubie had heard at Emory that "Whitaker will accept on his staff only men who will consent to pool their inner psychological experiences and problems," and the result was unusual "team spirit and loyalty."[82] Although the clinic left no evidence of this rule, its members were self-selected and hence inclined to seek intimacy for private growth and professional effectiveness. In the years before Whitaker's departure, the men served as cotherapists on cases and met weekly to work on coauthored articles. After he left, teams of therapists and their wives treated couples at the one of now two separate offices that kept the original name. All along, the families vacationed together, and when the Felders' son ran away from home, he took refuge, predictably, with the Malones. In the words of Ross Cox, who joined the clinic after giving up general practice for psychiatry in the mid-1960s, it was "an extremely intimate group."[83]

The satisfaction of living in close connection produced bittersweet memories after relocations, realignments, and retirements eroded the early coherence. An all-day symposium on the history of Atlanta psychotherapy in 1999, including Felder and William Phillips, who came on staff in the 1970s, ended with a long look at the problem of self-perpetuation. They remembered receiving applications from therapists that the doctors set aside, and even at Emory, Whitaker understood that the qualities of an "effective clinician" were "antithetical to the kind of attitude required to handle administrative problems." Although he recalled those years as his "administrative childhood," the men left Emory to escape its bureaucracy and neglected to formalize commonplace routines of their own like recruitment.[84]

Not surprisingly, charisma did the work instead. Patrick Malone's impression that Emory "students were just literally hanging off the rafters" to hear his father teach suggests how a sense of affinity and even calling drew new men later on. Cox, for example, who had been one of those students, consulted repeatedly with the group during the decade it took him to decide to bear "the stigma about being a psychiatrist" in exchange for career satisfaction. Emotional power also determined authority, much as natural gifts had singled out Malone's patient-therapists among the returning soldiers treated at the end of the war. Reminiscences of the clinic frequently turned at some point to the men who were leaders at each stage, and use of words like "genius" and "brilliant" for the founders by their successors was a sign of how much respect for talent created its own order.[85] Clearly, informality so perfectly suited the practice that it is hard to imagine any other organizational method. But motions of the spirit do not reliably produce institutional growth.

Across the country the postwar era was the heyday of outpatient psychotherapy based on healing conversation, and although the energy produced many experiments, practitioners outside the South seemed less tempted to quit supporting institutions for the sake of unrestrained freedom. Consider Carl Rogers (1902–87). Rogers was a professor of psychology at the University of Chicago in 1949 when he contacted John Warkentin about being treated by the Emory group. In the 1930s, he had been Warkentin's therapist in Rochester, where Rogers worked for the city's child services and Warkentin was a doctoral student, and now the tables were turned. Experiencing "panic states" and fearful that "I will go all to pieces in trying to get to the bottom" of the problem, Rogers turned to men with whom he felt kinship.[86] His most popular book, *On Becoming a Person* (1961), shows that Rogers, too, was redefining psychic difficulties philosophically, and *Client-Centered Therapy* (1951), his own case for dynamic doctor-patient relations, was in progress at the time of the correspondence.

Nothing came of Rogers's inquiry, but the communication offers a glimpse of a like-minded professional in a different region who took a dissimilar path. Rogers held positions at Ohio State, the University of Chicago, and the University of Wisconsin between 1940 and 1964, when, nearing an age of normal retirement, he left the mainstream for the Western Behavioral Sciences Institute. Were northern universities more flexible? Did their municipalities provide for the mentally ill at a level that did not require doctors to work overtime as administrators? Did the North depend less on the expertise of newcomers and so skirt contention between outsiders and old ways?[87] The eagerness of Rogers's employers to hire and sustain him as an innovator suggests that the answer to all three questions is yes. The Atlanta psychiatrists came in with fire, in contrast, but their professional isolation was a handicap, and their therapeutic skill did not help them build foundations.

The mood of regret among many who recalled the early days obscures how the Atlanta Psychiatric Clinic seeded the region, however. A participant in the 1999 colloquium noted how many local psychological professionals received their training therapy there, and two of the founding members, Rives Chalmers and Dick Felder, worked well beyond formal retirement. Patrick Malone continues a practice that bears the original name, and experiential psychotherapy as a theory achieved a clarity perhaps only possible in retrospect. The vitality of the unconscious, the nurturing power of relationships, and the ego involvement of the therapist appeared as simple precepts in *Experiential Psychotherapy*, published in 1991 by Felder and a younger coauthor, Avrum Weiss. With forewords by Whitaker and Malone, and even a note by Bingham Dai, a friend, the book bespoke the clinic's communal spirit and secured for its views a continued hearing.[88]

Christian Cures

When the Atlanta psychiatrists spoke of growth nearly as a matter of fulfilling one's destiny, they did so in a sea of Protestants. Their secular phrasing of human aspirations did not mean they opposed religion, and a number of them, including Whitaker, were churchgoers. Freedom was the precondition of experiential psychotherapy, however, and the chance of being considered "a Christian psychiatrist" made Felder, for one, "feel my hands getting tied."[89] Yet other southern healers deliberately practiced Christian therapy during the postwar years. Bible-based conversion, the time-honored southern path to personal renewal, was joined by pastoral counseling in liberal churches and a stunning revival of divine-healing ministries, led most visibly by white Pentecostal evangelists but affecting followers of both races. Southerners now had religious options that cultivated psychology and offered optimism about psychic health along with spiritual salvation. "Healing is your right," declared the *Shield of Faith* from Cleveland, Tennessee, in 1963, and no psychotherapist would deny this Pentecostal newspaper's profession that too many families experienced disobedient children, divorce, and "no peace of mind," and needed a helping hand. "Friend," the pastor coaxed in print with as much intimacy as fire, "eternity is calling you, and hell is a real place."[90] Whereas pastoral counseling made its appearance in seminaries and prosperous city churches, mental healing by prayer, touch, and charms was, though not quite the poor man's cure, the therapy of people on the margins. Although the revival's instantaneous healings were breathtaking, there was little to sustain health after the tent came down and the itinerant moved on, other than old-fashioned supports of preaching, Bible reading, and church fellowship.

Pastoral counseling was an adjunct of Christian liberalism in the sense that it borrowed secular theories and encouraged self-improvement, and although Americans typically think of the South as the heartland of born-again faith, an eagerness for reform appeared here and there in the region before church-based mentoring took root. Academic institutions helped promote the idea of human self-help. Frankie Adams of the Atlanta School of Social Work, for example, advised Martin Luther King Sr. on how to set up a nursery department at his Ebenezer Baptist Church in 1933. Whether either one had read Horace Bushnell's classic critique of revivalism, *Chris-*

tian Nurture (1847), both grasped the point: a child can be led gradually to faith by caring adults serving as steady agents of God's grace.[91]

Adams's role was to provide understanding of child development, and some Christian colleges similarly explored science to further their missions. Shortly after southern Methodists reunited with their northern peers in 1939, ending a century-old schism, the denomination's white Scarritt College in Nashville planned an exchange for its social work students. The young people would go to New York to learn psychiatry, and the northern sister institution would send students south for "rural experience." Scarritt aimed to train many of its graduates for "missionary work in some of the backward areas of the world," in the words of a foundation visitor, and soon the college was a prime site in the city for studying anthropology and linguistics.[92] Intellectual openness like this made liberal Christian schools perfect environments for launching pastoral counseling.

This background makes it less surprising that Wayne Oates (1917–99) completed a doctoral dissertation on Freudian theory and Christianity at Southern Baptist Theological Seminary in Louisville, Kentucky, before joining its faculty in 1947. Born again as a teenager in "a cotton-mill Baptist church" in South Carolina, Oates professed gratitude "for the rugged individualism of conversion theology" but devoted his career to a different model of Christian experience: faith nurtured by caring relationships in a church community.[93] Although his own counseling style remained constant, he developed a sharper vision of therapy's social meaning over time. His method, essentially nondirective, was "a *reciprocal* pilgrimage between counselor and counselee" based on mutual respect as God's creatures. Having offered this description in 1955, Oates made counseling the centerpiece of a "ministry of reconciliation" a decade later.[94]

Good listening in private settings was the standard for both pastoral and lay behavior in *Pastoral Counseling in Social Problems* (1966). No longer was the preacher "the tactless, loud-spoken, fist-waving authoritarian bully" Oates associated with the evangelical pulpit. "The pastor as a counselor is not seen" and solves problems quietly. So, too, the whole church was "a *teaching* community," actively watchful of its members. As Oates made counseling the model of Christian relations, he built on foundations of Baptist egalitarianism and southern populism. The notion that congregants should mentor families recalled the mutual discipline practiced by earlier Baptists, and the same communal ideal distanced Oates from the abuse of religious authority by "owners of farm and mill" that he saw as a child. "Perhaps the church has too often been the instrument whereby oppressors have oppressed the oppressed." "This is the burden which I bear as a Southern pastor," because clergymen were complicit.[95] Although pastoral counseling began among Christians comfortable with psychology in the urban North, Oates made it touch southern chords. A church given over to counseling helped remedy the region's inequities by restoring fellowship.

Oates also presented Christian therapy as the instrument of a latter-day Reformation of personal faith. Never forgetting that his goal for a counselee was supernatural, he explained impediments to belief in emotional terms, opening the door to a psychological cure. "Legalistic anxiety," for example, one type of mental burden analyzed in *Anxiety in Christian Experience* (1955), resembled both Martin Luther's traumatized effort to satisfy the letter of God's law and obsessive-compulsive disorder. Oates was sure not only that "therapeutic release" from conviction of sin was possible but that it was biblical, found in the "teachings of Jesus and Paul."[96] Explained this way, church-based therapy promised renewal for individuals as well as congregations.

Even so, Oates was not naive about tensions between religion and science, real or perceived. His writing tried to reassure parishioners that therapy would not weaken their faith and to build confidence in pastors intimidated by the secularism of professional psychology. Yet he admitted that psychological theories began with "naturalistic presuppositions" and said vehemently that insistence on "a one-on-one correlation between psychotherapeutic doctrine and Christian doctrine would reek with philosophical stupidity."[97] No form of postwar existential psychology, northern or southern, escaped pressures on its fragile synthesis of rational and irrational knowledge. Oates's career shows, however, that the challenge of balancing mind and soul could be an opportunity as much as a problem. In 1947, the same year he began teaching at the seminary, he became a consultant to the psychiatry department at the University of Louisville School of Medicine. Although he wrote mainly about church work, he also saw patients on wards, and he moved to the medical school full-time in 1974. The unsettled relation of nature and grace in Oates's thinking arguably helped extend the influence of his Christian counseling from churches to medical circles.[98]

The theory of divine healing of postwar Pentecostals was so systematic, in contrast, that religion and medicine appeared seamlessly joined. Whereas Oates's sources were a patchwork—he quoted Kierkegaard and Paul Tillich, Freud and Erich Fromm—godly cure was simple. All disease was by nature the same. Grateful testimonies from readers of the *White Wing Messenger*, published by the Church of God of Prophecy, acknowledged recovery from "a terrible nervous condition" alongside cures of colds, polio, and cancer.[99] Whether the affliction was mental or physical, the cause was possession by evil. W. V. Grant, an evangelist based in Dallas, offered advice in the mid-1950s in *Freedom from Evil Spirits: How to Be Set Free from Depression, Recession, and Repression*, and the concreteness of the threat to the sufferer lent urgency to the treatment. A. A. Allen's *The Curse of Madness* displayed "18 pictures of demons as seen and drawn by a demon possessed woman," accompanied by the admonition, "How would you like such creatures as your constant companions?"[100] Although Pentecostals clearly took the devil and his legions to be real, their theology of illness was more religiously conventional. "Worry is a product of unbelief," and it "makes people sick," warned the evangelist Louise Nankivell. She did not need to add that it is sin that blocks faith, and the atonement that makes healing possible. "By His Stripes," a reference to Jesus' suffering on Calvary, was a logical title for the space reserved in one journal for its readers' letters about cures.[101]

There was nothing strictly historical about God's presence in the Pentecostal's spiritually active cosmos, however, and divine healing truly meant that God worked miracles through faith. Yet preaching, the instrument of the revivalist, was less central to a healing ministry than were intimate, often tactile methods: prayer, fasting, and touch by an evangelist or a holy object. Oral Roberts prayed personally over thousands of anointed "handkerchiefs which are furnished by a group of spirit-filled women" and then distributed to sufferers, explained *Healing Waters* magazine in 1948. Subscribers to the *White Wing Messenger* used the truth-filled pages themselves. "My baby had a high fever," wrote a Tennessee mother, and "I placed the White Wing on him, prayed and promised God to testify to His healing power." Recovery was unambiguous and dramatic. When a woman fasting in a mental hospital vomited after being forcibly fed, "wonder of wonders, at that very moment the demon left her body never to return!"[102] Because

God was the physician, there was no reason to doubt that healing began with conviction.

Although believers could rejoice that divine healing was universally available, excitement about cures in Pentecostal circles had a particular history and geography. Like other psychologies with transcendent interests, the movement began outside the South. From the first days of Pentecostal spiritual awakening in Los Angeles in 1906, participants had hoped the wonders they witnessed were signs of Jesus' millennial return. Prophecies, visions, and speaking in tongues were more plentiful at the outset than miraculous cures. *Golden Grain*, a Los Angeles magazine, showed the dark spirit of Pentecostalism in 1935 when it announced the imminence of the coming of the anti-Christ as "A WORLD DICTATOR," and over the decades Pentecostals felt both trepidation and ecstasy stirred by belief in the end of the world.[103]

Excitement about medical recoveries in the late 1940s represented a moment of enthusiasm. Even the revival's publications displayed a new self-confidence bordering on worldliness. In contrast to the tightly printed format, broken up by biblical scenes, that gave *Golden Grain* the look of a tract, the successive magazines issued by Oral Roberts featured photographs of the evangelist and snappy phrases like "Turn Your Faith Loose."[104] Among spiritual gifts, mental health was now near the center of attention. Although one woman cited "mental trouble" as the reason for her letter to *Golden Grain* in 1928, far more of its correspondents at that time asked for prayers from fellow readers to give them "spiritual help" or relief from physical ills. Two decades later, writers to similar columns still mentioned afflictions of body, mind, and soul. The evangelists, however, perhaps attuned to national discussion of mental illness, emphasized psychological cures. "I pulled a chair up" to a woman ranting with "hysterical venom," Roberts wrote. "Healing power was surging through me," and "I saw the demons leering at me from her eyes and then quietly I commanded them, there were nine of them, to come out." Moved by "a sweet compassion," Roberts administered therapy of a kind, and he was rewarded by his patient's "radiant smile" and her profession, "I am free!"[105]

Although the Deep South had a near monopoly on the manufacture of tents used by itinerants, the region seemed initially cool to miraculous claims. "A few churches may elect to permit the flaming fire of revival to pass them," chastised a bishop of the Pentecostal Holiness Church from Franklin Springs, Georgia, in 1949, but they were mistaken. The "revival will sweep on and on preparing a people for the soon coming of Jesus."[106] The awakening had thundered into the South a year before, when Oral Roberts came from Tulsa for a monthlong tent meeting in Durham, North Carolina, where over 3,000 penitents were saved. Like Roberts, most of the healing evangelists lived in borderlands settled in recent memory by southerners, including Arkansas, Oklahoma, Texas, and California.[107]

Although Pentecostalism had migrated eastward well before the postwar excitement, its tone was more conservative in the South. At the same time that the *Pentecostal Holiness Advocate* in Georgia was denouncing the end of Prohibition in the mid-1930s, Aimee Semple McPherson printed advertisements for Los Angeles hairdressers, restaurants, and gas stations in her *Bridal Call Crusader*.[108] Who published the various magazines helps account for their regional tempers. Charismatic preachers like McPherson and Roberts launched their own ventures in the West, in contrast to denominational sponsorship in the Southeast. Socially, too, southern Pentecostals seemed more firmly rooted than their counterparts elsewhere. By 1955 the Church of God in Anniston, Alabama, a county seat, had moved from its original lamp-lit building into a former schoolhouse and then to a modern site with "tiled floors, rest rooms, church kitchen, nursery, pastor's study, store room and six Sunday School rooms."[109] Congregants of churches like these were up and coming, not desperately driven by poverty and ignorance to try any cure. In an environment where God's presence was unquestioned, divine healing was a reasonable idea.

Feelings expressed about medicine during the revival also closely matched southern mores. Accommodating distaste for doctors, trust in spiritual cures, and acceptance of death, divine healing drew on southerners' deepest instincts about sickness and treatment. Doctors themselves did not seem ill intended to Pentecostals so much as misguided. "The Psychiatrists know how to pick you to pieces, but they don't know how to put you back together," observed Roberts's *Healing Waters* during his stay in Durham. Physicians might yet be won over, the evangelists liked to repeat. They praised one doctor's admission in 1948 that his profession saw "human beings as machines," and in 1961 they felt encouraged that medicine was warming up to "acceptance of this miraculous [sic]."[110] It was surgery, virtually the only treatment at the time for serious disease, that focused fears of medicine. Operations were invasive, expensive, and required hospitalization, and published letters spoke joyfully of miracles that averted them. "The doctor said I needed the rest of my organs out," wrote a Kentucky woman afflicted with "female" trouble, "but they were afraid I would become insane if this were done."[111]

Prayer and touch, Pentecostalism's therapies, made every illness spiritual by definition. The premises resembled hoodoo, except for Christian monotheism, and the means were like conjure, too. A healer possessed a gift that made book learning unnecessary. Although the healing virtuosity of the evangelists inspired awe, the mood of prayer was democratic. "A Sister in Christ" in Mississippi addressed fellow readers of a journal, "Please pray for me to be completely healed and for my husband and 3 boys to be saved." Yet if the will of "the Great Physician" was death, hopes for health seemed instantly to yield. "Everything possible was done to save his life, but God saw fit to take him, and he died a victorious death," said one notice about a young man. The *White Wing Messenger* called its obituary column "Promoted to Heaven."[112] Southerners had long borne diseases as inevitable manifestations of evil, and Pentecostalism preached the joyous news that this need not be so. It drew, however, on southern aversion to medicine as an enterprise tainted by mortality, and yet when death, not recovery, was the outcome, believers showed no surprise or feelings of betrayal.

An evangelical healer could sway a crowd by presenting himself as a kindred sufferer, and for the Pentecostal itinerants, making the connection was not hard. Survivors of emotional roller coasters, they were arguments in the flesh that God does not shun the unstable. Some of the trials they described were not of their own making, including poverty-stricken childhoods and alcoholic parents, and adulthood traumas like nervous breakdowns and alcoholism seemed consequences of their nurture. William Branham remembered voices and visions as part of his boyhood, as if God were a surrogate parent. When his father, a bootlegger, tried to make him drink whiskey, he resisted with the aid of an "audible voice" that admonished, "Don't ever smoke, drink, or defile your body in any way, for there will be a work for you to do when you get older."[113] Episodes of incapacity recurred, however, in part because healers practiced what they preached and resisted conventional cures. A. A. Allen was arrested for drunk driving in 1955, and two years later Jack Coe died of polio when he arrived at a hospital too late to be saved. Rest was the only permissible natural remedy, and it was often used. By the summer of 1948, Branham needed "a protracted rest" after frequently praying "for the sick till one or two in the morning," and Roberts announced, "I am weary and plan on much rest" at the close of his Durham campaign.[114]

The effects of the evangelists' uneven and sometimes erratic behavior were mixed. To have public figures talk so openly about their personal struggles must have helped bring mental illness into the open among conservative Protestants. But the same crises disrupted their work. Roberts, consistently well dressed and businesslike, built an empire that *Life* magazine declared cynically in 1962 "is certainly due more to his organizational skill and his big budget (including his ability to meet it) than to spiritual or theological insight."[115] Founding a university and then becoming a Methodist in the 1960s, Roberts possessed a moderation that eluded others, like Branham, a man more and more convinced that these were the world's chaotic last days until his own death in a car accident in 1965. The postwar awakening consisted of spectacular moments accompanied by reminders of human frailty. It was not an environment where therapies to sustain health were very likely to develop.

Nor did the revivalists have a conventional social program to address inequalities often contributing to disease. Focused on the spirit, they did not pursue humanitarian reforms sometimes inspired by Christianity. The same absorption in godliness did lead them toward racial issues and politics, however. Although belief in spiritual equality made Pentecostalism biracial from its earliest days, white itinerants who visited the South seemed more self-consciously careful about segregation than were the region's homegrown Pentecostals. When Roberts was in Durham, his *Healing Waters* posted the ambiguous news that he granted "hundreds of requests from the colored people, to have a special service for them alone."[116] If the information was more than simple reporting, it seems a nod of respect to racial custom, though white readers might well wonder whether his services elsewhere were normally integrated. The southern Pentecostal press was almost silent about race, except for photographs. A stray notice about a "colored convention" in Mississippi in the Church of God of Prophecy suggests that segregation may have been too commonplace to mention routinely. Yet a picture of white and black leaders side by side was the cover of one issue of the same denomination's *White Wing Messenger* in 1955.[117] Whatever these conflicting hints about racial practice say, social justice was not the church's main goal.

Political commentary, far louder than notes about race, was driven more by circumstance than plan. Events made significant by their connection with millennial prophecy provoked discussion. The founding of Israel set off hopes for conversion of the Jews, and John Kennedy's run for the presidency stirred fears that the Pope would soon reign as the anti-Christ. "Temporal supremacy of the Pope is a fundamental dogma of the Catholic church," in the words of the *Voice of Healing*.[118] Public events seen through the lens of the book of Revelation may have helped convince one evangelist's readers that "America is going mad!" But the Pentecostal response was no more political than it was medical. Advertisements for books titled *American Presidents and Destiny* and *Praying to Change the World* appeared together in the *Voice of Healing* just before the 1960 election.[119] Faith was the only answer for problems that were spiritual at their foundation.

This was a compelling thought for many Americans as the revival spread. Spiritual healing must have profited from its likeness to other psychologies of a philosophical temper, and by 1954 the Roberts ministry alone was producing magazines, books, and films as well as planning campaigns that drew 1.4 million people just that year. Although some regions, like New England, were unreceptive, evangelists toured widely. Pennsylvania hosted healers in thirteen locations in 1955, for example, including Philadelphia and Pittsburgh.[120] Success predictably encouraged criticism. The layout of the *Life* feature about Roberts in 1962, showing rows of his secretaries at typewriters and businessmen at a board table, conveyed the impression the evangelist's real goal was moneymaking. The unspoken charge was that divine healing was deliberate deception, a belief echoed in accusations that therapeutic prayer was unscientific. Pentecostalism's opponents tried to reinforce the boundary between religion and science. Jack Coe was tried in Miami for practicing medicine without a license, and the United Lutheran Church took issue with faith healers who "fail to recognize as God's gift to man proven scientific methods."[121] The high pitch of healing enthusiasm had probably already passed by the early 1960s, when the critics grew vocal. Every revival has its own rhythm, driven by the difficulty of maintaining fervor. Yet before the excitement slackened, Americans heard again that soul, mind, and body are linked, and the spirit, if not the letter, of Pentecostal doctrine was welcomed. "Even some Episcopal ministers," *Time* reported, "conduct healing services."[122]

After the many decades when psychological ideas flowed southward with at best modest effect, this radical Christian variant stirred southern believers who were grateful for reassurance that God heals and indifferent to the method's status as science. Certainly this was not the first time in history that an extreme statement gained a wider hearing than cautious phrasings of a common premise. Bingham Dai, Ernst Borinski, Joseph Fichter, Atlanta's experiential psychiatrists, and Wayne Oates and fellow Christian counselors all opened doors to the thought that psychic health requires more than mental balance. The Pentecostal healers simply spoke without reserve. All envisioned healing holistically, insisting that means and ends transcending reason were welcome, and their common experience was to leave deeper marks on heads and hearts than on institutions. They affected the South by bringing ethics, metaphysics, and faith to bear on individual psychology. But the region's culture no less shaped them. Like frontier itinerants of earlier times, they gained and lost by being newcomers in southern communities: eager as the locals were for novelty, the strangers' unfamiliarity with the place and the people's distrust of anything more up to date than tradition itself posed obstacles to enduring innovation.

Through all the excitement, segregation remained. It is too easy to say that transcendent interests were a distraction from racial issues, although this often seemed true. The case of Martin Luther King Jr. not only prevents a simple judgment but also suggests that dedication to science might equally restrain social involvement. King's philosophy in a way epitomized the dual concern with human wellness and higher values of the existential healers, and yet it refused to become a psychology. Although he clearly listened to contemporary social science, his activism did not stop with therapy, and his principal language was theological. No one should be "forever fighting a degenerating sense of 'nobodiness,'" he declared more than once, because the "law of God" says that only a statute "that uplifts the human personality is just."[123] The psychological echo in his phrasing is unmistakable, but King did not devote himself to unraveling subjectivity, healing individuality, or advancing knowledge. In an era when more and more Americans were keenly interested in the mind, his psychological insight was most likely an asset. But at least in the South, being a Christian first and foremost was still the way to gain an audience. True as this was, psychological voices were heard, too, during desegregation.

| 5 | THE SHORT LIFE OF

SOUTHERN PSYCHOLOGY

The end of legal segregation mandated by the *Brown* ruling in 1954 seemed to promise that the South would soon catch up with the liberalism of which Americans of the era were proud. But the strident racial conservatism of rising southern psychologists made the prognosis less certain. This sharp rightward turn was to an extent a matter of generational change. For Lillian Smith, reflecting a year before her death in Georgia in 1966, it seemed that her work for racial justice was done. After her doctor remarked, "You've finished your big job, Miss Lil, all this segregation thin[g]," she realized that "in a big sense, I have 'finished;' it will all go now in its own way — like a big tidal wave — no matter what I write." Psychoanalysis had been her weapon. The guilt of white southerners who "betrayed the human spirit" by enforcing segregation left them with a "dread of the unconscious," asserted her *Killers of the Dream* in 1949. The best-selling book championed racial equity by refusing to allow a white American "to keep a safe distance from the profound depths of his own or another's nature."[1]

For Audrey Shuey, in contrast, psychology still had work ahead: halting school integration. Busy preparing a second edition of *The Testing of Negro Intelligence* for publication in 1966, Shuey believed she proved "the presence of native differences between Negroes and whites as determined by intelligence tests." The foreword, written by her former Columbia University mentor, made her out to be a "true scientist," and she presented the study's data as "objective, verifiable, and presumably accurate."[2] Now chair of the psychology department at Virginia's Randolph-Macon Woman's College, although Illinois-born, Shuey lent her discipline's authority to the segregationist cause.

As public figures, the two women most likely knew of each other, and their differences were a sign of accelerating changes in psychological thinking in the South brought on by the legal end of segregation. Shuey began with premises that natural endowment was more influential than nurture and that race as a measurable category of analysis was more serviceable than culture. Smith had probed the painful growth of personalities under the South's racial system. In the shadow of the *Brown* decision, the reinvention of a psychobiology of race challenged a belief like Smith's in a dynamic self. The South played host to the renewed contest between nature and nurture at the same moment that the region's distinctiveness seemed to be fading.

Anyone familiar with the southward migration of psychological knowledge after the turn of the century might have predicted how difficult it now was to keep focused on the South. For decades the region fascinated scientific outsiders as a dysfunctional culture on which to test competing ideas. The *Brown* mandate to desegregate public schools, and by extension all common sites, accented southern problems and put the environmental view of identity that underwrote *Brown* on the defensive. The dismantling of segregation was a protracted and public trauma, and psychologists and psychiatrists across the nation paid attention. They commented on southern school desegregation and the replication of racial isolation in northern ghettos. They realized that discrimination's subjective effects survived the legal end of Jim Crow, and they argued about why. Long-standing explanations about the influence of culture on personality came to seem superficial; radical theorists began to talk about social power, and conservative thinkers, about genetics as hidden impediments to personal growth. The Court had exposed the nation's most persuasive psychology to a nearly impossible real-world trial, and intellectual conflict followed. Analysts spoke increasingly of race as a personal trait unconnected with region. The concrete experience of segregation, with racial identities embedded in southern relationships, seemed a thing of the past.[3]

Southerners did not effectively protest their region's neglect. All along, southerners who engaged in the psychological sciences had struggled to find voices in conversations in which they were also the object of interest.

Now social upheaval made southern-born professionals either unusually quiet or fervent about racial matters by national standards. Moderate intellectuals of both races spoke guardedly about desegregation. Conservatives in the academy jumped to defend the racial status quo, joined by like-minded colleagues moving southward. Fear had been the mortar of segregation, and in the crisis, anxiety seemed to incline educated people to proceed by indirection or else with reckless abandon. Robert Coles of Harvard, visiting the South to chronicle school desegregation from a psychiatrist's perspective, saw the same tensions in ordinary people. The trepidation of the black child who daily summoned courage to walk past angry white parents outside her school matched the feeling of vulnerability in the woman who heckled her. "What she called the Negroes she feared herself to be; what she saw in that Negro child was herself, unhappy and isolated." "In no century has man been without his Souths and his wars," Coles wrote. The South had not fully lost its tragic uniqueness, although *Brown* made de facto segregation the national norm.[4] In the 1950s and 1960s, southerners trained in psychology had to approach their region either as a dangerous subject or cult object, and many said little about the local situation at all.

Southern psychology had a "short life," my chapter title contends. Its brevity was the result of human choices. Just when southerners grew accustomed to psychological thinking, professionals in the mental sciences, and not just in the South, turned away from troubling inquiries into southern minds and hearts. So long as emotional habits forged during segregation continued, however, science could not truly liberate. Three topics taken up by writers in psychological fields during the *Brown* era suggest how the South and its potential lessons came to be forgotten: the dissolution of segregation in the South, the reappearance of familiar racial patterns in the North, and the truth about how human nature is formed.

Southern Trauma

Enduring interest in children made southern schools a battleground in the 1950s and 1960s for contention over racial distinctions. In a nation attuned to psychology, the prospect of emotional upheaval stirred widespread curiosity. Objectivity proved difficult for observers, however, and few perceived the same situation. One writer in 1961 pictured a white child "forced into a predominantly Negro school," while a second explained that token black admissions to white classrooms by 1964 meant that "98.9 per cent of the South's Negro children were still segregated." A third noted that cities did little to reassign students until around 1970, when anti-integration litigation had run its course.[5] Whether the temper of school desegregation was violent transition or painful lethargy, it produced high emotions, situated as it was in the midst of the passing of a social order. Southern events not only drew the attention of psychological professionals but tested their acumen and courage.

Desegregation was undeniably a rich subject. The testimony of students and teachers involved in early experiments leaves no doubt that their experiences awoke new emotions. The physical proximity of the races, which was customary, was not the issue, Kenneth Clark pointed out. The emotional trigger was that now "*this implies equal status*," and those most intimately affected felt uncomfortable.[6] The anger of white parents daily protesting outside New Orleans schools and the fear of the black children who saw them were predictable. Robert Coles found both responses in interviews he conducted for *A Study of Courage and Fear*, the first volume of *Children of Crisis* (1964). But other southerners made unexpected self-discoveries. George, the child of segregationist parents, felt empathy for a black girl ostracized by fellow whites at his high school. He "began to feel openly sorry for Lois," and "when he thought they would be unobserved, he risked a smile at her." John, one of a tiny number of black students chosen to integrate Atlanta high schools, confided later to Coles, "I wished I was white when I was at school with whites," although "I never really could admit it to myself."[7]

For a white teacher from Alabama who volunteered for a racially mixed class, her awakening was in the past. When she discovered during graduate study in New York that a black female student was sharing the dorm's bathroom, she collapsed "as if I had been through a terrible nightmare," feeling "disgust, anger . . . toward the Negro woman for causing the crisis," and then, Coles continued in his own voice, "shame: that she, an educated woman, had behaved so irrationally." A black teacher realized the depth of her own racial pride when she faced school integration, which she opposed. "White people won't change until we've forced them to see us differently, because we are different, we've *become* different."[8] In all these cases, the rituals of segregation, conveying clear lessons about command and obedience, were replaced by unfamiliar emotions.

It seemed that every account of desegregation contained a psychological theory, even if the author was not a specialist. Speculation about human behavior, becoming habitual among Americans, showed up in books, although the analyses could cast more light on the writer than the subject. Two white commentators of nearly polar political orientations both pictured the South after *Brown* as a place of violence and delusion. "A racial estrangement" was the emotional pattern described by Benjamin Muse, commissioned to report by the liberal Southern Regional Council. Paternalistic whites shocked by black self-assertion felt so alienated that they stopped inviting "choruses from Negro colleges . . . to sing for white audiences" and "aiding and advising Negroes" at all, Muse explained in *Ten Years of Prelude* (1964). In the breach, "merchants of hate" such as local White Citizens' Councils and itinerant agitators drowned out moderate voices in the "hysteria and frenzy" that produced mobs and bloody confrontation.[9]

Carleton Putnam, in contrast, saw chaos descending from an orgy of miscegenation in *Race and Reason* (1961), a tract endorsed by an international alliance of right-wing academics. Although lust seemed the opposite of Muse's psychological mechanisms of betrayal and aggression, the disorderly effect was the same. Putnam revived a classic theory of degeneration rooted in nineteenth-century science: equality led to racial mixing that was genetically fatal to the superior race. Thoughts of African "human sacrifice cults," offered by Putnam as evidence that "the earth has never known a bloodier race than the African Negro," further launched a frightful image of the South's future. Conspirators were as much the real source of trouble, however, as they were for Muse. Even the Supreme Court was "under the hypnosis of the Boas school" and its claim that there are no innate racial differences, and Putnam reminded readers more than once that Franz Boas and his colleagues were Jews.[10] For all their differences, both Muse and Putnam believed that rational discernment had failed southerners and emotions were spinning out of control. It did not occur to them that black southerners experienced the peace of segregation as oppression or the new struggle as freedom. Here psychological presuppositions supported one-sided and provocative impressions.

Although professionals trained in the psychological sciences might be expected to bring sophistication to public discussion, there were influences that curtailed their involvement. One was the clinical tradition that kept psychotherapists focused on individuals. Social justice was simply not in the vocabulary of Winfred Overholser, the longtime superintendent of the government's St. Elizabeth's Hospital in Washington, D.C. As president of the American Psychiatric Association in 1948, he professed to put the stability of patients first when he argued that integration of VA hospitals would disrupt patient care. In 1952, when the use of psychological testimony in school desegregation cases was well known, he spoke only of the appearance of psychiatric experts at asylum commitments and criminal trials in lectures at Harvard he published as *The Psychiatrist and the Law*.[11] His narrow conception of the psychiatrist's responsibility seemed to some a disguise for prejudice. A black psychiatrist who knew him was contemptuous of Overholser's "soul-wrenching soliloquies" about his "blamelessness" for the all-white clinical staff at St. Elizabeth's.[12]

Although Overholser quite clearly opposed racial equality, patient treatment could genuinely compete with policy interests. Frederick Watts, a founder of Howard University's psychological counseling center after the war, became testy with an interviewer in the 1990s when she asked about black radicalism. "Again and again I keep telling you that I counseled people through this time of trouble" by offering them "faith, hope and love." The pressure to take a stand for racial equity weighed more heavily on black than white clinicians. There was so much to do and so few voices, and as a teacher of Kenneth and Mamie Clark during their undergraduate years at Howard, Watts was especially close to politically active professionals. Yet his preference was for one-on-one intimacy. "Education," he remembered with enthusiasm, "that was my cause!"[13] Psychotherapy's private temper most likely disinclined other practitioners as well from entering public debate.

How fragile the connection between sociology and personality was when closely examined may also have made clinicians wary of commenting on current events. The argument that segregation was psychologically harmful, convincing when Jim Crow arrangements were the object of study, might have been less persuasive when the variable was the vaguer notion of prejudice. *The Mark of Oppression* (1951) aimed to link individual pathology to "American Negro sociology," but the strands were tenuously joined. Abram Kardiner, a noted psychoanalyst, and his collaborator, Lionel Ovesey, found many of their twenty-five subjects scarred by early loss of parents, family dispersion, corporal punishment, and poverty. An impaired capacity for affective bonding, making one man "a lone wolf" and trapping a woman in a "solitary struggle for survival," was the result of childhood stress. Sexual impotence, frigidity, or homosexuality accompanied emotional isolation as both symptoms and causes. Although the people analyzed by the psychiatrists lived in New York, many had grown up in the South, and the project purported to measure "pressures [that] are subsumed under the heading of 'discrimination' and have been described with encyclopedic thoroughness by Myrdal and others." Detailed histories of their nurture made it nearly impossible, however, to distinguish the effects of racism from personal problems. The authors resolved the issue by declaration: "So much for the familial roots of R. R.'s low self-esteem. Let us take up next the influence of social factors." Both widely cited and criticized, Kardiner and Ovesey's book offered engrossing data and a bold conclusion: race prejudice crippled blacks in all their social interactions.[14] The logical risk involved in drawing conclusions about collective psychology from individual neuroses had the capacity to generate skepticism instead of faith in social psychology.

Psychological specialists in the South had additional reasons for remaining silent about desegregation's emotional costs. No matter what your sympathies, the topic of race relations was a minefield jeopardizing your career. The patients of one Virginia doctor called him to say "they didn't want to be caught going to a doctor who might become known as an integrationist." Among whites, a liberal physician probably felt most pressure, but the diversity of white opinion made it wise to be cautious. For black professionals, desegregation arguably decreased their already small numbers in the South. "Negro Doctors Leave Hate Ridden State," read a headline in a black Louisiana newspaper in 1956.[15] As agitation for equal public access exposed raw feelings, blacks with any mobility chose other regions. The chances were best for specialists, psychiatrists among them, although policies of American medical schools and hospitals meant that blacks made up less than 1 percent of board-certified specialists in 1957. Even now southern cities tried to avoid integrating hospital staffs by upgrading black-only facilities, and the response of one black doctor solicited for a contribution in Atlanta sums up the degrading situation of physicians of color: "I have had discrimination free all these years, why in the world would I want to pay for it now[?]"[16] In this restricted environment, commentary on civil rights by black professionals trained in psychology was understandably rare.

Some experts did describe desegregation, however, sensing that court-ordered racial mixing not only challenged southerners but tested mental science. As our society becomes "drab and lifeless," began Robert Coles, "the South still clings to its almost biblical struggles," forcing the region on the attention of anyone serious about understanding human nature.[17] Coles (b. 1928) lived in the South some time before discovering the problem of race. A young psychiatrist from Boston, he was drafted by the air force in 1958 and stationed in Biloxi, Mississippi. The South's "very distinctive life" was pleasant until he observed blacks scuffling over access to a white beach, whites protesting an integrated school, and professional meetings customarily excluding black colleagues.[18]

Even then Coles's decision to return south after his military discharge to chronicle desegregation was not predetermined. His father wondered why a married man would risk career advancement, but existential curiosity overruled practical concerns. How people, and particularly children, respond to extreme situations was a natural question for a man who had already treated boys and girls crippled by polio and who admired the psychoanalytic work of Erik Erikson, a personal friend, and Anna Freud, both Holocaust refugees. His family heritage also made social justice issues inescapable. His mother had volunteered in the Catholic Worker Movement, and his wife's family had been abolitionists. He stood, finally, in a line of northern scholars intrigued by the South's undisguised displays of emotion. Field-workers of earlier decades hoped to get close to the truth of human nature by studying taboo behavior like miscegenation and lynching. School desegregation seemed to appeal to Coles as a similar window on abnormal stress. Here was "a problem in human development," he reported to the American Psychiatric Association in 1963, seen in light of a "fatal and reciprocally stimulating engagement" of personality and society.[19]

Whatever excitement Coles felt about witnessing momentous events, his writing replaced the melodrama of lay observers with a matter-of-fact tone. His experience with mental illness told him that the southerners he interviewed were "ordinary" people with "pedestrian" goals in extraordinary circumstances. Consistently impressed by their adaptability, he was most amazed by the first black students to attend white schools. Reared to know "the rules of the game as they apply to Negroes," they had a "worldliness" that helped them manage their anger and fear. Through all, he conveyed assurance that integration was possible because southerners were not exotics but much like readers of the *Atlantic Monthly*, *New Republic*, and *New Yorker*, where he placed his essays.[20]

Coles's racial vision was so compelling that the near revolution he worked in psychiatry may be overlooked. Certified as a psychoanalyst, he took his skills out of the consulting room and hospital ward and into homes, schools, and streets. "The South freed me up," he recalled, yet not without professional skepticism. During his own analysis in New Orleans in the 1950s, undertaken for training, the doctor dropped his pencil when Coles introduced the subject of race. Some members of the Boston Psychoanalytic Society objected to his casual contacts with southern children. Visiting families at home and asking children too young to explain their feelings to draw pictures instead was a far cry from the classic couch and silent analyst. Still contributing to professional journals, Coles also acquired mastery at exploring behavior without jargon for popular readers.[21] His encounter with the South helped not only to normalize southerners for Americans but to make psychiatry more familiar as well.

In many ways Alvin Poussaint resembled Coles: both were northern born, Ivy League educated, and adept at applying psychiatry to social analysis. But Poussaint (b. 1934) was a black professional, a difference that made him more vulnerable in the South and sensitive to the depth of racial conflict. Going south as a psychiatrist in the civil rights movement, Poussaint felt distanced from his surroundings. Northern activists "invaded the South," he reflected in 1968. They lived "intimately together in the isolation of the South," subject to "battle-front" pressures.[22] Coles, like Poussaint, had spent time counseling civil rights workers, but he was still comfortable in the region. Poussaint's sense of disconnection, in contrast, seems the result of his heritage. Kenneth Clark once remarked to Coles that only a white person could move freely in the South, speaking with members of both races, as Coles did. Poussaint, facing customary racism from a different angle, could not have felt safe, no matter what his politics. Nor could he engage the South through family history. Born in Harlem, the grandchild of Haitian immigrants, Poussaint approached the legacy of

American slavery obliquely through his racial experience. On every score his alienation from the region seemed inevitable.[23]

Not surprisingly, then, his writing concentrated on the psychology of civil rights workers, although the movement's internal tensions made it seem an American microcosm. He described white female volunteers from the North who did not understand why blacks resented the women's self-satisfied altruism or worried that their equal and sometimes sexual relations with black male coworkers would bring reprisals from neighboring whites. He saw how the fragile self-esteem of black activists induced them to project blame for their own deficiencies onto white allies. The picture Poussaint drew was not the reassuring progress that Coles saw but interpersonal "chaos" leading to rejection of integration as a goal by partisans of black power. The South's tragic history stood in the background as the cause of strife. Black men had been "brainwashed for centuries" to revere white women and then brutalized on suspicion of getting too close to them, and although it might seem that self-awareness for all could now be liberating, Poussaint concluded that the past weighed too heavily in the South to permit success there. "In retrospect," he wrote after his departure, "one might argue that integration in the movement on the 'battle-ground' of the South was doomed to failure because of the profound effects which white racism, developed through centuries of indoctrination, has had on the psyche of both white and black Americans."[24] He had come close enough to the South to doubt its capacity for reform.

Coles and Poussaint returned north around 1970, both taking positions at Harvard Medical School and continuing to write about psychiatry and ethics. Although it had been clear from the first that their stays in the South would be temporary, Coles was more explicit about why he left. "The South is saying farewell now to many of its traditions and customs," he explained in 1972, or, in the words of a southerner he quoted, "The rest of America has come down here and taken us over—and we're giving up."[25] Where Coles felt resolution, Poussaint found provocation, as he worked to expose racism as a national trait. But neither seemed to wonder if southerners heard them or if they helped vitalize local debate about the region's psychology.

At least one southern professional had mixed feelings of self-criticism and insult in connection with northern observers. The president of the

Georgia Sociological and Anthropological Association in 1966 asked, "Why is it that Northern scholars conduct most of the studies of Southern race riots and nonviolent demonstrations," and if the reason "is the immunity of the stranger, why then are there not more Southern scholars studying these conditions in the North?" Even if national opinion smugly defined the South as the troubled subject, his colleagues were part of the problem: they "acquiesce to academic slavery and control by tactfully selecting noncontroversial areas of interest" that convey reassurance about "societal balance and stability."[26] The organization's other nine presidential addresses delivered between 1965 and 1974, collected in a book, silently confirmed his diagnosis of timidity. Covering urbanism, women, and, most self-reflexively, education, not one focused on race relations.[27]

Southern scholars who did speak about desegregation cannot be blamed for being careful. The transformation going on around them was profound. Lloyd C. Elam (1927–2008), the African American psychiatrist who became president of Meharry Medical College in 1967, had a responsibility to address southern issues as well as an institution to protect. Born in Arkansas and educated in the North, Elam was a new father in 1961 when he left Chicago for a faculty position at Meharry. As a "smaller city," Nashville seemed to him "more suitable for family life and raising children."[28] His administrative success as chair of the Department of Psychiatry was impressive. A unit that taught only a single, yearlong course in the late 1950s offered eleven classes in 1964 and sponsored a field study funded by the National Institutes of Health. Clear goals for psychiatrists likely to serve the urban poor accompanied these practical steps. Every "psychiatrist ultimately always teaches his patient something about personal and social freedom," Elam wrote, but the special challenges of cities required mental health professionals to have concrete skills. They did not quite have to be community organizers, but they did have to "identify the mental health problem—not just in terms of illness, but also in terms of the need for multiple avenues of problem solving" to cope with difficulties facing families.[29]

Racial considerations were understated in this vision. "Anti-Poverty Programs and the Psychiatrist" and "Urbanization: Implication for Mental Health" were the titles of typescripts outlining Elam's thoughts, and although problems of income, place of residence, and race were often interrelated, he downplayed color as a cause of disadvantage. To an extent,

Elam's audiences would have taken his attention to race for granted. The neighborhood served by Meharry's teaching hospital was nearly all black, and the college was experiencing a crisis of racial self-definition precipitated by integration. The future of the school, proud of sustaining black medicine in the South but now competing for its traditional students, was uncertain, although it began recruiting whites successfully in the early 1960s.[30]

With race so central to Meharry's mission, it is telling that Elam delivered his boldest remarks on desegregation abroad. Speaking at Oxford University in 1966 to the Medical Committee against War, he repeated his core principles, social concern and freedom, in connection with civil rights. His endorsement of activism by doctors was part of his conviction that desegregation was psychologically liberating. Can doctors, "a conservative group," stand silent while "the medical society refuses admission of Negroes to membership and 90% of the hospitals refuse Negro doctors staff privileges?" If they could not escape politics even when they were passive, better that they should bravely confront the status quo. "Preoccupation with the effects of the environment is an appropriate activity for physicians." Reform activism was also powerful therapy for doctors and patients alike. Elam put conventional psychiatry in perspective when he said, "More people had their self-esteem raised by racial desegregation than by numerous individual approaches to improve self-esteem such as psychotherapy."[31] He imagined every doctor as a psychiatrist, concerned with the spirit as well as the body, and also as a community leader, as a means to this end. It was a compelling ideal and yet for Elam an unusual subject.

Elam's command of both tact and principle was matched across the city by Frank Luton at Vanderbilt's medical school. "Dear Lloyd," he began a letter to Elam in 1968, asking for suggestions for a qualified successor to follow him as chair of the Vanderbilt psychiatry department, especially "persons who might sense the need for closer relationships between our two schools."[32] It is unlikely that Luton was thinking of black candidates. As the man who had sustained psychiatry at Vanderbilt for thirty-seven years, he might have been one of the southerners he described in 1958 as not "happy about the present direction of things" yet who "feel that integration is *inevitable*" and hope it can be accomplished "peacefully."[33] Among voluminous papers, Luton left only these remarks, part of a talk called "The Responsibility of the Psychiatrist in Desegregation," on the region's response to *Brown*.

He all but said he was uncomfortable evaluating social psychology, as if the invitation to speak about local school integration was a difficult assignment. "It is my role to teach doctors, medical students, nurses, school teachers and other disciplines, something about the basic principles underlying sick behavior," and race relations was a legitimate topic only because "such threatening experiences as the changes involved in desegregation" might cause "illness." Despite his hesitation, Luton's words revealed his wish for order and his faith in his fellow citizens to respect authority. "A committee composed of a psychiatrist, a colored social worker and the City Superintendent of Schools" devised a worthy plan, and there was evidence of compliance. "Many of the teachers did not agree with the principle of integration, but . . . since this was the law they were prepared to carry it out." At first he took only a white perspective, focusing on "the anxiety that comes from commanding threats to one's accustomed way of life." But by the end he showed understanding that there was another side: "The [black] parents were enthusiastic about the school and reported that their children were happy in the school." Still, he closed after several pages, saying, "the foregoing statements will suffice for the moment." The mentality of racial changes mandated by "people who are not aware of the nuances of our culture" was not an easy subject.[34]

Pained moderation like Luton's was little different from "left wing extremism" to southern segregationists, who nonetheless believed fatalistically that prudence was the academic norm. "You are a bright spot for me at Chapel Hill," wrote Jesse Helms in 1965 to Wesley Critz George (1888–1982) of the University of North Carolina. George agreed that his conservatism made him exceptional: "Agitators and nit wits are in the saddle at present."[35] North Carolina–born and Princeton-educated, George was an embryologist without psychological training. He extended a welcoming hand to incoming psychologists like Audrey Shuey and, by means of his contacts as well as his writings, decisively stamped scientific discussion of desegregation.[36]

George was strident, sincere, and uninterested in the individual psyche. First distracted from his research on primitive sea life when the university moved to admit Jews in 1933, he brought to every crisis the fervor of an absolutist. Rather than "make expediency one's guide," he lectured the university president on the Jewish issue, "it is far simpler, and gives one a greater feeling of confidence, to have a set of principles to steer one's course by." Then and later, his rule was "racial solidarity and racial antagonisms,—whether we observe say birds and thrushes or the races of man." Liberals who legislated contrary to natural law invited doom. Integration was equivalent to miscegenation and "the destruction of the white race in this country," he told a correspondent in 1944. Even Howard Odum, dangerously liberal in George's eyes, could not convince his colleague of the difference between the eugenic breeding of animals and human social mixing. "I can't see any relation between this and the scrub bull bred to registered jerseys," Odum replied patiently the same year.[37]

George's natural science background led him to fixate on the genetic traits of populations, to the point of ignoring individual variations. In yet another polemical letter, he professed that "the negroes are a genetically inferior race," all "indolent, wasteful, dirty, and stupid." Without room for accommodation, his mind-set made *Brown* seem one episode in an escalating conflict against, in his 1959 phrase, "communism and integration."[38] Instead of reacting to southern tensions with the understated diplomacy of Elam and Luton, George badgered politicians, turned out pamphlets, and organized grassroots resistance. An aging scientist who tucked away a letter from one of the family's former slaves among his papers, George was afraid for the South, but he was also outspoken.[39] Within the academy George developed a dogmatic and combative style.

George's disregard of the psychological complexity of individuals and groups, supported by his theory of racial biology, perhaps drew on the instinct of many white southerners to keep silent about troubling emotions. Odum, too, now ironically George's antagonist, took a restrained interest in the mind, and the impulse to look away seemed to dampen southern self-analysis overall. The voice of psychological professionals in public discussions of desegregation, though consistently intelligent, seemed thin. Commentaries seized on different human capacities: Coles found courage, Poussaint observed conflict, Elam envisioned liberation, and Luton noted deference. But these thoughts did not draw southern experts in general into a vigorous exploration of desegregation.

The region's special acquaintance with race as a component of human experience was precisely the circumstance that made it impossible to examine the current revolution in a forthright way. Desegregation as a legal process was also more and more limited to the South, as other states expeditiously revised racial laws, and Americans outside the region directed their attention elsewhere. As racism as a national problem superseded segregation as the object of concern, the South as a place seemed forgotten. A closer look, however, shows southern patterns of racial sociology and color consciousness being replicated in the North. To the extent that old-fashioned southernness persisted as a psychological condition, it seemed all too easily transplanted.

The Old South as a State of Mind

Because slavery had once been a national institution and racial prejudice survived the end of legal enslavement, the South was never the exclusive seedbed of American racism. Yet the migration of millions of southerners of both races to other regions during the first half of the twentieth century deepened racial awareness and conflict at their destinations. In part, the sheer rise in numbers of people of color in northern and western cities brought biases to the surface.[40] But it is also true that migrants carried their vulnerabilities along with them in their personalities. Abram Kardiner and Lionel Ovesey overstated this psychological reading of racial problems in 1951, making their *Mark of Oppression* a warning not to find roots for every difficulty in southern childhoods. Their psychoanalyses of African Americans who resettled in New York were too neat to be realistic: subjects who came north "in search of opportunity" bore "psychological scars" that shaped lives of urban anonymity.[41] So long as the authors considered the North a staging area for pathologies of southern origin, they overlooked how impersonal any city is, especially for newcomers.

Their core insight that migrants could not easily escape their backgrounds remains valid, however, and it is even clearer that scholars modified analytic methods once used in the South to explain northern racial stress. As the worst of the South seemed to take on new life elsewhere, human relocation tested the adaptability of psychological models devised in a southern setting. The intellectual outcome was mixed. Sometimes southern psychological science successfully explicated northern behavior; in other cases southern approaches were too easily modified, and not for the better. In particular, northern analysts reinterpreted race, a social experience in the South, as a personal attribute connected with skin color.

Kenneth Clark found the South at his doorstep when he recognized intractable segregation in New York in the 1960s, and his discovery typified the unsettling awareness that spread among northern social scientists. There was hope in the 1950s that northern freedom would gradually rehabilitate black migrants. Kardiner and Ovesey optimistically described Harlem-born subjects who were entering the middle class. Clark's wrenching *Dark Ghetto* of 1965, however, described dejection behind an "invisible wall."[42] As a young psychologist in New York around 1940, Clark avoided the field-study approach to black personality pioneered in southern locations in favor of controlled experiments whose presumed scientific validity made them compelling evidence for legal reform. His preference was not just strategic. In the same spirit in which Clark resisted pressure as a new black Ph.D. to settle for the usual job at a Jim Crow college, he declined to go south to collect data. He had a visceral disdain of segregation as a system of concession.[43]

Now, in *Dark Ghetto*, Clark not only admitted how emotionally charged it was for him to document black restriction in Harlem but rejected disinterested scientism as a sham. Only an "involved observer" could further social science's real goal: "helping society move toward humanity and justice with minimum irrationality, instability, and cruelty." Although he chose the term "ghetto" to link urban blacks with Jewish victimization, the book's arguments and solutions came clearly from southern social science.[44] The situation of Clark's "confined Negro" in a city slum was little different from the "biracial system" Charles S. Johnson named in 1941 in *Growing Up in the Black Belt*. White "taboos, compulsions, attitudes, and behavior," Johnson had said, "define the racial status of Negroes generally and Negro youth in particular." The deeper tragedy was that injustice perpetuated itself psychologically by teaching black children "a sense of personal inadequacy," in Johnson's words, or, as Clark now repeated, by acting "to corrode and damage the human personality." City schools, "separate and unequal," were part of the problem. Clark implored teachers to stop using their students' cultural disadvantage as an excuse and instead to teach with an "affirmative attitude."[45] Here his study's allusions to the historical and contemporary South, immersed in school reform, began to blur. Yet the shadow of the South on northern urban geography was in either case ominous, and Clark borrowed the field methods of southern scholarship to investigate city neighborhoods to explain where the North had gone wrong.

Discovery of racial patterns in the North that resembled those in the South did not simply prompt a return to tested strategies, however, but also pushed psychological studies toward innovation. Migration was one issue, not surprisingly, that claimed fresh attention. Although much social science fieldwork examined a single location at one point in time, sociologists of immigration had long contemplated mobility. In the late 1930s, Frazier's *The Negro Family in the United States* memorably applied the peasant model of W. I. Thomas, positing social disorganization at home and reorganization at the journey's end, to the black exodus from the American South. Even a sophisticated project like Frazier's that theorized about the migratory process focused on points of departure and destination, however, until Robert Coles moved along with his subjects. These were not southerners who relocated directly to northern cities but migrant farm laborers who traveled the Atlantic seaboard. Their personalities cast the psychology of displacement in a sharp, if oblique, light. Some rural kin of families Coles got to know through his work on school desegregation had taken to the road when their land in the Deep South wore out. In the mid-1960s, he investigated ten migratory families, black and white, for two years. His conclusions resembled Frazier's. Frazier believed that harmless habits of southern folk culture, such as relaxed sexuality, became problematic in northern cities. In the same way, Coles admired the migrants' easygoing childrearing but also noted sullen anger or flaring violence in adults provoked by their feelings of powerlessness. Children of such parents could not help but "learn a sense of their own weakness." Although Coles presented migrant families as members of an isolated "subculture," their story seemed heavily weighted with psychological lessons: most important, every form of marginalization was unhealthy segregation, and migration, if not a social dead end, was no clear solution.[46]

Studies like these that drove home the connection between segregation and maladjustment outside the South were persuasive, yet they were less commonly produced in psychological circles than were analyses that treated race as a personal trait. Color, meaning simply the shade of your skin, became a determinant of how you felt about yourself and how others rated you. In contrast to a southern conception of race, according to which visible features were inseparable from social position, racial identity now seemed a matter of appearance thought to influence self-esteem. Psychological testing and psychotherapy may almost be imagined to have created this private view of race by their own techniques. Diagnostic questionnaires and therapeutic sessions dealt with individuals separated from their environments, and in these artificial settings, skin color perhaps seemed a symbol of many ills. Yet however the reduction of race to pigmentation began, the shorthand gained enduring popularity in the North especially.

Academic interest in color was tenacious in part because African Americans were genuinely concerned about skin tone. When Charles Johnson questioned black youth in the rural South in the 1930s, they identified light-skinned people as superior in intelligence, morals, and beauty. He blamed prejudice for causing the "deep emotional disturbance" that prevented the teenagers from feeling self-love, but he placed this discussion near the end of a book concerned mainly with institutions like family, church, and school.[47] In contrast, *Color and Human Nature* (1941), a companion volume to Johnson's text in the AYC's black personality series, made physical appearance its organizing principle. Chapters on "darkskin," "lightskin," and "brownskin" groups, as well as the chapter "Volunteer Negroes and Other Passable People," concluded that a brown person enjoyed "a happy balance between social acceptance, perhaps too easily won by a lightskin individual, and the burden of proving himself, that may stimulate but also weigh down the darkskin individual."[48] Not surprisingly, the research site was Chicago, and the data source was interviews by a black psychiatrist, Walter Adams. Although his supervisor, W. Lloyd Warner, was an anthropologist, the book was so optimistic about assimilation that it was all but silent about social obstacles. It was "race, and race alone" that challenged the "national faith in the supremacy of individual merit," and because race was defined as a psychoneurosis caused by bodily features, cure was likely.[49] Even if the South's racial problems migrated north, they could be solved if race became an individual characteristic.

The happy thought that race without segregation was simply color gave the formula a protean life among psychiatrists and psychologists. Yet over time the habit of pondering physical traits without reference to sociology made appearance seem every bit as unyielding as southern custom. For Kardiner and Ovesey in 1951, who in the manner of *Color and Human Nature* catalogued their subjects as, for example, "medium brown" or "light tan," hue remained a social variable. Still, they saw that reactions to color could be overwhelming. One black man with "handsome Caucasian features, white skin, and straight hair" was "so burdened with guilt that his whole behavior is calculated not to alienate, offend, antagonize" others of his race.[50] It was a short step from recognizing the body as an absorbing obsession to believing that pigmentation had an unalterable natural meaning.

Classic physiological interpretations of racial character, overshadowed for many decades by social theories, in fact regained strength across the country in the late 1950s. Conservative psychologists cited white blood as the reason some black children scored higher than their peers on intelligence tests. In one instance in 1960, Henry E. Garrett, the longtime chair of the psychology department at Columbia, explained, "78% of these 103 bright Negro children reported some white ancestry."[51] Earlier analyses of skin color did not mean to resurrect a biological view of race and in fact sought just the opposite: to recast racial problems as personality disorders. Nonetheless, once appearance became the equivalent of race, the door opened wider to somatic theories. Even social liberals were encouraged to reconnect race and nature by this ahistorical discussion. The psychoanalyst Lawrence Kubie used the phrase "human need" in 1965 to explain feelings of repulsion toward both strangers and dark objects. Hoping to combat white prejudice by unmasking its genesis in disgust at excrement, he instead made bigotry seem a reflex of the universal capacity for self-hatred associated with the production of bodily waste. Although Kubie lobbied hard in the early 1960s for the admission of black students to Johns Hopkins's medical school, his alma mater, he articulated an essentialist view of color in a milieu where it was commonplace to equate race with physiognomy.[52]

Yet like most analysts of neuroses attributed to skin color, Kubie was at heart a clinician, confident that treatment remained the best hope for recovery. Northern psychiatrists of both races produced a literature about interracial therapy after the war intended mainly to guide doctors but also written with awareness that the sessions were a locus of racial encounter. The consulting room might, with care, serve to dismantle segregation, and on this intimate scale, conversation between therapist and patient addressed dysfunction with southern roots.

The location, however, was almost invariably the North. Economic disadvantage combined with feelings of shame about mental illness to deter blacks in every region from seeking therapy, and the scarcity of black psychiatrists collaborated with prejudice to keep whites from consulting blacks. These restraints began to loosen in northern cities. At first black patients visited segregated hospitals and saw doctors of their own race like Walter Adams, who practiced at Chicago's Provident Hospital beginning in the 1930s. Upward mobility brought blacks to white psychiatrists after midcentury, but it was the civil rights movement that helped reverse the roles. Liberal politics shaped the therapies described in "Transference and Countertransference in Interracial Analysis" (1968), coauthored by a white female analyst and a black male colleague in New York. The way the woman's activism made a bond with her black patient was less unusual than one white patient's trust of a black professional. The white man had sat by choice at the back of the bus when the army stationed him in the South, and now his decision to consult a black psychiatrist similarly challenged conventions of racial authority. Although the same racial pattern appeared in Alvin Poussaint's treatment of white female civil rights workers in Mississippi, the experience was exceptional there. It was not that white northerners were so much less prejudiced but that interracial counseling in the South was so rare.[53]

References to the South in published northern cases appeared only in passing in personal details about patients. Now race overshadowed place as a marker of social identity. Walter Adams, for example, used the phrases "Negro culture" and "Negro world" when he advised white psychiatrists in 1950 about how to understand blacks.[54] Even so, the specter of southern segregation seemed to inform the determination of white therapists to behave well in interracial sessions, as if they felt an obligation to right historical wrongs. Anxiety about making a mistake as a white authority figure was obvious in a paper about two black female patients published in 1952 by Janet Kennedy, a New York psychoanalyst. The Freudian idea of transference made Kennedy assume that the women would act out their neuroses in the relationship with the analyst, and because "Mrs. B" was troubled by color, it was fortuitous that "a white therapist provided the opportunity for a Negro to view a white person in a new light." Impressed by her symbolic role, Kennedy was torn between encouraging her patient's self-acceptance and standing as a racist presence in the woman's way. She wanted to make her patient "less fruitlessly rebellious against the restrictions of the culture," a thought she clarified carefully by concluding, "This was not an issue of *lowering* the patient's aspiration level, but *altering* it."[55]

A decade later, Robert Coles similarly presented interracial analysis as a test of the psychiatrist's professionalism and decency. The cultural stakes were high because "in the clinical situation we can hopefully expect the emergence of a mutual respect that laws and changed social practices can only herald." But the obstacles were formidable, too. Black patients feel "profound distrust and even hate of all whites, resentment of personal hurt and exploitation, and a sense of shame for being Negro, for wishing to be white, for talking at all about such matters to a white person, and for the very fact of feeling ashamed." "The therapist who looks closely at his own feelings" to confront "unconscious attitudes" about race is the most likely to elicit trust.[56] Self-awareness as a corrective to countertransference, the risk that the analyst instinctively projects his own neuroses in clinical interactions, was a standard psychoanalytic theme. Coles now politicized this mandate, because interracial therapy itself had a public meaning.

The popularity of psychotherapy in the postwar era was not enough, in the end, to make counseling a practical instrument of racial healing. Most publications on interracial arrangements cautiously downplayed social objectives and emphasized techniques for handling color in consultations, as if the writers did not want to be known as zealots or doubted that their methods were equal to the vast project of racial reconstruction. Kenneth Clark was cynical in *Dark Ghetto*, however, about the capacity of psychological professionals for self-criticism. He watched programs grow in Harlem "to bring these youngsters into a 'helping' relationship with a case worker, group worker, or remedial specialist" who often looked down on the children. Instead he planned a peer-controlled "subculture," complete with "insignia, slogans, rituals, rules," to promote student achievement. The "stress" would be "upon a restructured culture, or a new way of life, rather than upon a therapy."[57]

Clark's ambition did not match the direction of psychological care for black adults. Articles in the 1960s in the *Journal of the National Medical Association*, directed at black doctors, agreed that black patients received more medications than counseling. One reason was that inadequate access to physicians meant they arrived at a hospital sicker than did whites. The range of problems of the poor, added a Sacramento psychiatrist, made them "unready for the couch or any so-called classical method of treatment." New public funding through Medicare, bringing many patients to treatment for the first time, reinforced the incentive to make speedy progress. "Relief right now is the watchword of the hour," continued this clinician, "and it must be provided under the restrictions imposed by the agency sponsoring him." Psychotherapy remained a luxury, and even if more African Americans had been able to afford it, the number of practitioners willing to confront racial issues was small. "Also, as is known, many Caucasian psychiatrists prefer not to or refuse to treat Negro patients," casually noted a black researcher at the National Institutes of Health in 1965.[58] Clinical reports of interracial counseling were successful in the sense that they underscored the sociological component of all psychological distress. By the same token, therapy was at best a modest answer to the nation's racial dilemma.

To only a small extent did northern psychological strategies that aimed at disentangling race relations include a clear picture of southern segregation as the immediate predecessor of current events. Perhaps this was natural. Many migrants of southern origin interviewed in northern cities or seen in therapy had left home sufficiently long before that their children and even grandchildren were northerners. Even so, professionals outside the South also downplayed regional characteristics. *Black Rage* (1968), for example, omitted the history of Jim Crow by treating slavery as the catalyst of modern black pathology. Written by two black psychiatrists practicing in California, William Grier and Price Cobbs, the book explained that black families, today "in deep trouble," were a "latter-day version" of slave families. Unable to protect their children, black parents for generations tried to defend sons and daughters by training them to behave as slaves. The rise of Malcolm X as an "authentic hero" reflected the conversion of "depression and grief" as forms of self-hatred into a healthy "tidal wave of fury and rage."[59]

The argument was psychologically compelling but historically simplified. The "folk" stage of black culture between slavery and urban migration, albeit a problematic concept in Frazier's *Negro Family*, was absent here, despite the fact that a good number of northern blacks at least remembered rural life under segregation or had kin in the South. The authors' emphasis on slavery made the South the mythic heartland of American racism, at the same time that reducing bondage to its psychological components diminished the region's social importance. Rather than a source of tragedy, the recent South seemed no more than a provincial variant of the North, where whites displayed "mild exaggerations of tendencies common to most Americans" and took "a contempt and hatred for blacks" to "irrational extremes."[60] The substantial truth in the idea that prejudice was a common American fault made the logic credible. But disregard of the experience of Jim Crow had to make finding a national solution to racial problems all the harder.

Scant inquiry into southern roots in this body of northern writing did not mean that the works cast no light on the transplantation of the legacy of segregation. Like earlier southern fieldwork, investigations of the urban ghetto recognized that there was a psychology to racial separation. Whether migrants brought attitudes north with them or indigenous racism duplicated the South's invisible walls, separate was no more equal in one region than another, and the personalities of both races bore the consequences. Yet patterns of racial behavior in the North seemed more detached from law and custom than in the South. Discussions of color as a personal characteristic and of psychotherapy as a site of adjustment tried to make sense of racial identity in a situation in which race was less a cornerstone of social order than an individual trait. All these analytic strands echoed established southern themes, including the psychologies of inequity, color, and racial etiquette. Interregional comparisons, though, were rare, and by passing quickly by southern lessons, northern professionals came close to treating race as just another neurosis.

The urgency of examining the North's own racial problems was one reason for their haste. But northern scholars, like the migrants they studied, seemed also to bypass the South as an unpleasant memory. In the shadow of new vocabulary coined by northerners to decipher their region's racial psychology, southerners continued to reflect on psychological matters. Most publicly, when racial conservatives joined the international debate about the comparative influence of human genetics and cultural variables on individual development, they made a regional agenda one component of global science.

The Southern Battleground in the War for Human Nature

Human nature was on the minds of American scientists at midcentury, and questions about race and region could seem petty by comparison. The new book Abram Kardiner published in 1961 did not dwell on racial differences, as had his *Mark of Oppression*, but instead focused on human sameness. *They Studied Man* began with Darwin, ended with Freud, and in between praised a century-long line of cultural anthropologists, including Kardiner's colleagues at Columbia University, Franz Boas and Ruth Benedict. A title more faithful to his subjects' appreciation of social diversity might have used a term like "cultures" or "peoples." "Man," however, revealed Kardiner's awareness that the sciences' enduring debate about the comparative influence of nature and nurture was turning back toward natural endowment. He was one of the intellectuals now "remembering Darwin," in the words of the historian Carl Degler.[61]

Scientific excitement following publication of research on DNA by James Watson and Francis Crick in the journal *Nature* in 1953 was one catalyst. Chromosomes promised to be the means of genetic transmission behind natural selection. But the *Brown* decision, the most visible practical application of the nurture position, simultaneously reopened environmental theory to scrutiny. School desegregation became a test case for the premise that new circumstances would produce racial equality, and the experiment did not go well. Southern white resistance to integration led scholars on the left, particularly northern blacks, to conclude that hidden power arrangements made culture intractable. At the same time, one group of white psychologists, opposed to reform, stepped up efforts to prove that blacks were inferior by nature. When some of them migrated south to what they took to be the welcoming atmosphere of the region's white colleges, they added a regional component to the national and international controversy over human development. Preserving southern segregation became their cause, but prosecuting white racial dominance globally by means of science was their final ambition.

The logic of *Brown* raised the issue of human nature even before the case's consequences were apparent, and scientific discussion first gained momentum outside the South. Although the justices made use of the idea of cultural variability, their foundation was ethical absolutes. Equality was at the forefront of their reasoning that separate schools were "inherently unequal," and behind the premise of universal rights was the idea of each person's fundamental value.[62] Psychological commentary by liberals picked up this affirmation of common humanity to underscore white responsibility and black entitlement. It was a short step to reflection about the human character.

School desegregation fascinated Robert Coles, for example, because it laid bare elemental emotions. In an existential mood, his initial volume of *Children of Crisis* presented itself as "a study of courage and fear" evoked by moral struggle.[63] More defensively, black psychiatrists went out of their way to assert the races' uniform mental structure after the mid-1960s, as if their own focus on the racial achievement gap inadvertently highlighted black backwardness. There was almost nothing about nature in Kenneth Clark's *Prejudice and Your Child* of 1955. "How Children Learn about Race" was the title of the opening chapter, which attributed psychology to "acquired patterns." *Black Rage* said explicitly in 1968, in contrast, that the "mental functioning" of the races was identical, and Alvin Poussaint, with his coauthor James Comer, was even clearer in *Black Child Care* in 1975: "There is no distinct black psychology or white psychology."[64] As discussion shifted from social differences as the problem to common capacity as a justification for reform, the axis of debate remained the moral imperative behind *Brown*. Natural rights provoked thoughts about basic humanity.

These books stressing the unity of the species as a rationale for democracy were also reacting, however, to psychologists who believed social groups were endowed with unequal intelligence. Nowhere, North or South, did scientific commitment to natural differences wholly disappear in the midst of professional excitement about the psyche's dynamic potential. The international coterie that converged in 1960 to launch the conservative journal *Mankind Quarterly* chose the South as a home site, but its members' work gained momentum elsewhere during World War II as a respectable variant of mainstream social science. In 1943 the *Journal of Educational Psychology* published uneven test scores for black and white children in Richmond public schools that Frank McGurk (1910–95) used to recommend "separate norms for the Negroes." His care to avoid stating a cause for the races' unequal performance most likely helped make the study acceptable, as did its appearance of compatibility with scholarly interest in human variation. When he defended "classification of the

Negro child in relation to others of his race, culture, opportunities," he seemed respectful of black mores. Clever phrasing did not keep later critics from understanding that "the McGurk thesis" was "that Negroes have less capacity for education than whites," as *Time* magazine explained in 1956.[65] But any discussion of social pluralism in earlier years may have seemed enough like cultural theory to win a hearing.

Perhaps this is why the assessment of the personalities of New York Jewish college students by Audrey Shuey (1900–1978) in 1944 was so seriously received. Beginning with traits commonly attributed to Jews, she observed whether teachers identified the characteristics in individual young people. Where there was a match, she concluded that Jews really were "more gregarious, slightly less stable emotionally," and had "a greater percentage of aggressiveness as well as a smaller percentage of timidity."[66] *Commentary*, a journal begun in 1945 by the American Jewish Committee, called Shuey's research a "significant study" the next year, in part because its reviewer shared her assumption that Jews were a distinctive group. Whether the source of difference was genetic or cultural, an issue with crucial implications for social policy, received no comment.[67] Shuey's experiment entered the literature as yet another study of ethnic identity.

Her enduring purpose was to unveil "native differences" among populations, however, and like her scholarly allies, Shuey relied on the era's faith in science to make her conclusions seem true to nature. "It is possible to determine personality traits scientifically," declared her *Commentary* respondent with characteristic optimism, and proponents of race-based intelligence made sure their research appeared judicious, comprehensive, and objective.[68] McGurk's Richmond study claimed the virtue of factuality: he was "not concerned with the question whether the Negro is or is not as intelligent as the white" and merely reported "the scores which the two races make on three standard tests."[69] Understated yet suggestive arguments were matched by sweeping breadth. Far more typical than McGurk's local study were surveys of the hundreds of publications comparing test results for the races. Shuey collected studies reaching back to World War I for the first edition of *The Testing of Negro Intelligence* in 1958, and by 1966 her second edition swelled to more than 500 pages. When tests conducted in every region by researchers of both races showed blacks achieving lower scores, she praised their "remarkable consistency" as evidence of accuracy. Silence was her frequent response to the authors' own interpretations. "Engel observed that many of the families had come from Southern rural areas where schooling was so limited that their children presented a serious retardation problem when they entered a well-organized city school system," she noted before moving to the next set of statistics. She pointed to substandard professionalism to explain contradictions when all else failed. "Unfortunately," data indicating black promise gathered by the pioneering black psychologist, Herman Canady, may have been "due to rapport established between examiner and colored S[ubjects], to some unrecognized bias on the part of the examiner, or to some other factor."[70] Shuey's criticism of Canady made her seem reliable by contrast.

The sincerity of these psychologists' belief in their own scientific rigor did not lead them to social disengagement but made them all the more eager to shape public policy. Although desegregation cases clearly pertained to their theory of differential intelligence, the breadth of their racial and ethnic concerns meant that the South was not foreordained as the place of their practical efforts. It was the testimony of Henry Garrett (1894–1973) against integration in 1952 in a Virginia case, *Davis v. County School Board*, however, that sparked his alliance with Shuey, McGurk, and others.[71]

At first glance, the conservative psychologists seemed to put the argument about natural intelligence on the table to counter the idea of cultural agency, but the deeper issue was the source of individual value. They did not have to deny the right to freedom. They simply treated equal opportunity as less significant than a single quality: intelligence. Ina Brown, a white anthropologist at Scarritt College in Nashville, called their emphasis misplaced. The races' unequal IQ scores were "common knowledge," she wrote dismissively in 1960 in a review of the first edition of Shuey's book. Even if there were "some native differences between Negroes and Whites . . . we have no way of proving that such differences do exist while the evidence of socio-cultural differences is overwhelming." Phrased crisply as a nature-culture issue for readers of the *American Anthropologist*, Brown's logic quietly drew attention to inexcusable injustice. Nature promised equal rights to all, irrespective of intelligence, Brown implied, making Shuey's analysis, even if true, "much ado about nothing."[72]

The journal must have agreed, because its editors ran the review of Shuey's book in the miscellaneous category "Other." Through much of the 1950s, the psychologists committed to natural hierarchy had no secure audience, and they remained a largely undistinguished group of northern scholars. Although Shuey left New York for Randolph-Macon Woman's College by the middle of the war, Garrett stayed at Columbia until 1955, and McGurk taught at Villanova, outside Philadelphia, once he completed his doctorate at Catholic University in 1951. But converging circumstances made the South more attractive: the psychologists' new visibility in mounting debate about desegregation and their employers' resulting embarrassment. Beginning in 1956, when McGurk aired his views in *U.S. News and World Report*, "Villanova has censored me stiffly," he confided to Wesley Critz George, adding, "I am itching to come south."[73] Although Garrett took a position at the University of Virginia and McGurk found work at Alabama College, in the light of liberal pressures at home, their moves were an exile.

The appearance of northern social analyses citing power as the opponent of the reconstruction of personality may also have made the conservative psychologists eager to relocate to a friendlier region. Kenneth Clark never imagined that desegregated schools would easily change children, but slow progress made him wonder about "a culture that predisposes the individual to develop some form of prejudice." By 1960 he believed entrenched interests were responsible. "Events within the last five years have indicated that many of the individuals who control the political, social, and economic power necessary to effect significant and positive social change in race relations are not willing to do so," he told an audience of psychologists. Instead they are "exploiting racial issues for the perpetuation of personal political power."[74]

Clark's analysis reflected growing conviction about the reality of "institutionalized racism," words Alvin Poussaint chose for a speech in 1987. The position radicalized the nurture argument. Categorically rejecting biological differences between the races as a "genetic trap," Poussaint indicted "the whole institutional system."[75] Overseas in Africa, Frantz Fanon, the Caribbean-born psychiatrist, memorably called for revolutions in *The Wretched of the Earth* (1961) to uproot social orders devoted to "systematic negation of the other person." American black professionals more moderately envisioned black-controlled "alternative institutions," as Poussaint said.[76] But for them, old-fashioned cultural theory failed to acknowledge how imbedded the individual psyche was in a nexus of self-interest.

There was virtually no counterpart in the South to this line of thinking, perhaps less because extremism was risky for black professionals there than because it was a luxury. To declare that a nearly conspiratorial coalition held the key to progress belonged to a bold style of discourse that in a way was an end in itself. Whereas the power argument succeeded if it energized a mass audience, tasks in the South seemed more humble. Lloyd Elam of Meharry was not openly critical of a demonstrator who was convinced "that he can change the social structure of many generations now," but Elam's main goal was to provide at least rudimentary mental health care where there was little or none.[77] "Behavioral Blocks to Learning," a talk he delivered to teachers, adhered to simple behaviorism for the sake of effectiveness. "I do not want you to be better psychologists—you have your hands full being teachers," he began, and so he skipped "organic causes of learning problems" to deal with the practical difficulties he outlined, including "early negative conditioning" and "fear of learning."[78]

Elam's outreach to teachers was consistent with his vision of the psychiatrist as a community problem solver, and he acted throughout on the assumption that the problems of African Americans had overwhelmingly social roots. Loyalty to nurture reasoning among black psychiatrists does not mean they ignored new research on inheritance. Elam may well have read "Medical Genetics and Modern Medicine" by a Howard University professor in the *Journal of the National Medical Association* in 1968.[79] Yet because the article focused on hereditary disease in families, not supposed racial differentials, it did not veer into politically charged areas of theory. For a southerner like Elam, genetics may have seemed a useful addition to an eclectic set of premises. Being one step removed from the science wars heating up outside the South offered Elam the option of avoiding a theoretical stand.

Any reader of southern psychological literature during the era of renewed interest in natural endowment might well guess the race of an author, however. Although open champions of white superiority were a minority in the southern academy, a white scholar was far more likely to make evolution the anchor of a social theory acknowledging natural limits, cultural hierarchy, and institutional stability. This was the temper of work in the 1960s by John T. Doby of Emory University.

Not a racial extremist or even a native southerner, Doby articulated a latter-day social Darwinism. A habit of understatement averted potential objections from racial liberals to his textbook *Introduction to Social Psychol-*

ogy (1966). Omitting the subject of racial intelligence, Doby explained, "The genotype provides the biological potentialities, and the environment for opportunities—for good or bad." Nearly incontestable in the abstract, the rule was compatible with conservative psychologists' experiments in racial genetics. When Doby imagined twins born in an Australian tribe who were raised separately, with one brother excelling at hunting at home and his sibling in America mastering calculus, he seemed to honor cultural variety. But two pages later, references to "the more backward society" and "the more advanced society" placed cultures on a continuum of progress determined by Western values.[80] The notion that all societies can be classified in a natural arrangement carried a reassuring message about order in a decade distinguished by its social violence, and Doby's definition of culture similarly emphasized stable "customary patterns." "Culture is the derived system of human solutions to recurring human events, experiences, and conditions," and, by implication, anyone who tampered with mores risked losing "rational control of the forces which release human potentialities" and enable "man . . . 'to make himself.'"[81] Like the concept of folkways coined by William Graham Sumner at the turn of the century and later adopted by Howard Odum, Doby's explanation made culture seem enduring because it was intertwined with nature itself. There was no room in the model for the possibility of injustice or for deliberate reform.

To be sure, *Social Psychology* (1965), a competing textbook by Roger Brown of Harvard, similarly explained culture as "the totality of shared, transmitted guides to behavior," and we might think all surveys resembled each other until a second look shows Brown's greater interest in human uniqueness, personality development, and social change.[82] Whereas nearly half of Doby's book placed "man" firmly in nature as a "species" and "sociocultural animal," Brown devoted just one chapter in nearly 800 pages to animal behavior and instead explored traits like morality and individuality that set humans apart.[83] He observed, too, that "culture always does contain a certain amount of latent internal contradiction," which he judged unhealthy, and he treated stereotyping as one such problem. "Leaders of opinion in the United States disapprove of stereotypes," Brown wrote unequivocally, in contrast to Doby, who made it a point "to distinguish between stereotyping and prejudice" and praised the former for "providing continuity or relative constancy and organization in perception."[84]

These details added up to differing impressions of how a society's psychology worked, one view favoring dynamism and diversity and the other inheritance and cohesion. As the authors situated their books along a liberal-conservative political axis, regionalism took a back seat. Although Doby's analysis offered new reasons to respect tradition, the academy's style now disregarded place, and his choice of a New York publisher indicates his expectation of a national audience. For Odum in years gone by, conservatism was inseparable from southernness. The value of a stable hierarchy, conceived in relation to race, was the South's lesson for other Americans. Doby retained Odum's even deeper faith in evolution as the natural law underwriting social success. But the South was invisible in the broad strokes he used to sketch biological transformation over many millennia. Rather than an exponent of southern traditionalism, he was a man of conservative leanings who happened to live in the South.

He was not alone. The South drew two kinds of right-of-center psychological theorists during desegregation who had more explicit political goals than Doby. The academic group was a tight-knit cadre whose members generally used statistics to demonstrate natural differences among social groups. In so doing they translated old racial stereotypes into respectable science. In tune with the racial and ethnic comparisons published by McGurk and Shuey in the 1940s, R. Travis Osborne (b. 1913) used "factor analysis" and "heritability ratios" two decades later to argue that blacks had less inherent mathematical skill than whites. Having earned a doctorate in psychology at the University of Georgia following wartime naval service, Osborne spent his career there. In 1982 he joined McGurk to edit a supplement to *The Testing of Negro Intelligence* that included data collected by Shuey before her death.[85]

Henry Garrett, who wrote introductions for Shuey's earlier editions, was a neighbor in Charlottesville, Virginia, of Carleton Putnam (1901–98).[86] The latter, a self-styled native "Yankee" and former airline executive, broadcast racial determinism with bravado. His *Race and Reason*, propaganda without a scientific veneer, represented a second type of vehicle for right-wing psychology, and because he spoke so bluntly, Putnam underscored the appeal of the South as a location for the entire group. The region resembled the last outpost of "white civilization." Not only did like-minded intellectuals bear a responsibility to aid segregation's defenders, but they might get a hero's welcome. The mayors of Birmingham and New Orleans gave Putnam keys to their cities, Mississippi celebrated "Race and

Reason" day, and Louisiana distributed thousands of copies of his book free to students and state officials. Although the professors were not feted in a carnival style, they may well have felt valued in an area where a greater number of whites agreed with their racial ideas.[87]

Their affinity with the South's white conservatives, however, remained one piece of a broader crusade. References to psychological studies by Garrett, Shuey, and McGurk were the intellectual underpinning for emotional polemics about desegregation such as *Race and Reason*, as well as the lawyerly presentation *The Southern Case for School Segregation* (1962) by James Jackson Kilpatrick, the editor of the *Richmond (Va.) News Leader*.[88] The psychologists willingly assisted the segregationists. Kilpatrick thanked Garrett for material, and Garrett wrote an introduction for Putnam's book.[89] But the professors' true cause was intellectual politics and, specifically, defense of the nature argument.

The goal connected them with the national and international Far Right. When *Mankind Quarterly* began publication in Edinburgh in July 1960, the name of everyone in the southern circle except for Osborne appeared on the masthead as an editor or a board member, along with a list of other sponsors that included a former adviser on eugenics to Mussolini. Not surprisingly, Garrett used his space in the journal's first number to attack the cultural ideas of his former colleague at Columbia, Otto Klineberg. For a worldwide audience, desegregation was too parochial a theme.[90] The wish to participate in scientific debate conceived to be universal ironically ended with ever-growing intimacy with social extremists. Shuey, McGurk, and Osborne accepted grants from the Pioneer Fund, a philanthropy said to promote intolerance under the guise of "racial betterment," and white supremacist organizations like the Christian Party still cite their work. Although these proponents of innate racial differences lived in the South, they felt they belonged to the sprawling ultraconservative movement.[91]

Their outlook suggests why southern white psychology as practiced in colleges and universities missed opportunities to address regional problems. Although this circle's polemical mind-set was unusual, their response to provincialism and sensitivity to race were not. Across the country the revolt of partisans of evolution against the hegemony of cultural theory pushed scholarly discourse toward elemental questions, and participants who felt marginal to the discussion tried all the harder to appear in command of the topic of the hour. In this spirit John Doby urged the Southern

Sociological Society in 1970 to embrace the "unity of science" made possible by the idea of "adaptation." Southerners needed to keep up, he implied, and imitation of national trends was the way. Summarizing the latest theories on human genetics, communication, and cognition, he made no mention of local applications, as if regionalism were a dead end.[92] Field studies, the longtime staple of social scientists allied with policy makers, were also poorly adapted to rule about evolutionary premises. Even more, an environmental approach, increasingly identified with northern liberals of both races, was suspect in the white South for that simple reason. Together these currents of intellectual politics had a cumulative effect: to favor the nature argument in white scholarship and discourage attention to region. In a southern college community, it may have seemed reasonable to situate yourself in relation to national issues. The South that was isolated, poor, and socially segregated did not elicit the interest of the new biological theorists.

When these advocates insisted that genetic capacity was integral to the subject of race, scientific debate completed a historical circle: a somatic view of racial psychology had been the intellectual starting point for Jim Crow. There is nothing inherently racist about theories of natural inheritance, nor are they uniquely southern. But they have been used in America to close off inquiry about human beings, and segregation in particular thrived on reasoning that rendered black individuals two-dimensional. The irony was that now desegregation breathed new life into a self-styled science of racial inequality, and the psychological disciplines revealed their potential to limit attention to personality as well as encourage it. Racial genetics remained just one strand of mental science in the postwar South. On a day-to-day basis, doctors, teachers, social workers, clergy, and the populations they served, black and white, expected individuals to be able to transform themselves, especially if treated with the substantial body of psychological knowledge that had come into existence. Private optimism about repair of the mind and emotion had little public counterpart in hopes for social reconstruction, however. Southernness as a problem or, more positively, as an opportunity had no advocate, and individuals had to struggle for their own mental health in a culture still uncertain about collective self-knowledge.

THE SCIENCES OF THE

SELF AS AN INSTRUMENT OF

SOUTHERN SELF-KNOWLEDGE

By the end of segregation, the South had acquired a storehouse of psycho-logical ideas that did justice to the early faith of the new mental sciences that the mind could be explicated. The self that so widely attracted notice at the turn of the century was imagined to be individualized and flexible, and mastery of its secrets promised control of personal and perhaps human destiny. Southerners, along with many others, explored personality devel-opment, group dynamics, and existential healing. The psychological fields expanded in southern colleges and universities, and private practices and public agencies offered therapies. Southern experts entered the postwar debate that restored natural endowment to respectability as a component of identity.

During the same era, segregation gave southern society a unique and troubled character, and yet the psychological disciplines as practiced there, intellectual tools of self-discovery by their very nature, did not foster investigation of an immediate human dilemma. Reasoned problem solv-ing directed at racial ills, though sincere, was sporadic, and many analysts skimmed over segregation's essential lesson about race: that racial identi-ties and prejudices have deep cultural roots in America that do not yield easily to scientifically guided social adjustments. The South's reputation as the nation's anomaly oddly contributed to a habit of scientific generaliza-tion. If a researcher could treat the region as a curious object of inquiry, and of no personal interest, abstract laws of behavior were the expected outcome. Northern and southern investigators belonging to both races sensed the limitations of this logic. The South was more than a site, and they approached their work with a variety of interests. Their common feelings of shame and anger about segregation nonetheless sought resolution in the impersonality of science.

The growing uniformity of American culture irrespective of region may now make the history of psychological knowledge under Jim Crow seem irrelevant. Even if the human sciences failed to deliver deliberate progress, social improvement occurred. The South's isolation declined, and racial exclusion diminished. Out-migration from the region began to reverse itself in the 1960s as a temperate climate, low prices, and deliberate boosterism attracted outsiders to southern communities.[1] The end of Jim Crow made racial mixing the national standard. By some measures integration quickly gained ground. Eighty percent of black medical students attended previously all-white schools by the end of the 1970s, nearly reversing the pattern of just a decade before, when three-quarters of them trained at Howard and Meharry. Countervailing signs of failure to achieve racial equity at least were not limited to the South. The proportion of American medical students belonging to minority groups remained a small 8 percent between 1975 and 1990 and, according to some surveys, even declined.[2] Peculiarly southern problems might be safely dismissed as simply residual. One study of Medicare's performance in patient care in all fifty states and two territories, published in 2000, ranked six southern states among the ten least effective, and a regional analysis of the same program in 2005 identified race as the crucial variable: "In particular, the percentage of a state's Medicare population that is black is inversely related to the quality of medical care."[3] Segregation looms dimly behind this persistent racial inequality and regional shortcoming, but the survey's lack of historical information makes it impossible to discern either past or future directions with any assurance.

One thing is certain: history now plays little role in popular southern commentaries on mental wellness. Consider the way Rosalynn Carter and Walker Percy, both perceptive southerners, turn the debate about treatment of mental illness into a discussion of human nature in the abstract. Social structure, southern or otherwise, seems unimportant as a cause or cure of psychological disorders in Carter's *Helping Someone with Mental Illness* (1998). Beginning with today's medical commonplace that "most mental illnesses are biologically based" and hence responsive to medication, Carter advises families on how to restore "a loved one" to health.[4] In so doing she upends once-dominant views of personality formation. Families or, more broadly, civilizations are not riddled with conflicts that make people ill; now culture is the benign setting of personal distress. Closer to home, Carter's reasoning defies the body of southern data used in the past to demonstrate that racial injustice contributes to psychological damage. Instead, by presenting mental illness as "an equal opportunity problem," potentially afflicting anyone, Carter offers mental health reform as a democratic—and biracial—crusade.[5] This strenuous reading of a simple argument aimed at nonspecialists should not discredit Carter's good intentions. Yet it is striking that a southerner, reared in a region generally believed a half century ago to distort the personalities of both races alike, slights the burdens imposed by custom on individuals.

As if in dialogue with Carter, *The Thanatos Syndrome* (1987), the last novel by Louisiana author Walker Percy, rejects physiological psychology as practiced by "brain engineers, neuropharmacologists, chemists of the synapses" with a rebel yell. If there was ever a story pitting regional preservation against science, on one level this is it. Its villain is Dr. Robert Comeaux, a transplanted Yankee named "Como" before his move southward. Funded, like northern researchers of earlier years, by the federal government and a wealthy foundation, Comeaux secretly alters the chemistry of the drinking water to stop "the decay of the social fabric." "Tom, we're talking about caring," he explains to the hero, a local psychiatrist, although when the consequence is mass pedophilia at a boarding school, the dark potential of therapeutic empathy is exposed.[6] The reader cannot mistake Percy's cynicism about scientistic psychiatry when he links Comeaux's project with eugenics and involuntary euthanasia, most notoriously practiced by Nazi doctors. In the end the Yankee thankfully goes home, as Dr. Como (so called again) returns to New York to work in a Planned Parenthood clinic.

Yet Percy's book succeeds only modestly as an argument for regional self-assertion despite its attentiveness to geography. Although saturated with love of the South, *The Thanatos Syndrome* turns to metaphysics and myth, not to the region and its history, for resolution. In the late 1940s, Percy gave up plans to become a psychiatrist, converted to Catholicism, and began writing fiction, and the novel follows his own path from science to religion. It is the muddled Father Smith, suffering from dementia, who explains the destructive folly of using reason to engineer human life, and his alternative to control is compassion. He operates a hospice. The priest's growing incapacity suggests Percy's doubts about the church's ability to lead. Nonetheless, he is clear that no natural solution, including regional self-consciousness, can bring personal peace.

The South still remains valuable for Percy as a soulful environment for healing. For one thing, the races unite against the intruder. When black as well as white children are victimized at the school, adults of both races work equally hard to save them all. These southerners speak a common language. At one point Tom converses with an elderly black janitor in "a six-layered exchange beyond the compass of any known science of communication but plain as day to Frank and me." "One would have to be a Southerner, white or black, to understand the complexities" of the dialogue.[7] It is far more likely that a white writer like Percy would find this intricacy charming. Race relations is one subject he is unwilling to explore with an analytical eye. Although he eagerly introduces regionalism into a conversation about mental health, his South is too good to be true.

Set side by side, the views of mental healing offered by Carter and Percy take the form of a contest between science and faith. What they share, though, is a longing for an unshakable cure. From the outset, psychological study and therapy in America stirred elevated hopes for enlightenment about human beings that matched equal fears of mental derangement. Because the psyche presents itself as the seat of identity, the prospect of gaining control of the mind and emotions by means of insight impelled investigators, including these two southerners, to search for answers that seemed reliably truthful.

Historical study of the rise of psychological inquiry in the South, in contrast, leads away from resolution rather than toward it. History as a discipline typically exposes human limitations that are not simple enough to respond easily to deliberate correction. The southward migration of the idea of an indeterminate self during the era of segregation in America was no exception. Although nearly everyone involved in the transmission of psychological knowledge between regions meant well, their science stopped short of painful honesty about the inhumanity in their midst. Their instinct to look away compels our own reflection.

NOTES

Abbreviations

ASU	Special Collections, Carol Grotnes Belk Library, Appalachian State University, Boone, N.C.
AUC	Archives and Special Collections, Robert W. Woodruff Library, Atlanta University Center, Atlanta
Fisk	Special Collections, John Hope and Aurelia Elizabeth Franklin Library, Fisk University, Nashville
GEB Archives	General Education Board Archives, Rockefeller Archive Center, Sleepy Hollow, N.Y.
Howard	Special Collections, Moorland-Spingarn Research Center, Howard University, Washington, D.C.
JNMA	*Journal of the National Medical Association*
LC	Manuscript Division, Library of Congress, Washington, D.C.
MMC	Meharry Medical College Archives, Nashville
MPL	Memphis Public Library and Information Center, Memphis
RF Archives	Rockefeller Foundation Archives, Rockefeller Archive Center, Sleepy Hollow, N.Y.
UGA	Hargrett Rare Book and Manuscript Library, University of Georgia Libraries, Athens
UNC	Southern Historical Collection, Wilson Library, University of North Carolina at Chapel Hill
VUMC	Annette and Irwin Eskind Biomedical Library Historical Collection, Vanderbilt University Medical Center, Nashville

Introduction

1. My understanding of this transformation has been most shaped by Edwin G. Boring, *A History of Experimental Psychology*, 2d ed. (New York: Appleton-Century-Crofts, 1950); Dorothy Ross, *G. Stanley Hall: The Psychologist as Prophet* (Chicago: University of Chicago Press, 1972); Edward S. Reed, *From Soul to Mind: The Emergence of Psychology from Erasmus Darwin to William James* (New Haven, Conn.: Yale University Press, 1997); Bruce Kuklick, *The Rise of American Philosophy: Cambridge, Massachusetts, 1860–1930* (New Haven, Conn.: Yale University Press, 1977); Nathan G. Hale Jr., *Freud and the Americans: The Beginnings of Psychoanalysis in the United States, 1876–1917* (New York: Oxford University Press, 1971); Yosef Haym Yerushalmi, *Freud's Moses: Judaism Terminable and Interminable* (New Haven, Conn.: Yale University Press, 1991); Charles Darwin, *The Expression of the Emotions in Man and Animals* (1872; repr., Chicago: University of Chicago Press, 1965); George W. Stocking Jr., *Race, Culture, and Evolution: Essays in the History of Anthropology* (New York: Free Press, 1968); and Carl N. Degler, *In Search of Human Nature: The Decline and Revival of Darwinism in American Social Thought* (New York: Oxford University Press, 1991).

2. Boring, *History of Experimental Psychology*, 505.

3. On segregation as a system of customs with psychological components, see esp. Jennifer Ritterhouse, *Growing Up Jim Crow: How Black and White Southern Children Learned Race* (Chapel Hill: University of North Carolina Press, 2006); Melton A. McLaurin, *Separate Pasts: Growing Up White in the Segregated South* (Athens: University of Georgia Press, 1987); and John Dollard, *Caste and Class in a Southern Town*, 2d ed. (New York: Harper, 1949). On segregation as a legal arrangement, see C. Vann Woodward, *The Strange Career of Jim Crow*, 3d ed. (New York: Oxford University Press, 1974). On segregation as a component of late-nineteenth-century southern development, see Edward L. Ayres, *The Promise of the New South: Life after Reconstruction* (New York: Oxford University Press, 1992), chap. 6. On the medical diagnosis and treatment of African Americans from slavery to the turn of the twentieth century, see Todd L. Savitt, *Race and Medicine in Nineteenth- and Early-Twentieth-Century America* (Kent, Ohio: Kent State University Press, 2007). General works on the South following *Plessy v. Ferguson* include Jack Temple Kirby, *Rural Worlds Lost: The American South, 1920–1960* (Baton Rouge: Louisiana State University Press, 1987); John Egerton, *Speak Now against the Day: The Generation before the Civil Rights Movement* (New York: Knopf, 1994); and J. William Harris, *Deep Souths: Delta, Piedmont, and Sea Island Society in the Age of Segregation* (Baltimore: Johns Hopkins University Press, 2001), pts. 2–3. On the ideological nature of psychological ideas, see esp. Michel Foucault, *Madness and Civilization: A History of Insanity in the Age of Reason* (1961; repr., New York: Random House, 1965).

4. The percentage of African Americans living in the South in 1900 was 89.7 percent. Daniel M. Johnson and Rex R. Campbell, *Black Migration in America: A Social Demographic History* (Durham, N.C.: Duke University Press, 1981), 73. In 1930, 78.2 percent of African Americans still lived in the South. Charles S. Johnson, *Growing Up in the Black Belt: Negro Youth in the Rural South* (1941; repr., New York: Schocken

Books, 1967), xxiii. According to the 2000 census, 54.8 percent of African Americans lived in the South; African Americans (those who responded to the census that they were black only) then constituted 12.3 percent of all Americans. Jesse McKinnon, "The Black Population: 2000," Census 2000 Brief 01-5 (U.S. Census Bureau, Aug. 2001), 2–3, ⟨http://www.census.gov/prod/2001pubs/c2kbr01-5.pdf⟩ (June 14, 2008).

5. See esp. C. Vann Woodward, "The Search for Southern Identity," in *The Burden of Southern History*, 3d ed. (Baton Rouge: Louisiana State University Press, 1993), 321–38; Bertram Wyatt-Brown, *Southern Honor: Ethics and Behavior in the Old South* (New York: Oxford University Press, 1982); and Christine Leigh Heyrman, *Southern Cross: The Beginnings of the Bible Belt* (New York: Knopf, 1997).

6. I. A. Newby, *Jim Crow's Defense: Anti-Negro Thought in America, 1900–1930* (Baton Rouge: Louisiana State University Press, 1965), 28–29. Newby was most likely thinking of classic statements of racial theory such as Arthur de Gobineau, *The Inequality of Human Races*, trans. Adrian Collins (ca. 1853; repr., New York: Fertig, 1967), and Madison Grant, *The Passing of the Great Race; or, The Racial Basis of European History* (New York: Scribner, 1916). Southern writers who produced works of significant intellectual stature about the races tended to belong to an earlier period, for example, J. C. Nott and George R. Gliddon, *Types of Mankind; or, Ethnological Researches, Based upon the Ancient Monuments, Paintings, Sculpture, and Crania of Races, and upon Their Natural, Geographical, Philological, and Biblical History* (Philadelphia: Lippincott, Grambo, 1854). On Nott and Gliddon, see William Stanton, *The Leopard's Spots: Scientific Attitudes toward Race in America, 1815–1859* (Chicago: University of Chicago Press, 1960), 45–81.

7. Dorothy Ross emphasizes this historical tendency in *The Origins of American Social Science* (Cambridge: Cambridge University Press, 1991), esp. chaps. 2, 10.

8. See the text of *Brown v. Board of Education* in Kenneth B. Clark, *Prejudice and Your Child*, 2d ed. (Boston: Beacon Press, 1963), 156–65. Although the *Brown* decision was a national ruling, the opinion's choice of words — such as "Negro race," "Northern States," and "segregation" — was a good deal more concrete than the broad way the word "race" has come to be used. Ibid., 157 (first and second quotations), 156 (third quotation). For commentaries on the social sciences in relation to the *Brown* case, see Daryl Michael Scott, *Contempt and Pity: Social Policy and the Image of the Damaged Black Psyche, 1880–1996* (Chapel Hill: University of North Carolina Press, 1997); John P. Jackson Jr., *Social Scientists for Social Justice: Making the Case against Segregation* (New York: New York University Press, 2001); and Walter A. Jackson, *Gunnar Myrdal and America's Conscience: Social Engineering and Racial Liberalism, 1938–1987* (Chapel Hill: University of North Carolina Press, 1990).

9. Lawrence K. Frank, "Society as the Patient," *American Journal of Sociology* 42 (1936): 335–44.

10. Hadley Cantril, *The Psychology of Social Movements* (1941; repr., New York: Wiley, 1963), 85. Although humanistic works since the 1980s almost universally take race to have a cultural meaning only, scholars in biological and social sciences most influenced by the revival of evolutionary theory may criticize cultural explanations of racial identity as superficial. See, for example, Steven Pinker, *The Blank Slate: The Modern Denial*

of Human Nature (New York: Penguin, 2002). For a historical analysis of the resurgent popularity of biological explanations, see Degler, *In Search of Human Nature*, pt. 3. I wish to make an argument different from either of these: that history is an inevitable component of culture and that its influence can best be apprehended in specific societies.

11. C. R. Garvey, "List of American Psychological Laboratories," *Psychological Bulletin* 26 (1929): 652–60; R. H. Gillespie, "General Report" (typescript, Third Annual Educational Conference, University of Mississippi, Oxford, July 1–2, 1937), 23–24, box 93, folder 834, series 1.1, GEB Archives; "Bibliography" (typescript, Tougaloo College Health Education Workshop, Greenville, Miss., 1948), box 542, folder 5811, series 1.3, GEB Archives. I did not count two experimental psychology laboratories in Texas.

12. I know of no comprehensive study of the psychological fields in southern higher education. Research on southern institutions for the mentally ill and disabled includes Samuel B. Thielman, "Southern Madness: The Shape of Mental Health Care in the Old South," in *Science and Medicine in the Old South*, ed. Ronald L. Numbers and Todd L. Savitt (Baton Rouge: Louisiana State University Press, 1989), esp. 262–75; Peter McCandless, *Moonlight, Magnolias, and Madness: Insanity in South Carolina from the Colonial Period to the Progressive Era* (Chapel Hill: University of North Carolina Press, 1996); Edward J. Larson, *Sex, Race, and Science: Eugenics in the Deep South* (Baltimore: Johns Hopkins University Press, 1995); and Steven Noll, *Feeble-Minded in Our Midst: Institutions for the Mentally Retarded in the South, 1900–1940* (Chapel Hill: University of North Carolina Press, 1995). Because these works generally focus on reform, they demonstrate that mental health care in the South consisted of more than unenlightened traditionalism. Nonetheless, they also suggest that the South adopted medical innovations slowly.

13. William James explained the stream of consciousness in *The Principles of Psychology* (New York: Holt, 1890), vol. 1, chap. 9; G. Stanley Hall focused on personal growth in *Adolescence*, 2 vols. (1904; repr., New York: Arno Press, 1969); and John B. Watson emphasized observable learned behavior in *Behaviorism* (New York: Norton, 1924), esp. chap. 1. On the interdisciplinary trend that enhanced fieldwork in psychological study, see Anne C. Rose, "Putting the South on the Psychological Map: The Impact of Region and Race on the Human Sciences during the 1930s," *Journal of Southern History* 71 (2005): 321–56. A few examples of the enduring devotion of psychologists to testing include Carl C. Brigham, *A Study of American Intelligence* (Princeton, N.J.: Princeton University Press, 1923); Lewis M. Terman and Catharine Cox Miles, *Sex and Personality: Studies in Masculinity and Femininity* (1936; repr., New York: Russell and Russell, 1968); and T. W. Adorno, Else Frenkel-Brunswik, Daniel J. Levinson, and R. Nevitt Sanford, *The Authoritarian Personality* (New York: Harper, 1950).

14. On the early employment decisions of Du Bois, who was born in Great Barrington, Massachusetts, see David Levering Lewis, *W. E. B. Du Bois: Biography of a Race, 1868–1919* (New York: Holt, 1993), chaps. 7–8. On the birthplaces of the three southerners, see, respectively, Boring, *History of Experimental Psychology*, 529; Kerry W.

Buckley, *Mechanical Man: John Broadus Watson and the Beginnings of Behaviorism* (New York: Guilford Press, 1989), 1; and Eli Zaretsky, editor's introduction to *The Polish Peasant in Europe and America*, by William I. Thomas and Florian Znaniecki, ed. Eli Zaretsky (Urbana: University of Illinois Press, 1987), 8. The individuals I name as prominent in the movement to reenvision human beings as indeterminate were men who had unusual influence on southern ideas.

15. James L. Pate, "The Southern Society for Philosophy and Psychology," in *No Small Part: A History of Regional Organizations in American Psychology*, ed. James L. Pate (Washington, D.C.: American Psychological Association, 1993), 2–5. On the oscillation of educated southerners between pride and self-doubt, see Michael O'Brien, *Conjectures of Order: Intellectual Life and the American South, 1810–1860* (Chapel Hill: University of North Carolina Press, 2004), 1:6–7, 45–48, and William R. Taylor, *Cavalier and Yankee: The Old South and American National Character* (New York: Harper and Row, 1961), 18.

16. Peter G. Cranford, *But for the Grace of God: The Inside Story of the World's Largest Insane Asylum, Milledgeville* (Augusta, Ga.: Great Pyramid Press, 1981), 108, 139. The muckraking critic of psychiatric care Albert Deutsch began his visit to Milledgeville with the expectation that southern institutions would be worse than mental hospitals elsewhere; he found that conditions in Georgia were poor but comparable to conditions across the country. Albert Deutsch, *The Shame of the States* (1948; repr., New York: Arno Press, 1973), 88–90.

17. Helen Leland Witmer, *Psychiatric Clinics for Children, with Special Reference to State Programs* (New York: Commonwealth Fund, 1940), 60, 83; Bertram Wyatt-Brown, *The House of Percy: Honor, Melancholy, and Imagination in a Southern Family* (New York: Oxford University Press, 1994), 248, 251, 253–55.

18. Clifford Whittingham Beers, *A Mind That Found Itself: An Autobiography* (1907; repr., Pittsburgh: University of Pittsburgh Press, 1981), 76 (first quotation), 72 (second quotation), 78 (third quotation).

19. Newby, *Jim Crow's Defense*, 115.

20. A. H. Witmer, "Insanity in the Colored Race in the United States," *Alienist and Neurologist* 12 (1891): 19–30; Robert Bennett Bean, "Some Racial Peculiarities of the Negro Brain," *American Journal of Anatomy* 5 (1906): 353–432; Mary O'Malley, "Psychoses in the Colored Race: A Study in Comparative Psychiatry," *American Journal of Insanity* 71 (1914): 309–37; E. M. Green, "Psychoses among Negroes: A Comparative Study," *Journal of Nervous and Mental Disease* 41 (1914): 697–708; John E. Lind, "The Dream as a Simple Wish-Fulfilment in the Negro," *Psychoanalytic Review* 1 (1914): 295–300; Arrah B. Evarts, "The Ontogenetic against the Phylogenetic Elements in the Psychoses of the Colored Race," *Psychoanalytic Review* 3 (1916): 272–87. Bean did his research at the Anatomical Research Laboratory of Johns Hopkins, and Green was identified as director of the Georgia State Sanitarium at Milledgeville. On their professional movements, see R. J. Terry, "Robert Bennett Bean, 1874–1944," *American Anthropologist*, n.s., 48 (1946): 70–74, and Cranford, *But for the Grace of God*, 74. O'Malley, Lind, and Evarts were said to be affiliated with the Government Hospital for the Insane, later re-

named St. Elizabeth's Hospital. Witmer was located in Washington, D.C., and, because St. Elizabeth's was the principal mental hospital in the city, presumably worked there as well.

21. G. Stanley Hall to Francis C. Sumner, Feb. 14, 1917, box 45 (B1-6-12), folder "Francis C. Sumner," G. Stanley Hall Papers, Archives and Special Collections, Robert Hutchings Goddard Library, Clark University, Worcester, Mass. Sumner's 1927 Guggenheim Fellowship application conveys his continuing interest in psychoanalysis. "Separate Document (No. 2), Plan for Study," manuscript, [1927], box "Correspondence, Smith-Tobias," folder "Francis Sumner," Mordecai Johnson Papers, collection 178-12, Howard. See also Robert V. Guthrie, *Even the Rat Was White: A Historical View of Psychology* (New York: Harper and Row, 1976), chap. 7.

22. Roger K. Thomas, "An Historical Overview of the Department of Psychology at the University of Georgia," ⟨http://www.uga.edu/psychology/about/history.htm⟩ (June 14, 2008). See also my discussion of Austin Southwick Edwards, the first chair of the department, in chapter 1.

23. McLaurin, *Separate Pasts*, 13.

24. On the etiquette of space, see ibid., 13–14. On the use of names and titles, see Benjamin E. Mays, *Born to Rebel: An Autobiography* (New York: Scribner, 1971), 80–82. On black patronage of white doctors, see Mays, *Born to Rebel*, 87, 140. On considerations governing where blacks and whites sat in cars, see McLaurin, *Separate Pasts*, 91–92. Segregation in some cases led to physical separation of the races unknown in the past. Lewis Killian notes that white suburban children had no exposure to black children, black barbers no longer shaved white customers, and whites now declined to visit black churches. Lewis M. Killian, *White Southerners*, rev. ed. (Amherst: University of Massachusetts Press, 1985), 25. The purpose of segregation was much less to maintain physical distance than to enforce reminders of racial inequality, however, as the psychologist Kenneth Clark observed. Kenneth B. Clark, *Dark Ghetto: Dilemmas of Social Power* (New York: Harper and Row, 1965), 22.

25. Fred Hobson, *Tell about the South: The Southern Rage to Explain* (Baton Rouge: Louisiana State University Press, 1983). Hobson indicates in a headnote that his title comes from Faulkner's *Absalom, Absalom!* (1936).

26. On the history and psychology of autobiography, by white and black authors, as a southern literary form, see O'Brien, *Conjectures of Order*, 2:671–82. By explaining the honor ethos of the historic white South as socially focused rather than introspective, Bertram Wyatt-Brown casts light on the southern preference for theatrical forms of self-expression. To the extent that social judgments were the basis of individual identity in an honor culture, any speaker needed to carefully conceal as well as reveal and to control audience responses by literary mechanisms. Wyatt-Brown, *Southern Honor*, esp. 45–47.

27. Walter White, *Rope and Faggot: A Biography of Judge Lynch* (1929; repr., New York: Arno Press, 1969), 57; Mays, *Born to Rebel*, 26. White devoted an entire chapter of *Rope and Faggot*, "Sex and Lynching" (chap. 4), in an effort to explain why white southerners

commonly justified lynching as a response to black sexual assault, which in White's view was mistaken.

28. McLaurin, *Separate Pasts*, 39.

29. Lawrence J. Friedman, *The White Savage: Racial Fantasies in the Postbellum South* (Englewood Cliffs, N.J.: Prentice-Hall, 1970), 127 (first quotation), 128 (second and third quotations); Howard W. Odum, *Rainbow round My Shoulder: The Blue Trail of Black Ulysses* (Indianapolis: Bobbs-Merrill, 1928), 67 (fourth quotation), 25 (fifth quotation), 100 (sixth quotation).

30. William H. Grier and Price M. Cobbs, *Black Rage* (New York: Basic Books, 1968), 62–63 (first through fourth quotations); Robert Coles, "Southern Children under Segregation," 27, Report for the American Psychiatric Association, typescript, May 6, 1963, box 474, folder 5045, series 1.3, GEB Archives (fifth through seventh quotations). *Black Rage* belongs to a body of literature on the psychology of race, and the authors did not intend their conclusions to pertain only to the South.

31. See esp. Johnson, *Growing Up in the Black Belt*, 1–37, 53–70; Allison Davis and John Dollard, *Children of Bondage: The Personality Development of Negro Youth in the Urban South* (1940; repr., New York: Harper and Row, 1964), esp. 28–35; and Ritterhouse, *Growing Up Jim Crow*. See also the literature on race and childrearing without a southern focus, including Gordon W. Allport, *The Nature of Prejudice* (Reading, Mass.: Addison Wesley, 1954), chaps. 18–19, and James P. Comer and Alvin F. Poussaint, *Raising Black Children: Two Leading Psychiatrists Confront the Educational, Social, and Emotional Problems Facing Black Children* (1975; repr., New York: Plume, 1992).

32. Harry Crews, *A Childhood: The Biography of a Place* (New York: Harper and Row, 1978), 57–58. Lillian Smith tells an almost identical story in Lillian Smith, *Killers of the Dream* (New York: Norton, 1949), 26–30. Following the discovery that Janie, a light-skinned girl taken into Smith's childhood family on the presumption that she was white, was really black, it was Smith who communicated the news to Janie. The issue in the crises of both Crews and Smith was not simply that segregation was divisive but that the authors as white children so easily became agents of injustice.

33. Mays, *Born to Rebel*, 38.

34. W. J. Cash, *The Mind of the South* (New York: Vintage, 1941), 48 (quotation), 46–60.

35. Johnson, *Growing Up in the Black Belt*, 71 (first quotation); McLaurin, *Separate Pasts*, 89 (second and third quotations). Among Johnson's examples of teenagers' fantasies, a girl took refuge from restricted opportunities in religion, the son of a farmhand dreamed of escape, and a boy imagined where he might go to college if he were white. Johnson, *Growing Up in the Black Belt*, 11, 19, 37.

36. William Alexander Percy, *Lanterns on the Levee: Recollections of a Planter's Son* (1941; repr., New York: Knopf, 1966), 286–87.

37. Patrick T. Malone, interview by the author, July 30, 2002, Atlanta. Dollard, who had Freudian training, made sexual attraction across racial lines an analytical cornerstone of his book *Caste and Class in a Southern Town*, esp. chap. 7.

38. Following earlier considerations of southern lawlessness such as Charles S. Sydnor, "The Southerner and the Laws," *Journal of Southern History* 6 (1940): 3–23, works that set southern violence in a national context as a result of the turmoil of the 1960s included Howard Zinn, *The Southern Mystique* (New York: Knopf, 1964), 238; Sheldon Hackney, "Southern Violence," *American Historical Review* 74 (1969): 906–25; and John Shelton Reed, "'To Live—and Die—in Dixie': A Contribution to the Study of Southern Violence," *Political Science Quarterly* 86 (1971): 429–43.

39. Clarence Cason, *90 Degrees in the Shade* (1935; repr., Westport, Conn.: Negro Universities Press, 1970), 79.

Chapter 1

1. "Souvenir Program: Dedication Services, Recreation Building, U.S. Veterans' Hospital, Tuskegee, Alabama, June 25, 1927," box 90, folder "1923. U.S. Veterans Hospital #91" (hereafter cited as folder "1923"), Robert Russa Moton Papers, Tuskegee University Archives, Tuskegee University, Tuskegee, Ala. Although Robert Russa Moton, principal of Tuskegee Institute, was eager to have the hospital adjacent to his school and offered the federal government 300 acres for a maximum of $7,000, at least some black veterans opposed the proposed Alabama location for what would be the only VA hospital in the country serving African Americans. See Robert Russa Moton to the Secretary of the Treasury, Nov. 17, 1921, box 90, folder "1923," Moton Papers, and John W. Love, "National Committee on Negro Veteran Relief," n.d., attached to J. R. A. Crossland to James O. F. Thomas, Oct. 28, 1921, box 85, folder 596, Moton Papers. On the hospital's origins, see also "The U.S. Veterans' Hospital, Tuskegee, Ala., Colonel Joseph Henry Ward," *JNMA* 21 (1929): 65–67; J. H. Ward, "U.S. Veterans' Hospital, Tuskegee, Alabama," *JNMA* 22 (1930): 133–34; Clifton O. Dummett and Eugene H. Dibble, "Historical Notes on the Tuskegee Veterans Hospital," *JNMA* 54 (1962): 133–38; Herbert M. Morais, *The History of the Negro in Medicine* (New York: Publishers, 1967), 113–16; and Jeanne Spurlock, "Early and Contemporary Pioneers," in *Black Psychiatrists and American Psychiatry*, ed. Jeanne Spurlock (Washington, D.C.: American Psychiatric Association, 1999), 4–5.

2. "Calhoun Ordered Back to Tuskegee" (typescript, July 21, 1923), published in the *Montgomery Advertiser*, July 22, 1923, box 90, folder 669, Moton Papers. The number 700 was cited in "An Editorial in the [New York] *Sun* and the *Globe*" (typescript, July 5, 1923), box 95, folder 670, Moton Papers.

3. George E. Ijams to Robert Russa Moton, Mar. 1, 1923, box 95, folder 670, Moton Papers (first quotation); Warren G. Harding to William W. Brandon, May 1, 1923 (typescript copy), box 90, folder 669, Moton Papers (second quotation). Ijams, who was acting director of the Veterans Bureau, did not doubt that there would be a sufficient number of black orderlies, attendants, and laborers; his skepticism focused on finding African Americans for medical, nursing, and managerial positions. The intensity of the controversy is impossible to convey briefly. In a way characteristic of many participants, the NAACP fanned emotion by charging that sheets supposedly used for the

Ku Klux Klan procession had been taken from the hospital itself. [Walter F. White] to Helen L. Ryan, August 21, 1923; NAACP, "Release Wednesday Morning, July 25," news release, both in box 125, folder 941, Moton Papers.

4. "Confidential Memorandum for Mr. Sanders. Subject: Recreational and Assembly Building for the U.S. Veteran's Hospital at Tuskegee, Alabama," n.d., box 125, folder 941, Moton Papers. Sources differ about whether Fuller trained three or four black psychiatrists, but records in the Moton Papers suggest that George C. Branche, Simon O. Johnson, and Toussaint T. Tildon were among the first. Robert H. Sharpley proposes that Fuller (1872–1953) himself had been asked to head the psychiatry unit at Tuskegee but declined. "Solomon Carter Fuller" in *Psychoanalysis, Psychotherapy, and the New England Medical Scene, 1894–1944*, ed. George E. Gifford Jr. (New York: Science History/USA, 1978), 192–93. Once it became clear that black doctors would replace white ones, L. B. Rogers, the hospital's first medical director, who was white, tried to recruit ten black psychiatrists by contacting the National Medical Association. See "The Veterans' Hospital," *JNMA* 15 (1923): 203–4. Johnson may have been the first to arrive; his name appears as recording secretary for a board reviewing personnel problems. "Report of Proceedings, Findings and Recommendations," Dec. 22, 1923, box 95, folder 670, Moton Papers. Charles Prudhomme, a psychiatrist who practiced at the hospital from 1939 until 1943, is the source of the report that the VA encouraged the diagnosis of syphilis in cases of mental illness. Charles Prudhomme and David F. Musto, "Historical Perspectives on Mental Health and Racism in the United States," in *Racism and Mental Health: Essays*, ed. Charles V. Willie, Bernard M. Kramer, and Bertram S. Brown (Pittsburgh: University of Pittsburgh Press, 1973), 52–53. Prudhomme and Musto offer an account of the career of Solomon Fuller in "Historical Perspectives on Mental Health and Racism," 48–54.

5. Robert Russa Moton to Frank T. Hines, May 5, 1927, box 139, folder 1085, Moton Papers.

6. Thomas Pearce Bailey, *Race Orthodoxy in the South, and Other Aspects of the Negro Question* (1914; repr., New York: Negro Universities Press, 1969), 10 (quotation). On the military testing, see Clarence S. Yoakum and Robert M. Yerkes, *Army Mental Tests* (New York: Holt, 1920), and Carl C. Brigham, *A Study of American Intelligence* (Princeton, N.J.: Princeton University Press, 1923). Inattention at the hospital to the classification of patients by illness appears, for example, in a communication by J. R. A. Crossland, an African American doctor and early advocate of black physicians, who put racial identity at the forefront when he counted the hospital's 400 black patients and personnel and contrasted them with 6 white staff members. J. R. A. Crossland to George Woodson, Jan. 8, 1923, box 90, folder 669, Moton Papers. In later years, correspondents still struggled with what to call the psychiatric patients. Moton referred to "one of the neurotics" in a letter to J. H. Ward, Mar. 15, 1934, and Ward wrote in reply about the hospital's "neuropsychiatric beneficiaries," Mar. 24, 1934, both in box 188, folder 1607, Moton Papers.

7. Melton A. McLaurin, *Separate Pasts: Growing Up White in the Segregated South* (Athens: University of Georgia Press, 1987), 102 (first quotation); Trudier Harris, *Sum-*

mer Snow: Reflections from a Black Daughter of the South (Boston: Beacon Press, 2003), 123 (subsequent quotations).

8. Lillian Smith, *Killers of the Dream* (New York: Norton, 1949), 211. John Egerton notes the lack of a developed religious liberalism—tolerant, optimistic, and socially conscious—in the South in *Speak Now against the Day: The Generation before the Civil Rights Movement* (New York: Knopf, 1994), 43–44.

9. W. J. Cash, *The Mind of the South* (New York: Vintage, 1941), 214.

10. Helen Leland Witmer, *Psychiatric Clinics for Children, with Special Reference to State Programs* (New York: Commonwealth Fund, 1940), 57, 35 (quotation).

11. Hortense Powdermaker, *After Freedom: A Cultural Study of the Deep South* (1939; repr., New York: Russell and Russell, 1966), 285.

12. Erskine Caldwell, *Deep South: Memory and Observation* (New York: Weybright and Talley, 1966), 116.

13. Harry Crews, *A Childhood: The Biography of a Place* (New York: Harper and Row, 1978), 80 (first quotation), 81 (second quotation), 82 (third quotation).

14. Mary O'Malley, "Psychoses in the Colored Race: A Study in Comparative Psychiatry," *American Journal of Insanity* 71 (1914): 325 (first quotation); Peter G. Cranford, *But for the Grace of God: The Inside Story of the World's Largest Insane Asylum, Milledgeville* (Augusta, Ga.: Great Pyramid Press, 1981), 155 (subsequent quotations). Trudier Harris emphasized the importance in the African American community of communicating with God about sorrows in an interview by the author, May 15, 2004, University of North Carolina, Chapel Hill.

15. E. M. Green, "Psychoses among Negroes: A Comparative Study," *Journal of Nervous and Mental Disease* 41 (1914): 707.

16. O'Malley, "Psychoses in the Colored Race," 324.

17. E. E. Evans-Pritchard, *Witchcraft, Oracles, and Magic Among the Azande* (1937; abr., Oxford: Oxford University Press, 1976), 16 (first quotation), 1 (second quotation). Evans-Pritchard discussed the prominence of health problems and the means of cure in ibid., 5, 37, 176. See also Evans-Pritchard's consideration of magic in relation to social scientists' views of tribal religions in *Theories of Primitive Religion* (Oxford: Oxford University Press, 1965). Not all early anthropologists agreed with Evans-Pritchard's interpersonal interpretation of magic. Bronislaw Malinowski, for example, presented magic as an instrument meant to manipulate nature in *Magic, Science, and Religion and Other Essays*, ed. Robert Redfield (Boston: Beacon Press, 1948). The psychoanalyst Gregory Zilboorg predictably took a more psychological perspective on magic in *The Medical Man and the Witch during the Renaissance* (1965; repr., New York: Cooper Square, 1969).

18. Zora Hurston, "Hoodoo in America," *Journal of American Folk-Lore* 44 (1931): 333 (first and second quotations), 414 (third quotation). The personal problems mentioned appear in ibid., 329, 335, 339–40, respectively. Hurston reported the use of Jesus' picture in ibid., 344, and of Job in ibid., 362. See also the contemporaneous examination of hoodoo, based on southern fieldwork, by Newbell Niles Puckett, *Folk Beliefs of the*

Southern Negro (Chapel Hill: University of North Carolina Press, 1926), chaps. 3–8, as well as Jeffrey E. Anderson, *Conjure in African American Society* (Baton Rouge: Louisiana State University Press, 2005), esp. chap. 5, and Sharla M. Fett, *Working Cures: Healing, Health, and Power on Southern Slave Plantations* (Chapel Hill: University of North Carolina Press, 2002). Anderson offers a helpful discussion of the terms "conjure" and "hoodoo," which he identifies as folk practices distinct from Voodoo and Santería, both more formal religious systems, in *Conjure in African American Society*, ix–xii.

19. Michael MacDonald, *Mystical Bedlam: Madness, Anxiety, and Healing in Seventeenth-Century England* (Cambridge: Cambridge University Press, 1981), 8, 198–230.

20. Peter McCandless, *Moonlight, Magnolias, and Madness: Insanity in South Carolina from the Colonial Period to the Progressive Era* (Chapel Hill: University of North Carolina Press, 1996), 37, 205.

21. Charles W. Chesnutt, "Po Sandy" and "Sis' Becky's Pickaninny," in *The Conjure Woman and Other Conjure Tales*, ed. Richard H. Brodhead (Durham, N.C.: Duke University Press, 1983), 44–54, 82–93. For whatever reason, Chesnutt made Aunt Peggy a free woman. "The Goophered Grapevine" in ibid., 36. Brodhead explains Chesnutt's awareness of the political and moral problems connected with portraying black traits that white readers would consider primitive in his editor's introduction, ibid., 14.

22. "Sis' Becky's Pickaninny," 82.

23. Annie's husband sides with the doctor's science when he tells Uncle Julius that former slaves will not achieve progress unless they give up superstition for reason and common sense, but Chesnutt undercuts this opinion when he shows Uncle Julius's story to be the instrument of Annie's "ultimate recovery." Ibid., 82–84, 92–93. Despite this message in the stories, Chesnutt's journals, representing an earlier period in his life (1874–82), show his distaste for black folk beliefs when he was an aspiring man of letters. See *The Journals of Charles W. Chesnutt*, ed. Richard H. Brodhead (Durham, N.C.: Duke University Press, 1993), esp. 14, 21–22. The complexity of his own position as a well-educated African American seemed finally to leave Chesnutt (1858–1932) unresolved about black folk culture.

24. MacDonald, *Mystical Bedlam*, 128. MacDonald notes that caring for the insane in early modern England was the responsibility of families. Ibid., 4.

25. McCandless, *Moonlight, Magnolias, and Madness*, 160–61.

26. Ocie [?] Lila Harrison to Charlie May Simon Fletcher, condolence card, n.d., box 33B, folder 14, series 5, John Gould Fletcher Papers, collection MS F63, Special Collections Division, University Libraries, University of Arkansas, Fayetteville. The coroner's statement that the death was an "apparent suicide" appeared in a clipping, "Obituary," *Little Rock Daily News*, May 11, 1950, 22, box 33B, folder 14, series 5, Fletcher Papers.

27. William Alexander Percy, *Lanterns on the Levee: Recollections of a Planter's Son* (1941; repr., New York: Knopf, 1966), 26 (first quotation), 348 (second quotation). Percy mentioned Sigmund Freud and Carl Jung in ibid., 76.

28. Ibid., 310. For an external account of these events, see Bertram Wyatt-Brown, *The House of Percy: Honor, Melancholy, and Imagination in a Southern Family* (New York: Oxford University Press, 1994), 254–56, 271–75. On the honor ethos, see Bertram Wyatt-Brown, *Southern Honor: Ethics and Behavior in the Old South* (New York: Oxford University Press, 1982).

29. Mental abnormalities may have made blacks more vulnerable to lynch mobs, instead of leading them to be judged by whites to be less responsible for their actions. Walter White reported that a black man in the Milledgeville State Hospital was lynched by a mob in 1925 after he killed a nurse "in one of his periodic fits of dementia." Walter White, *Rope and Faggot: A Biography of Judge Lynch* (1929; repr., New York: Arno Press, 1969), 33.

30. Michael J. Bent and Ellen F. Greene, *Rural Negro Health: A Report on a Five-Year Experiment in Health Education in Tennessee* (Nashville: Julius Rosenwald Fund Southern Office, 1937), 19 (first quotation), 59 (second quotation). Bent and Greene noted the declining use of home medications of all kinds in ibid., 49.

31. E. H. Abington, *Back Roads and Bicarbonate: The Autobiography of an Arkansas Country Doctor* (New York: Vantage Press, 1955), 114. Abington also called the traveling salesmen "comedians" (ibid.). Their adventures in marketing the product in Arkansas, Kansas, Oklahoma, and Texas appear in chap. 7.

32. John Gould Fletcher, diary, July 11, 1945, "Diary 1945," box 11, folder 105, series 2, Fletcher Papers (first quotation); shopping list, ca. May 14, 1949, diary "March 1, 1949–June 1, 1949," box 12, folder 119, series 2, Fletcher Papers (second quotation). On the Wallace facility, see untitled list of Memphis-area hospitals (typescript, [1935]), folder "Memphis-Hospitals," Memphis and Shelby County Room, MPL. Memoirs that emphasize drinking include Crews, *Childhood*, 12, 49, and McLaurin, *Separate Pasts*, 27–28. Thomas D. Clark suggests the effects of Progressive legislation on removing narcotics and alcohol from over-the-counter products in *Pills, Petticoats, and Plows: The Southern Country Store* (1944; repr., Norman: University of Oklahoma Press, 1963), 189, 202–4.

33. Crews, *Childhood*, 84. Crews recalled the reason for using Auntie's hair in ibid., 76–77.

34. Smith, *Killers of the Dream*, 113.

35. An early psychiatrist articulated the commonplace view that blacks were more natural, in the sense of being more animal-like, when he wrote that "the colored race is so much nearer its stage of barbarism" than whites. Arrah B. Evarts, "The Ontogenetic against the Phylogenetic Elements in the Psychoses of the Colored Race," *Psychoanalytic Review* 3 (1916): 274.

36. Abington, *Back Roads and Bicarbonate*, 72. J. Edward Perry (b. ca. 1870), a black contemporary of Abington (b. 1873), had a similar recollection: "There was a general fear of hospitals in the minds of the people of both races. To induce people to go for examination was almost impossible." J. Edward Perry, *Forty Cords of Wood: Memoirs of a Medical Doctor* (Jefferson City, Mo.: Lincoln University, 1947), 259.

37. Damon Sauve, "Everything Is Optimism, Beautiful and Painless: A Conversation with Harry Crews," in *Getting Naked with Harry Crews*, ed. Erik Bledsoe (Gainesville: University of Florida Press, 1999), 323–24.

38. A poignant example of the cultural misunderstandings involved in health care is Trudier Harris's account of how well-meaning white dentists extracted the permanent teeth of black children in her public school in Tuscaloosa around 1950 instead of filling the cavities. Harris, *Summer Snow*, chap. 4 ("Dental Charity").

39. Charles Victor Roman, *Meharry Medical College: A History* (Nashville: Sunday School Publishing Board of the National Baptist Convention, 1934), 85 (first and second quotations); Hurston, "Hoodoo in America," 320 (third and fourth quotations).

40. Clarence Cason told this story about his father, an Alabama doctor, in *90 Degrees in the Shade* (1935; repr., Westport, Conn.: Negro Universities Press, 1970), vii–viii. The quotations from Abington appear in *Back Roads and Bicarbonate*, 110 (first quotation), 157 (second quotation). Abington's racist remarks were not casual; he was a determined segregationist. He referred to "lily-white territory" (65) and argued that miscegenation inevitably produced inferior offspring (157).

41. Carl A. Whitaker and Thomas P. Malone, *The Roots of Psychotherapy* (New York: Blakiston, 1953), viii (first quotation), 40 (second quotation), 41 (third quotation). Although neither Whitaker nor Malone was a native southerner, Whitaker sensed an affinity between his program and the South when he described Atlanta to an official of the Rockefeller Foundation: "I am amazed at how fertile the soil is and it offers the opportunity of doing what I feel is rather a pioneering job at teaching psychiatry." Carl A. Whitaker to Robert S. Morrison, Jan. 27, 1947, box 127, folder 1120, RG 1.2, series 200A, RF Archives. Whitaker did not seek to evoke a southern medical style specifically so much as to teach doctors the personal engagement of traditional practice.

42. Frank H. Luton and Paul L. Boynton, "A Study of Mental Health Needs in Tennessee: A Report to Honorable George H. Cate, Commissioner of Institutions and Public Welfare" (typescript, Dec. 1938), chap. 4, [5] (first quotation), chap. 3, [3] (second quotation), box 7, folder 2, Frank H. Luton Papers, VUMC. Among Luton's papers is an invitation to a 1953 meeting to discuss sterilization, accompanied by informational documents. Edward L. Bridges (Tennessee public service director) to Frank H. Luton, July 2, 1953, box 6, folder 46, Luton Papers. Supplemental materials, presumably provided by Bridges, include "Sterilization of Mental Defectives" (typescript); T. G. Peacock, "Georgia Program for Sterilization" (typescript); and *Sterilizations Reported in the United States to January 1, 1954* (New York: Human Betterment Association of America, 1954). There is no evidence that Luton attended the meeting or became involved in the eugenics initiative. The principal study of southern eugenics is Edward J. Larson, *Sex, Race, and Science: Eugenics in the Deep South* (Baltimore: Johns Hopkins University Press, 1995). On mental institutions during slavery, see Samuel B. Thielman, "Southern Madness: The Shape of Mental Health Care in the Old South," in *Science and Medicine in the Old South*, ed. Ronald L. Numbers and Todd L. Savitt (Baton Rouge: Louisiana State University Press, 1989), esp. 262–75. McCandless makes a solid argument that

therapeutic efforts in antebellum public asylums in South Carolina declined after the Civil War because of the institutions' financial hardship; see *Moonlight, Magnolias, and Madness*, esp. chap. 13. On similar institutions in the South and elsewhere, see Steven Noll, *Feeble-Minded in Our Midst: Institutions for the Mentally Retarded in the South, 1900–1940* (Chapel Hill: University of North Carolina Press, 1995); David J. Rothman, *Conscience and Convenience: The Asylum and Its Alternatives in Progressive America* (Boston: Little, Brown, 1980); and Gerald N. Grob, *The Mad among Us: A History of the Care of America's Mentally Ill* (New York: Free Press, 1994), esp. chaps. 6–9.

43. Quoted in McCandless, *Moonlight, Magnolias, and Madness*, 109. Observations about public access to the Tennessee hospital are in Luton and Boynton, "Study of Mental Health Needs in Tennessee," chap. 3, [3].

44. McLaurin, *Separate Pasts*, 15–17.

45. *R. L. Polk's 1901 Memphis City Directory*, 94, microfilm, MPL; *R. L. Polk's 1910 Memphis City Directory*, between 2060 and 2061, microfilm, MPL. The title of the city directory varied; I use a single title in notes for the sake of clarity.

46. Although Jacqueline Anne Rouse states in her introduction to the finding aid for the Neighborhood Union Collection that the project originated in 1908, clinical records began in the mid-1910s. The Neighborhood Union Collection, 1908–1961 (1995), v, AUC. Among illnesses seen at one location, the Summerhill Clinic, in 1917, there were cases of "senile asthenia" (May 18), "shylisis [*sic*] and measles" (May 15), and "hereditary syphilis" (May 17). Typescript, box 5, folder 13, Neighborhood Union Collection, AUC.

47. A. S. Edwards, *The Fundamental Principles of Learning and Study* (Baltimore: Warwick and York, 1920), 64 (first quotation), 175 (second quotation). On the British psychological tradition, represented in the United States by the émigré Edward Bradford Titchener of Cornell University, Edwards's first doctoral adviser, see Edwin G. Boring, *A History of Experimental Psychology*, 2d ed. (New York: Appleton-Century-Crofts, 1950), 219–45, 410–20. Titchener and Edwards both earned doctorates under the pioneering German psychologist Wilhelm Wundt. Boring, *History of Experimental Psychology*, 316–47. For biographical information on Edwards and his efforts to make psychology a laboratory science in Georgia, see Roger K. Thomas, "An Historical Overview of the Department of Psychology at the University of Georgia," ⟨http://www.uga.edu/psychology/about/history.htm⟩ (June 14, 2008). On the habit in southern higher education of considering psychology a foundational discipline when its subject remained the normative mind, see James L. Pate, "The Southern Society for Philosophy and Psychology," in *No Small Part: A History of Regional Organizations in American Psychology*, ed. James L. Pate (Washington, D.C.: American Psychological Association, 1993), 12.

48. "A Feudal Land" is the subtitle of part 1 of Egerton, *Speak Now against the Day*, and refers here to the South during the years 1932–38. The southern statistic, which included college graduates of both races, appears in ibid., 26. "Middletown" was Muncie, Indiana. Robert S. Lynd and Helen Merrill Lynd, *Middletown: A Study in American Culture* (1929; repr., New York: Harcourt, Brace, Jovanovich, 1956), 183.

49. Mark Twain, *The Adventures of Huckleberry Finn* (New York: Holt, Rinehart, and Winston, 1948), 3 (first and second quotations), 16 (Jim's hair-ball).

50. William Faulkner, *The Sound and the Fury* (New York: Vintage, 1946), esp. "April Seventh, 1928."

51. Charlie May Simon, *Johnswood* (New York: Dutton, 1953), 57 (first quotation); [Lillian Smith], "A Brief Account of Things from 1954–64" (manuscript, n.d.), 24, box 1, folder 1, Lillian E. Smith Papers, collection 1283, UGA (second quotation).

52. Author's Questionnaire, 3, Apr. 8, 1940, folder 58, series 2, subseries 1, Joseph L. Morrison Papers, collection 3787, UNC. Please note that in Cash's typescripts there may be multiple pages of the same number, missing pages, and writing on fronts and backs of pages. On the Author's Questionnaire, the date 1936 also appears; it is possible that Cash began the form in 1936 and finished it when he completed his book.

53. W. J. Cash to Blanche W. Knopf, Mar. 9, 1936, folder 57, series 2, subseries 1, Morrison Papers (first quotation); W. J. Cash to Paula Snelling, Mar. 10, 1938, folder 57, series 2, subseries 1, Morrison Papers (second quotation); W. J. Cash to R. P. Harriss, Mar. 10, 1941, folder 60, series 2, subseries 1, Morrison Papers (third quotation).

54. "Application for John Simon Guggenheim Memorial Fellowship" (Oct. 20, 1932), 1, folder 56, series 2, subseries 1, Morrison Papers (first and second quotations); "1941 [Guggenheim] Application" (typescript, Oct. 1940), 1, folder 59, series 2, subseries 1, Morrison Papers (third and fourth quotations); Author's Questionnaire, 3 (fifth and sixth quotations). Biographies of Cash include Joseph L. Morrison, *W. J. Cash: Southern Prophet* (New York: Knopf, 1967), and Bruce Clayton, *W. J. Cash: A Life* (Baton Rouge: Louisiana State University Press, 1991). See also Paul D. Escott, ed., *W. J. Cash and the Minds of the South* (Baton Rouge: Louisiana State University Press, 1992).

55. "Application for John Simon Guggenheim Memorial Fellowship," 2, 3 (first and second quotations); W. J. Cash to Paula Snelling, June 27, 1938, folder 57, series 2, subseries 1, Morrison Papers (third quotation).

56. Claude B. Squires quoted in Morrison, *W. J. Cash*, 56. On the tests at Johns Hopkins, see ibid., 56, 137.

57. On Cash's friendship with his doctor, see Morrison, *W. J. Cash*, 79–80. On Adolf Meyer, see Barbara Sicherman, "The New Psychiatry: Medical and Behavioral Science, 1895–1921," in *American Psychoanalysis: Origins and Development*, ed. Jacques M. Quen and Eric T. Carlson (New York: Brunner/Mazel, 1978), 20–37.

58. Author's Questionnaire, 3 (quotation). Cash named Watson in his article "Close View of a Calvinist Lhasa," published in *American Mercury* in 1933 and cited in Joseph L. Morrison, "The Obsessive Mind of W. J. Cash," *Virginia Quarterly Review* 41 (1965): 280. On Watson, see Kerry W. Buckley, *Mechanical Man: John Broadus Watson and the Beginnings of Behaviorism* (New York: Guilford Press, 1989), esp. 3–4. Although both of Cash's biographers note that he read Freud (Morrison, "Obsessive Mind," 280; Clayton, *W. J. Cash*, 58), his reading was grounded in classical authors. On his 1940 Guggenheim application, Cash listed Ecclesiastes, Homer, Chaucer, Montaigne, and Shakespeare, among many others. "1941 [Guggenheim] Application," 3.

59. W. J. Cash, "The Mind of the South," *American Mercury* 18 (1929): 185, 187.

60. Morrison, *W. J. Cash*, 64 (first quotation), 65 (second and third quotations).

61. W. J. Cash to Alfred Knopf, May 17, 1936, folder 57, series 2, subseries 1, Morrison Papers (first quotation); W. J. Cash to Alfred Knopf, July 27, 1940, folder 59, series 2, subseries 1, Morrison Papers (second quotation); Cash, "Mind of the South," 187 (third quotation).

62. Mary Cash Maury, "The 'Mysterious' Suicide of W. J. Cash" (typescript, n.d.), 8, box 6, series 2, subseries 1, Morrison Papers. Mary wrote this and several similar accounts of her short marriage at the request of Joseph Morrison. See Joseph Morrison to Mary Cash Maury, Sept. 9, 1964, folder 68, series 2, subseries 1, Morrison Papers.

63. W. J. Cash to R. P. Harriss, Mar. 10, 1941, folder 57, series 2, subseries 1, Morrison Papers (first quotation); Maury, "'Mysterious' Suicide," 9A.

64. Maury, "'Mysterious' Suicide," 13. Most scholars of Cash have struggled to explain his suicide. See Morrison, *W. J. Cash*, chap. 6; Clayton, *W. J. Cash*, chap. 9; and Bertram Wyatt-Brown, "Creativity and Suffering in a Southern Writer," in Escott, *W. J. Cash*, 38–64. A number of obituaries are in folder 60, series 2, subseries 1, Morrison Papers.

65. *Life Is My Song: The Autobiography of John Gould Fletcher* (New York: Farrar and Rinehart, 1937), 368. Although Fletcher did not name the hospital where he was a patient during this period (winter 1932–33), it was the notorious Royal Bethlehem Hospital—"Bedlam"—in London. Ben F. Johnson III, *Fierce Solitude: A Life of John Gould Fletcher* (Fayetteville: University of Arkansas Press, 1994), 195.

66. Johnson, *Fierce Solitude*, 147 (first quotation); Charlie May Simon Fletcher to Tema and George Cohen, Nov. 7, 1944, box 39, folder 78, series 5, Fletcher Papers (second and third quotations). Charlie May told the Cohens about the attempted suicide in a letter dated Oct. 27, 1944 (same folder), adding, "I feel like I'm in a madhouse when I'm around that family." Fletcher's hospitalizations occurred in 1926, 1932–33, 1934, and 1944–45; in 1932 he attempted suicide by jumping from a window. Johnson, *Fierce Solitude*, 195. Fletcher's depressions began in 1907, when he was a student at Harvard, and recurred approximately every five years. Johnson, *Fierce Solitude*, esp. 28–31.

67. Charlie May Fletcher to John Gould Fletcher, Feb. 17, 1949, box 47, folder 376, series 2, Fletcher Papers (first quotation); manuscript notes by L. Turner, R.N., 1934, box 33A, folder 7, series 5, Fletcher Papers (second and third quotations); Fletcher, *Life Is My Song*, 318 (fourth quotation), 319 (fifth quotation). Whether the 1934 incident occurred at a Little Rock or Memphis hospital is unclear. A report of electric shock therapy appears in Fletcher, diary, Feb. 7, 1945, "Diary 1945"; the use of Luminal appears in manuscript notes by L. Turner; and references to shots appear in his diary, June 30, July 1, July 3, 1945, "Diary 1945."

68. Fletcher, diary, July 25, 1945, "Diary 1945" (first quotation); Charlie May Fletcher to Tema and George Cohen, Dec. 12, 1944, box 39, folder 78, series 5, Fletcher Papers (second quotation). Fletcher noted in his 1945 diary on May 10 that his wife had asked him for a separation for the second time.

69. Ellen Herman shows that psychology increased its visibility in American society

because of the war, both in relation to the emotional well-being of men and women in the military and other wartime issues. Ellen Herman, *The Romance of American Psychology: Political Culture in the Age of Experts, 1940–1970* (Berkeley: University of California Press, 1995), esp. chap. 4.

70. Fletcher, diary, Sept. 23, 1939, untitled diary, box 9, folder 86, series 2, Fletcher Papers (first quotation); Fletcher, diary, Feb. 6–7, 1949, "Diary Mar.–June 1949," box 12, folder 119, series 2, Fletcher Papers (second and third quotations); Fletcher, diary, Sept. 19, 1926, 1926 diary, box 5, folder 56, series 2, Fletcher Papers (fourth quotation); Fletcher, diary, Feb. 6–7, 1949, "Diary Mar.–June 1949" (fifth quotation). Despite the dates on the cover of "Diary Mar.–June 1949," the first entry is Nov. 1, 1948.

71. Fletcher argued against a utilitarian and democratic system of education and for schooling that promoted self-mastery in conditions of leisure for a white elite. John Gould Fletcher, "Education, Past and Present," in Twelve Southerners, *I'll Take My Stand: The South and the Agrarian Tradition*, ed. Louis D. Rubin Jr. (1930; repr., Baton Rouge: Louisiana State University Press, 1962), 93–121. Although there was no anti-Semitism here, this was an element in the thinking of Christian conservatives such as T. S. Eliot, an acquaintance of Fletcher in England at a time when Eliot was moving from modernism to Anglicanism. Fletcher wrote in his diary that he got drunk with Eliot on Aug. 2, 1926, 1926 diary.

72. Fletcher, diary, ca. Nov. 12, 1945–Feb. 11, 1946, "Sept. 21, 1945–Feb. 28, 1946" diary, box 11, folder 107, series 2, Fletcher Papers. On Fletcher's suicide, see Johnson, *Fierce Solitude*, 251–54. Condolence cards, obituaries, and other papers relating to his death are in box 33B, folder 14, series 5, Fletcher Papers.

73. Fletcher seemed to describe an ideal state when he found "mountains of meat, fruit, candy, cigarettes, and liquor" in San Francisco. Fletcher, diary, Aug. 1, 1945, "Diary 1945." He smoked five packs of cigarettes on Aug. 10, 1938 (1938 diary, box 9, folder 83, series 2, Fletcher Papers), and twenty-two cigarettes on a bad night, Dec. 9, 1939 (untitled diary). He had gone to a water cure when Charlie May wrote to him about a doctor overseeing his "baths." Jan. 1948, box 47, folder 376, series 2, Fletcher Papers.

74. Fletcher's version of the Lord's Prayer appears in Fletcher, diary, n.d., "Apr. 1, 1945–Sept. 21, 1945" diary, box 11, folder 106, series 2, Fletcher Papers. His self-styled creed appears in his diary, Nov. 23, 1949, "Diary Mar.–June 1949," box 12, folder 119, series 2, Fletcher Papers. He noted here that he had written these thoughts down months before, on July 18.

75. Fletcher, diary, Nov. 1, 1948 (first and second quotations), Nov. 21, 1948 (third quotation), Nov. 1, 1948 (fourth quotation), all in "Diary Mar.–June 1949." Fletcher discussed Merton's book in his diary on Nov. 19, 1948, in ibid.

76. Fletcher, diary, April 28, 1945, "Diary 1945."

77. Ralph McGill, "Miss Smith and Freud," *Atlanta Constitution*, Nov. 24, 1949, 18B.

78. Lillian Smith to Guy B. Johnson, June 12, 1944, in *How Am I to Be Heard? Letters of Lillian Smith*, ed. Margaret Rose Gladney (Chapel Hill: University of North Carolina

Press, 1993), 86 (first, second, and third quotations); Lillian Smith to Lawrence Kubie, June 2, 1955, in ibid., 168 (fourth quotation); Menninger quoted in "Report from Lillian Smith on Killers of the Dream," Feb. 18, 1950, in ibid., 131 (fifth quotation).

79. McGill, "Miss Smith and Freud," 18B. On these events in Smith's life, see Anne C. Loveland, *Lillian Smith: A Southerner Confronting the South* (Baton Rouge: Louisiana State University Press, 1986), esp. 113, 129, 176–77, and, especially on the fire, Lillian Smith to Denver Lindley, Dec. 1?, 1955, in Smith, *How Am I to Be Heard*, 179–81. The years of appearance of her cancers were 1953, 1955, 1958, 1960, 1963, and 1965.

80. Lillian Smith to Charles S. Johnson, July 28, 1955, in Smith, *How Am I to Be Heard*, 176.

81. Lawrence Kubie to Lillian Smith, Oct. 17, 1949 (first quotation); Lawrence Kubie to Lillian Smith, Apr. 11, 1961 (second quotation); Lillian Smith to Lawrence Kubie, Sept. 30, 1954 (third quotation); Lawrence Kubie to Lillian Smith, July 30, 1954 (fourth quotation); Lawrence Kubie to Lillian Smith, Oct. 6, 1954 (fifth, sixth, and seventh quotations), all in box 57, folder "Lillian Smith," Lawrence S. Kubie Papers, LC. For his work on the psychology of creativity, see Lawrence S. Kubie, *Neurotic Distortion of the Creative Process* (Lawrence: University of Kansas Press, 1958). On his liberalism, he wrote to Smith periodically between 1958 and 1965 about his efforts to integrate Johns Hopkins's medical school and the psychiatric profession. See box 15, folder 58, Smith Papers. There was a romantic quality to their relationship, particularly on the part of Kubie, who seemed swept away by Smith's writing. Lawrence Kubie to Storer Lunt, Oct. 17, 1949, box 57, folder "Lillian Smith 404-782-3196," Kubie Papers. Lawrence Kubie (1896–1973) was divorced for the second time in 1948 and remarried briefly in 1962–63; Smith remained single throughout her life. "Biographical Note," Lawrence Kubie Finding Aid, LC.

82. On plans for his trip in March 1966, see Lillian Smith to Lawrence Kubie, Nov. 5, 1965, box 57, folder "Lillian Smith," Kubie Papers.

83. Lawrence Kubie to Lillian Smith, Sept. 2, 1955 (first quotation); Lawrence Kubie to Lillian Smith, Aug. 30, 1956 (second and third quotations), both in box 57, folder "Lillian Smith 404-782-3196," Kubie Papers. He wrote to the cancer specialist, Henry P. Randall, Aug. 24, 1955, box 57, folder "Lillian Smith," Kubie Papers. Elisabeth Kübler-Ross's contemporaneous classic, *On Death and Dying* (New York: Macmillan, 1969), esp. 25–33, is in part a plea for greater candor with all patients on the part of doctors, caregivers, and family members. Kübler-Ross's interviews with dying patients suggest that truthfulness about the severity of a person's illness was not then the norm.

84. Lillian Smith to Lawrence Kubie, Sept. 30, 1954, box 57, folder "Lillian Smith," Kubie Papers (first quotation); Lillian Smith to Lawrence Kubie, Jan. 30, 1957, box 57, folder "Lillian Smith 404-782-3196," Kubie Papers (second quotation).

85. Lillian Smith to Lawrence Kubie, Jan. 30, 1957 (first quotation); Lillian Smith to Paul Tillich, Nov. 17, 1959 (second and third quotations); Lillian Smith to Dorothy Canfield Fisher, Mar. 10, 1956 (fourth quotation), in Smith, *How Am I to Be Heard*, 205, 234, 198.

86. [Smith], "Brief Account of Things," 34 (first and second quotations); Smith to

Tillich, Nov. 17, 1959 (third quotation), and Smith to Kubie, Jan. 30, 1957 (fourth and fifth quotations), in Smith, *How Am I to Be Heard*, 233, 205.

87. Smith, *Killers of the Dream*, 24 (first quotation), 25 (second quotation). Smith made many lists of writers, psychoanalysts among them, who influenced her. In *Killers of the Dream*, for example, she mentioned Sigmund Freud, Karl Menninger, Sandor Ferenczi, Hanns Sachs, and Géza Róheim (10–11).

88. Lillian Smith to Lawrence Kubie, Oct. 10, 1957, in Smith, *How Am I to Be Heard*, 219.

89. [Lillian Smith], "What Books Influenced Me? And What Use?" (typescript, n.d.), 41, box 1, folder 1, Smith Papers. Smith's biographer notes that she was secretive. Loveland, *Lillian Smith*, 193.

90. Richard Robbins, *Sidelines Activist: Charles S. Johnson and the Struggle for Civil Rights* (Jackson: University of Mississippi Press, 1996), 176. Bobby himself referred to his "minor 'breakdowns'" as well as other times of forthright search for help in a letter to his mother, Marie, Feb. 2, 1957, box 154, folder 3 ("Robert, 1938–64"), Charles S. Johnson Papers, Fisk. Robbins notes that the daughter of Charles S. Johnson did not release family correspondence to him (*Sidelines Activist*, xi), suggesting the family's continuing wish for privacy about this and other matters. Robbins's fullest discussion of Bobby appears in *Sidelines Activist*, 211–12 n. 27.

91. Robert Johnson to Charles Johnson, Apr. 7, 1954, box 154, folder 3, Charles S. Johnson Papers.

92. Robert Johnson to Marie Johnson, 1947, box 154, folder 3, Charles S. Johnson Papers. His father tried to reverse Bobby's rejection by the doctoral program of the University of Chicago's Department of Sociology. Charles Johnson to Everett C. Hughes, Sept. 7, 1946, box 154, folder 3, Charles S. Johnson Papers. On Bobby's drinking, see Robert Johnson to Charles Johnson, May 15, 1955, box 154, folder 3, Charles S. Johnson Papers. On his divorce, see Robert Johnson to Charles and Marie Johnson, Apr. 8, 1956, and Feb. 2, 1957, box 154, folder 3, Charles S. Johnson Papers.

93. Robert Johnson to Charles Johnson, Apr. 7, 1954. Although the letter began "Dear Dad," he slipped into addressing both parents.

94. Robbins, *Sidelines Activist*, 165.

95. Robert Johnson to Charles Johnson, May 15, 1955 (first quotation), Apr. 7, 1954 (second quotation), May 15, 1955 (third quotation), box 154, folder 3, Charles S. Johnson Papers. In a letter to his mother following his father's death in Oct. 1956, Bobby demonstrated greater psychological awareness than earlier, including references to laboratory experiments using rats and to psychiatric commonplaces. Robert Johnson to Marie Johnson, Feb. 2, 1957, box 154, folder 3, Charles S. Johnson Papers. Whether he had received more therapy by this time or picked up psychological knowledge through his work is unclear. He appears in all his letters to be a person of self-awareness who struggled to communicate with his parents. In his Feb. 2, 1957, letter to his mother, he described his two-sided personality: on the one hand, a man of "great potential," and on the other, "uncertain, anxious, nervous, under strain, drinking, insomnia-type, withdrawing, funny combination of complance [*sic*] and rebellion." For Charles Johnson's

tribute to Harry Stack Sullivan, see Charles Johnson, "The Contribution of Harry Stack Sullivan to Sociology" (typescript, address delivered at Hunter College, New York, Oct. 14, 1951), box 159, folder 20, Charles S. Johnson Papers.

96. Robert Johnson to Charles Johnson, n.d. (first quotation); Robert Johnson to Charles and Marie Johnson, n.d. (second quotation), both in box 154, folder 4, Charles S. Johnson Papers.

97. Janice D. Stanton to Robert B. Johnson, Dr. and Mrs. Maurice [Patricia Johnson] Clifford, Jeh V. Johnson, and Dr. and Mrs. Charles S. Johnson Jr., June 26, 1952; Charles Johnson to Charles S. Johnson Jr., Feb. 1, 1945; Charles Johnson to Robert Johnson, Feb. 1, 1945, all in box 144, folder 3, Charles S. Johnson Papers. It is true that Stanton was communicating with the children while the Johnsons were in Europe; it seems, however, that Charles Johnson's letter to her contained business mixed with travel news, and she extracted the latter for the children. He similarly asked his wife to serve on university committees by means of notes sent from the office typed by a secretary. Charles Johnson to Marie Johnson, Sept. 5 and 14, 1953, box 144, folder 8, Charles S. Johnson Papers. Both sons trained in the air force at Tuskegee, Alabama, during the war, and Johnson now advised them to set up an "airline transport service."

98. Robert Johnson to Charles and Marie Johnson, n.d. (first quotation); Robert Johnson to Charles and Marie Johnson, n.d. (second quotation); Robert Johnson to Patricia Johnson Clifford, n.d. (third quotation), all in box 154, folder 4, Charles S. Johnson Papers. What finally happened to Bobby is unclear. Although Robbins writes in *Sidelines Activist* (37) that he became a professor of sociology at Central State College in Wilberforce, Ohio, the college has no record of his employment. I am grateful to Sheila Darrow, who searched college and local records for me, without result. Sheila L. Darrow, e-mail message to the author, Apr. 22, 2005. Without a record of his last place of residence, I have not been able to obtain an obituary.

99. McCandless, *Moonlight, Magnolias, and Madness*, 198.

100. Lloyd C. Elam, "Development of the Department of Psychiatry at Meharry Medical College," in Spurlock, *Black Psychiatrists and American Psychiatry*, 69. Biographical information on Elam appears in a sketch in *Modern Medicine*, Jan. 15, 1975, 57, clipping, Lloyd Charles Elam Papers, MMC.

101. All the Percys were treated in Baltimore: Walker Percy of Birmingham entered Sheppard and Enoch Pratt Hospital in 1911; his sister Lady Percy McKinney of Knoxville was treated at Phipps Psychiatric Clinic in 1917; his son, Le Roy, also of Birmingham, went to Phipps in 1925; and Le Roy's son, Phinizy, of Greenville, Mississippi, was taken there for nightmares in 1932. Wyatt-Brown, *House of Percy*, 248, 251, 253, 275.

102. Le Roy Percy to Hampton Springs Hotel, Hampton Springs, Fla., Oct. 31, 1928, reel 7 (1922–28), Percy Family Papers, Mississippi Department of Archives and History, Jackson. On Camille's treatment at the Battle Creek Sanitarium, Battle Creek, Mich., and the Glen Springs Sanitarium, Watkins, N.Y., see Le Roy Percy to Battle Creek Sanitarium, Sept. 17, 1928, reel 7, and William Alexander Percy to Lucy R. Watkins, Sept. 3, 1921, reel 8 (1929), Percy Family Papers. Note that the Le Roy Percy of

Greenville, Mississippi, who wrote these letters and was the husband of Camille was not the Le Roy Percy of Birmingham who was hospitalized for depression.

103. On these personal connections, see Anne C. Rose, "Putting the South on the Psychological Map: The Impact of Region and Race on the Human Sciences during the 1930s," *Journal of Southern History* 71 (2005): 321–22. Sullivan was a psychiatrist at the Sheppard-Pratt hospital in the 1920s, not Phipps Psychiatric Clinic, where Le Roy was a patient, but he may have been called in by his friend Adolf Meyer, the founder of Phipps. Sullivan's connection with Johnson, who completed graduate work in sociology under Robert Park at the University of Chicago, may have been through Edward Sapir, an anthropologist at Chicago in the 1920s and Sullivan's friend and collaborator. See Helen Swick Perry, *Psychiatrist of America: The Life of Harry Stack Sullivan* (Cambridge, Mass.: Harvard University Press, 1982), chaps. 23, 27, 28. See also Harry Stack Sullivan, "Memorandum of a Psychiatric Reconnaissance," appendix to Charles S. Johnson, *Growing Up in the Black Belt: Negro Youth in the Rural South* (1941; repr., New York: Schocken Books, 1967), 328–33.

104. Percy to Battle Creek Sanitarium, Sept. 17, 1928.

105. On the development of health institutions by the Battle Creek Adventists, see Ronald L. Numbers, *Prophetess of Health: Ellen G. White and the Origins of Seventh-Day Adventist Health Reforms*, rev. ed. (Knoxville: University of Tennessee Press, 1992), esp. chap. 5.

106. The quotation described P. J. Sparer, in Jane Sanderson, "'Policy with God' Pays Off Well," *Memphis Press-Scimitar*, Sept. 6, 1971, clipping, Biography Files, Memphis and Shelby County Room, MPL. For Sparer's biography, see "Dr. P. J. Sparer, Noted Psychiatrist," *Memphis Press-Scimitar*, Oct. 10, 1977, clipping, Biography Files, Memphis and Shelby County Room, MPL. The history of Nicholas Gotten, the doctor with Confederate ancestry, appears in Christina Lambard, "Dr. Gotten Had Illustrious Neurosurgery Career," *Memphis Commercial Appeal*, Oct. 17, 1996, A13, clipping, and "Nicholas Gotten" (typescript, n.d.), both in Biography Files, Memphis and Shelby County Room, MPL. The latter also appears in James D. Porter, *Confederate Military Heroes* (Atlanta: Confederate, 1899), 8:509. On the training of Gartly and Ramsay at Battle Creek and their Canadian origins, see Wayne Chastain, "Gartly-Ramsay Plans to Close January 1," *Memphis Press-Scimitar*, Dec. 15, 1972, clipping, folder "Gartly-Ramsay Hospital," Memphis and Shelby County Room, MPL.

107. "Gartly & Ramsay Hospital" advertisement, *R. L. Polk's 1910 Memphis City Directory*, between 2060 and 2061, microfilm, MPL.

108. Chastain, "Gartly-Ramsay Plans to Close" (quotation). Fletcher referred to "Dr. Turner" in his diary, Jan. 2 and 3, 1945, "Diary 1945." This was most likely Carrol C. Turner, who became chief of staff of Gartly-Ramsay Hospital in 1933 ("Dr. Turner Is Named Hospital Staff Head," *Memphis Commercial Appeal*, Jan. 27, 1933, clipping, folder "Gartly-Ramsay Hospital," Memphis and Shelby County Room, MPL) and who is described as the only full-time psychiatrist then in Memphis in D. C. McCool and Carrol C. Turner, "Psychiatry," in *History of Medicine in Memphis*, ed. Marcus Stewart

and William Black Jr. (Jackson, Tenn.: McCourt-Mercer Press, 1971), 283. By the time Fletcher arrived in Memphis, Turner may have established his own hospital; he nonetheless began at Gartly-Ramsay. On Faulkner's connection with the hospital, see Wayne Risher, "Salvation Army Taking Hospital Site," *Memphis Commercial Appeal*, July 16, 1998, clipping, folder "Gartly-Ramsay Hospital," Memphis and Shelby County Room, MPL, and Patricia M. LaPointe (curator, Memphis and Shelby County Room), e-mail message to the author, May 11, 2003.

109. Buckley, *Mechanical Man*, 39–41.

110. For biographical information on Luton, see "Noted Psychiatric Doctor F. H. Luton Dies," *Nashville Tennessean*, Oct. 11, 1986?, clipping, folder "Frank Harper Luton, M.D., 1898–1979," Luton Papers. On his attitude toward returning home to practice, see Frank H. Luton to Evelyn Ridley, Feb. 14, 1930, box 1, folder 2, Luton Papers. His reform work led in 1938 to Luton and Boynton, "Study of Mental Health Needs in Tennessee." Meyer's phrase appears in Adolf Meyer to Edward Bradford Titchener, Sept. 18, 1909, box 2, folder Aug.–Sept. 1909, Edward Bradford Titchener Papers, collection 14-23-545, Division of Rare and Manuscript Collections, Cornell University Library, Ithaca, N.Y. A decade later, Meyer described his view of "a biological psychology as one of the 'natural sciences.'" Adolf Meyer to Edward Bradford Titchener, Nov. 5, 1918, box 5, folder June 6–Dec. 31, 1918, Titchener Papers.

111. "Boston Rites Monday for Dr. Moore, Poet: Cancer Fatal to Psychiatrist, Member of Vanderbilt Fugitives," *Nashville Tennessean*, Sept. 21, 1957, clipping, folder 2, Merrill Moore Papers, VUMC.

112. Moore's literary production was calculated by Henry W. Wells, *Poet and Psychiatrist: Merrill Moore, M.D.; A Critical Portrait* (New York: Twayne, 1955), 220. Frost wrote an obituary, "Merrill Moore, 1903–1957," *Harvard Medical Alumni Bulletin* 32 (1958): 25, clipping, folder 2, Moore Papers, VUMC. Moore is identified as Frost's psychiatrist in "Boston Rites Monday for Dr. Moore." On the Fugitives' reunion, see Ralph Morrissey, "The Fugitives Return," *Vanderbilt Alumnus*, May–June 1956, clipping, folder 2, Moore Papers, VUMC. The article appeared originally in the *New York Times Magazine*.

113. Merrill Moore to Frank Luton, Oct. 14, 1932 (quotation); Merrill Moore to Frank Luton, Oct. 2, 1932; Merrill Moore to Frank Luton, Apr. 18, 1941, all in folder 2, Moore Papers, VUMC. On his swimming, see Wells, *Poet and Psychiatrist*, 224, and Frost, "Merrill Moore." On the disposition of his body, see the obituary in the *Nashville Banner*, Sept. 20, 1957, clipping, folder 2, Moore Papers, VUMC.

114. [Merrill Moore], untitled typescript (n.d.), box B-174, folder "Third Grade," Merrill Moore Papers, LC (quotation). I base my inference about Hirsch on the fact that he taught Moore Yiddish and my inference about Starr on his name and Moore's persistence in using him as a source of assistance for Holocaust refugees. Starr was Moore's companion on a trip to Europe in 1928. On these relationships, see Wells, *Poet and Psychiatrist*, 60, 64. Moore was identified as a Methodist in his obituary in the *Nashville Banner*, Sept. 20, 1957. On the placement of Holocaust refugees at traditionally black colleges (in which Moore had no part), see Gabrielle Simon Edgcomb, *From Swastika to Jim Crow: Refugee Scholars at Black Colleges* (Malabar, Fla.: Krieger, 1993).

115. Merrill Moore to Hanns Sachs, Aug. 26, 1939, box B-48, folder "Hanns Sachs, 1939," Moore Papers, LC. Wells notes Moore's training analysis with Sachs in *Poet and Psychiatrist*, 113. It was a matter of bitter disappointment to Moore that the Boston Psychoanalytic Society denied his application for admission. Merrill Moore to Hanns Sachs, Aug. 24, 1939, box B-48, folder "Hanns Sachs, 1939," Moore Papers, LC. On these favors for Sachs, see Merrill Moore to Hanns Sachs, Mar. 29, 1936; Merrill Moore to Milton Lord (director, Boston Public Library), Nov. 3, 1936; CAP, Harcourt, Brace, and Company to Merrill Moore, Nov. 30, 1936; and Merrill Moore to Hanns Sachs, Jan. 31, 1936, all in box B-48, folder "1936," and Merrill Moore to Hanns Sachs, Mar. 3, 1938, box B-48, folder "1938," Moore Papers, LC.

116. Merrill Moore to Hanns Sachs, Aug. 3, 1938, box B-48, folder "1938," Moore Papers, LC. See also Merrill Moore to Israel Newman, Sept. 16, 1938, box B-48, folder "1938," Moore Papers, LC. On Starr's assistance with publishing, see Milton Starr to Hanns Sachs, Oct. 21, 1938, and [B.?] Davis, W. B. Ziff Company, to Milton Starr, n.d., both in box B-48, folder "1938," Moore Papers, LC. Moore tried to find a job for an Austrian legal scholar at Vanderbilt. Merrill Moore to Dean E. C. Arnold, Vanderbilt Law School, Sept. 15, 1936 (typescript copy), box B-48, folder "1936," Moore Papers, LC. He intervened with the Starrs to provide financial aid for other refugee scholars. See Hanns Sachs to Merrill Moore, June 15, 1939, and Milton Starr to Merrill Moore, Sept. 15, 1939, box B-48, folder "1939," Moore Papers, LC. He also tried to help with the unsuccessful immigration of Walter Benjamin. Merrill Moore to Hanns Sachs, Nov. 7, 1939, box B-48, folder "1939," Moore Papers, LC.

117. Hanns Sachs to Merrill Moore, Feb. 24, 1938, box B-48, folder "1938," Moore Papers, LC.

118. Robert A. Lambert to Willard C. Rappleye, Jan. 22, 1938, box 136, folder 1257, series 1.1, GEB Archives. On Williams, see his "Personal History Record and Application for Fellowship," Mar. 26, 1931; "Medical Examination," n.d.; and "Agreement" (to take a position at Howard after the fellowship), Mar. 26, 1931, all in box 28, folder 268, series 1.1, GEB Archives. On Dai, see Lawrence K. Frank to Tracy B. Kittredge, Feb. 17, 1932, and John Dollard to Stacy May, Dec. 17, 1932, box 408, folder 4829, RG 1.1, series 200s, RF Archives.

119. On Dai's career in the American South, see chapter 4. Hernandez and Williams had to pledge to return to black medical schools as a condition of accepting Rockefeller funding. On Williams's selling real estate, see Spurlock, "Early and Contemporary Pioneers," 7. On the inquiry about Hernandez's credentials, see D. G. Gill to General Education Board, June 16, 1955, and Katherine E. Oster to D. G. Gill, June 21, 1955, both in box 136, folder 1257, series 1.1, GEB Archives. On his career path, see [Mary Nieves Hernandez], "Rafael Hernandez, Sr." (typescript, n.d.), and Mary Nieves Hernandez, untitled offprint, *BPA Quarterly* 17 (1988): 4–5, both in folder "Meharry Medical College, Biographical Collection, Hernandez, Rafael, Sr., 1897–1976," MMC.

120. For a sense of E. Y. Williams's scholarly contribution, see his "Some Observations on the Psychological Aspects of Suicide," *Journal of Abnormal Psychology* 21 (1936): 260–65, and "The Incidence of Mental Disease in the Negro," *Journal of Negro Educa-*

tion 6 (1937): 377–92. For a sample of Dai's work, see *Becoming Fully Human: The Works of Bingham Dai*, rev. ed., ed. Sally Atkins (Boone, N.C.: Appalachian State University and Atkins, 1997).

121. Prudhomme and Musto, "Historical Perspectives on Mental Health and Racism," 45.

122. P. J. Pesare ("S. A. Surgeon," Venereal Disease Division, U.S. Public Health Service) to Theodore Bauer (chief, Venereal Disease Division, U.S. Public Health Service), Oct. 14, 1948, box 17, folder "Report on Medical Activities at Tuskegee 1948," RG 442 (Tuskegee Syphilis Study Administrative Records, 1929–1972), National Archives and Record Administration, Southeast Region, Atlanta. James H. Jones did not emphasize that the syphilis experiment was centered at a hospital primarily devoted to psychiatry and controlled by black psychiatrists in his classic study, *Bad Blood: The Tuskegee Syphilis Experiment* (New York: Free Press, 1981).

Chapter 2

1. "Montgomery County" (typescript, n.d.), 2, box 2, folder "1940–1946 General Education Board," Jackson Davis Papers, collection MSS 3072, Special Collections, University of Virginia Library, Charlottesville.

2. Paul B. Foreman to Robert D. Calkins, May 13, 1947 (first quotation); Benjamin Mays, "He, Too, Was Southern: America Produced No Finer Spirit Than Jackson Davis," *Pittsburgh Courier*, n.d., clipping (second quotation), both in box 2, folder "1947, Letters of Condolence for the Death of Jackson Davis," Davis Papers.

3. Jackson Davis, diary, Aug. 16, 1911, "The National Diary 1911," box 1, Davis Papers (first quotation); Davis, diary, Feb. 7, 1913, "The National Diary 1913," box 1, Davis Papers (second and third quotations). He noted his horse-and-buggy travel in his diary on Dec. 8, 1911, "National Diary 1911." W. W. Brierly of the GEB certified Davis's need for gasoline in "Statement," May 12, 1942, attached to "Application for Supplemental Gasoline Ration Card," box 2, folder "1940–1946 General Education Board," Davis Papers. Brierly reported that Davis traveled 9,504 miles by car in 1941.

4. On Davis's piety, see, e.g., his reflections on a Presbyterian Bible class in his diary, June 18, 1911, "National Diary 1911." For biographical information on Davis, see William A. Link, "Jackson Davis and the Lost World of Jim Crow Education," in *Jackson Davis and the Lost World of Jim Crow Education*, ed. Edward Gaynor and Rebecca Yocum (Charlottesville: Rector and Visitors of the University of Virginia, 2000), 7–16; William A. Link, *A Hard Country and a Lonely Place: Schooling, Society, and Reform in Rural Virginia, 1870–1920* (Chapel Hill: University of North Carolina Press, 1986), esp. 185–88; and Raymond B. Fosdick, *Adventure in Giving: The Story of the General Education Board, a Foundation Established by John D. Rockefeller* (New York: Harper and Row, 1962), passim.

5. This was not the first time in American history that hopes for children spurred a reappraisal of human nature. Distaste at the prospect of infant damnation among

Calvinists who loved their children drove an initial wedge in New England Puritanism during the seventeenth and eighteenth centuries and led the way to faiths more tolerant of choice, effort, and progress. The Puritans' affection for their unconverted children motivated the Half-Way Covenant of the mid-seventeenth century, and the erosion of belief in original sin 100 years later grew in part from revulsion at the idea of eternal judgment of infants. See Perry Miller, *The New England Mind: From Colony to Province* (Boston: Beacon Press, 1961), chaps. 6–8, and Conrad Wright, *The Beginnings of Unitarianism in America* (Boston: Starr King Press, 1955), 85–89.

6. Franklin C. McLean, "Report on Meharry Medical College" (typescript, Mar. 27, 1934), 10, box 135, folder 1250, series 1.1, GEB Archives.

7. Booklists, 7, accompanying H. J. Thorkelson to Thomas E. Jones, Oct. 18, 1928, box 138, folder 1278, series 1.1, GEB Archives. The cover letter indicated that the GEB would add $15,000 to its initial pledge of $400,000 toward a new Fisk library. For a breakdown of the numbers of students pursuing various courses of study, see "Fisk University Office of Alumni Secretary and Alumni Occupational Directory," box 138, folder 1278, series 1.1, GEB Archives. The Peabody proposal, titled "Fourteen Four-Year Undergraduate Curricula Each Leading to B.S. Degree, Combining in a Single Curricula for Training High School Teachers," accompanied Bruce R. Payne to General Education Board, Dec. 26, 1925, box 147, folder 1364, series 1.1, GEB Archives. Payne, Peabody's president, reported that the college currently had 3,573 students. On Progressivism in northern education, see Lawrence A. Cremin, *The Transformation of the School: Progressivism in American Education, 1876–1957* (New York: Knopf, 1969), esp. chaps. 4, 6, and Maurice R. Berube, *American School Reform: Progressive, Equity, and Excellence Movements, 1883–1993* (Westport, Conn.: Praeger, 1994), chaps. 1–3. On Progressivism in southern education, see Louis R. Harlan, *Separate and Unequal: Public School Campaigns and Racism in the Southern Seaboard States, 1901–1915* (1958; repr., New York: Atheneum, 1968); Henry Allen Bullock, *A History of Negro Education in the South: From 1619 to the Present* (Cambridge, Mass.: Harvard University Press, 1967), chaps. 4–7; James D. Anderson, "Northern Foundations and the Shaping of Southern Black Rural Education, 1902–1935," *History of Education Quarterly* 18 (1978): 371–96; James D. Anderson, *The Education of Blacks in the South, 1860–1935* (Chapel Hill: University of North Carolina Press, 1988), esp. chaps. 4–7; Link, *Hard Country and a Lonely Place*, pt. 2; William A. Link, *The Paradox of Southern Progressivism, 1880–1930* (Chapel Hill: University of North Carolina Press, 1992), esp. chaps. 5, 9; James L. Leloudis, *Schooling in the New South: Pedagogy, Self, and Society in North Carolina, 1880–1970* (Chapel Hill: University of North Carolina Press, 1996), esp. xiii, 229–31; and Adam Fairclough, *Teaching Equality: Black Schools in the Age of Jim Crow* (Athens: University of Georgia Press, 2001), esp. chaps. 1–2. Harlan notes how often positions in school administrations had been political sinecures in *Separate and Unequal*, 136. Looking beyond schools, John Chynoweth Burnham shows that Progressivism was connected with the psychology of the era in "Psychiatry, Psychology and the Progressive Movement," *American Quarterly* 12 (1960): 457–65.

8. G. Stanley Hall, "The Contents of Children's Minds," *Princeton Review* 11 (1883): 249–72.

9. The nineteenth-century idea of organic growth directed the attention of intellectuals to child nurture. Influential philosophical statements concerning individual development that anticipated Hall's scientific method include A. Bronson Alcott, *Record of a School: Exemplifying the General Principles of Spiritual Culture*, 2d ed. (Boston: Russell, Shattuck, 1836); Ralph Waldo Emerson, "Nature" (1936), in *Selected Writings of Ralph Waldo Emerson*, ed. William H. Gilman (New York: Signet, 1965), 181–224; Horace Bushnell, *Christian Nurture* (1847; repr., New Haven, Conn.: Yale University Press, 1967); and primary selections in David Brion Davis, ed., *Antebellum American Culture: An Interpretive Anthology* (Lexington, Mass.: Heath, 1979), chaps. 2, 4. Leading statements on the relationship of psychology to the instruction of children produced by Hall's peers include William James, *Talks to Teachers on Psychology and to Students on Some of Life's Ideals* (1899; repr., Cambridge, Mass.: Harvard University Press, 1983), and John Dewey, *Democracy and Education: An Introduction to the Philosophy of Education* (1916; repr., New York: Macmillan, 1926). Hall was nonetheless the first to try to establish child nurture on a scientific basis, and as his stature increased, he predictably became a target of criticism. Psychologists at Columbia University, especially James McKeen Cattell, Edward Thorndike, and Robert Woodworth, who devised statistical measures for child assessment used in experimentation and testing, charged Hall with being too impressionistic. For an overview of their work, see Edwin G. Boring, *A History of Experimental Psychology*, 2d ed. (New York: Appleton-Century-Crofts, 1950), esp. 532–40, 559–70. For critiques of Hall, see Dorothy Ross, *G. Stanley Hall: The Psychologist as Prophet* (Chicago: University of Chicago Press, 1972), esp. chap. 17. Perhaps as late as World War II, these scholarly controversies primarily affected southern schools indirectly, usually by means of the northern graduate education of southern educators or the books they read in their field.

10. Hall, "Contents of Children's Minds," 263 (first and second quotations), 265 (third quotation).

11. Ibid., 255–56 (first quotation), 257 (second quotation).

12. Ibid., 254 (first and second quotations), 264 (third and fourth quotations). On racial ideas and their influence on common speech, see George W. Stocking Jr., *Race, Culture, and Evolution: Essays in the History of Anthropology* (New York: Free Press, 1968); Elazar Barkan, *The Retreat of Scientific Racism: Changing Concepts of Race in Britain and the United States between the World Wars* (Cambridge: Cambridge University Press, 1992); and Anne C. Rose, "'Race' Speech—'Culture' Speech—'Soul' Speech: The Brief Career of Social-Science Language in American Religion during the Fascist Era," *Religion and American Culture* 14 (2004): 83–108.

13. Hall, "Contents of Children's Minds," 272 (first quotation), 270 (second quotation). Sources on Hall to supplement Ross's excellent biography, *G. Stanley Hall*, include Nathan G. Hale Jr., *Freud and the Americans: The Beginnings of Psychoanalysis in the United States, 1876–1917* (New York: Oxford University Press, 1971), 100–104; Cremin,

Transformation of the School, esp. chap. 4; and G. Stanley Hall, *Life and Confessions of a Psychologist* (New York: Appleton, 1923), esp. chap. 9.

14. Odum's dissertation at Clark was published as "Religious Folk-Songs of the Southern Negroes," *American Journal of Religious Psychology and Education* 3 (1909): 265–365; it was followed by a second dissertation at Columbia that was more openly racist, *Social and Mental Traits of the Negro: Research into the Conditions of the Negro Race in Southern Towns; A Study in Race Traits, Tendencies and Prospects* (1910; repr., New York: AMS Press, 1968). On Odum, see Michael O'Brien, *The Idea of the American South, 1920–1941* (Baltimore: Johns Hopkins University Press, 1979), chaps. 2–4. On Sumner, see Robert V. Guthrie, *Even the Rat Was White: A Historical View of Psychology* (New York: Harper and Row, 1976), chap. 7. An analysis of the controversy concerning Sumner's letters to the *Worcester (Mass.) Gazette* in 1918 appears in Guthrie, *Even the Rat Was White*, 179–81. For Hall's warm, if patronizing, support of Sumner during the controversy, see [G. Stanley Hall?], untitled typescript describing the affair, n.d.; Philip H. Churchman to G. Stanley Hall, May 27, 1918; and A. G. Bullock to G. Stanley Hall, June 3, 1918, all in box 45 (B1-6-12), folder "Francis C. Sumner," G. Stanley Hall Papers, Archives and Special Collections, Robert Hutchings Goddard Library, Clark University, Worcester, Mass.

15. A. H. Witmer, "Insanity in the Colored Race in the United States," *Alienist and Neurologist* 12 (1891): 24 (first quotation); Owen A. R. Berkeley-Hill, "The 'Color Question' from a Psychoanalytic Standpoint," *Psychoanalytic Review* 11 (1924): 252 (second and third quotations). For an examination of similar issues in colonial India, see Dinesh Bhugra, "The Colonized Psyche: British Influence on Indian Psychology," in *Colonialism and Psychology*, ed. Dinesh Bhugra and Roland Littlewood (New Delhi: Oxford University Press, 2001), 46–76.

16. Thomas Pearce Bailey, *Race Orthodoxy in the South, and Other Aspects of the Negro Question* (1914; repr., New York: Negro Universities Press, 1969), 107. Black social scientists and physicians were prominent among those who soon launched direct and sustained critiques of the doctrine of racial limitations to individual development. See, e.g., E. Franklin Frazier, "Psychological Factors in Negro Health," *Journal of Social Forces* 3 (1925): 488–90; C. V. Roman, "The Negro's Psychology and His Health," *Hospital Social Service* 11 (1925): 89–95; and E. Y. Williams, "The Incidence of Mental Disease in the Negro," *Journal of Negro Education* 6 (1937): 377–92. They built on an intellectual foundation laid by W. E. B. Du Bois. See esp. *The Souls of Black Folk* (1903; repr., New York: Modern Library, 1996), esp. chap. 1. Physiological views of race have persisted as a generally muted emphasis in psychological writing. See Graham Richards, "'It's an American Thing': The 'Race' and Intelligence Controversy from a British Perspective," in *Defining Difference: Race and Racism in the History of Psychology*, ed. Andrew S. Winston (Washington, D.C.: American Psychological Association, 2004), 137–69; Andrew S. Winston, Bethany Butzer, and Mark D. Ferris, "Constructing Difference: Heredity, Intelligence, and Race in Textbooks, 1930–1970," in Winston, *Defining Difference*, 199–229; Andrew S. Winston, "Science in the Service of the Far Right:

Henry E. Garrett, the IAAEE, and the Liberty Lobby," *Journal of Social Issues* 54 (1998): 179–210; and William H. Tucker, *The Funding of Scientific Racism: Wickliffe Draper and the Pioneer Fund* (Urbana: University of Illinois Press, 2002).

17. Odum, *Social and Mental Traits of the Negro*, esp. 46–48.

18. On the students' religious affiliations, see John J. Mullowney, "The Annual Report of Meharry Medical College and Hospital for 1936–1937" (typescript, n.d.), 10, box 135, folder 1250, series 1.1, GEB Archives. On the Baptists, see Paul Harvey, *Redeeming the South: Religious Cultures and Racial Identities among Southern Baptists, 1865–1925* (Chapel Hill: University of North Carolina Press, 1997).

19. Charles S. Johnson, *Growing Up in the Black Belt: Negro Youth in the Rural South* (1941; repr., New York: Schocken Books, 1967), 157 (first and second quotations), 156 (third quotation).

20. "Report of the Health Education Workshop" (typescript, Okolona College, Okolona, Miss., June 14–15, 1948), 12, box 542, folder 5811, series 1.3, GEB Archives. Similarly, a discussion topic at an earlier teachers' conference in South Carolina sounded more moralistic than psychological: "How to Promote Intelligence, Conservation and Economy." See "Conference on Negro Education to Be Held at Orangeburg, September 20th and 21st, 1917" (typescript), box 131, folder 1200, series 1.1, GEB Archives.

21. "Report of the Negro Summer School" (typescript, Anderson, S.C., July 23–Aug. 16, 1918), box 132, folder 1209, series 1.1, GEB Archives. Lectures at a "People's College" connected with Fisk University in the late 1930s similarly blended Christianity and mental health. In a course titled "Mental Hygiene," the instructor described religion as a "mental stabilizer" in one lesson and presented "Our Lord" as "an example of peace happiness and all that is good" in another. Lesson 4, "Mental Stabilizers and Safeguards to Mental Health" (first quotation), and "What's Right? What's Wrong" (second and third quotations), box 1, folder 10, Charles S. Johnson Papers, Social Center, Fisk. The course may have been taught by Sara R. Blake, named as the teacher of "Psychology" on an attendance form dated Apr. 25, 1939, box 1, folder 20, Charles S. Johnson Papers, Social Center.

22. "Appendix: Coahoma County [Miss.] Schools," in "Health Studies in Coahoma County in the Schools for Negroes" (typescript, n.d.), box 542, folder 5809, series 1.3, GEB Archives. William Link argues that an ingrained resistance to change on the part of local communities contributed to their neglect of schools in *Hard Country and a Lonely Place*, x. W. E. B. Du Bois taught at a black rural school in Tennessee during summers between his undergraduate years at Fisk in the 1880s; he left a moving account in *Souls of Black Folk*, chap. 4. For a sense of the social and medical obstacles to education, see Jack Temple Kirby, *Rural Worlds Lost: The American South, 1920–1960* (Baton Rouge: Louisiana State University Press, 1987), and John Ettling, *The Germ of Laziness: Rockefeller Philanthropy and Public Health in the New South* (Cambridge, Mass.: Harvard University Press, 1981), esp. prologue.

23. *Jeanes Teacher* 2 (1937): 2, box 131, folder 1206, series 1.1, GEB Archives. The newsletter mentioned acquisitions of seats and desks (5), blackboards (7), and pianos,

trees, flowers, and fresh paint (13). This is the only issue of the newsletter I have seen. All subsequent citations of *Jeanes Teacher* refer to this issue.

24. "Report of the Demonstration School" (typescript, University of Mississippi, Oxford, 1936), 5 (first quotation), 4 (second and third quotations), box 93, folder 834, series 1.1, GEB Archives.

25. Mildred S. Topp to J. S. Vandiver, May 2, 1940, box 97, folder 874, series 1.1, GEB Archives.

26. The phrase was the subtitle of "Northern Aid to Negroes Attacked," *New York Herald*, Apr. 25, 1901, clipping, folder 290, series 6.2, Southern Education Board Papers, collection 680, UNC (hereafter cited as SEB Papers). The figure of $325 million appears in Fosdick, *Adventure in Giving*, 1.

27. The language of sectional reconciliation and nationalism more widely stamped the movement to reform southern education. An official document described an earlier Conference on Christian Education in the South held in West Virginia in 1898 as an "opportunity for acquaintance and fellowship between representative people from both the North and the South." "Origin, Purposes and Plans of the Conference for Education in the South" (typescript, n.d.), 2, folder 269, series 6.1, SEB Papers. Similarly, Wallace Buttrick, first executive officer of the GEB, offspring of the SEB in 1902, explained his mission as aiding education throughout the country in "The Beginning and Aims of the General Education Board," *Addresses and Proceedings, National Education Association of the United States*, 1903, 121. Behind the conciliatory tone, the South by 1900 seemed less an immoral opponent to northerners and increasingly a place of charming emotion and local color, as Anne Rowe has shown in *The Enchanted Country: Northern Writers in the South, 1865–1910* (Baton Rouge: Louisiana State University Press, 1978).

28. E. D. Crumpacker, "Disenfranchisement of Negroes," *Chicago Tribune*, Mar. 24, 1901, clipping, folder 290, series 6.2, SEB Papers; Fannie Barrier Williams, "Negroes Down South and Up North," *Chicago Times-Herald*, Oct. 8, 1899, clipping, folder 285, series 6.2, SEB Papers.

29. The major philanthropies active in the South came into being over the course of many decades, beginning with the establishment of the George F. Peabody Fund in 1867 and ending with the founding of the Julius Rosenwald Fund in 1917 and including the Slater Fund, Phelps-Stokes Fund, Carnegie Foundation, Rockefeller Foundation, GEB, and Jeanes Fund in the intervening years. At least at the beginning, they were allied with a Protestant evangelical impulse to educate the freedmen. None of the founders intended to support reform in perpetuity; when the initial funds were exhausted, as they were for the Peabody Fund in 1914, for example, the philanthropy would cease operation. For an overview of the organizations, see Bullock, *History of Negro Education in the South*, chap. 5. See also histories of specific charities, including Fosdick, *Adventure in Giving*; Raymond Fosdick, *The Story of the Rockefeller Foundation* (New York: Harper, 1952); and Edwin Embree and Julia Waxman, *Investment in People: The Story of the Julius Rosenwald Fund* (New York: Harper, 1949). Scholars offer differing interpretations of the philanthropies' goals. William Link argues that their moderation

led them to focus on white education (*Hard Country and a Lonely Place*, esp. 173–74). James Anderson believes that they focused on black education to guarantee a stable and productive work force ("Northern Foundations," esp. 374–75). James Leloudis emphasizes their wish to produce an individualized sense of self unimpeded by traditional bonds (*Schooling in the New South*, esp. xiii, 229–31). Not only is there much underlying agreement among these views, but together they capture the inevitable variety of motives in so protean an enterprise.

30. "Millions of Dollars for South's Schools," *New York World*, Apr. 21, 1901, clipping, folder 290, series 6.2, SEB Papers. For an instance of government matching of foundation subsidies, see reports on South Carolina summer schools for black teachers around 1920 (e.g., "Report of Bettis Academy Summer School" [typescript, Trenton, S.C., July 5–31, 1920]) in box 132, folder 1209, series 1.1, GEB Archives. Evidence of Works Progress Administration involvement is in *Jeanes Teacher*, 7–9, and forms used to apply for WPA support in box 1, folder 4, Charles S. Johnson Papers, Social Center. One indication of the business orientation of the philanthropies was the advice to young men routinely dispensed by Robert C. Ogden, a Philadelphia businessman and the inspiration behind the SEB. See, e.g., Robert C. Ogden, "Getting and Keeping a Business Position," *Saturday Evening Post*, Nov. 4, 1899, 345–46, clipping, folder 285, series 6.2, SEB Papers.

31. Dewey, *Democracy and Education*, 62 (first quotation), part of chap. 1 title (second quotation), part of chap. 2 title (third quotation).

32. A. D. Mueller, *Progressive Trends in Rural Education: An Interpretative Discussion of Some of the Best Tendencies in Rural Education* (New York: Century, 1926), 98 (first and second quotations), 317 (third quotation), 321 (fourth and fifth quotations). On the rural education movement, see Cremin, *Transformation of the School*, 75–83.

33. Catherine B. Johnson, *Jeanes Teacher*, 12 (first and section quotations); Myrtle Swindell, questionnaire response, May 19, 1921 (third quotation), Annie Pruitt, questionnaire, May 16, 1921 (fourth quotation), and B. C. [?] Williams, questionnaire response, n.d. (fifth quotation), all in box 17, folder "Miss Annie Pruitt—Questionnaires and Replys [*sic*] about North Carolina School and Home Agencies" (hereafter cited as folder "Miss Annie Pruitt"), Howard W. Odum Papers, collection 3167, UNC. Medical and dental clinics held in schools, possibly for adults as well as students, were mentioned in Z. V. Mose, questionnaire response, n.d., box 17, folder "Miss Annie Pruitt," Odum Papers.

34. Mary G. Linton, questionnaire response, n.d. (first and second quotations); N. W. Britton, questionnaire response, n.d. (third quotation), both in box 17, folder "Miss Annie Pruitt," Odum Papers.

35. With the cost of the 500 schools totaling $500,000 and hence the average cost of a building just $1,000, it is clear that the schoolhouses were not elegant. "History and Development of Negro Education in South Carolina" (typescript, State Department of Education,1949), 11, box 131, folder 1206, series 1.1, GEB Archives. The professions of the Jeanes teachers are found in *Jeanes Teacher*, 2 (first quotation), 13 (second quotation). There were cases in which community-oriented teaching may have helped chil-

dren. At Fisk University's People's College in the 1930s, a teacher followed the lecture "Introduction to the Study of Mental Hygiene" with two talks titled "Training Children for Failure" and a third titled "The Psychological Aspects of Marriage." See course materials for "Mental Hygiene," box 1, folder 10, Charles S. Johnson Papers, Social Center. This teacher was college educated, however, and received practical support from the university.

36. "Don't Like Yankees: Let the Darkey Work at a Trade or Hoe Cotton," *North Carolina Morning Post*, Apr. 25, 1901 (first quotation); Julian Hawthorne, "Poor Whites in the South Must Be Educated for the Sake of the Negro," *Philadelphia North American*, Apr. 23, 1901 (second and third quotations), both clippings in folder 290, series 6.2, SEB Papers. Although scholars differ about whether black schools or white were the original focus of the northern philanthropies (see n. 29), I base my emphasis on their mission to blacks on the clippings collection of the SEB, where the majority of articles saved focus on the situation of African Americans. In October 1899, for example, articles clipped included "Negro Education: Booker T. Washington Addresses Baptist Social Union," *Chicago Inter-Ocean*, Oct. 4, 1899; "The Negro of the New South," *New York Outlook*, Oct. 1899; "Voice of the Press: Not Promising for the Negro," *San Francisco Bulletin*, Oct. 2, 1899; and "Race Prejudice Growing," *New York Evening Post*, Oct. 23, 1899, all in folder 285, series 6.2, SEB Papers. Whereas public policy affirmed that children of both races would benefit (e.g., Buttrick, "Beginning and Aims of the General Education Board"), I interpret the pattern of clippings as an indication of the organizers' private interests. The aim to aid black schools did not mean that equality was the northerners' goal, however, or even that funding to schools would be equitable. In addition, Harlan argues that southern white administrators effectively diverted funding intended for black students to white ones in *Separate and Unequal*, 269.

37. J. E. Swearingen to E. C. Sage, Mar. 6, 1919 (first quotation); Jackson Davis to Wallace Buttrick, May 31, 1919 (subsequent quotations), both in box 131, folder 1200, series 1.1, GEB Archives. The Mississippi professor was Stanley Wright, a teacher of mathematics at Mississippi Agricultural and Mechanical College, who wrote to Wallace Buttrick, Nov. 5, 1914; W. H. Smith was the Mississippi official who contacted Abraham Flexner about a black school agent, Nov. 22, 1915, both in box 97, folder 871, series 1.1, GEB Archives.

38. W. F. Bond to Leo M. Favrot, Mar. 1, 1932, box 99, folder 893, series 1.1, GEB Archives.

39. "Report of the First Teacher Health Education Workshop in Washington County" (typescript, Tougaloo College Extension Summer School, Greenville, Miss., June 7–July 9, 1948), box 542, folder 5811, series 1.3, GEB Archives. The statistic about black teachers appears in Bond to Favrot, Mar. 1, 1932.

40. Buttrick, "Beginning and Aims of the General Education Board," 121.

41. "Virginia's Forgotten Children" (clipping, Co-operative Education Association of Virginia, connected with Patron's Day), Oct. 30, 1914, box 188, folder 1766, series 1.1, GEB Archives.

42. On the white project, see "A Proposal to Establish a Permanent Cooperative

Child Health Study at Woman's College, Greensboro, North Carolina" (typescript, n.d.); Arthur R. Mann to Fred McCuistion, interoffice correspondence, Oct. 6, 1941; "General Education Board, Grant in Aid: Southern Program-White" (typescript, Dec. 11, 1941); E. W. McHenry, "Report to the General Education Board Re Trip to Alabama, Tennessee, and Virginia, July 3–20, 1942" (typescript), heading 6, all in box 542, folder 5814, series 1.3, GEB Archives. On the black project, see James E. Shephard to Fred McCuistion, Jan. 29, 1942; Fred McCuistion to James E. Shephard, Feb. 11, 1942; James E. Shephard to Albert R. Mann, Aug. 28, 1942; [James E. Shephard?], "Proposed Health Program for North Carolina College" (typescript, n.d.); W. W. Brierly to James E. Shephard, Dec. 31, 1942; James E. Shephard to W. P. Jacobs, Oct. 1, 1943; and W. W. Brierly to James E. Shephard, Oct. 27, 1944, all in box 543, folder 5816, series 1.3, GEB Archives. The shift in funding was a virtual trade: the GEB had given $6,000 to the Woman's College in early 1942 to be used over three years, and the organization allocated North Carolina College for Negroes $8,800 in late 1944. The Woman's College was located in Greensboro, and the College for Negroes, in Durham.

43. Davis, diary, Oct. 6, 1911, "National Diary 1911."

44. "Interviews—Conference of Child Guidance Psychiatrists at Princeton Inn, Princeton, New Jersey" (typescript, April 20–22, 1934), box 370, folder 3865 (first quotation); [H. Payne], "Conference on Personality Study, Princeton, N.J." (typescript, Jan. 18–20, 1935), 4 (second quotation), 7 (third quotation), box 370, folder 3866, both in series 1.3, GEB Archives. The psychologist who used both of these expressions was Max Wertheimer. On the foundation's hopes for the conference, see Lawrence K. Frank, "Subject: Conference of Psychologists to Formulate Methods of Studying Personality in Terms of the Gestalt Theory" (typescript, n.d.), box 370, folder 3866, series 1.3, GEB Archives. Frank signed here by his initials, a common practice for GEB officials' in-house memorandums. In this and subsequent instances, I have indicated the person's name for the sake of simplicity, unless the initials are part of a title.

45. "Excerpt from letter dated 6/11/38—S. Bayne-Jones to AG [Alan Gregg]" (first quotation); [Arnold Gesell?], "Summary Statement: The Yale Clinic of Child Development," 6 (second quotation); Prof. Arnold Gesell, interview by AG [Alan Gregg], Oct. 20, 1938, New Haven, Conn., 2 (third and fourth quotations), all typescripts in box 376, folder 3925, series 1.3, GEB Archives. Gregg conceded privately after his interview of Oct. 1938 that part of Gesell's problem was his connection with the Yale Institute of Human Relations, heavily endowed by the Rockefeller Foundation and filled with conflict (Gesell, interview, 1). On the Institute of Human Relations, see Anne C. Rose, "Putting the South on the Psychological Map: The Impact of Region and Race on the Human Sciences during the 1930s," *Journal of Southern History* 71 (2005), esp. 346–50.

46. Florence M. Read to Trevor Arnett, May 14, 1936 (first quotation); Lawrence K. Frank to Trevor Arnett, "Subject: Spelman College Nursery School and Parent Education Project," May 28, 1936 (second and third quotations), both in box 394, folder 4130, series 1.3, GEB Archives. Because Read, acting president of Atlanta University by the summer of 1936, spoke of "research" and Frank, a foundation official, articulated more

modest goals, there may have been a quiet conflict between southern and northern intentions.

47. R. H. Gillespie, "General Report" (typescript, Third Annual Educational Conference, University of Mississippi, Oxford, July 1–2, 1937), 17, box 93, folder 834 (first quotation); "Rural School Organization and Management" (course outline, Hampton Institute, summer session, 1936), box 188, folder 1764 (second quotation), both in series 1.1, GEB Archives. On psychology's role in teacher training at Peabody College in Nashville, see, e.g., "Fourteen Four-Year Undergraduate Curricula Each Leading to B.S. Degree, Combining in a Single Curricula for Training High School Teachers," typescript accompanying Bruce R. Payne to General Education Board, Dec. 26, 1925, box 147, folder 1364, series 1.1, GEB Archives.

48. Davis, diary, July 15, 1911, "National Diary 1911."

49. John W. Ritchie, *Primer of Sanitation*, in *Sanitation and Physiology, Consisting of Primer of Sanitation and Human Physiology in One Volume* [separate pagination], 3d ed. (Yonkers: World Book, n.d.), 144 (first and second quotations); Walter Frank Cobb, *Health for Body and Mind* (New York: Appleton-Century, 1936), chap. 8 title (third quotation), 116 (fourth quotation), 389 (fifth quotation), 410 (sixth quotation). Link names the *Primer of Sanitation* as a book commonly taught in southern schools in *Paradox of Southern Progressivism*, 207. In the same study, he emphasizes the importance of health education in the reform program and notes that tradition-minded southerners tended to oppose it. Link, *Paradox of Southern Progressivism*, chaps. 5, 9. Cobb's works, including *Health for Body and Mind*, figured prominently on a list of books on mental health in a bibliography distributed to black teachers at a Tougaloo College workshop in 1948. "Bibliography" (typescript, Tougaloo College Health Education Workshop, Greenville, Miss., 1948), box 542, folder 5811, series 1.3, GEB Archives.

50. Robert Bennett Bean, *The Races of Man: Differentiation and Dispersal of Man* (New York: University Society, 1932), 35 (first quotation), 95 (second quotation), 19 (third quotation and photograph). On Bean, see R. J. Terry, "Robert Bennett Bean, 1874–1944," *American Anthropologist*, n.s., 48 (1946): 70–74.

51. Joseph Peterson and Lyle H. Lanier, *Studies in the Comparative Abilities of Whites and Negroes* (Baltimore: Williams and Wilkins, 1929), 151. The GEB also organized testing in the South at the end of World War I, in part, an official memorandum stated, because of the "very large number of psychologists and those skilled in conducting educational tests and measurements" who were "now being demobilized" and were presumably available for service. Memorandum C, "Virginia Survey" (typescript, n.d.), box 188, folder 1767, series 1.1, GEB Archives. The agency explained the testing as an effort to compare racial achievements in a civilian setting. The advisory role of Robert M. Yerkes, who supervised the army testing that gave evidence of the races' unequal intelligence, suggests that the foundation was not skeptical about the methods or results of previous testing. See Robert M. Yerkes to Abraham Flexner, Nov. 5, 1919, box 188, folder 1767, series 1.1, GEB Archives. The GEB's tolerance of segregation makes its trust of Yerkes and the testing process unsurprising.

52. "Camp John Hope" (brochure, n.d.), box 5, folder 2, Frankie V. Adams Papers,

AUC (first and second quotations). Adams (1902–79) taught at the Atlanta School of Social Work (renamed the Atlanta University School of Social Work), 1931–64. Her religious orientation is suggested by her involvement in the YMCA and YWCA. [Karen L. Jefferson], biographical sketch, 3, Adams Papers. In addition, she corresponded with Martin Luther King Sr. about opening a nursery department at his church school (July 11, 1933, box 4, folder 19, Adams Papers), and she directed "An Evening of Xmas Plays," as the program title described the event, presented at three churches in 1936, box 4, folder 30, Adams Papers.

53. Mrs. William B. Stone to Lillian Smith, June 13, 1944 (first and second quotations); response from parent of Collin Wilcox on form titled "A Candid Photograph of Your Daughter," 1944 (third, fourth, and fifth quotations), both in box 68, folder 2, Lillian E. Smith Papers, collection 1283, UGA. Smith described the camp as "a nationally famous camp for girls" in an untitled promotional statement signed "Miss Lil" (box 68, folder 2, Smith Papers), but the parents' questionnaire responses indicate that most were from southern coastal cities. They did not belong to a social class whose members would visit a public clinic, and none of the girls seems to have been treated privately for psychological problems. Smith encouraged and responded to her patrons' interest in child development.

54. [Lillian Smith], "My Various Journeys. Travel, etc." (typescript, n.d.), 6 (first quotation), 7 (second quotation), box 1, folder 1, Smith Papers; "Candid Photograph" (third and fourth quotations); "Cherokee" scrapbook, 1944, loose page of instructions (fifth, sixth, and seventh quotations), entry for July 3, 1944 (eighth and ninth quotations), box 70, Smith Papers.

55. "History and Development of Negro Education in South Carolina," 7 (first quotation), 10 (second quotation); Percy Bell quoted in "Attitudes of Some of Our Leading Mississippians toward Negro Education, 1938," list of testimonies filed with P. H. Easom to L. S. Rogers, Aug. 9, 1938, box 97, folder 873, series 1.1, GEB Archives (third quotation). The eighteen quotations favoring black education were presumably collected by Easom, the GEB-employed supervisor of Mississippi's black schools, to influence Rogers, the state superintendent of education.

56. Dr. Howard W. Odum, interview by Arthur R. Mann, Dec. 15, 1942, University of North Carolina, Chapel Hill (first and second quotations), and Fred McCuistion, marginal note on ibid. (third quotation), box 459, folder 4886, series 1.3, GEB Archives.

57. Dabney S. Lancaster to Fred McCuistion, Mar. 7, 1944, box 187, folder 1756, series 1.1, GEB Archives.

58. "Proposed Plan for Child Study and Mental Health Workshop" (typescript, University of Arkansas and State Department of Education, Little Rock Center, Aug. 7–25, 1950), box 495, folder 5282 (first quotation); "Outline for Better Mental Health" (typescript, Child Health Conference, Woman's College of the University of North Carolina, June 9–July 18, 1942), box 542, folder 5814 (subsequent quotations), both in series 1.3, GEB Archives. Christopher Lasch has been the most articulate critic of a therapeutic orientation and its potential to foster social neglect; see *The Culture of Narcissism: American Life in an Age of Diminishing Expectations* (New York: Norton, 1978).

59. "Report of Negro Summer School" (Anderson, S.C., 1918), box 132, folder 1209, series 1.1, GEB Archives.

60. "Why Don't Parents Visit the School" (song connected with Patron's Day, Oct. 30, 1914), box 188, folder 1766, series 1.1, GEB Archives (first and second quotations); Floy C. Mitchum, *Jeanes Teacher*, 10 (third quotation). Evidence of improved attendance is in *Jeanes Teacher*, 4–5.

61. Davis, diary, July 18, 1911, "National Diary 1911" (quotation). Selected photographs taken by Davis have been published in Gaynor and Yocum, *Jackson Davis and the Lost World of Jim Crow Education*.

62. On building projects at Vanderbilt, see "Report on Vanderbilt Univ. Medical School. Read at Meeting of G.E.B., December 13, 1934" (typescript), box 153, folder 1415, and W. F. Hoffman, "Medical Unit Beneficiary of Big Grant," no source, July 1, 1935, clipping, box 153, folder 1419, both in series 1.1, GEB Archives. The report noted that more than $3 million had been contributed to the medical school for its physical plant over the past fifteen years (2); the clipping noted that the GEB gave an additional $2.5 million to the school in the early 1930s. Its new academic building and hospital were completed in 1925. On the negotiations connected with the construction of Meharry's new medical school and hospital (1928–31), see James Summerville, *Educating Black Doctors: A History of Meharry Medical College* (University: University of Alabama Press, 1983), 66–68, and "Bishop Nicholson to Give Dedication Speech at Meharry," no source, 1931, clipping, box 136, folder 1253, series 1.1, GEB Archives, which cited the cost of the buildings as $2 million.

63. "Psychiatry—Dr. Luton" (typescript, Apr. 19, 1933), 7, box 3, folder 96 (first quotation); "Psychiatry" (typescript, Jan. 26, 1938), 2, box 3, folder 100 (second quotation); Spafford Ackerly to Frank H. Luton, Apr. 11, 1938, box 1, folder 7 (third and fourth quotations), all in Frank H. Luton Papers, VUMC.

64. "Report on Vanderbilt Univ.," 2 (first and second quotations); "The Flexner Report" (excerpt) in Herbert M. Morais, *The History of the Negro in Medicine* (New York: Publishers, 1967), 226 (second quotation). On the black medical schools that closed, see Morais, *History of the Negro in Medicine*, 227–28. The largest group of Howard medical students (1944–45) came from New York, followed in order by students from Washington, D.C., Pennsylvania, South Carolina, and Maryland. John W. Lawlah, "Annual Report of the College of Medicine, 1944-1945" (typescript, July 21, 1945), 10, box 28, folder 263, series 1.1, GEB Archives. Meharry drew its largest number (1937–38) from Texas, followed in order by Virginia, Ohio and Tennessee (tied), and Florida, New York, North Carolina, and South Carolina (all tied). Mullowney, "Annual Report." On Vanderbilt's medical school, see Timothy C. Jacobson, *Making Medical Doctors: Science and Medicine at Vanderbilt since Flexner* (Tuscaloosa: University of Alabama Press, 1987). On Meharry, see Charles Victor Roman, *Meharry Medical College: A History* (Nashville: Sunday School Publishing Board of the National Baptist Convention, 1934), and Summerville, *Educating Black Doctors*. On the teaching of psychiatry in particular, see Lloyd C. Elam, "Development of the Department of Psychiatry at Meharry Medical College," in *Black Psychiatrists and American Psychiatry*, ed. Jeanne Spurlock (Washing-

ton, D.C.: American Psychiatric Association, 1999), 67–75. For an informative overview of the difficulties facing black doctors, see Paul B. Cornely, "The Economics of Medical Practice and the Negro Physician," *JNMA* 43 (1951): 84–92.

65. On Fisk University, see Joe E. Richardson, *A History of Fisk University, 1865–1946* (University: University of Alabama Press, 1980). The GEB Archives, series 1.1, include folders on George Peabody College for Teachers in box 147 and on Scarritt College for Christian Workers in box 155.

66. "Account of Interview with Dr. Leathers—Dec. 29, 1933" (typescript), box 153, folder 1415, series 1.1, GEB Archives (first quotation); "Report on Vanderbilt Univ.," 1 (second quotation). W. S. Leathers, the medical school dean, made a concerted effort to gain support for psychiatry. In a letter to Alan Gregg at the GEB, he cited the even more dramatic statistic that 25–50 percent of the hospital's patients had "significant psychiatry difficulties." W. S. Leathers to Alan Gregg, Dec. 23, 1933, box 153, folder 1415, series 1.1, GEB Archives.

67. Although the philanthropies did not make public the logic of their focus on medical schools, there is evidence to suggest their reasoning. In the case of the Rockefeller Foundation's campaign against hookworm disease around 1910, the philanthropists sought to cure a medical problem for which success in a reasonable amount of time was possible, according to Ettling, *Germ of Laziness*, 209. In other words, they were concerned about their image. Aiding state asylums could not have yielded either quick or generally positive results and certainly would have deflected attention from teaching and research. The psychiatrist Lawrence S. Kubie, for example, was excited to see that a group of Emory University psychiatrists was "free from the financial and practical administrative burdens of running psychiatric wards" when he visited them after World War II. Lawrence Kubie to F. C. Redlich, May 18, 1949, 2, box 127, folder 1120, RG 1.2, series 200A, RF Archives. Frank Luton confirmed the commonplace impression that state mental hospitals were embroiled in politics and mainly served a custodial function in Frank H. Luton and Paul L. Boynton, "A Study of Mental Health Needs in Tennessee: A Report to Honorable George H. Cate, Commissioner of Institutions and Public Welfare" (typescript, Dec. 1938), chap. 1, [1], box 7, folder 2, Luton Papers.

68. On Vanderbilt's lack of facilities for inpatient psychiatric care, see [Alan Gregg?], typescript, notes on discussion with Dr. H. J. Morgan, Mar. 31, 1931, box 153, folder 1415, series 1.1, GEB Archives. On the same situation at Meharry's Hubbard Hospital, see Frank H. Luton, "Facilities in Middle Tennessee Contributing to Mental Hygiene" (typescript, n.d.), [1], attached to Frank H. Luton to Ethel Panter, Dec. 18, 1951, box 7, folder 27, Luton Papers. On conditions at Nashville City Hospital, see subheading "Visit to Nashville City Hospital with Dr. Mullowney" (typescript, May 30, 1931), box 136, folder 1260, series 1.1, GEB Archives. The data on Central State Hospital are in Luton and Boynton, "Study of Mental Health Needs in Tennessee," chap. 3, [1, 9].

69. "AG [Alan Gregg] Diary," Apr. 5, 1931, box 153, folder 1415, series 1.1, GEB Archives (quotation). He played golf on Apr. 4. On the conflict between the Methodist bishops and Vanderbilt, see Edwin Mims, *The Advancing South: Stories of Progress and Reaction* (Garden City, N.Y.: Doubleday, Page, 1926), 159–68, and Jacobson, *Making*

Medical Doctors, 71. In contrast, the Methodist Church continued to be involved in Meharry's affairs. See, e.g., Summerville, *Educating Black Doctors*, 57, as well as "Bishop Nicholson to Give Dedication Speech at Meharry," for the religious tenor of the program to dedicate the new campus. The GEB's tolerance of religion at Meharry seems a reflection of the foundation's lower expectations for scientific work at black institutions.

70. J. L. Cuninggim (president, Scarritt College for Christian Workers), interview by Arthur R. Mann, Feb. 21, 1941, Nashville, Tenn. (typescript), box 154, folder 1435, series 1.1, GEB Archives. The quotation is Mann's paraphrase of Cuninggim's opinion. Over the next decade, the GEB warmed up to Scarritt College, not only because its study of the social sciences as an adjunct of mission work was sophisticated but also because the college took "a liberal position in both racial and economic matters," to quote Mann's impression when he returned the following year. J. L. Cuninggim, interview by Arthur R. Mann, Jan. 22, 1942, Nashville, Tenn. (typescript), box 154, folder 1435, series 1.1, GEB Archives. Mann continued, "It is the one institution in Nashville where Negroes and whites can sit down to lunch together."

71. Lawrence K. Frank, "Society as the Patient," *American Journal of Sociology* 42 (1936): 339 (first and second quotations); Allen Tate, "Remarks on the Southern Religion," in Twelve Southerners, *I'll Take My Stand: The South and the Agrarian Tradition*, ed. Louis D. Rubin Jr. (1930; repr., Baton Rouge: Louisiana State University Press, 1962), 173 (third and fourth quotations). Frank was an outspoken advocate of scientific standards for all manner of social problems. See, e.g., his wish to develop an "inventory" of culture in "Study of Comparative Culture" (typescript, n.d.), [1], box 408, folder 4828, RG 1.1, series 200s, RF Archives. On his career, see Margaret Mead, "Lawrence Kelso Frank, 1890–1968," *American Sociologist* 4 (1969): 57–58. Although Frank worked at the Rockefeller Foundation through the early 1930s, the affiliation noted in the cited article was the Josiah Macy Jr. Foundation. On Tate, see O'Brien, *Idea of the American South*, chap. 7.

72. Typescript of clinical dialogue, n.d., 27, box 3, folder 97, Luton Papers (all quotations). Representative lectures include "Psychobiology—4th Lecture, 1932" (Apr. 6, 1932), folder 95; "Outline of Psychopathology" (n.d.), folder 92; "Lecture to City Hospital Nurses, Nov. 5, 1931, Child Psychology," folder 94; and "Psychiatry—Dr. Luton" (Apr. 19, 1933), all in box 3, Luton Papers. Luton served on the professional advisory board of the Presbyterian Church in the United States. See correspondence accompanying Frank H. Luton to Rev. William B. Oglesby, May 14, 1976, box 2, folder 26, Luton Papers.

73. "Psychiatry" (Jan. 12, 1938), 4 (first quotation), 5 (second quotation), box 3, folder 100, Luton Papers; "Psychiatry—Dr. Luton" (Apr. 19, 1933), 9 (third quotation), 4 (fourth and fifth quotations).

74. *Meharry News*, July 1928, *Catalogue Edition*, in composite volume, *Meharry News, 1928–34*, MMC (first quotation); J. W. D. Grant to John J. Mullowney, Sept. 16, 1916, box 1, folder "Correspondence, General. Grandy, J. M.—Rosenwald, Julius, 1915–1935," John J. Mullowney Papers, MMC (second quotation). Note that two letters from Grant

are dated Sept. 16, 1916. The Bureau of Human Betterment produced literature in the 1950s favoring sterilization. See its brochure, *Sterilizations Reported in the United States to January 1, 1954* (New York: Human Betterment Association of America, 1954), box 6, folder 46, Luton Papers. Meharry faculty salaries appear in "Meharry Medical College Budget Analysis, 1938–39" (typescript), box 135, folder 1250, series 1.1, GEB Archives. The highest salary, $5,000, went to the professor of surgery; the allocation for the lecturer in psychiatry was $300. One lower-paid position ($160) was "medical history-ethics, juris," but this seems to have been an occasional course offering rather than a faculty line. Rafael Hernandez, who taught psychiatry, also gave instruction in several other specialties, bringing his total salary into a reasonable range. With respect to the college's religious orientation, Mullowney sent a document, "Points for Serious Consideration [Confidential]," to its Methodist group of trustees through Dr. M. J. Holmes, Board of Education, Methodist Episcopal Church, Chicago, Mar. 26, 1934, box 1, folder "Correspondence, General. Grandy, J. M.—Rosenwald, Julius, 1915–1935," Mullowney Papers. In effect, he seems to have hoped to marshal denominational rivalries to help resist GEB pressure to merge Meharry with Fisk, founded by Congregationalists. On Mullowney, see Summerville, *Educating Black Doctors*, 60–79.

75. William E. Miller to Rockefeller Foundation, July 9, 1933, box 135, folder 1257, series 1.1, GEB Archives (first quotation); McLean, "Report on Meharry Medical College," 7 (second quotation).

76. "Points for Serious Consideration," 1. Mullowney's condescension resembled the thought among whites that blacks were too uncivilized to be mentally ill. See Charles Prudhomme and David F. Musto, "Historical Perspectives on Mental Health and Racism in the United States," in *Racism and Mental Health: Essays*, ed. Charles V. Willie, Bernard M. Kramer, and Bertram S. Brown (Pittsburgh: University of Pittsburgh Press, 1973), 36.

77. [W. S. Leathers], "Memorandum Concerning Expansion of the Vanderbilt Medical School and Hospital" (typescript, Apr. 1931), 2, box 153, folder 1415 (first and second quotations); Robert A. Lambert to Willard C. Rappleye, Jan. 22, 1938, box 136, folder 1257 (third and fourth quotations), both in series 1.1, GEB Archives. On Hernandez's psychiatric training, see [Mary Nieves Hernandez], "Rafael Hernandez, Sr." (typescript, n.d.), 2, and Mary Nieves Hernandez, *BPA Quarterly* 17 (1988): 4–5, untitled offprint, both in folder "Meharry Medical College, Biographical Collection, Hernandez, Rafael, Sr., 1897–1976," MMC.

78. Frank H. Luton to Otto Billig, Dec. 13, 1956, box 2, folder 11, Luton Papers. Although Hernandez's name appeared, for example, in Meharry's *School of Medicine Bulletin* in July 1941 (7), Dec. 1945 (33), 1958–59 (12), and June 1964 (16), he mainly held positions elsewhere, first in the army during the war and later in veterans' hospitals. [Hernandez], "Rafael Hernandez, Sr.," 3–4.

79. Thomas E. Jones, copy of communication (letter or speech) to Franklin D. Roosevelt, Nov. 17, 1934 (first quotation); John Mullowney to Thomas Elsa Jones, Nov. 19, 1934 (second quotation), both in box 139, folder 1283, series 1.1, GEB Archives. The white professor who commuted was Ina Brown. See "Interview: JD [Jackson Davis],

Sept. 25, 1943, Scarritt College, Nashville, Tennessee," box 155, folder 1436, series 1.1, GEB Archives. In his 1934 evaluation of Meharry at the GEB's request, Franklin McLean of the University of Chicago suggested that the college would benefit from closer ties with Vanderbilt School of Medicine. McLean, "Report on Meharry Medical College," 9. Segregation seems to have impeded this idea; the extent of interaction was apparently occasional teaching at Meharry by Vanderbilt professors.

80. Ernest W. Goodpasture to Harvie Branscomb, Jan. 7, 1949, 4, box 1, folder 16, Luton Papers (first quotation); "Community Failure," 1948, clipping, no source, box 136, folder 1253, series 1.1, GEB Archives (second quotation); Mary Jane Brooks, "Meharry, Hubbard May Be Moved from This City," no source, 1947, clipping, box 136, folder 1253, series 1.1, GEB Archives (third quotation).

81. Edward A. Turner to Robert A. Lambert, June 29, 1943, box 135, folder 1244, series 1.1, GEB Archives.

82. "Community Failure" (first quotation); McLean, "Report on Meharry Medical College," 3 (second quotation). Information on alumni giving, 1915–47, appears in Brooks, "Meharry, Hubbard May Be Moved."

83. Frank H. Luton to Ernest W. Goodpasture, Feb. 17, 1949, box 1, folder 16, Luton Papers.

84. Frank H. Luton to William F. Roth Jr., May 8, 1946, box 1, folder 13, Luton Papers (first and second quotations). The men's club mentioned in this letter was the Exchange Club. Menninger came to address Tennessee legislators on mental health reform and to raise money for the Menninger Foundation. William C. Menninger to Frank H. Luton, Feb. 9, 1957; Frank H. Luton to Gov. Frank G. Clement, Feb. 25, 1957; James L. Bomar (state representative) to William C. Menninger, Mar. 8, 1957, all in box 2, folder 38, Luton Papers.

85. Frank H. Luton to Hugh J. Morgan, Mar. 24, 1947, box 1, folder 14, Luton Papers (first and second quotations); Frank H. Luton to Ernest W. Goodpasture, Aug. 14, 1945, box 1, folder 12, Luton Papers (third quotation). On his research, see also [Frank H. Luton], "Proposed Mental Health Demonstration" (typescript, ca. 1934–35), box 2, folder 3, Luton Papers.

86. Goodpasture to Branscomb, Jan. 7, 1949, 1 (first quotation), 2 (second quotation).

87. Frank H. Luton to E. E. Landis, July 7, 1949, box 1, folder 16, Luton Papers (first and second quotations); Frank H. Luton to Spafford Ackerly, Mar. 30, 1938, box 1, folder 7, Luton Papers (third quotation). Luton had worked in the mid-1930s for the Section on Neurology and Psychiatry of the Southern Medical Association, moving up through the ranks to serve as its president in 1938. See, e.g., "Preliminary Program of Section on Neurology and Psychiatry — Southern Med. Ass'n" (n.d.), box 1, folder 7, Luton Papers. He served later as vice president of the American Psychiatric Association, 1965–66. "Curriculum Vitae," folder "Frank Harper Luton, M.D., 1898–1979," Luton Papers. A 1931 report described his initial position as "part-time." "Vanderbilt University Medical School — Visit by Alan Gregg April 1931" (typescript), 2, box 153, folder 1415, series 1.1, GEB Archives.

88. [Hernandez], "Rafael Hernandez, Sr." On Hernandez, see also Jeanne Spurlock, "Early and Contemporary Pioneers," in Spurlock, *Black Psychiatrists and American Psychiatry*, 5–6.

89. [Hernandez], "Rafael Hernandez, Sr.," 5.

90. [Luton], "Proposed Mental Health Demonstration," 1 (first and second quotations). The other studies were Michael J. Bent and Ellen F. Greene, *Rural Negro Health: A Report on a Five-Year Experiment in Health Education in Tennessee* (Nashville: Julius Rosenwald Fund Southern Office, 1937), and Johnson, *Growing Up in the Black Belt*. Although the one Tennessee county that Johnson included among eight total southern counties was Nashville's own Davidson County, the focus of his work was rural. Johnson, *Growing Up in the Black Belt*, v, xxi. In her national survey, Helen Witmer concurred with Luton on the need to take mental health care for children to rural areas. Helen Leland Witmer, *Psychiatric Clinics for Children, with Special Reference to State Programs* (New York: Commonwealth Fund, 1940), x.

91. [Luton], "Proposed Mental Health Demonstration," 9 (first, second, and third quotations). The psychiatrist was William F. Roth Jr., described in Frank H. Luton to H. R. Wahl, June 14, 1946, box 1, folder 13, Luton Papers. See also Frank H. Luton to William F. Roth Jr., Apr. 26, 1935, box 1, folder 4, Luton Papers. Virginia Kirk, a student of Arnold Gesell at Yale, worked in the community as a psychologist. Virginia Kirk to Frank H. Luton, Oct. 25, 1942, box 1, folder 10, Luton Papers. Luton described the ten-year plan in a letter to Chester L. Reynolds, Feb. 26, 1935, box 2, folder 63, Luton Papers. Whether the project ended because its objectives were so broad or its continuation was jeopardized by the war is unclear. Roth entered the navy, although whether he volunteered or was drafted is unknown as well.

92. Luton, "Facilities in Middle Tennessee Contributing to Mental Hygiene," [2].

93. "Psychiatry—Dr. Luton" (Apr. 19, 1933), 4 (first quotation); "Psychiatry" (Jan. 26, 1938), 7 (second quotation). On the improvements at Vanderbilt hospital, see Luton, "Facilities in Middle Tennessee Contributing to Mental Hygiene," [1]. On medications used at Central State Hospital in the 1930s, see Luton and Boynton, "Study of Mental Health Needs in Tennessee," chap. 3, [11]. In the case of Metrozol, used for psychosis, families of patients had to purchase the medication. Under the heading "Psychotherapy," the investigators wrote, "Little individual treatment can be done." Luton and Boynton, "Study of Mental Health Needs in Tennessee," chap. 3, [11]. For a hospital that made no attempt to group patients by the nature of their illnesses, consider the 1931 GEB report titled "Visit to Nashville City Hospital with Dr. Mullowney," where the observer was shocked to see "patients being distributed according to sex and race and without regard to their nature of the ailment, i.e., the white female ward contains medical, surgical, obstetrical and pediatric cases."

94. Luton, "Facilities in Middle Tennessee Contributing to Mental Hygiene," [4] (first, second, and third quotations), [1] (fourth and fifth quotations).

95. "Visit to Nashville City Hospital with Dr. Mullowney."

96. "Flexner Report" quoted in Morais, *History of the Negro in Medicine*, 226. The

Flexner Report provided data on all seven of the Jim Crow medical schools in operation in 1910 Ibid., 227–28.

97. "Memphis in Front Rank as Hospital and Clinic Center," *Memphis Commercial Appeal*, Apr. 23, 1933, clipping, folder "Memphis-Hospitals," Memphis and Shelby County Room, MPL. The academic connections of Memphis psychiatrists seem to have been mainly a trend of the post–World War II era. The obituary of Dr. Richard Bunting did not note a university affiliation. *Memphis Press-Scimitar*, Oct. 2, 1935, clipping, folder "Memphis-Hospitals," Memphis and Shelby County Room, MPL. Carrol Turner, who began to practice in sanitariums in the 1930s, and P. J. Sparer, who arrived in Memphis in 1951, were both professors at the medical school of the University of Tennessee. On Turner, see Jerry L. Robbins, "'Mr. Anonymous' Goodfellows Gift Aids Christmas Fund," *Memphis Press-Scimitar*, Nov. 17, 1980, clipping, Biography Files, Memphis and Shelby County Room, MPL. On Sparer, see "Dr. P. J. Sparer, Noted Psychiatrist," *Memphis Press-Scimitar*, Oct. 10, 1977, clipping, Biography Files, Memphis and Shelby County Room, MPL.

98. Robert Coles, telephone interview by the author, July 27, 2005. The scholar was Erwin Wexberg, then a member of the Department of Neuropsychiatry of Louisiana State University Medical School, who wrote "The Comparative Racial Incidence (White and Negro) of Neuropsychiatric Conditions in a General Hospital," *Tri-State Medical Journal* 13 (1941): 2694–96.

99. Richard E. Felder, interview by the author, July 29, 2002, Gainesville, Ga. One may also note the situation in Washington, D.C., a border city that was southern by custom. E. Y. Williams was Howard University's principal psychiatrist in the 1930s and 1940s. His application for support for advanced study includes biographical information. "The Rockefeller Foundation: Personal History Record and Application for Fellowship: Ernest Y. Williams" (typescript, Mar. 26, 1931), box 28, folder 268, series 1.1, GEB Archives. Howard medical students, mostly of northern background (see n. 64), were permitted to train at the federal government's massive St. Elizabeth's Hospital for the mentally ill in the 1930s during the directorship of William Alanson White. White's successor, Winfred Overholser, excluded them. Prudhomme and Musto, "Historical Perspectives on Mental Health and Racism," 43–44. Harry Stack Sullivan's Washington School of Psychiatry attracted white southern doctors during and after World War II. Among them were Rives Chalmers, a faculty member at Emory University after the war, and members of the New Orleans Psychoanalytic Society acquainted with Robert Coles in the early 1960s. Rives Chalmers, interview by the author, July 29, 2002, Atlanta; Coles, interview. On Sullivan's school, see Helen Swick Perry, *Psychiatrist of America: The Life of Harry Stack Sullivan* (Cambridge, Mass.: Harvard University Press, 1982), chaps. 38, 40.

100. "Memphis in Front Rank as Hospital and Clinic Center."

101. Luton to Roth, May 8, 1946. Luton mentioned his and a colleague's private practices in his letter to Goodpasture, Aug. 14, 1945. The practice of a Memphis psychiatrist was noted in "Dr. Richard Bunting, Neurologist, Dies," *Memphis Commercial Appeal*,

Oct. 1, 1935, clipping, Biography Files, Memphis and Shelby County Room, MPL. I have seen no record that black psychiatrists before the 1950s treated paying patients, although it is very likely that they did.

102. Frank H. Luton to Charles Riley, Feb. 14, 1930, box 1, folder 2, Luton Papers.

103. "Psychiatry" (Jan. 26, 1938).

104. Typescript (n.d.), 27, box 3, folder 97, Luton Papers.

105. Edward L. Bridges (Tennessee public service director) to Frank H. Luton, July 2, 1953, box 6, folder 46, Luton Papers. Among the handouts were "Sterilization of Mental Defectives" (typescript, n.d.); T. G. Peacock, "Georgia Program for Sterilization" (typescript, n.d.); and Sterilizations Reported in the United States to January 1, 1954, all in box 6, folder 46, Luton Papers.

106. "Dr. Richard Bunting, Neurologist, Dies."

107. Howard C. Warren to Edward Bradford Titchener, Oct. 21, 1921, box 3, folder July 29, 1921–Dec. 29, 1921, Edward Bradford Titchener Papers, collection 14-23-545, Division of Rare and Manuscript Collections, Cornell University Library, Ithaca, N.Y. (first and second quotations); Jane Gentry Smith, "The Mystery of the Mind: A Biography of William McDougall" (Ph.D. diss., University of Texas, 1980), 220 (third quotation). I rely on Smith's dissertation for biographical information unless otherwise noted. See also McDougall's autobiography, "William McDougall," in A History of Psychology in Autobiography, ed. Carl Murchison (1930; repr., New York: Russell and Russell, 1961), 1:191–223, and an assessment by his protégé, Cyril Burt, "The Permanent Contributions of McDougall to Psychology," British Journal of Educational Psychology 25 (1955): 10–22.

108. William McDougall, "World Chaos," in Religion and the Sciences of Life, with Other Essays on Allied Topics (Durham, N.C.: Duke University Press, 1934), 208.

109. Bruce Kuklick, The Rise of American Philosophy: Cambridge, Massachusetts, 1860–1930 (New Haven, Conn.: Yale University Press, 1977), 459–60. McDougall did send a telegram to Duke's president, William Preston Few, on October 4, 1926, that read, "Accepted—McDougall." Quoted in Smith, "Mystery of the Mind," 256. But this resolution followed prolonged negotiation, primarily about salary. See Smith, "Mystery of the Mind," 247–56, and Robert F. Durden, The Launching of Duke University, 1924–1949 (Durham, N.C.: Duke University Press, 1993), 112–14.

110. On the younger group of psychologists who defended racial differences, see chapter 5. These writers focused narrowly on measurable intelligence, and although McDougall championed psychology as an experimental science, his own work far more resembled speculative philosophy than the cut-and-dried outlook he called mechanism or behaviorism. For this reason I imagine tension between McDougall and later professionals who might otherwise seem allies. For typical critiques of scientific narrowness, see William McDougall, "Psychical Research as a University Study" (1926), in William McDougall: Explorer of the Mind; Studies in Psychical Research, ed. Raymond Van Over and Laura Oteri (New York: Garrett, 1967), 76, and William McDougall, "Religion and the Sciences of Life" (1932), in McDougall, Religion and the Sciences of Life, 7–8.

111. William McDougall, "Whither America?" (1931), in McDougall, *Religion and the Sciences of Life*, 259. Despite McDougall's profession to Few that he found the South charming (Smith, "Mystery of the Mind," 250), it is not clear when he visited the region before he accepted Duke's offer.

112. William McDougall, foreword to *Extra-Sensory Perception*, by J. B. Rhine (1934; repr., Boston: Branden Press, 1964), xv. Similarly, McDougall's comment about the beauty of American colleges (see n. 111) appeared in a footnote.

113. William McDougall to William Few, Apr. 23, 1926, quoted in Smith, "Mystery of the Mind," 250. Another reference to his age appeared in a letter to Few, Apr. 16, 1926, quoted in ibid., 249.

114. McDougall, "Religion and the Sciences of Life," 13 (first quotation), 15 (second quotation). The essay appeared originally in the *South Atlantic Quarterly*, published by Duke. Note the places of publication of other principal books by McDougall during this period: *World Chaos: The Responsibility of Science* (New York: Covici, Friede, 1932), *The Frontiers of Psychology* (New York: Appleton-Century, 1934), and *The Riddle of Life: A Survey of Theories* (London: Methuen, 1938). During his years in America, he in fact often published concurrent British and American editions of texts. Early and late reports that convey the tenor of his Lamarckian experiments are William McDougall, "An Experiment for the Testing of the Hypothesis of Lamarck," *British Journal of Psychology* 17 (1926–27): 267–304, and William McDougall, "Fourth Report on a Lamarckian Experiment," *British Journal of Psychology* 28 (1937–38): 321–45. The idea that acquired characteristics are inherited, formulated by Jean-Baptiste de Lamarck (1744–1829), was sufficiently vital in the mid-nineteenth century to underwrite Darwin's work, but it was rejected by most biologists after the rediscovery of the genetic experiments of Gregor Mendel (1822–84) at the turn of the twentieth century. See Stocking, *Race, Culture, and Evolution*, chap. 10. For McDougall's account of his acquaintance with J. B. Rhine and Rhine's wife and collaborator, Louisa, see McDougall, foreword to Rhine, *Extra-Sensory Perception*, xv. No matter how controversial the Rhines' work in parapsychology was, it also enjoyed an enduring popularity. See, e.g., J. B. Rhine, ed., *Progress in Parapsychology* (Durham, N.C.: Parapsychology Press, 1973).

115. William McDougall, *Is America Safe for Democracy? Six Lectures Given at the Lowell Institute of Boston, under the Title "Anthropology and History, or the Influence of Anthropologic Constitution on the Destinies of Nations"* (New York: Scribner, 1921), 157 (first quotation); William McDougall, *The Group Mind: A Sketch of the Principles of Collective Psychology with Some Attempt to Apply Them to the Interpretation of National Life and Character* (Cambridge: Cambridge University Press, 1921), 300 (second quotation), 301 (third quotation). McDougall had a self-disparaging habit and felt that he had no audience, particularly among scholars (see McDougall, "William McDougall," esp. 206, 223), but two of his books, *An Introduction to Social Psychology* (1908) and *Psychology: The Study of Behavior* (1912), each sold more than 100,000 copies. See J. Wainwright Evans, introduction to Van Over and Oteri, *William McDougall*, 19–20.

116. McDougall, *Group Mind*, 300. McDougall's eugenic ideas figured in much of

his writing, but key texts include "Family Allowances: A Practical Eugenic Suggestion" (1906) and "Family Allowances as a Eugenic Measure" (1933), both in McDougall, *Religion and the Sciences of Life*, 132–71.

117. Accounts of McDougall's efforts for the Department of Psychology are in Smith, "Mystery of the Mind," 254–70, and Durden, *Launching of Duke University*, 112–18. Smith mentions the dissertation on mediumship as the first on the subject in a psychology program ("Mystery of the Mind," 265), and Durden explains the controversy over the use of departmental funding for experiments in parapsychology, which led to their continuation under the sponsorship of private donors (*Launching of Duke University*, 117). For national data on doctorates in psychology awarded 1884–1948, see Robert S. Harper, "Tables of American Doctorates in Psychology," *American Journal of Psychology* 62 (1949): 579–87.

118. Although Lyman trained African Americans in psychiatry during the summer of 1941, a more ambitious plan to recruit an integrated study body did not materialize. For an overview of the project that stressed its experimental rather than social value, see the program proposal (typescript, n.d.), box 2, folder "African American Employees, 1940–1942," Richard S. Lyman Papers, Archives Department, Duke University Medical Center, Durham, N.C. In letters to northern colleagues, Lyman said quite openly that he hoped a modest acquaintance with basic psychiatry would lead gifted blacks into the specialty. Richard S. Lyman to Cyrus C. Sturgis, Oct. 2, 1941; Richard S. Lyman to Theophile Raphael, Oct. 2, 1941, both in folder "African American Employees, 1940–1942," Lyman Papers. The Rosenwald Fund refused to support the program on social grounds, saying that it was too bold. M. O. Bousfield to Richard Lyman, April 29, 1941, folder "African American Employees, 1940–1942," Lyman Papers. It appears that the Rockefeller Foundation offered enough funding to cover the summer course. N. C. Newbold to Dr. John Ferrell, Mar. 27, 1941, folder "African American Employees, 1940–1942," Lyman Papers.

119. McDougall, *Group Mind*, 4 (first and second quotations), 201 (third quotation); McDougall, *Is America Safe for Democracy?*, 54 (fourth quotation). McDougall explained his therapeutic work with British soldiers in *Group Mind*, viii. He was psychoanalyzed by Carl Jung in Zurich after the war, "so far as that process is possible for so hopelessly normal a personality as mine." McDougall, "William McDougall," 211.

120. McDougall, "World Chaos," 208. True to the theoretical phraseology of much writing on the characters of the races, McDougall typically spoke more comfortably about race as a natural category than about any particular race, making it less surprising that he now declined to write about southern blacks. In *Is America Safe for Democracy?*, his first work produced for an American audience as part of Boston's annual Robert Lowell Memorial Lecture Series, McDougall said that he was forced to focus on African Americans because of the extensive scholarship about them (53). Although he more typically analyzed the so-called European races—Nordic, Alpine, and Mediterranean—McDougall had participated in an anthropological expedition to the Pacific in 1898–99, exposing him personally to dark-skinned peoples. See Charles Hose and William McDougall, *The Pagan Tribes of Borneo*, 2 vols. (1912; repr., New York: Barnes

and Noble, 1966). In later years, he admired the Japanese for their discipline, traditionalism, and artistic cultivation. William McDougall, "Japan or America: An Open Letter to H.I.M. the Emperor of Japan" (ca. 1926–27), in McDougall, *Religion and the Sciences of Life*, 103–12. Whatever inclinations led McDougall to remain silent about African Americans in the South, however, it was clear that he believed them to be inferior.

Chapter 3

1. Clarence Cason, *90 Degrees in the Shade* (1935; repr., Westport, Conn.: Negro Universities Press, 1970), ix (first and second quotations), 43 (third quotation), 175 (fourth quotation).

2. Publicity blurb attached to Marjorie Bond to Clarence E. Cason, including handwritten marginal comment by Cason to Bond, Jan. 23, 1935, folder 2 (first through fourth quotations); Clarence E. Cason to Marjorie Bond, Jan. 10, 1935, folder 2 (fifth quotation); Clarence E. Cason to W. T. Couch, Dec. 16, 1934, folder 1 (sixth quotation), all in Clarence E. Cason folders, Records of the University of North Carolina Press, collection 40073, subgroup 4, series 1, University Archives, Wilson Library, University of North Carolina, Chapel Hill.

3. Cason, *90 Degrees in the Shade*, 123. For his recollection of the lynching during his childhood, see ibid., 111–13. For an account of Cason's state of mind on the day of his death as explained by a friend, see James Saxon Childers to W. T. Couch, mid-May 1935, folder 2, Cason folders. The reaction of his editor, W. T. Couch, appears in Couch's letter to Cason's widow, Louise R. Cason, May 22, 1935, folder 2, Cason folders. Cason died on May 7.

4. Walter White, *Rope and Faggot: A Biography of Judge Lynch* (1929; repr., New York: Arno Press, 1969), 6 (first quotation); Howard W. Odum, "Lynchings, Fears, and Folkways," *Nation*, Dec. 30, 1931, 719 (second quotation); Harry Stack Sullivan, "Memorandum of a Psychiatric Reconnaissance," appendix to Charles S. Johnson, *Growing Up in the Black Belt: Negro Youth in the Rural South* (1941; repr., New York: Schocken Books, 1967), 332 (third quotation).

5. Herbert A. Miller, "Some Psychological Considerations of the Race Problem," in *The Health and Physique of the Negro American*, ed. W. E. Burghardt Du Bois (Atlanta: Atlanta University Press, 1906), 53 (first quotation), 55 (second quotation). The essay was reprinted from *Bibliotheca Sacra* (1906); Miller's title was "Dr.," but whether he was a doctor of medicine or philosophy is unclear. Franz Boas, the Columbia University anthropologist who became an outspoken opponent of racialism, participated in the conference at Atlanta University out of which Du Bois's book grew; even so, the volume generally treated race as a matter of physiology, for example by displaying photographic portraits to depict black physical types and equating race with bloodlines, esp. 18, 31, 35.

6. Mary O'Malley, "Psychoses in the Colored Race: A Study in Comparative Psychiatry," *American Journal of Insanity* 71 (1914): 310 (first and second quotations), 311 (third quotation). On the transition from biological to cultural explanations of human

societies in Western culture, see especially George W. Stocking Jr., *Race, Culture, and Evolution: Essays in the History of Anthropology* (New York: Free Press, 1968), esp. chaps. 8, 10, and 11; Elazar Barkan, *The Retreat of Scientific Racism: Changing Concepts of Race in Britain and the United States between the World Wars* (Cambridge: Cambridge University Press, 1992); Carl N. Degler, *In Search of Human Nature: The Decline and Revival of Darwinism in American Social Thought* (New York: Oxford University Press, 1991), pt. 2; and Anne C. Rose, "Putting the South on the Psychological Map: The Impact of Region and Race on the Human Sciences during the 1930s," *Journal of Southern History* 71 (2005): 321–56. Also see scholarship that suggests that physiological explanations never disappeared, including Andrew S. Winston, Bethany Butzer, and Mark D. Ferris, "Constructing Difference: Heredity, Intelligence, and Race in Textbooks, 1930–1970," in *Defining Difference: Race and Racism in the History of Psychology*, ed. Andrew S. Winston (Washington, D.C.: American Psychological Association, 2004), 199–229. Works by southern black scholars who were active in this debate include C. V. Roman, "The Medical Phase of the South's Ethnic Problem," *JNMA* 8 (1916): 150–52; C. V. Roman, "The Negro's Psychology and His Health," *Hospital Social Service* 11 (1925): 89–95; and E. Franklin Frazier, "Psychological Factors in Negro Health," *Journal of Social Forces* 3 (1925): 488–90.

7. Lawrence J. Friedman, *The White Savage: Racial Fantasies in the Postbellum South* (Englewood Cliffs, N.J.: Prentice-Hall, 1970), 169 (first quotation), 76 (second quotation).

8. Frank Tannenbaum, *Darker Phases of the South* (1924; repr., New York: Negro Universities Press, 1969), 3 (first quotation), 38 (second quotation); Odum, "Lynchings, Fears, and Folkways," 719.

9. White, *Rope and Faggot*, 19. On the reappearance of the Klan, see John Egerton, *Speak Now against the Day: The Generation before the Civil Rights Movement* (New York: Knopf, 1994), 47–48. For a year-by-year table of the number of lynchings, see Robert L. Zangrando, *The NAACP Crusade against Lynching, 1909–1950* (Philadelphia: Temple University Press, 1980), 6–7.

10. White, *Rope and Faggot*, 19 (first and second quotations); Lillian Smith, *Killers of the Dream* (New York: Norton, 1949), 62 (third quotation). Hadley Cantril chose five groups as case studies for *The Psychology of Social Movements* (1941; repr., New York: Wiley, 1963), including lynch mobs (93–122), the Nazi Party (210–70), Father Divine's kingdom, the Oxford Group, and followers of the Townsend Plan.

11. Tannenbaum, *Darker Phases of the South.*

12. Ibid., 33 (first quotation), 31 (second quotation). On the American use of Freudian ideas as justification for freedom from repression, see Nathan G. Hale Jr., *The Rise and Crisis of Psychoanalysis in the United States: Freud and the Americans, 1917–1985* (New York: Oxford University Press, 1995), chap. 4.

13. Cantril, *Psychology of Social Movements*, 111 (first quotation), 112 (second quotation); Roger Brown, *Social Psychology* (New York: Free Press, 1965), 753–56. Judging by Cantril's citations, his emphasis on the ego as an adaptive mechanism owed intellectual debts not only to neo-Freudians, such as Anna Freud, but to the Gestalt psychologists'

insistence on the unique character of a whole perceptual field and to social applications of Freudianism in America by John Dollard and his colleagues at Yale's Institute of Human Relations, among others. Helpful primary sources on these complex, interconnecting trends include Anna Freud, *The Ego and the Mechanism of Defense* (New York: International Universities Press, 1946); Wolfgang Köhler, *The Task of Gestalt Psychology* (Princeton, N.J.: Princeton University Press, 1969); and John Dollard, Leonard W. Doob, Neal E. Miller, O. H. Mowrer, and Robert R. Sears, *Frustration and Aggression* (New Haven, Conn.: Yale University Press, 1939). Secondary sources include Hale, *Rise and Crisis of Psychoanalysis*, 48–49, 232–35, and Lewis A. Coser, *Refugee Scholars in America: Their Impact and Their Experiences* (New Haven, Conn.: Yale University Press, 1984), pt. 2. The work of game theorists at Massachusetts Institute of Technology and leading American universities during the postwar era is highlighted by Sylvia Nassar in *A Beautiful Mind: The Life of Mathematical Genius and Nobel Laureate John Nash* (New York: Simon and Schuster, 1998), esp. chap. 16.

14. Brown, *Social Psychology*, 733.

15. Gustave Le Bon, *The Crowd: A Study of the Popular Mind*, 2d ed. (Dunwoody, Ga.: Berg, n.d.), 2 (first quotation), ix (second quotation), xviii (third quotation), xiv (fourth quotation). The distinction between individual and collective psychologies was also the intellectual underpinning of William McDougall, *The Group Mind: A Sketch of the Principles of Collective Psychology with Some Attempt to Apply Them to the Interpretation of National Life and Character* (Cambridge: Cambridge University Press, 1921), esp. pt. 1. Writing before he arrived in America, McDougall did not enter the debate about the Klan, but his text attests to the popularity of analysis of the psychology of collective bodies.

16. White, *Rope and Faggot*, 9 (first, second, and third quotations); Cantril, *Psychology of Social Movements*, 113 (fourth quotation); Tannenbaum, *Darker Phases of the South*, 25 (fifth quotation). With respect to other themes that followed Le Bon more closely, White wrote that lynch mobs revealed the region's mental decay in *Rope and Faggot*, 156, and Tannenbaum and Cantril, respectively, emphasized the psychological suggestibility of mobs in *Darker Phases of the South*, 34, and *Psychology of Social Movements*, 113, 117.

17. Arthur F. Raper, *The Tragedy of Lynching* (Chapel Hill: University of North Carolina Press, 1933), 38. Background on Raper is in Arthur F. Raper, *Preface to Peasantry: A Tale of Two Black Belt Counties* (Chapel Hill: University of North Carolina Press, 1936), v–vi, and J. William Harris, *Deep Souths: Delta, Piedmont, and Sea Island Society in the Age of Segregation* (Baltimore: Johns Hopkins University Press, 2001), esp. 307–11. Although Raper's lynching study was commissioned by a southern organization, it was funded by a grant from the Julius Rosenwald Fund. See Jacquelyn Dowd Hall, *Revolt against Chivalry: Jessie Daniel Ames and the Woman's Campaign against Lynching*, rev. ed. (New York: Columbia University Press, 1993), 160–61.

18. Raper, *Tragedy of Lynching*, 11, 3, 34.

19. "Black's White," *Time*, Jan. 24, 1938, 8 (first quotation); William Faulkner, *Intruder in the Dust* (1948; repr., New York: Vintage, 1972), 154 (second quotation). The

headlines appeared in connection with the lynching of Claude Neal in Florida; see, respectively, *New York Times*, Oct. 27, 1934, and *Daily Worker*, [Nov. 27, 1934], clippings, box 2 (scrapbook), John Dollard Papers, group 1758, Manuscripts and Archives, Yale University Library, New Haven, Conn. The handwritten date on the *Daily Worker* clipping may be erroneous; the actual date of the article was most likely Oct. 27, because the lynching occurred during the night of Oct. 26. The Gallup poll results appear in Zangrando, *NAACP Crusade against Lynching*, 148. Zangrando chronicles White's devotion to national antilynching legislation throughout his study.

20. Bilbo quoted in Zangrando, *NAACP Crusade against Lynching*, 150.

21. "Black's White," 9.

22. George F. Milton, chair of the Southern Commission on the Study of Lynching, acknowledged Chivers's role in his introduction to Raper, *Tragedy of Lynching*, v. On Chivers, see *Atlanta School of Social Work Bulletin, 1929–30*, 5, AUC. Raper put a happy face on the cooperation of local whites during fieldwork for his later study, *Preface to Peasantry*, vi, but his data gatherers were in fact harassed in the countryside, as Harris explains in *Deep Souths*, 307. Hall notes that the Commission on Interracial Cooperation, the parent organization of the commission on lynching, had a "colored advisory committee," including John Hope of Atlanta University, Charles S. Johnson of Fisk, and Robert Moton and Monroe Work of Tuskegee Institute. Hall, *Revolt against Chivalry*, 161. Although Raper thanked Johnson and Hope warmly in *Preface to Peasantry*, vi–vii, there is no evidence that they helped behind the scenes with his lynching project.

23. Zangrando, *NAACP Campaign against Lynching*, 33, 173. Similarly, G. Franklin Edwards reports that E. Franklin Frazier, as the young director of the Atlanta School of Social Work, fled the city after threats to his life following the publication of his essay "The Pathology of Race Prejudice," *Forum* 70 (1927): 856–62. G. Franklin Edwards, "E. Franklin Frazier," in *Black Sociologists: Historical and Contemporary Perspectives*, ed. James E. Blackwell and Morris Janowitz (Chicago: University of Chicago Press, 1974), 93.

24. Tannenbaum, *Darker Phases of the South*, 8 (first quotation); Cantril, *Psychology of Social Movements*, 90 (second quotation); Tannenbaum, *Darker Phases of the South*, 34 (third quotation).

25. Faulkner, *Intruder in the Dust*, 136–37 (first, second, and third quotations), 238 (fourth quotation). The image of the menacing white lynch mob was so powerful that it seemed to carry over into descriptions of civil rights confrontations. Although part of the reason for the likeness in portrayals of lynching and prosegregation crowds was the similarity of social circumstances, the earlier language itself must have resonated so deeply with writers and audiences involved in desegregation that it was difficult to avoid its use. For example, Robert Coles, the Harvard psychiatrist, wrote in his children's book, *The Story of Ruby Bridges* (New York: Scholastic, 1995), that "a large crowd of angry white people gathered" to keep the first black child from crossing the color line at a New Orleans school. He continued, "Some wanted to hurt her," and "the city and state police did not help Ruby" (no pagination). As a matter of literary construction and emotion, in other words, writings on lynch mobs survived declining lynch

violence, the failure of the legislative campaign, and the disappearance of sociological debate.

26. [Charles S. Johnson], "Discussion," 4, of James S. Plant, "Community Planning for the Emotional Needs of the Child" (typescript, n.d.), box 129, folder 10, Charles S. Johnson Papers, Fisk (first and second quotations); Johnson, *Growing Up in the Black Belt*, 78 (wording repeated from the typescript), xxi (third quotation), 134 (fourth quotation). On the White House conference, the first session of which convened on Apr. 26, 1939, see "The White House Conference on Children in a Democracy, Jan. 18–20, 1940" (typescript), box 129, folder 3, Charles S. Johnson Papers.

27. Allison Davis and John Dollard, *Children of Bondage: The Personality Development of Negro Youth in the Urban South* (1940; repr., New York: Harper and Row, 1964); E. Franklin Frazier, *Negro Youth at the Crossways: Their Personality in the Middle States* (1940; repr., New York: Schocken Books, 1967); W. Lloyd Warner, Buford H. Junker, and Walter A. Adams, *Color and Human Nature: Negro Personality Development in a Northern City* (Washington, D.C.: American Council on Education, 1941). In the case of Johnson, *Growing Up in the Black Belt*, the phrase "formation of personality" appears on p. 1. Raymond B. Fosdick explained that the GEB suggested the formation of the AYC to the American Council on Education. The AYC began in 1935 and had $1.35 million at its disposal by 1942, most of the resources presumably from the GEB. See Raymond B. Fosdick, *Adventure in Giving: The Story of the General Education Board, a Foundation Established by John D. Rockefeller* (New York: Harper and Row, 1962), 244–45.

28. Charles S. Johnson to E. Franklin Frazier, Mar. 13, 1929, box 131-11, folder 13, E. Franklin Frazier Papers, Howard.

29. Robert Ezra Park, "Education in Its Relation to the Conflict and Fusion of Cultures," in *Race and Culture*, ed. Everett Cherrington Hughes (Glencoe, Ill.: Free Press, 1950), 280. Various dates for Park's retirement from Chicago and connection with Fisk appear in secondary sources, perhaps because he made the transition to retirement gradually. I cite the date offered by his former Chicago colleague, Ernest W. Burgess, in "Social Planning and Race Relations," in *Race Relations, Problems and Theory: Essays in Honor of Robert E. Park*, ed. Jitsuichi Masouka and Preston Valien (Chapel Hill: University of North Carolina Press, 1961), 15. A biographical entry on the American Sociological Association's website, however, gives the date as 1933. "Robert Ezra Park," ⟨http://www.asanet.org/cs/root/leftnav/governance/past_officers/presidents/robert_e_park⟩ (June 14, 2008).

30. Robert E. Park, "Personality and Cultural Conflict," in *Race and Culture*, 357–71; Robert E. Park, "Mentality of Racial Hybrids," in *Race and Culture*, 389.

31. My identification of Park's students is based on a full list of names of his doctoral students provided in Burgess, "Social Planning and Race Relations," 18. Based on the same list, his students who spent a significant part of their careers in the South included Lewis Copeland (Fisk University), Bingham Dai (Fisk and Duke universities), Frazier (Atlanta School of Social Work and Fisk), and Charles S. Johnson (Fisk). Biographical information on Park is in Robert E. Park, "An Autobiographical Note,"

in *Race and Culture*, v–ix; Burgess, "Social Planning and Race Relations," 13–25; and Robert L. Hall, "E. Franklin Frazier and the Chicago School of Sociology," in *E. Franklin Frazier and Black Bourgeoisie*, ed. James E. Teele (Columbia: University of Missouri Press, 2002), 49–57. I have drawn on Edwards's description of Park's specialties in "E. Franklin Frazier," 101, 111. Park believed in teaching as a means of influence, and his widely used text, coauthored with Ernest W. Burgess, *Introduction to the Science of Sociology*, sold 30,000 copies between its publication in 1921 and 1943, when it went out of print. Morris Janowitz, introduction to Blackwell and Janowitz, *Black Sociologists*, vii. The text, available in a revised third edition (Chicago: University of Chicago Press, 1969), offers a comprehensive view of his approach to the discipline.

32. Edward Sapir, "Cultural Anthropology and Psychiatry," in *Selected Writings of Edward Sapir in Language, Culture and Personality*, ed. David G. Mandelbaum (Berkeley: University of California Press, 1949), 515. Also relevant to Sapir's growing interest in psychiatry is "The Unconscious Patterning of Behavior in Society" (1927) in *Selected Writings of Edward Sapir*, 544–59. For the professional collaboration of Sullivan and Sapir, see, e.g., Harry Stack Sullivan, "A Note on the Implications of Psychiatry, the Study of Interpersonal Relations, for Investigations in the Social Sciences," and Edward Sapir, "The Contribution of Psychiatry to an Understanding of Behavior in Society," *American Journal of Sociology* 42 (1937): 848–61, 862–70. On their personal relationship, see Helen Swick Perry, *Psychiatrist of America: The Life of Harry Stack Sullivan* (Cambridge, Mass.: Harvard University Press, 1982), esp. chap. 28. For a penetrating reminiscence of Sullivan, see David McKenzie Rioch, "Recollections of Harry Stack Sullivan and of the Development of His Interpersonal Psychiatry," *Psychiatry* 48 (1985): 141–58.

33. Rockefeller officials negotiated with both the University of Chicago and Yale to see which institution would make a more substantial contribution to the seminar's support. See Edmund E. Day to John V. Van Sickle, 1–2, Dec. 9, 1930, box 408, folder 4828, RG 1.1, series 200s, RF Archives. I have used the title of the seminar that appears in Edward Sapir to Stacy May, May 22, 1933, box 408, folder 4830, RG 1.1, series 200s, RF Archives. Sullivan was one of the visiting social scientists who made presentations to the Yale seminar. See Bingham Dai, "Diary of the Seminar on the Impact of Culture upon Personality" (manuscript, 1932–33), 124–36, box 1, folder 1.5, Bingham Dai Papers, ASU.

34. "Memorandum on Impact of Culture on Personality" (typescript, n.d.), 1 (first quotation); LKF [Lawrence K. Frank], "Study of Comparative Culture" (typescript, n.d.), 2, 3 (second and third quotations), both in box 408, folder 4828, RG 1.1, series 200s, RF Archives. Donald Slesinger referred to the seminar as "Larry's study" in a memorandum to Edmund Ezra Day, Mar. 18, 1930 (box 408, folder 4828, RG 1.1, series 200s, RF Archives), indicating that the seminar was the brainchild of Lawrence Frank. On Frank, see Margaret Mead, "Lawrence Kelso Frank, 1890–1968," *American Sociologist* 4 (1969): 57–58. Sapir, who did not begin with political aspirations for the seminar, called it "a decided success" in his letter to Stacy May of the foundation, May 22, 1933.

35. No return travel funding was provided at the outset for seminar members from Japan, China, and India. Lawrence K. Frank to Edmund E. Day, Feb. 6, 1932, box 408, folder 4829, RG 1.1, series 200s, RF Archives. Initially, the reasons may not have been political or military problems at home, although these soon affected some participants. For example, Bingham Dai returned to the University of Chicago to pursue a doctorate at the end of his year at Yale, and he wished to practice psychiatry in China. Mrs. Bingham (Vivian) Dai, interview by the author, Oct. 16, 2005, Asheville, N.C. Although he held a position at Peiping Union Medical College from 1935 to 1939, the Japanese occupation of China forced him to leave the country. He was unable to return after the war because of the rise of communism. See his autobiographical reflections in "Psychoanalysis in China before the Revolution: A Letter from Bingham Dai," *Transcultural Psychiatric Research Review* 21 (1984): 280–82.

36. Powdermaker explained her wish to extend her work on New Haven's black community to Mississippi in a letter to Mark May, Sept. 27, 1933, box 12, folder 114, series II, Institute of Human Relations Papers, RU 483, Manuscripts and Archives, Yale University Library. She had visited the Delta region to do preliminary research in 1932. Her in-house reports suggest the evolution of the southern work. Hortense Powdermaker, "Report on Negro Study," Nov. 6, 1933; Hortense Powdermaker, "Plan for Continuation of the Negro Research for the Next Academic Year," Feb. 5, 1934, box 12, folder 114, series II, Institute of Human Relations Papers. I describe the intellectual conflicts the research in Mississippi provoked in "Putting the South on the Psychological Map," esp. 337–53. Powdermaker published her research on Mississippi as *After Freedom: A Cultural Study of the Deep South* (1939; repr., New York: Russell and Russell, 1966). She recalled her southern fieldwork in her excellent autobiography, *Stranger and Friend: The Way of an Anthropologist* (New York: Norton, 1966), pt. 3.

37. John Dollard, *Caste and Class in a Southern Town*, 2d ed. (New York: Harper and Brothers, 1949), 23. Although Dollard's analysis with Sachs is often mentioned in the secondary literature—for example, Neal E. Miller, "John Dollard (1900–1980)," *American Psychologist* 37 (1982): 2—the only explanation of its meaning to him that I have found appears in Bingham Dai's journal. On the basis of a conversation with Dollard, Oct. 21, 1932, Dai recorded that Dollard was attracted to psychoanalysis at the University of Chicago by academic interests first in statistical measurement and then in social psychology. An analyst at Worcester (Mass.) Hospital gave him preliminary training before he went abroad. Dollard professed to be focused on "the technique of analysis" while accepting "some of the concepts" of Freud. Dai, "Diary of the Seminar," 54. When Dollard asked Yale University Press to send complimentary copies of the first edition of *Caste and Class in a Southern Town* to colleagues and friends, Sachs's name appeared on the "personal copies" list. Box 21, folder 52, series III, Institute of Human Relations Papers.

38. Dollard, *Class and Caste in a Southern Town*, 23 (first and second quotations), 269 (third quotation), 268 (fourth quotation), 267 (fifth quotation), 361 (sixth and seventh quotations).

39. "Yale Sociologist in New Book Bares Rivalry of Races in the South," *New Haven*

(Conn.) Register, Mar. 21, 1937, clipping, box 2, Dollard Papers. Slightly different versions of an interview of Dollard by William R. Ferris provide his later reflections on his southern experience. John Dollard, interview by William R. Ferris, March 14, 1975, New Haven, Conn. (typescript), box 1, folder 4, Dollard Papers; William R. Ferris, "John Dollard: Caste and Class Revisited," *Southern Cultures* 10 (2004): 7–18.

40. Donald Davidson, "Gulliver with Hay Fever," review of *Caste and Class in a Southern Town*, by John Dollard, *American Review* 9 (1937): 155, copy in box 2, Dollard Papers.

41. Ibid. (first and second quotations); W. E. B. Du Bois, "Southern Trauma," review of *Caste and Class in a Southern Town*, by John Dollard, *North Georgia Review* 2 (1937–38): 9, copy in box 2, Dollard Papers (third and fourth quotations); Lyle H. Lanier, "Mr. Dollard and Scientific Method," review of *Caste and Class in a Southern Town*, by John Dollard, *Southern Review* 3 (1938): 663 (fifth quotation), 664 (sixth quotation).

42. E. F. Frazier, "Racial Cultures and Conflict," *Christendom*, n.d., 506–7, copy in box 2, Dollard Papers; Davidson, "Gulliver with Hay Fever," 168.

43. James R. Angell to John Dollard, June 28, 1937, box 1, folder 2, Dollard Papers. In what seems a terribly small world, Angell, an experimental psychologist, was the head of the Department of Psychology at the University of Chicago at the turn of the century. Kerry W. Buckley, *Mechanical Man: John Broadus Watson and the Beginnings of Behaviorism* (New York: Guilford Press, 1989), 37. See also "James Rowland Angell" in *A History of Psychology in Autobiography*, ed. Carl Murchison (Worcester, Mass.: Clark University Press, 1936), 3:1–38.

44. Davis and Dollard, *Children of Bondage*, 9. Although it may seem illogical to claim the identity of behaviorism and psychoanalysis, Dollard stood in an established American tradition on the issue. In a book that introduced Freud to many Americans, *The Freudian Wish and Its Place in Ethics* (New York: Holt, 1915), Edwin B. Holt used Freud's sense of the complexity of human identity to complicate behaviorism, but he also argued that the behaviorists and Freud already shared an environmental orientation absent in the work of psychologists who emphasized introspection as the path to self-knowledge. See Holt, *Freudian Wish*, 199, 204. Dollard credited his Yale colleague, Neal Miller, with introducing him to behaviorism in Davis and Dollard, *Children of Bondage*, xiv.

45. Douglas Southall Freeman to Raymond B. Fosdick, Jan. 5, 1938, folder 5965 (first quotation); "$110,000 Goes for a National 2-Year Survey," *Washington Tribune*, Jan. 15, 1938, clipping, folder 5966 (second quotation); "A Proposal for a Study of Negro Youth" (typescript submitted Apr. 6, 1936, for Oct. 1936 meeting of AYC personnel), 3, folder 5966 (third quotation), all in box 558, RG 1.3, GEB Archives.

46. "Proposal for a Study of Negro Youth," 2 (first and second quotations); [Allison Davis], "A Proposal for a Study of the Racial Factor in the Personality Development of Negro Youth" (typescript, n.d.), 4 (third quotation), 5 (fourth and fifth quotations), box 558, folder 5965, RG 1.3, GEB Archives. Davis is identified as the author of the latter document in Homer P. Rainey to Edmund E. Day, Feb. 16, 1937, box 558, folder 5965, RG 1.3, GEB Archives.

47. "Proposal for a Study of Negro Youth," 2. The committee that prepared the report included two black members, Charles S. Johnson and Charles H. Thompson, the editor of the *Journal of Negro Education*, as well as two representatives of the Department of the Interior and a GEB officer.

48. For biographical information on Johnson, Frazier, and Davis, respectively, see Richard Robbins, *Sidelines Activist: Charles S. Johnson and the Struggle for Civil Rights* (Jackson: University of Mississippi Press, 1996); Edwards, "E. Franklin Frazier," 85–117; Hall, "E. Franklin Frazier," 47–67; and Dallas L. Browne, "Across Class and Culture: Allison Davis and His Works," in *African-American Pioneers in Anthropology*, ed. Ira E. Harrison and Faye V. Harrison (Urbana: University of Illinois Press, 1999), 168–90. Sullivan's contributions to the book series include "Memorandum of a Psychiatric Reconnaissance" in Johnson, *Growing Up in the Black Belt*, 328–33, and "Warren Wall" in Frazier, *Negro Youth at the Crossways*, 208–34. In his introduction to the latter book, St. Clair Drake explains that Sullivan also conducted twenty interviews for Frazier, xvii. The most complete list of advisers to the project appears in "$110,000 Goes for a National 2-Year Survey." Charles Johnson; Will W. Alexander, a white liberal from Georgia; and Robert M. Hutchins, the president of the University of Chicago, were members of the advisory group, along with government representatives, journalists, social workers, and labor leaders. Perhaps they had a say in research assignments.

49. Monroe Work to Robert L. Sutherland, Apr. 20, 1938, 4, box 558, folder 5965, RG 1.3, GEB Archives.

50. Johnson, *Growing Up in the Black Belt*, 301 (quotation), 19, 71, 223 (fantasy), 90 (education), 251 (parental protection). Johnson acknowledged his debts to colleagues in ibid., v–vi. Names of Johnson's staff appear in [Robert L. Sutherland], "Report on the Negro Youth Study" (typescript, 1940), 2, box 558, folder 5965, RG 1.3, GEB Archives. Sutherland is the likely author based on thematic connections between the report and Fred McCuistion to Robert L. Sutherland, June 28, 1940, box 558, folder 5965, RG 1.3, GEB Archives.

51. Davis and Dollard, *Children of Bondage*, 265 (first and second quotations), ix (third quotation). Although Dollard must have helped present the behavioral division between classes in psychological terms, this view of class relations may also be attributed to W. Lloyd Warner, an anthropologist who had recently moved from Harvard to the University of Chicago. Davis (M.A., Harvard, 1932, and Ph.D., Chicago, 1942) worked with Warner at both institutions and served as principal author of a field study described as "directed by W. Lloyd Warner" and for which Warner wrote an introduction about caste and class, Allison Davis, Burleigh B. Gardner, and Mary R. Gardner, *Deep South: A Social Anthropological Study of Caste and Class* (Chicago: University of Chicago, 1941).

52. St. Clair Drake, introduction to Frazier, *Negro Youth at the Crossways*, ix (quotation). On community resources, see ibid., chap. 7 ("Social Movements and Ideologies") and appendix B ("Supplementary Information on the Institutions, Social Movements and Ideologies, and Social Pathology of the Negro Community in Washington, D.C."). Although Frazier never lost sight of social facts and avenues for concrete action, his

view of class relations remained psychologically informed, to the extent that he offered a heavily cultural interpretation of social class in his later work, *Black Bourgeoisie* (Glencoe, Ill.: Free Press, 1957).

53. [Sutherland], "Report on the Negro Youth Study," 6.

54. Ira Reid, interview by ARM [Arthur R. Mann], Oct. 27, 1939, Atlanta University, interoffice memorandum, box 558, folder 5965, RG 1.3, GEB Archives. Reid stressed the "independence" of the projects, each one using "different techniques and formulae," and he seemed to attribute the fact "that each author wished his studies to be published separately" to careerism (Mann's words). Although the case studies were published, Reid also wrote a short additional summary of the project's findings, *In a Minor Key: Negro Youth in Story and Fact* (1940; repr., Westport, Conn.: Greenwood Press, 1971).

55. Allison Davis to R. J. Havighurst, Sept. 20, 1939, box 558, folder 5965, RG 1.3, GEB Archives.

56. Fred McCuistion to Floyd W. Reeves, Dec. 4, 1939, box 558, folder 5965, RG 1.3, GEB Archives (first quotation); McCuistion to Sutherland, June 28, 1940 (second and third quotations). Donald J. Shank requested the names of GEB state agents for the purpose of marketing from Arthur Mann, Apr. 3, 1940, box 558, folder 5965, RG 1.3, GEB Archives. McCuistion enclosed a list of summer schools in his June 28 letter to Sutherland. The prices of publications appear in a clipping from the *Committee Youth Problems Bulletin*, 1942, box 558, folder 5966, RG 1.3, GEB Archives.

57. McCuistion to Reeves, Dec. 4, 1939. Most audiences in the North were at the University of Chicago or Yale. The authors reached some southerners when Johnson spoke to the Southern Sociological Society, Reid distributed free mimeographed information in Atlanta, and Sutherland addressed adult educators in Austin, Texas. [Sutherland], "Report on the Negro Youth Study," 4-5. The proposal for the guidance clinics appears in Robert L. Sutherland, "A Recommendation for a Demonstration Project in the Personality Adjustment of Negro Youth" (typescript, stamped as received, Oct. 27, 1939), esp. 3, box 558, folder 5965, RG 1.3, GEB Archives. On the prominent role of Department of the Interior officials at the outset, see n. 47.

58. [Sutherland], "Report on the Negro Youth Study," 1 (first quotation); Sutherland, "Recommendation for a Demonstration Project," 2 (second quotation).

59. Discussion about locations for fieldwork is most fully documented in Work to Sutherland, Apr. 20, 1938. Still, much of the logic was not recorded.

60. Johnson, *Growing Up in the Black Belt*, xxiii.

61. The black scholars who left the South could not have been naive about the presence of racism in the North as well. During meetings in New York concerning the youth project, the Commodore Hotel refused Frazier a room, and the GEB declined to complain. Robert Havighurst wrote to Robert Sutherland that he had "not been explicit enough in my suggestions to you concerning securing rooms for the negro members of the group." Sutherland could protest to the hotel, Havighurst continued, but because "I am not so directly involved, I hesitate to make an issue when the hotel management might say that we had not done everything possible at our end to prepare for a favor-

able reception." Robert Havighurst to Robert Sutherland, Apr. 12, 1939, box 558, folder 5965, RG 1.3, GEB Archives.

62. Earl Warren writing for the Court, "Text of the Supreme Court Opinions, May 17, 1954," in Kenneth B. Clark, *Prejudice and Your Child*, 2d ed. (Boston: Beacon Press, 1963), 159.

63. Ibid., 164. The title of Myrdal's book is not italicized in the text. The names of scholars involved in the black youth project who also contributed to Mydral's book are in Gunnar Myrdal, *An American Dilemma: The Negro Problem and Modern Democracy* (1944; repr., New York: Harper and Row, 1962), lii. On the broader effect of the social sciences on the *Brown* decision, see esp. Walter A. Jackson, *Gunnar Myrdal and America's Conscience: Social Engineering and Racial Liberalism, 1938–1987* (Chapel Hill: University of North Carolina Press, 1990); Daryl Michael Scott, *Contempt and Pity: Social Policy and the Image of the Damaged Black Psyche, 1880–1996* (Chapel Hill: University of North Carolina Press, 1997), esp. chaps. 5–7; and John P. Jackson Jr., *Social Scientists for Social Justice: Making the Case against Segregation* (New York: New York University Press, 2001).

64. Thirty-five signatures follow "The Effects of Segregation and the Consequences of Desegregation: A Social Science Statement" in Clark, *Prejudice and Your Child*, 177–78. Thirty-two names appear at the end of a document of the same title, dated Sept. 22, 1952, in *Landmark Briefs and Arguments of the Supreme Court of the United States: Constitutional Law*, ed. Philip B. Kurland and Gerhard Casper (Arlington, Va.: University Publications of America, 1975), 60–61. Johnson's name appears only on the second list. Unless Clark was simply wrong, I infer that the additional signatures were added when the Court reconsidered *Brown* in 1954. Perhaps the documents were refiled, although official Supreme Court records contain only the 1952 version of the social scientists' statement. Perhaps, in contrast, the subsequent signers added their names publicly but not legally. I count thirteen names of scholars located in New York City on the list in Kurland and Casper's collection. Fifteen signers from New York City are on the list compiled by Clark.

65. Alain Le Roy Locke, *The New Negro: An Interpretation* (New York: Boni, 1925), book title (first quotation); Kenneth Clark to the editors of *Time*, Oct. 11, 1939, box 14, folder 1, Kenneth Bancroft Clark Papers, LC (second, third, and fourth quotations); Kenneth Clark to Mamie Clark, May 1, 1939, box 3, folder 7, Clark Papers (subsequent quotations). Mamie's letter to Kenneth about the rejection by Minnesota was dated Apr. 29, 1939, box 3, folder 7, Clark Papers. Kenneth often called Mamie "Katherine" during these years; for the sake of simplicity, I have not used "Katherine" to identify her letters, although that name may appear in the salutation or closing. For the same reason, I use only her married name throughout. A sample of the Clarks' early experiments is Kenneth B. Clark and Mamie K. Clark, "Segregation as a Factor in the Racial Identification of Negro Pre-School Children: A Preliminary Report," *Journal of Experimental Education* 8 (1939): 161–63. Kenneth had previously served as a "psychological investigator" for E. Franklin Frazier's *Negro Youth at the Crossways*. E. Franklin Frazier

to Kenneth Clark, Feb. 18, 1938, box 14, folder 1, Clark Papers. On their collaboration, see also Kenneth Clark to Francis Sumner, Jan. 12, 1937, and E. Franklin Frazier to Kenneth Clark, Nov. 20, 1938, Jan. 28, 1939, all in box 14, folder 1, Clark Papers. The Clarks developed experiments to test children's awareness of color in part through their doctoral work at Columbia under the psychologists Otto Klineberg (Kenneth's adviser) and Henry Garrett (Mamie's adviser). Still, the earliest experiments began as Mamie's master's thesis in the Department of Psychology at Howard University, where the couple had been undergraduates, under the supervision of the department chair, Francis C. Sumner. See [Mamie Clark], "Clinical Experience" (typescript, n.d.), box 9, folder 4, Clark Papers. The Clarks' discussion of Kenneth's job placement was ongoing during the early years of their marriage. Although Charles H. Thompson, dean of the College of Liberal Arts at Howard, wrote to Kenneth about a job possibility at Virginia State College for Negroes (Jan. 6, 1939, box 14, folder 1, Clark Papers), it seems often to have been Mamie who was receptive to openings in segregated colleges and who suggested them to her husband. See Mamie Clark to Kenneth Clark, 1938–40, box 3, folder 8, Clark Papers, and Mamie Clark to Kenneth Clark, May 20, 1939, box 3, folder 7, Clark Papers. When Mamie was in New York and Kenneth was at Hampton, she wrote, "Write to me often — you can even talk about Hampton." "Wed. night," [1941?], box 3, folder 8, Clark Papers. I infer that her greater tolerance of the segregated South was the result of her southern background. Mamie's father, Harold Hilton Phipps, was identified as "Dr." and manager of the Pythian Hotel, Bath House, and Sanitarium, in Hot Springs, Arkansas, according to the hotel's letterhead. Among many accounts of Clark's connection with the *Brown* litigation, see esp. Kenneth B. Clark, "Racial Progress and Retreat: A Personal Memoir" (1993), in *Toward Humanity and Justice: The Writings of Kenneth B. Clark, Scholar of the 1954* Brown v. Board of Education *Decision*, ed. Woody Klein (Westport, Conn.: Praeger, 2004), 190–95.

66. Mamie Clark to Kenneth Clark, July 6, 1936, box 3, folder 8, Clark Papers. For a discussion of the use of "Katherine" as Mamie's name, see Mamie Clark to Kenneth Clark, Mar. 15, 1938, and his response, Mar. 16, 1938, both in box 3, folder 1, Clark Papers. The Clarks named their first child and only daughter Katherine.

67. [Kenneth Clark] to [Harold Phipps], draft, n.d., box 5, folder 4, Clark Papers. The couple were married in New York on Apr. 14, 1938. Mamie Clark to Kenneth Clark, Apr. 19, 1939, box 3, folder 7, Clark Papers. Although the collection does not contain Phipps's letter to Clark, Clark had written to Phipps about the romance, June 9, 1937, and Phipps responded cordially, if not warmly, July 19, 1937, both in box 3, folder 7, Clark Papers. In his letter of June 9, Clark explained that he met Mamie when he was in charge of freshman orientation at Howard in 1934 and she was an incoming student. The extensive correspondence in the collection attests to his single-minded devotion to her.

68. "Effects of Segregation and the Consequences of Desegregation" in Clark, *Prejudice and Your Child*, 171 (first quotation), 170 (second quotation).

69. Charles S. Johnson, *Shadow of the Plantation* (1934; repr., New Brunswick, N.J.: Transaction Publishers, 1996), 5 (first quotation); Robert E. Park, introduction to ibid.,

xx (second quotation); Frank Lawrence Owsley, *Plain Folk of the Old South* (1948; repr., Chicago: Quadrangle, 1965), title of chap. 3, 90 (third quotation). I have chosen these instances of word usage to indicate the diversity of scholars who applied this language to a variety of human subjects. Johnson, a southern black writer, and Park, a northern white one, were referring to African Americans, whereas Owsley, a southern white, was speaking about antebellum white farmers.

70. Howard W. Odum, "Religious Folk-Songs of the Southern Negroes," *American Journal of Religious Psychology and Education* 3 (1909): 268.

71. Howard W. Odum, "Folk and Regional Conflict as a Field of Sociological Study," in *Folk, Region, and Society: Selected Papers of Howard W. Odum*, ed. Katherine Jocher, Guy B. Johnson, George L. Stimpson, and Rupert B. Vance (Chapel Hill: University of North Carolina Press, 1964), 246.

72. Odum, "Lynchings, Fears, and Folkways," 720.

73. Howard W. Odum, "The Folkways, the Mores, the Technicways," excerpt from *Understanding Society: The Principles of Dynamic Sociology* (1947), in Odum, *Folk, Region, and Society*, 264 (first quotation), 266 (second quotation). Some of Odum's analysis here closely follows the thinking of his dissertation adviser at Columbia, Franklin Henry Giddings, whose late lectures Odum edited and published after Giddings's death as *Civilization and Society: An Account of the Development and Behavior of Human Society* (New York: Holt, 1932), esp. chap. 5. For a general discussion of Odum, see Michael O'Brien, *The Idea of the American South, 1920–1941* (Baltimore: Johns Hopkins University Press, 1979), chaps. 2–4. For an incisive analysis of the relationship between Odum's ideas of regionalism and folk culture, see Michael James Milligan, "The Contradictions of Public Service: A Study of Howard Odum's Intellectual Odyssey" (Ph.D. diss., University of Virginia, 1994), esp. chap. 5.

74. Odum, "Folkways, the Mores, the Technicways," 257 (first quotation); William Graham Sumner, *Folkways: A Study of the Sociological Importance of Usages, Manners, Customs, and Morals* (1906; repr., New York: New American Library, 1960), 20 (second quotation). Although folk studies and behavioral psychology generally stood in intellectual opposition to one another at this time, behaviorism also nearly made a reflective mind as traditionally conceived irrelevant to an understanding of human action. This similarity suggests an odd kinship between Odum and behaviorists such as John B. Watson. For an informative discussion of contention among psychologists in the 1920s over behaviorism, see Jane Gentry Smith, "The Mystery of the Mind: A Biography of William McDougall" (Ph.D. diss., University of Texas, 1980), chap. 8.

75. Sumner, *Folkways*, 57 (first and second quotations), 58 (third quotation), 59 (fourth quotation). Sumner discussed his memorable distinction between the brutish "masses" and powerful "classes" in ibid., 54–59.

76. Wilhelm Wundt, *Elements of Folk Psychology: Outlines of a Psychological History of the Development of Mankind*, rev. ed. (London: Allen and Unwin, 1922). Odum criticized Wundt in Howard W. Odum and Harry Estill Moore, *American Regionalism: A Cultural-Historical Approach to National Integration* (New York: Holt, 1938), 416. Although he also stated reservations about Wundt in "Folk and Regional Conflict as a Field of Socio-

logical Study," 242, Odum was enough of a traditionalist to be wary of modern freedoms. Consider his praise of "people in isolated areas [who] are natural and free" but who also have an "inner consistency and unity, of spiritual and religious motivation, in contrast to the more individualistic behavior of individuals in large cities." Howard W. Odum, "Folk Culture and Folk Society," excerpt from *Understanding Society*, in Odum, *Folk, Region, and Society*, 225.

77. Odum, "Folk Culture and Folk Society," 227. Odum and Moore's *American Regionalism* likewise called culture a "gestalt" of "various factors," 413. For a retrospective summary of the Gestalt viewpoint, see Köhler, *Task of Gestalt Psychology*.

78. Odum and Moore, *American Regionalism*, 417 (first and second quotations); R. R. Marett, *Psychology and Folk-Lore* (New York: Macmillan, 1920), 25 (third and fourth quotations).

79. Odum, "Folk and Regional Conflict as a Field of Sociological Study," 242 (first quotation); Howard W. Odum, "The Technicways in Modern Society," excerpt from *Understanding Society*, in Odum, *Folk, Region, and Society*, 270 (second quotation). Freud's foray into social theory is *Civilization and Its Discontents* (1930), trans. and ed. James Strachey (New York: Norton, 1961).

80. Odum, "Folk and Regional Conflict as a Field of Sociological Study," 246. Odum and Moore's *American Regionalism*, for example, includes page-long quotations from Odum's other publications, as well as equally lengthy excerpts from other research.

81. Howard W. Odum, *Social and Mental Traits of the Negro: Research into the Conditions of the Negro Race in Southern Towns; A Study in Race Traits, Tendencies and Prospects* (1910; repr., New York: AMS Press, 1968), 39 (first, second, and third quotations), 13 (fourth quotation).

82. Katherine Jocher, Guy B. Johnson, George L. Stimpson, and Rupert B. Vance, preface to Odum, *Folk, Region, and Society*, x. Milligan argues, in contrast, that Odum very gradually voiced agreement with environmental explanations of racial character between the 1910s and 1940s in "Contradictions of Public Service," 131–32, 299–300. My sense is that Odum's expressions of agreement with the emerging social science consensus about cultural components of racial identity still did not mean that he formulated a consistent view of dynamic racial psychology.

83. Howard W. Odum, *Rainbow round My Shoulder: The Blue Trail of Black Ulysses* (Indianapolis: Bobbs-Merrill, 1928), 67 (first quotation), 39 (second quotation), 316 (third quotation). Odum's *Wings on My Feet: Black Ulysses at the Wars* (Indianapolis: Bobbs-Merrill, 1929) and *Cold Blue Moon: Black Ulysses Afar Off* (Indianapolis: Bobbs-Merrill, 1931) became increasingly retrospective; the second in the trilogy focused on Ulysses as a soldier during the world war and the third simply made him the narrator of a melancholy tale of an antebellum family, black and white. Perhaps a folk treatment of contemporary blacks was too controversial or else the direction of the series simply represented a failure of imagination. Scholars of both races surprisingly spoke as if Odum's rough, migratory hero were a real social type, although good manners may have contributed to respectful references. See Park, introduction to Johnson, *Shadow of the Plantation*, xxi, and E. Franklin Frazier, *The Negro Family in the United States*, rev.

ed. (Chicago: University of Chicago Press, 1966), 210. These allusions at least suggest that Odum's series was widely known.

84. Odum, "Lynchings, Fears, and Folkways," 720 (first quotation); Odum, "Folk and Regional Conflict as a Field of Sociological Study," 240 (second quotation).

85. Newbell N. Puckett, "Religious Folk-Beliefs of Whites and Negroes," *Journal of Negro History* 16 (1931): 22 (first quotation); B. A. Botkin, "Folk and Folklore," in *Culture in the South*, ed. W. T. Couch (Chapel Hill: University of North Carolina Press, 1935), 580 (second and third quotations), 579 (fourth quotation); Puckett, "Religious Folk-Beliefs," 35 (fifth quotation). Newbell Niles Puckett (1898–1967) was a native of Mississippi. He earned a doctorate at Yale and spent his teaching career at Western Reserve University in Cleveland. Wayland Hand, "Newbell Niles Puckett," *Journal of American Folklore* 80 (1967): 341–42. Benjamin A. Botkin (1901–75) was born in Boston and spent most of his career as a writer in Washington and New York. See Michael L. Murray, "Benjamin Botkin," *Voices: The Journal of New York Folklore* 27 (2001), ⟨http://www.nyfolklore.org/pubs/voic27-3-4/botkin.html⟩ (June 10, 2008).

86. Puckett, "Religious Folk-Beliefs," 35. See also Puckett's elaborate *Folk Beliefs of the Southern Negro* (Chapel Hill: University of North Carolina Press, 1926), published in Odum's Social Study Series.

87. Johnson, *Growing Up in the Black Belt*, 280.

88. Robert E. Hemenway quoted in M. Genevieve West, *Zora Neale Hurston and American Literary Culture* (Gainesville: University of Florida Press, 2005), 85. For a sense of Hurston's immersion in folklore, see her *Mules and Men* (1935; repr., New York: Harper and Row, 1990); "Hoodoo in America," *Journal of American Folk-Lore* 44 (1931): 318–417; and *Dust Tracks on the Road: An Autobiography*, 2d ed. (Urbana: University of Illinois Press, 1984). West explains that Hurston's autobiography was criticized for its tendency to blur or obscure facts, as if Hurston treated her life as folklore. West, *Zora Neale Hurston and American Literary Culture*, chap. 5. On the rebirth of interest in black folklore, and in hoodoo along with it, between the late 1920s and 1940s, see Jeffrey E. Anderson, *Conjure in African American Society* (Baton Rouge: Louisiana State University Press, 2005), 10–16.

89. Frazier, *Negro Youth at the Crossways*, 29. West explains Hurston's position on Brown in *Zora Neale Hurston and American Literary Culture*, 226.

90. Johnson, *Shadow of the Plantation*, 6 (first and second quotations); Robert Redfield, *Tepoztlán* (1930), quoted in Park, introduction to Johnson, *Shadow of the Plantation*, xxi (third quotation); Johnson, *Shadow of the Plantation*, 5 (fourth quotation), 4 (fifth quotation).

91. Johnson, *Shadow of the Plantation*, 103 (first quotation), 125 (second quotation).

92. William I. Thomas and Florian Znaniecki, *The Polish Peasant in Europe and America*, ed. and abr. Eli Zaretsky (Urbana: University of Illinois Press, 1987), 191 (first quotation), 205 (second quotation).

93. Ibid., 11 (first quotation), 63 (second quotation). On the life stages, see ibid., 298–304. Although Thomas was arrested for sexual immorality in 1918, lost his job, and had no choice but to reside in Poland during the 1920s (Zaretsky, introduction to

ibid., 23–24), he was one of the top choices of Rockefeller officials to lead the seminar on culture and personality at Yale and in fact participated in the 1932–33 group on an ongoing basis. See [Frank], "Study of Comparative Culture," 1, and Dai, "Diary of the Seminar," esp. 81–82.

94. Charles S. Johnson, "Negro Personality Changes in a Southern Community," in *Race and Culture Contacts*, ed. E. B. Reuter (New York: McGraw-Hill, 1934), 208–27. This is a fascinating transitional piece, because Johnson highlighted "personality" in the title and on the first two pages (208–9), then titled the next two subheadings "A Peasant Group" and "Changing Folkways" (210–11).

95. Frazier, *Negro Family*, 15.

96. Ibid., 211 (first quotation), 363 (second quotation), 100 (third and fourth quotations). Although Thomas had left the University of Chicago by the late 1920s, when Frazier completed his doctoral work with Robert Park, scholars take for granted Frazier's indebtedness to *The Polish Peasant*. See Zaretsky, introduction to Thomas and Znaniecki, *Polish Peasant*, 5, and Edwards, "E. Franklin Frazier," 93–103.

97. Frazier, *Negro Family*, 19 (first quotation), 88 (second quotation), 361 (third quotation), 190 (fourth and fifth quotations). For similar thoughts in Freud, see *Civilization and Its Discontents*, esp. chap. 5.

98. E. Franklin Frazier, *The Negro Church in America* (New York: Schocken Books, 1964), 77. The book grew out of the Frazer Lecture in Social Anthropology he delivered at the University of Liverpool in 1953. His study *Black Bourgeoisie*, published in France as *Bourgeoisie Noir* (1955) before its English publication in 1957, strenuously blended an array of psychological ideas that bore little resemblance to Thomas's drives, including insecurity, self-hatred, and self-delusion, with the Marxian notion of ideology as a false consciousness. Among the black sociologists who rose to prominence in the 1930s, Frazier was the most sensitive to the social applications of psychology and continued to apply a variety of concepts to his scholarship.

99. Donald Davidson, "Howard Odum and the Sociological Proteus," in *The Attack on Leviathan* (Chapel Hill: University of North Carolina Press, 1938), 287 (first quotation), book title (second quotation); Rupert B. Vance, *Human Geography of the South: A Study in Regional Resources and Human Adequacy*, 2d ed. (Chapel Hill: University of North Carolina Press, 1935), ix (third quotation). Although Davidson was a traditionalist, he was intrigued by the use of social science to protect established mores. See also Donald Davidson, "Regionalism as Social Science," *Southern Review* 3 (1937): 209–24.

100. Although Odum's ideological phrasing of folk theory, with conservative racial overtones, seemed increasingly out of place in a nation moving toward desegregation, study of folklore itself continued. In Odum's own generation, for example, Frank Owsley published his acclaimed book, *Plain Folk of the Old South*, in 1948. More recent is the research of Charles Joyner, especially his historical consideration of the development of the field of southern folk culture, "The South as a Folk Culture: David Potter and the Southern Enigma," in *Shared Traditions: Southern History and Folk Culture* (Urbana: University of Illinois Press, 1999), 141–50.

101. Daniel Patrick Moynihan, *The Negro Family: The Case for National Action* (the

"Moynihan Report," 1965), in *The Moynihan Report and the Politics of Controversy*, ed. Lee Rainwater and William L. Yancey (Cambridge, Mass.: MIT Press, 1967), 64.

102. Ibid., 65 (first quotation), 75 (second quotation). Rainwater and Yancey explain that the wording about pathology derived from Clark in their introduction to *Moynihan Report and the Politics of Controversy*, 6.

103. William Alexander Percy, *Lanterns on the Levee: Recollections of a Planter's Son* (1941; repr., New York: Knopf, 1966), 304 (first quotation), 298 (second quotation).

Chapter 4

1. T. W. Adorno, Else Frenkel-Brunswik, Daniel J. Levinson, and R. Nevitt Sanford, *The Authoritarian Personality* (New York: Harper, 1950). The various names for the personality type appear throughout the study; earlier versions of the theory did not put the word "authoritarian" so much in the foreground. See, e.g., Else Frenkel-Brunswik, Daniel J. Levinson, and R. Nevitt Sanford, "The Anti-Democratic Personality," in *Readings in Social Psychology*, ed. Theodore M. Newcomb and Eugene L. Hartley (New York: Holt, 1947), 531–41, and Else Frenkel-Brunswik, "A Study of Prejudice in Children," *Human Relations* 1 (1948): 295–306. For a discussion of the F scale, see Adorno et al., *Authoritarian Personality*, chap. 7. For an assessment of the theory's wide and continuing influence, see Peter Suedfeld, "A TAProot of Social, Personality, and Political Psychology: Authoritarianism Yesterday, Today, and Tomorrow," *PsycCRITIQUES* 51 (2006), ⟨http://www.apa.org/psyccritiques/⟩. I thank William H. Tucker for a copy of the article. Some of the European-born intellectuals most intimately connected with the project, particularly Adorno and Max Horkheimer, were not psychologists but instead social theorists of the Frankfurt School. Frenkel-Brunswik, also a major contributor, was a child psychologist who studied in Vienna with Karl and Charlotte Buehler. On these émigrés, see Lewis A. Coser, *Refugee Scholars in America: Their Impact and Their Experiences* (New Haven, Conn.: Yale University Press, 1984), 38, 90–101. Even a brief look at the book's organization reveals that anti-Semitism was the catalyst for research. Along the same lines, the American Jewish Committee sponsored its publication.

2. Adorno et al., *Authoritarian Personality*, 234 and passim.

3. Thomas F. Pettigrew, "Regional Differences in Anti-Negro Prejudice," *Journal of Abnormal and Social Psychology* 59 (1959): 35. Works by American analysts of the South who paid lip service to authoritarian theory but used its own measures to chip away at its universality also include E. Terry Prothro and John A. Jensen, "Interrelations of Religious and Ethnic Attitudes in Selected Southern Populations," *Journal of Social Psychology* 32 (1950): 45–49; Richard Christie and John Garcia, "Subcultural Variation in Authoritarian Personality," *Journal of Abnormal and Social Psychology* 46 (1951): 457–69; E. Terry Prothro, "Ethnocentrism and Anti-Negro Attitudes in the Deep South," *Journal of Abnormal and Social Psychology* 47 (1952): 105–8; Thomas F. Pettigrew, "Desegregation and Its Chances for Success: Northern and Southern Views," *Social Forces* 35 (1957): 339–44; J. Allen Williams Jr., "Regional Differences in Authoritarianism," *Social Forces* 45 (1966): 273–77; and Russell Middleton, "Regional Differences in Prejudice,"

American Sociological Review 41 (1976): 94–117. The Dutch scholar Jos Meloen, in contrast, showed no skepticism about the broad utility of the F scale. See Jos D. Meloen, "The F Scale as a Predictor of Fascism: An Overview of 40 Years of Authoritarian Research," in *Strength and Weakness: The Authoritarian Personality Today*, ed. William F. Stone, Gerda Lederer, and Richard Christie (New York: Springer-Verlag, 1993), 47–69. None of the American authors was a southerner living in the South at the time he wrote, with the exception of Thomas Pettigrew, a native Virginian who taught for one year (1956–57) at the University of North Carolina. Southern scholars of both races avoided the authoritarian theory as, presumably, too categorical. See, e.g., a key assessment of the South's racial future in the region's premier social science journal at a pivotal moment for both this theory and segregation: Guy B. Johnson, "A Sociologist Looks at Racial Desegregation in the South," *Social Forces* 33 (1954): 1–10. In this presidential address to the Southern Sociological Society, Johnson made no mention of the authoritarian personality.

4. Prothro and Jensen reported a small correlation between church attendance and racial liberalism in "Interrelations of Religious and Ethnic Attitudes," 48. Pettigrew, in contrast, found religious practice to be connected with racial prejudice, as shown in "Regional Differences in Anti-Negro Prejudice," 32. Middleton rejected Pettigrew's claim of a clear influence of churchgoing on racism in "Regional Differences in Prejudice," 105. Although it would be too much to argue that religion was a central theme of the southern studies, the authors consistently treated the possible effect of faith on prejudice as a serious and an open-ended question. The claim that the white southern Protestant majority was not unusually anti-Semitic or anti-Catholic reinforced a positive view of southern piety as an obvious component of regional character. See, e.g., Pettigrew, "Regional Differences in Anti-Negro Prejudice," 30, and Middleton, "Regional Differences in Prejudice," 103. Slightly differently, E. Terry Prothro and John A. Jensen argued that southern blacks were not anti-Semitic in "Comparison of Some Ethnic and Religious Attitudes of Negro and White College Students in the Deep South," *Social Forces* 30 (1952): 426–28. The postwar revival across America's triple melting pot of Protestants, Catholics, and Jews makes it unsurprising that tolerance of religion figured in the American response to authoritarian theory. On the surge in religious interest, see Sydney E. Ahlstrom, *A Religious History of the American People* (New Haven, Conn.: Yale University Press, 1972), chap. 56. All this is not to say that *The Authoritarian Personality* spoke in a monotone about religious belief. For instance, a section reporting empirical work by an American junior coauthor was less dismissive of faith as unreason than collaborative analysis by Europeans influenced by a blend of Marxism and psychoanalysis. Adorno et al., *Authoritarian Personality*, 208–21, 233–26. Horkheimer's connection of prejudice with "irrational or anti-rational beliefs" made it predictable, however, that American religious habits, southern or otherwise, would clash with the theory. Max Horkheimer, preface to Adorno et al., *Authoritarian Personality*, ix.

5. Among scholarly works on the history of humanistic and existential psychology, see esp. E. Brooks Holifield, *A History of Pastoral Care in America: From Salvation to*

Self-Realization (Nashville: Abingdon Press, 1983), chap. 7, and Susan E. Myers-Shirk, *Helping the Good Shepherd: Pastoral Counselors in a Psychotherapeutic Culture, 1925–1975* (Baltimore: Johns Hopkins University Press, 2009). As excellent background, see Heather D. Curtis, *Faith in the Great Physician: Suffering and Divine Healing in American Culture, 1860–1900* (Baltimore: Johns Hopkins University Press, 2007). An early formal critique of the somatic orientation of early psychotherapy was Otto Rank, *Psychology and the Soul: A Study of the Origin, Conceptual Evolution, and Nature of the Soul* (1930), trans. Gregory C. Richter and E. James Lieberman (Baltimore: Johns Hopkins University Press, 1998). Rank reacted in part to Sigmund Freud's dismissal of spirituality in *The Future of an Illusion* (1927). American works before the war that spoke of mental healing in comparatively religious or philosophical terms include Rollo May, *The Art of Counseling* (1939; repr., Nashville: Abingdon Press, 1967), and Karl Menninger, *Love against Hate* (New York: Harcourt, Brace and World, 1942). C. P. Snow memorably called for an intellectual rapport between science and the humanities in his Rede Lecture at Cambridge in 1959. See *The Two Cultures: And a Second Look* (Cambridge: Cambridge University Press, 1965). But in America the cross-fertilization was already well under way, visible in such influential works as Joshua Loth Liebman, *Peace of Mind* (New York: Simon and Schuster, 1946); Seward Hiltner, *The Counselor in Counseling: Case Notes in Pastoral Counseling* (New York: Abingdon-Cokesbury Press, 1950); Paul Tillich, *The Courage to Be* (1952; repr., New Haven, Conn.: Yale University Press, 2000); Martin Buber, *The Knowledge of Man*, ed. Maurice Friedman, trans. Maurice Friedman and Ronald Gregor Smith (London: Allen and Unwin, 1965); Gregory Zilboorg, *Psychoanalysis and Religion*, ed. Margaret Stone Zilboorg (London: Allen and Unwin, 1967); and Howard Kirschenbaum and Valerie Land Henderson, eds., *Carl Rogers: Dialogues; Conversations with Martin Buber, Paul Tillich, B. F. Skinner, Gregory Bateson, Michael Polanyi, Rollo May, and Others* (Boston: Houghton Mifflin, 1989). Ellen Herman does not focus on the philosophical movement in her otherwise thorough study of the war's impact on the mental sciences, *The Romance of American Psychology: Political Culture in the Age of Experts, 1940–1970* (Berkeley: University of California Press, 1995), nor does Gerald N. Grob in his informative survey *The Mad among Us: A History of the Care of America's Mentally Ill* (New York: Free Press, 1994), esp. chaps. 7–9. On the war's consequences for psychoanalysis in particular, see Nathan G. Hale Jr., *The Rise and Crisis of Psychoanalysis in the United States: Freud and the Americans, 1917–1985* (New York: Oxford University Press, 1995), esp. chaps. 11, 13, 14, and 16.

6. Although few Americans would question that the modern South is the Bible Belt, scholars explain that it was not until the nineteenth century that the region became the heartland of Protestant evangelicalism. See esp. Christine Leigh Heyrman, *Southern Cross: The Beginnings of the Bible Belt* (New York: Knopf, 1997), and David Edwin Harrell Jr., "The South: Seedbed of Sectarianism," in *Varieties of Southern Evangelicalism*, ed. David Edwin Harrell Jr. (Macon, Ga.: Mercer University Press, 1981), 45–57. Randall J. Stephens similarly explains the migration of Pentecostalism into the South near the turn of the twentieth century in *The Fire Spreads: Holiness and Pentecostalism in the American South* (Cambridge, Mass.: Harvard University Press, 2008). Other espe-

cially helpful points of entry into the literature on twentieth-century southern religion are Beth Barton Schweiger and Donald G. Mathews, eds., *Religion in the American South: Protestants and Others in History and Culture* (Chapel Hill: University of North Carolina Press, 2004), and David L. Chappell, *A Stone of Hope: Prophetic Religion and the Death of Jim Crow* (Chapel Hill: University of North Carolina Press, 2004).

7. Ernst Borinski, interview by John Jones (archivist, Mississippi Department of Archives and History), Jan. 13, 1980 (transcript), 9, box 1, folder 1, Ernst Borinski Papers, Mississippi Civil Rights Collection, L. Zenobia Coleman Library, Tougaloo College, Tougaloo, Miss. Despite Borinski's profession of comfort in Mississippi, the dinners he cooked for Jones were not local cuisine; they included knockwurst, sauerbraten, and marinated herring. One evening Jones observed that the meal consisted of "things that I'd never put in my mouth before tonight," suggesting that Borinski set limits on his assimilation. Ernst Borinski, interview by John Jones, Mar. 9, 1980 (transcript), 1, box 1, folder 1, Borinski Papers.

8. Robert E. Park to Bingham Dai, Oct. 12, 1938, box 1, folder 1.2, Bingham Dai Papers, ASU. Dai's correspondence with Richard Lyman concerning his employment in Beijing indicates that Lyman sought Dai for his interdisciplinary training, community interests, and psychoanalytic experience. See Richard S. Lyman to Bingham Dai, Jan. 15, 1935; Bingham Dai to Richard S. Lyman, May 7, 1935; and Richard S. Lyman to Bingham Dai, Mar. 25, 1935, all in box 2, folder 2.18, Dai Papers. The subject of Dai's dissertation was the sociology of opium addiction. Bingham Dai, *Opium Addiction in Chicago* (1937; repr., Montclair, N.J.: Patterson Smith, 1970). On Dai's first contacts with Dollard and Sullivan, leading to his analysis by Sullivan, see Bingham Dai, "Diary of the Seminar on the Impact of Culture upon Personality" (manuscript, 1932–33), 106–7, 124–36, box 1, folder 1.5, Dai Papers. For insight into his analytic style in China, see Bingham Dai, "Divided Loyalty in War: A Study in Coöperation with the Enemy," *Psychiatry* 7 (1944): 327–40. For information on Dai's professional goals in China, his escape, and his family life, I am indebted to the late Vivian Dai, his wife, and Meiling Dai, his daughter, whom I interviewed in Asheville, N.C., on Oct. 16, 2005. Details about Dai's personal life noted here are from that interview unless otherwise noted. Biographical background on Dai is in Sally Atkins, "The Search for Self-Knowledge," in *Becoming Fully Human: The Works of Bingham Dai*, rev. ed., ed. Sally Atkins (Boone, N.C.: Appalachian State University and Atkins, 1997), 3–5; Bingham Dai, "Psychoanalysis in China before the Revolution: A Letter from Bingham Dai," *Transcultural Psychiatric Research Review* 21 (1984): 280–82; Paul L. Adams, "Tribute to Bingham Dai, August 14, 1986" (typescript), and "Curriculum Vitae: Bingham Dai, Ph.D." (typescript, n.d.), both in the author's possession. Copies of these two items are also in the Dai Papers, as are copies of all his publications.

9. Bingham Dai to Richard S. Lyman, May 5, 1943, box 2, folder 2.18, Dai Papers. Dai worked in New York for the Chinese News Service. The phrase "sociological clinic" appears in Bingham Dai, "Some Problems of Personality Development among Negro Children," in *Sociological Foundations of the Psychiatric Disorders of Childhood: Proceedings of the Twelfth Institute of the Child Research Clinic of the Woods School, . . . in Collabora-*

tion with the School of Medicine of Duke University (Durham, N.C., November 1945), 78, 99. For his research at Fisk, see also Bingham Dai, "Negro Personality and the Learning Process," *Harvard Educational Review* 16 (1946): 173–93.

10. For the details of Lyman's plan to teach psychiatry to African Americans, see chapter 2, esp. n. 118. Although there was no psychiatrist on the original faculty of the School of Medicine at Duke in 1931, forty-one psychiatrists, including Dai, had served on the faculty at one time or another by 1950, most with titles indicating that their specialty was "neuropsychiatry," though a few were called neurosurgeons or neurologists. *The First Twenty Years: A History of the Duke University Schools of Medicine, Nursing and Health Services, and Duke Hospital, 1930–1950* (Durham, N.C.: Duke University, 1952), 106–17. Dai's name appears in ibid., 108. Lyman founded the Department of Neuropsychiatry in 1940 with the help of a Rockefeller Foundation grant. Ibid., 18. The "foreign fellows" are listed in ibid., 127–28. On Dai's teaching responsibilities and tenuous employment, see "Neuropsychiatry Staff Members and the Courses They Teach" (typescript, Mar. 15, 1945), box 4, folder "Teaching 1945," and letters between Lyman and Dai, box 2, folder "Dr. Bingham Dai, 1943–1947," Richard S. Lyman Papers, Archives Department, Duke University Medical Center, Durham, N.C. On Lyman, see Emily Glenn, "Biographical/Historical Note," in "Guide to the Richard S. Lyman Papers, 1935–1959," ⟨http://archives.mc.duke.edu/mcalymanr_html⟩ (June 14, 2008). The collection reveals Lyman's diverse interests in the mental hygiene movement, the training of conscientious objectors as psychiatric caregivers, and racial reform. Wartime expansion of psychiatric treatment across the country offered Lyman a favorable atmosphere in which to experiment at Duke. His ambitious efforts did not seem anchored in a coherent medical philosophy, however, and he seemed to flounder after the war as government involvement in mental health through the VA system imposed a maze of new regulations. He spent the 1950s, the last decade of his life, at Meharry Medical College.

11. Borinski, interview by Jones, Jan. 13, 1980, 4 (first and second quotations), 5 (third quotation).

12. Ibid., 8 (first quotation); Ernst Borinski, interview by Roger B. Brown (transcript, ca. 1980–81), box 1, folder 1, Borinski Papers (second quotation). The Brown interview was one of a series of taped discussions with Borinski conducted by students under the supervision of Jerry Ward, a Tougaloo College faculty member. The Jones interviews offer the most detailed picture of Borinski's life, but see also Gabrielle Simon Edgcomb, *From Swastika to Jim Crow: Refugee Scholars at Black Colleges* (Malabar, Fla.: Krieger, 1993), chap. 8. He does not appear in Lewis Coser's otherwise informative study, *Refugee Scholars in America*, because of Coser's northeastern focus.

13. Borinski, interview by Jones, Jan. 13, 1980, 20.

14. Ernst Borinski, interview by John Jones, Jan. 27, 1980 (typescript), 10, box 1, folder 1, Borinski Papers.

15. Thomas J. Shields, S.J., to Joseph Fichter, June 30, 1937, box 1, folder 1, Joseph H. Fichter, S.J., Papers, collection 12, Special Collections and Archives, J. Edgar and Louise S. Monroe Library, Loyola University, New Orleans. Information on why

Fichter had to move south to join the Jesuits is in William J. Byron, "Fr. Joseph Fichter, Sociologist and Lover of Causes, Dead at 85," *National Catholic Reporter*, Mar. 11, 1994, 14, and Thomas Clancy, S.J., "Jesuit Father Fichter Asked Tough Questions," *New Orleans Clarion Herald*, Mar. 10, 1994, 10, both uncatalogued clippings in Fichter Papers, as well as in R. Bentley Anderson, *Black, White, and Catholic: New Orleans Interracialism, 1947–1956* (Nashville: Vanderbilt University Press, 2005), 21–22. Anderson untangles confusing information about Fichter's early years. Thomas Shields, S.J., gave Fichter permission to purchase books on Renaissance-era Jesuits, Oct. 16, 1939, box 1, folder 1, Fichter Papers. Between 1934 and 1942, the year of his ordination, Fichter published forty-six articles, the majority in *America*, the *Catholic World*, and *Commonweal*. "Published Articles: Joseph H. Fichter" (uncatalogued typescript, n.d.), Fichter Papers. Fichter did spend time outside the South when he earned bachelor's and master's degrees at St. Louis University in the 1930s and pursued theological study at St. Mary's College in Kansas in the 1940s. Additional biographical information is in his own "Vita Brevis" (uncatalogued typescript, n.d.), Fichter Papers; Joseph H. Fichter, *One-Man Research: Reminiscences of a Catholic Sociologist* (New York: Wiley, 1973); and Jeffrey K. Hadden and Theodore E. Long, eds., *Religion and Religiosity in America: Studies in Honor of Joseph H. Fichter* (New York: Crossroad, 1983), 1–14. Fichter's history may profitably be placed against the background of the transformation of Catholics from southern outsiders to insiders during the civil rights era. See Andrew S. Moore, *The South's Tolerable Alien: Roman Catholics in Alabama and Georgia, 1945–1970* (Baton Rouge: Louisiana State University Press, 2007).

16. Harry L. Crane, S.J., to Joseph H. Fichter, Sept. 14, 1944, box 1, folder 3, Fichter Papers. Although scholars typically say that Fichter's Harvard degree was in the field of sociology, he in fact earned his doctorate in the Department of Human Relations. See Fichter, *One-Man Research*, 1, and the letterhead of correspondence to Fichter from Talcott Parsons, May 28, 1947; Gordon Allport, Oct. 6, 1947; and Carle C. Zimmerman, Sept. 2, 1948, all in box 1, folder 3, Fichter Papers. The difference is noteworthy because the name reflected the unit's commitment to interdisciplinary work. Allport, a member of Fichter's doctoral committee, took sufficient interest in psychology, for example, to have written *Personality: A Psychological Interpretation* (1937). Fichter's summer study in sociology at the University of North Carolina in 1945 has also been underestimated. He acquired a reputation as an expert on regionalism in Catholic circles; for example, Maurice V. Shean, C.O., asked him to explain a "basic, regional approach" to a Catholic conference on racial issues, Dec. 4, 1950, box 1, folder 5, Fichter Papers. See correspondence connected with his acceptance at North Carolina, W. W. Pearson to Joseph H. Fichter, Apr. 3, 1945, and June 9, 1945, as well as "[Short?] List — Books Still Needed in Sociology Department, Spring 1949" (typescript), which included Howard W. Odum and Harry Estill Moore's *American Regionalism*, all in box 47, folder 6, Fichter Papers.

17. Bingham Dai, "The Patient as a Person," in *Sociology and Psychological Studies in Neuropsychiatry in China*, ed. Richard S. Lyman (Peiping: Vetch, 1939), reprinted in Atkins, *Becoming Fully Human*, 18.

18. Bingham Dai, "Personality Problems in Chinese Culture," *American Sociological*

Review 6 (1941): 688 (first quotation); Atkins, "Search for Self-Knowledge," 5 (second quotation).

19. For the repeated description of the basic psychology course, see *Loyola University Bulletin*, 1930–31, 75; 1933–41, 73; and 1949–50, 96, all in Special Collections and Archives, Monroe Library. The dates refer to bound volumes sometimes containing bulletins for several academic years. Additional psychology courses appeared outside the philosophy department without displacing philosophy's offering. For example, the Department of Education and Physical Education offered two general psychology courses as well as educational, business, and applied vocational psychology, according to *Loyola University Bulletin*, 1933–41, 55.

20. [Joseph H. Fichter] to Thomas Shields, St. Anthony, 1946, box 1, folder 3, Fichter Papers. Fichter often dated correspondence by the liturgical calendar rather than providing standard Gregorian dates.

21. *Tougaloo News: Catalogue Number*, 1923–24, 20, Archives of Coleman Library (quotations). Although the catalogue titles vary, I use *Tougaloo News* throughout for the sake of clarity. On moral regulations, see *Tougaloo News*, 1922–23, 8, 13, and 1924–25, 17, Archives of Coleman Library. Reverend Ludwig T. Larsen began teaching at Tougaloo in 1935 and at various times taught religion, philosophy, psychology, and the social sciences. See faculty lists in *Tougaloo News*, 1940–41, 1946–47, and 1951–52, Archives of Coleman Library. Based on headings of fliers for Borinski's Social Science Forum, Tougaloo added "Southern Christian" to its name from about 1956 to 1964. See box "Social Science Forums/Announcements/Fliers," folder "Social Science Forums," Borinski Papers. Like Loyola, Tougaloo added specialized psychology classes in connection with teacher preparation without displacing more traditional offerings. For example, courses on educational psychology, childhood, and adolescence appear in *Tougaloo News*, 1930–31, 23, Archives of Coleman Library.

22. "Pre-Christmas Social Science Forum" (flier, Dec. 5, 1951), box "Forums/Announcements/Fliers," folder "Social Science Forums," Borinski Papers. See also "Pre-Easter Social Science Forum" (flier, Apr. 1, 1953), box "Forums/Announcements/Fliers," folder "Social Science Forums," Borinski Papers.

23. Although Fichter was only an assistant professor when he began as a regular faculty member at Loyola in 1947, recognition of his mastery of sociology led to his appointment as chair of the department. See *Loyola University Bulletin*, 1949–50, 13. Sociology courses for the same year appear in ibid., 102–3. Fichter had urged Loyola administrators to develop a school of social work, distinct from the sociology department, before he returned with his Ph.D. See Fichter to Shields, St. Anthony, 1946. Borinski's courses appear in *Tougaloo News*, 1949–50, 44–45, Archives of Coleman Library. The later psychology courses are mentioned in *Tougaloo News*, 1965–66, 89–90, Archives of Coleman Library.

24. Bingham Dai, "My Experience of Psychotherapy: Some Reasons for My Relative Freedom from Fatigue" (1979), in Atkins, *Becoming Fully Human*, 52.

25. Bingham Dai, "Freedom, Discipline and Personal Security," *Progressive Education* 26 (1949): 70 (first and second quotations), 73 (third quotation). Another instance of

Dai's use of "self" appears in "Culture, Self and Ethnocentrism" (typescript, paper for conference of the International Council of Psychologists, ca. 1960), box 2, folder 2.9, Dai Papers. Here he argues characteristically that no individual self can be understood apart from its social surroundings (13). In "The Growth of the Self" ([typescript, n.d.], box 2, folder 2.9, Dai Papers), prepared for Mead's Philosophy 321, Dai contended that the self, understood as a matter of self-consciousness, is a social product (esp. 6, 15). For a straightforward primary work of European ego psychology, see Anna Freud, *The Ego and the Mechanisms of Defence*, trans. Cecil Baines (New York: International Universities Press, 1946). On the American movement, see Hale, *Rise and Crisis of Psychoanalysis*, chap. 13. In a different mood, Leon Saul's letters counseled Dai to read Freud, Karl Abraham, and Sandor Ferenczi as foundational figures. Leon Saul to Bingham Dai, June 29, 1938, Jan. 4, 1939, both in box 1, folder 1.4, Dai Papers. Dai emphasized that both Asian and Western thinking permitted optimistic assessments of human nature in "Science and Wisdom: A Psychologist Finds in the Wisdom of Religions Answers Similar to Those of Modern Psychiatry: A Talk with Bingham Dai," *Duke Alumni Register* 43 (1957), esp. 35. His affirmation of the synergy of East and West accelerated from this point onward. See Bingham Dai, "Being Fully Human: A Chinese Ideal of Mental Health" (1981), in Atkins, *Becoming Fully Human*, 55–64, and similar pieces in that volume. But Dai deliberately integrated world philosophies from the outset. See, e.g., references to Chinese and Buddhist thought in Dai, "Growth of the Self," 13, 22. He explained the extent of his psychotherapeutic practice at Duke, which included all medical and neurological residents, in a letter to E. Mark Stern, Apr. 8, 1979, box 2, folder 2.12, Dai Papers. Sally Atkins, Jack Mulgrew, and Murray Scher underscore Dai's reliance on dreams, as well as his eventual rejection of Freud's presuppositions, in "Dreams without Interpretation: The Dreamwork of Bingham Dai" (1997), in Atkins, *Becoming Fully Human*, 81–85.

26. Dai, "Some Problems of Personality Development among Negro Children," 71. He repeated the thought in ibid., 96. The question of black identity was logically connected for Dai with the problem of prejudice, which he wrote about almost simultaneously in "Some Problems of Inter-Cultural Collaboration for World Peace," in *Approaches to World Peace*, ed. Lyman Bryson, Louis Finkelstein, and Robert M. MacIver (New York: Conference on Science, Philosophy and Religion, 1944), 124–42.

27. Saul to Dai, June 29, 1938. Curiosity about the applicability of psychoanalytic theory to Chinese individuals was palpable when Saul explained that he could not suppress all personal details about Dai "since the whole point would be the role of the Chinese culture." Nor was Saul's inquisitiveness unique: "Harry Stack Sullivan has already announced that he has analyzed seven or eight Chinese." Eagerness for cross-cultural comparisons places Dai's contemporaneous publications about his practice in China in an odd light: on the one hand, they simply expanded scientific knowledge, but on the other, they asserted the humanity of Asian patients to a skeptical West. See his "Personality Problems in Chinese Culture" and "Divided Loyalty in War."

28. Bingham Dai, "Thirty Years of My Life (An Autobiography)" (typescript, 1932), 35, box 1, folder 1.8, Dai Papers.

29. Ibid., 41; Dai, "Culture, Self and Ethnocentrism," 9.

30. Dai, "Thirty Years of My Life," 44 (first quotation), 45 (second quotation). Dai explained his study of Asian philosophies and religions in ibid., 35–36. He criticized Christian ethnocentrism in "Some Problems of Inter-Cultural Collaboration," esp. 127, 131–33. Dai may have understated his early commitment to Christianity in later writings. In "Thirty Years of My Life," he reported that he experienced conversion at a revival at age eighteen (26) and made contradictory statements about whether he ever aimed to become a minister, denying the goal at one point (27) but saying elsewhere that new interests "led me away from the Christian ministry" (44).

31. Dai, "Thirty Years of My Life," 45 (first and third quotations); Horney quoted in Dai, "Science and Wisdom," 35 (second quotation).

32. Borinski, interview by Jones, Jan. 13, 1980, 27.

33. Ibid., 23 (first and second quotations), 24 (third and fourth quotations). On Tougaloo's Social Science Laboratory and the Social Science Forums that grew out of it, see Borinski, interviews by Jones, Jan. 13, 1980, 21–22, and Jan. 27, 1980, 25. Notable speakers, as advertised in fliers, included Medgar Evers, the state secretary of the NAACP, July 20, 1955; Allard Lowenstein, then the New York field secretary of the Collegiate Council of the United Nations, Feb. 7, 1957; Eudora Welty, Aug. 8, 1958; William Kuntsler, a New York attorney, Nov. 7, 1962; Bernard Law, then serving on the Natchez-Jackson delegation to the Second Vatican Council, Nov. 17, 1965; and Sidney Mintz, a professor of anthropology at Harvard, Mar. 12, 1969. Box "Forums/Announcements/Fliers," folder "Social Science Forums," Borinski Papers.

34. Joseph H. Fichter to "Father Provincial," Mar. 22, 1955 (first quotation); [Joseph H. Fichter] to [Robert C. Harnett, S.J.?], Feb. 11, 1955 (second quotation), both in box 1, folder 9, Fichter Papers.

35. Joseph H. Fichter, *Southern Parish*, vol. 1, *Dynamics of a City Church* (Chicago: University of Chicago Press, 1951), 1. Note the title and assignment of a volume number, indicating his plan for the series; this, however, was the only volume published. In light of the interest of sociologists at the University of Chicago in southern fieldwork, dating back to Robert Park in the 1910s, the publication of Fichter's book by the University of Chicago Press makes sense. Fichter seems to have approached W. Lloyd Warner, the Chicago anthropologist, to secure publication of his book by the university press. See W. Lloyd Warner to Joseph H. Fichter, Aug. 19, 1948, box 1, folder 3, Fichter Papers.

36. Thomas J. Shields to Joseph H. Fichter, Feb. 24, 1948 (first, second, and third quotations); Sister Mary Frances to Joseph H. Fichter, Feb. 4, 1948 (fourth quotation), both in box 1, folder 3, Fichter Papers. On Allport's role, consider his letter to Fichter, Oct. 6, 1947, in which he wrote, "I am wondering whether you are carrying out your threat to hold a mixed seminar at Loyola and St. Xavier?" Box 1, folder 3, Fichter Papers.

37. Joseph H. Fichter to Louis Radelet, St. Edward [ca. Oct. 5], 1950, box 1, folder 5, Fichter Papers (first and second quotations). The encyclical is "Mystici Corpus Christi: Encyclical of Pope Pius XII on the Mystical Body of Christ, June 29, 1943," in *The Papal*

Encyclicals, 1939–1958, ed. Claudia Carlen (Raleigh, N.C.: Pierian Press, 1990), 38–61. For instances in which Fichter used the phrase "mystical body," see *Southern Parish*, 1:265; a public letter to fellow members of the Commission on Human Rights signed "yours in the unity of the mystical body," Sept. 10, 1953, *Christian Impact*, Oct. 1953, clipping, box 47, folder 1, Fichter Papers; and "Sermon Preached by Rev. Joseph H. Fichter, S.J., Mater Dolorosa—October 2, 1949" (typescript), box 65, folder 16, Fichter Papers. Many of his sermons and addresses at this time focused on racial issues. See Joseph H. Fichter, "Good Friday Sermon" (Mater Dolorosa Church, Mar. 26, 1948), and Joseph H. Fichter, "Commencement Address—Xavier University—Friday Morning, July 30, 1948," both typescripts in box 65, folder 16, Fichter Papers. On Fichter's racial goals for Loyola, see Anderson, *Black, White, and Catholic*, esp. 23–24, 46–47.

38. James McBride Dabbs quoted in Joseph H. Fichter, "American Religion and the Negro," *Daedalus* 94 (1965): 1095.

39. Ibid., 1098.

40. "The Way with Children," *Christian Impact*, Oct. 1953, 2, was a reprint of J. H. Pollack, "Are You Raising a Bigot?" *Everyman's Magazine*, n.d., box 47, folder 1, Fichter Papers. The expert was Benjamin Pasamanick, M.D., of Ohio State, who spoke on Mar. 11, 1956. See "An Opportunity for You to Hear the Truth about 'Racial Intelligence'" and "Noted Psychiatric Expert Ridicules Argument That Race Is the Cause of Mental Inferiority," *Christian Impact* fliers, n.d., box 47, folder 3, Fichter Papers. See also "Says Negroes Are Equal If Given Chance," *New Orleans Times-Picayune*, Mar. 12, 1956. This article about the lecture, reprinted in the back of the second flier, suggests that an interracial discussion, including faculty members from Tulane and Dillard universities, followed the talk. The Catholic Church did address its concerns about psychology in a way that permitted a distinctive psychological tradition. See Henryk Misiak and Virginia M. Staudt, *Catholics in Psychology: A Historical Survey* (New York: McGraw-Hill, 1954); Christopher J. Kauffman, *Ministry and Meaning: A Religious History of Catholic Health Care in the United States* (New York: Crossroad, 1995), 237, 284–87; and Benedict Neenan, *Thomas Verner Moore: Psychiatrist, Educator, and Monk* (New York: Paulist Press, 2000).

41. Dr. Vincent Daly (psychologist, Mississippi State Hospital), "The Psychology of Culture Changes and Culture Conflicts" (flier, ca. 1950); Dr. W. L. Jaquith (director, Mississippi State Hospital), "Are We Normal or Insane[?]—Community and Institutional Responsibilities for Mentally Ill Citizens" (flier, ca. 1950), both in box "Forums/Announcements/Fliers," folder "Social Science Forums," Borinski Papers. See also announcements for Anthony San Angelo, "Public School Teachers and Mental Disturbances of Students" (June 18, 1958), and Alvin W. Wolfe, "The Anthropological Conception of Race . . ." (Mar. 7, 1962), both in box "Forums/Announcements/Fliers," folder "Social Science Forums," Borinski Papers, and Vincent Daly, "Psycho-Pathology of Crime," *Tougaloo News*, Oct. 1951, 1, Archives of Coleman Library.

42. Dai's name appears on the list of signers of "The Effects of Segregation and the Consequences of Desegregation: A Social Science Statement" in *Landmark Briefs and Arguments of the Supreme Court of the United States: Constitutional Law*, ed. Philip B. Kur-

land and Gerhard Casper (Arlington, Va.: University Publications of America, 1975), 60–61, and, following the same text, also in Kenneth B. Clark, *Prejudice and Your Child*, 2d ed. (Boston: Beacon Press, 1963), 177–78. Charles S. Johnson's name appears only on the second list, as one of three names presumably added later. For further discussion of the documents and signatures, see chapter 3, n. 64.

43. Atkins, "Search for Self-Knowledge," 5 (first quotation); George Kriegman, "Bingham Dai and Wu-Wei," in Atkins, *Becoming Fully Human*, 9 (subsequent quotations).

44. Borinski, interview by Jones, Jan. 27, 1980, 10 (quotation). Edgcomb notes Borinski's living arrangements on campus in *From Swastika to Jim Crow*, 127. He lived in a nearby house, however, at the time of the Jones interviews. Borinski, interview by Jones, Jan. 13, 1980, 1. On the experiences of other Holocaust refugees at traditionally black colleges, see Edgcomb, *From Swastika to Jim Crow*, xiii and passim.

45. Fichter, "Vita Brevis."

46. RSM [Robert S. Morrison], "Emory University School of Medicine, Atlanta, Georgia, Tuesday, February 1, 1949," interoffice memorandum, [1], box 127, folder 1120, RG 1.2, series 200A, RF Archives.

47. Carl A. Whitaker and Thomas P. Malone, *The Roots of Psychotherapy* (New York: Blakiston, 1953), 98 (first quotation); Carl A. Whitaker, John Warkentin, Thomas P. Malone, and Richard E. Felder, "Experiential Psychotherapy: Evaluation of Relatedness," *Journal of Existential Psychiatry* 3 (1963): 247 (second quotation); Carl A. Whitaker and John Warkentin, "The Therapist as a Prototype," in *Challenges of Humanistic Psychology*, ed. James F. T. Bugental (New York: McGraw-Hill, 1967), 242 (third quotation).

48. On the evolution of the name, see Richard E. Felder and Avrum Geurin Weiss, *Experiential Psychotherapy: A Symphony of Selves* (Lanham, Md.: University Press of America, 1991), xx. Felder recalled both here and in an interview that the final name emerged within two or three years of the founding of the practice in the mid-1950s. Richard E. Felder, interview by the author, July 29, 2002, Gainesville, Ga. The first use of "experiential" that I have found in print, however, is the title of Whitaker et al., "Experiential Psychotherapy," in 1963. For another philosophical (versus historical) description of the approach, see Kareen Malone, Tom Malone, Ray Kuckleburg, Ross Cox, John Barnett, and David Barstow, "Experiential Psychotherapy: Basic Principles," *Pilgrimage* 10 (Spring–Fall/Winter 1982), offprint in the author's possession. I thank Patrick T. Malone for his gift of this text and many other offprints by or about members of the Atlanta Psychiatric Clinic.

49. [Morrison], "Emory University School of Medicine," [2]. For Whitaker's recollections, see Carl Whitaker, *Midnight Musings of a Family Therapist*, ed. Margaret O. Ryan (New York: Norton, 1989), 19–34.

50. Whitaker, *Midnight Musings*, 18 (first quotation), 19 (second quotation). For Whitaker's wartime experiences, see ibid., 15–19. Biographical information about Whitaker and Warkentin is in their essay "Therapist as a Prototype," 240. Whitaker earned an M.D. (1936) and M.A. (psychology, 1941) at Syracuse University; Warkentin completed a Ph.D. at the University of Rochester (psychology, 1938) and an M.D. at

Northwestern University (1942). On Whitaker, see also his "Emory University: Faculty Personnel Record," a form he completed Nov. 28, 1946, folder "Carl Whitaker," Biographical Files, Special Collections and Archives, Robert W. Woodruff Library, Emory University, Atlanta. For general discussions of the war's relation to psychological developments, see Herman, *Romance of American Psychology*, esp. chaps. 2–4, and Grob, *Mad among Us*, chaps. 7–9.

51. Thomas P. Malone, "Analysis of the Dynamics of Group Psychotherapy Based on Observations in a Twelve-Month Experimental Program," *Journal of Personality* 16 (1948): 253 (first quotation), 268 (second quotation). Whitaker recalled that he knew of Malone when he was still at Oak Ridge (*Midnight Musings*, 21); given the usual time delay for publications, I speculate that it was nonetheless Malone's research with soldiers, so similar in tone to Whitaker's emerging approach, that appealed to Whitaker, along with their instinctive rapport. Biographical information on Malone is in "Dr. Thomas P. Malone, Assistant in Psychiatry" (typescript, n.d.); "2/9/49 Malone" (typescript); and "Class of 1940" (typescript, n.d.), all in folder "Thomas P. Malone," Biographical Files, Special Collections and Archives, Woodruff Library; as well as Patrick T. Malone, interview by the author, July 30, 2002, Atlanta. There is disagreement about Malone's date of birth. "Dr. Thomas P. Malone" indicates that he was born in 1918, but a memorial booklet prepared by his family contains the date 1919. "A Remembrance: A Memorial to his Life, Thomas Patrick Malone, October 1, 1919–December 5, 2000" (January 14, 2001), in the author's possession. I have used the family's date. Morrison of the Rockefeller Foundation was so impressed by Malone's research ability that he told Malone that his medical studies were misdirected, inducing Malone to admit that "his motivation is largely the wish for a union card." Malone paraphrased in [Morrison], "Emory University School of Medicine," [3]. Morrison urged the psychiatrists to conduct research in collaboration with Emory's psychology department, an alternative that would have dovetailed more closely with Malone's skills than Whitaker's.

52. Rives Chalmers, interview by the author, July 29, 2002, Atlanta; Felder, interview. See also biographical entries on Chalmers and Felder, respectively, in *Fellows and Members of the American Psychiatric Association, Biographical Directory, as of January, 1983* (Washington, D.C.: American Psychiatric Press, 1983), 193, 346. On Chalmers, see also *Fellows and Members of the American Psychiatric Association, Biographical Directory, as of January, 1989* (Washington, D.C.: American Psychiatric Press, 1989), 251. On Felder, see also *Who's Who in Medicine and Healthcare, 1997–1998* (n.p.: Reed Elsevier, 1996), 350.

53. Chalmers, interview (quotation). On his options and choices after the war, see ibid. On his marriage to Elizabeth (Buba) Yates in 1944, see "Director," *Converse College Magazine*, Fall 1955, clipping, folder "Rives Chalmers," Biographical Files, Special Collections and Archives, Woodruff Library. Chalmers's aunt was a professor of Latin at Converse, and his wife was a graduate of the college. William R. Phillips, who joined the staff of the Atlanta Psychiatric Clinic in 1972, also emphasized the lure of Atlanta when he called it a "mecca" for the rural South. *Our History in Psychotherapy*, videotape

of symposium including Earl C. Brown, Richard Felder, and Phillips, coordinated by Tom Query, Apr. 24, 1999 (Clarksville, Ga.: Foothills Workshop), audiotape copy in the author's possession. The late Richard Felder brought the event to my attention and lent me the tape, and Tom Query permitted me to make an audio copy of it.

54. Felder, interview. Ross Cox, who became associated with the group in the mid-1960s, met with a similar reaction from his family. Ross and Nancy Cox, interview by the author, July 28, 2002, Cumming, Ga. A list of the original personnel at Emory appears in "Postgraduate Training Syllabus, Department of Psychiatry, Emory University School of Medicine, Emory University, in Conjunction with Grady Memorial Hospital and Lawson VA Hospital" (typescript, n.d.), 3, box 127, folder 1120, RG 1.2, series 200A, RF Archives. I have not discussed William H. Kiser and his wife, Ellen Finley Kiser, pediatricians before they became psychiatrists, or Nan Johnson, a psychiatric social worker who came with Whitaker and Warkentin from Oak Ridge. Although Johnson did not join the Atlanta Psychiatric Clinic, the Kisers did; they did not contribute to the group's publications, however. Graduates of Johns Hopkins School of Medicine, they were friends of the psychoanalyst Lawrence Kubie. Lawrence Kubie to F. C. Redlich, May 18, 1949, 5–6, box 127, folder 1120, RG 1.2, series 200A, RF Archives.

55. Carl Whitaker to Robert Morrison, Jan. 27, 1947, box 127, folder 1120, RG 1.2, series 200A, RF Archives.

56. [Morrison], "Emory University School of Medicine," [1]. For information on Grady Memorial Hospital, which served the local population, as well as psychiatric facilities at Emory Hospital and Lawson VA Hospital, see "Postgraduate Training Syllabus," 1, and Odom Fanning, "Grady to Install Mental [sic] Ill Facilities," Atlanta Journal, Oct. 6, 1948, clipping, folder "Carl Whitaker," Biographical Files. On Milledgeville, see "State Aid to Mentally Ill Praised," Atlanta Journal, Sept. 26, 1952, and "Emory and Milledgeville," no source, Oct. 1959, both clippings in folder "Rives Chalmers," Biographical Files.

57. William Rottersman quoted in Frank A. Smith (executive director, Georgia Association for Mental Health), "Outline of Community Mental Health Program Activities Currently Carried On by GAMH Chapters and Other State-Wide Organizations" (typescript, May 16, 1960), 2, box 78, folder 10, Lillian E. Smith Papers, collection 1283, UGA. On the women's clubs, see ibid., 7.

58. "Sterilization of Mental Defectives" (typescript, n.d.), filed with Ed L. Bridges to Frank Luton, July 2, 1953, box 6, folder 46, Frank H. Luton Papers, VUMC (first quotation); "Hines Will Probe Hospital Status," no source, n.d., clipping, box 95, folder 670, Robert Russa Moton Papers, Tuskegee University Archives, Tuskegee University, Tuskegee, Ala. (second quotation). Note that the black patients in Atlanta were already in a VA hospital and were not necessarily mental patients. The number of Georgia sterilizations appears in *Sterilizations Reported in the United States to January 1, 1954* (New York: Human Betterment Association of America, 1954), 2, box 6, folder 46, Luton Papers. By far the most sterilizations over the decades occurred in California (more than 11,000 mentally ill in contrast to a total of 1,130 in Georgia). Georgia, however,

had not yet acted to restrict the practice. See also T. G. Peacock, "Georgia Program for Sterilization" (typescript, n.d.), box 6, folder 46, Luton Papers.

59. Felder and Weiss, *Experiential Psychotherapy*, 25 (first quotation); Whitaker and Warkentin, "Therapist as a Prototype," 244 (second quotation).

60. Carl Whitaker, "The Use of a Limited Objective in Psychiatric Teaching" (typescript, n.d.), 2, attached to Carl Whitaker to Alan Gregg, Sept. 28, 1950, box 127, folder 1120, RG 1.2, series 200A, RF Archives (first quotation); Whitaker to Gregg, Sept. 28, 1950 (second quotation).

61. Kubie to Redlich, May 18, 1949, 4 (first and second quotations), 5 (third and fourth quotations). Kubie also explained the year-by-year training of the students in ibid., 3–4.

62. Whitaker to Gregg, Sept. 28, 1950 (first quotation); Whitaker, "Use of a Limited Objective," 4 (second and third quotations).

63. John Warkentin, "An Experience in Teaching Psychotherapy by Means of Group Therapy," *Progressive Education*, May 1955: 81, offprint in the author's possession. Some students expressed similar concerns when they met with Kubie: "These said that they would like to learn more about diagnosis, that they wanted to know what to tell families, that they wanted more help on prognosis and more idea [*sic*] about what to do about psychoses, and about the administrative and medico-legal problems involved." Kubie to Redlich, May 18, 1949, 4.

64. Malone, interview. Biographical folders for Rives Chalmers, John Warkentin, and Thomas P. Malone in Special Collections and Archives, Woodruff Library, all contain notes, presumably inserted by Emory University, indicating that the psychiatrists resigned in September 1955; a similar note in Whitaker's folder indicates the year more generally as 1955–56. Although the conflict was philosophical, money seems to have been a catalyst. Whitaker recalled that at no time was Emory willing or able to fund the psychiatry program fully. Whitaker, *Midnight Musings*, 20. Perhaps the university used budget cuts to remove the controversial program; Ross Cox remembered funding reductions. Cox, interview.

65. Rives Chalmers was the speaker covered in "Child Happiness Explained to P-TA," *Northside News*, Feb. 12, 1953, clipping, folder "Rives Chalmers," Biographical Files. He was also the lecturer or discussion leader for "Dental Group to See Film about Children," *Atlanta Journal*, Apr. 24, 1950, and "Nurses, Doctors Talk Workers' Emotional Ills," *Atlanta Constitution*, June 23, 1955, both clippings in folder "Rives Chalmers," Biographical Files. Whitaker spoke about "New Developments in Social Welfare in Atlanta," reported in "Sheltering Arms Elects Mrs. Griffen," *Atlanta Journal*, Sept. 25, 1949, clipping, folder "Carl Whitaker," Biographical Files. "Decatur Rotary to Hear Whitaker," *Atlanta Journal*, Aug. 19, 1953, reported his lecture on mental health, and he led a discussion on "family problems" following a play staged by the Atlanta section of the American Council of Jewish Women, "Council to Stage Play Feb. 21," *Atlanta Journal*, Feb. 16, 1955, both clippings in folder "Carl Whitaker," Biographical Files.

66. Wylly Folk St. John, "Emory Doctors Test Love as a Cure for Insanity," *Atlanta*

Journal and Constitution Magazine, Dec. 16, 1951, 9, clipping, folder "Carl Whitaker," Biographical Files (first quotation); Wylly Folk St. John, "Marry If You Want to Stay Sane," *Atlanta Journal and Constitution Magazine*, Feb. 21, 1954, 15, clipping, folder "John Warkentin," Biographical Files (second and third quotations).

67. Whitaker and Malone, *Roots of Psychotherapy*, viii (quotation). Writings for general practitioners include Richard E. Felder, Thomas P. Malone, John Warkentin, and Carl A. Whitaker, "Organic Psychoses as Picked Up in Psychiatric Examination," *Journal of the Medical Association of Georgia* 49 (1960): 56–59; Carl A. Whitaker, "The Ambulatory Schizophrenic Patient," *Journal of the Medical Association of Georgia* 49 (1960): 125–26; and John Warkentin, Richard E. Felder, Thomas P. Malone, and Carl A. Whitaker, "The Usefulness of Craziness," *Medical Times*, June 1961, all offprints in the author's possession.

68. Whitaker, *Midnight Musings*, 20. He repeated his regard for Gregg in ibid., 54.

69. Alan Gregg, *The Furtherance of Medical Research* (New Haven, Conn.: Yale University Press, 1941), 23 (first quotation); [Morrison], "Emory University School of Medicine," 2 (second quotation). Gregg's book consisted of his contributions to annual lectures endowed by the Dwight Harrington Terry Foundation on "Religion in the Light of Science and Philosophy." He spoke about sponsored medical research as innovative in *Furtherance of Medical Research*, 14–15.

70. Whitaker and Malone, *Roots of Psychotherapy*, vii (first quotation), 83 (second quotation), 105 (third quotation).

71. John Warkentin, Carl A. Whitaker, and Thomas Malone, "Social Origins of Delusions," *Southern Medical Journal* 52 (1959): 1418–20; Carl A. Whitaker, "Communication in Brief Psychotherapy with the Non-Psychotic Patient," *Diseases of the Nervous System* 18 (1957): 2–7, both offprints in the author's possession.

72. Whitaker, "Communication in Brief Psychotherapy," 3. Patrick Malone's impression was that Whitaker "wanted to be able to teach and keep writing and learning." Malone, interview. Wisconsin offered his father, Thomas Malone, a position at the same time, but he declined it. Looking back in his autobiography, Whitaker seemed to charge Emory with insisting on a scientism that psychotherapy could not deliver: "It [the arrangement with Emory] worked for ten years before 'they' (who is *they*?) realized that psychotherapy was not a science." Whitaker, *Midnight Musings*, 48. It is significant that Whitaker identified art versus science as an issue, although I believe that he simplified an internal ambivalence in hindsight by casting it as a bureaucratic dilemma.

73. Richard E. Felder, "Music of the Interview," *Voices* 4 (1968): 41–42, offprint in the author's possession; Felder and Weiss, *Experiential Psychotherapy*.

74. Kubie to Redlich, May 18, 1949, 4. Kubie was referring specifically to the "record room" of the Phipps Psychiatric Clinic in Baltimore, overseen for decades by Adolf Meyer, Kubie's teacher, inducing Kubie to quip, "Poor old Adolf." Ibid., 5.

75. Carl Whitaker, ed., *Psychotherapy of Chronic Schizophrenic Patients* (Boston: Little, Brown, 1958), chaps. 3 (transcript of session on "orality" moderated by Whitaker), 6

(session on "countertransference" moderated by Malone). The group hosted a total of ten conferences on schizophrenia beginning in 1950; this volume contains the only published proceedings. Whitaker, *Midnight Musings*, 26.

76. Whitaker, *Chronic Schizophrenic Patients*, 65 (first quotation), 74 (second quotation), 147 (third, fourth, and fifth quotations), 27 (sixth quotation). Whitaker recalled discovering Melanie Klein's theory of infant sexuality in the late 1930s in *Midnight Musings*, 12. See also Klein's most influential work of the period, *Love, Guilt and Reparation* (1937), excerpted in Melanie Klein, *Love, Guilt and Reparation and Other Works, 1921–1945* (1975; repr., London: Virago Press, 1988), 306–43. Late in life Whitaker remembered being aware of the difficulty of communicating with practitioners outside his group; they had to translate their "revered code words" into widely understandable language. Whitaker, *Midnight Musings*, 33. The wish to build bridges may have motivated the use here of then-popular Freudian concepts. The best-documented presentation of Whitaker's therapeutic style, free, in fact, of Freudian terms, belongs to a later period and so does not help unravel motivations of the 1950s. Augustus Y. Napier with Carl A. Whitaker, *The Family Crucible* (New York: Harper and Row, 1978). An earlier interview with him is less revealing. "The Growing Edge: An Interview with Carl A. Whitaker," in *Techniques of Family Therapy*, by Jay Haley and Lynn Hoffman (New York: Basic Books, 1967), 265–360.

77. Thomas Patrick Malone and Patrick Thomas Malone, *The Art of Intimacy* (New York: Prentice Hall, 1987), 36. Sources of epigraphs in Whitaker and Malone, *Roots of Psychotherapy*, include Kahlil Gibran, xvii; e. e. cummings, 8; Ecclesiastes, 40; Freud, 59; Whitman, 80; and Shakespeare, 159. Among group members, Felder most strongly articulated the aspiration to discover the commonalities of all psychotherapy: "So everything that applies to experiential therapy applies to psychotherapy in general. . . . We said that whatever kind of psychotherapy you do, what we say is psychotherapy applies to what you do." Felder, interview.

78. Whitaker, *Chronic Schizophrenic Patients*, 21. Note that it was John Rosen, a Philadelphia psychiatrist, who introduced this use of "black" and "white" into the conversation, but other participants repeated the terms in ibid., 21–23, 157. It is the lack of self-consciousness about the usage that is so arresting from a historical distance. Chalmers noted that at a time before widespread insurance coverage for mental health care, the group served paying patients. Chalmers, interview. In the early years of the practice, the cost of a session was five dollars, according to Felder, *Our History in Psychotherapy*.

79. "Leaders of Tomorrow: Emory Claims 26 of Atlanta's 100," *Emory Alumnus*, June 1953, 41, clipping, folder "Rives Chalmers," Biographical Files. Additional clippings about Chalmers's civic activities include "Emory and Milledgeville," no source, n.d.; Katherine Barnwell, "Rehabilitation Center Pushed by C.[hamber] of C.[ommerce]," *Atlanta Constitution*, Mar. 2, 1955; and Jack Nelson, "Mental Health Committee Asks Indeterminate Terms for Deviants," *Atlanta Constitution*, Sept. 23, 1955, all clippings in folder "Rives Chalmers," Biographical Files. Chalmers mentioned his friendship with King in his interview. Felder recalled Chalmers's focus on community service in his interview. "Mental Hygiene Group to Discuss Prejudice" (*Atlanta Constitution*, Mar.

19, 1951, 3, clipping, folder "Thomas P. Malone," Biographical Files), noting Malone's involvement, was a tiny notice compared with other clippings about the psychiatrists in Emory's files. Mention of the black family as patients appears in Felder and Weiss, *Experiential Psychotherapy*, 152.

80. Although I have questioned in my own work how much this generalization applies to the transcendentalists, America's preeminent romantics, the statement is certainly true for Ralph Waldo Emerson, a key figure, and many later reformers influenced by him. See Anne C. Rose, *Transcendentalism as a Social Movement, 1830–1850* (New Haven, Conn.: Yale University Press, 1981), as well as Leigh Eric Schmidt, *Restless Souls: The Making of American Spirituality* (San Francisco: HarperSanFrancisco, 2005), and Sydney E. Ahlstrom, *A Religious History of the American People* (New Haven, Conn.: Yale University Press, 1972), chaps. 36–37, 60.

81. Whitaker, *Chronic Schizophrenic Patients*, 211–14.

82. Kubie to Redlich, May 18, 1949, 4.

83. Cox, interview. On the group's use of multiple therapists for a patient and their cooperative writing, see Whitaker, *Midnight Musings*, 18, 26, 29, 33; Felder and Weiss, *Experiential Psychotherapy*, xvii–xxi; and Whitaker, *Chronic Schizophrenic Patients*, 214. Nancy Miller Phillips offers an account of experiences that led up to her participation in couples therapy in "The Pilgrimage of the Therapist's Wife," *Pilgrimage* 8 (1980): 209–11, offprint in the author's possession. On the couples approach, see also Cox, interview; Felder, interview; and Malone, interview. Patrick Malone remembered annual fishing trips that he and his father took with Whitaker and his son in Malone and Malone, *Art of Intimacy*, 30–31. Felder told the story about his son during the symposium recorded in *Our History in Psychotherapy*. Cox recalled that the group purchased land north of Atlanta in hopes of establishing a retreat center. Cox, interview.

84. Whitaker, *Midnight Musings*, 21. He felt his failure as an administrator so strongly that he used "impotent" and "impotence" to describe his feelings at Emory and in connection with his outreach work for the Georgia Department of Mental Health. Ibid., 21, 22. The discussion of applications for positions at the clinic was recorded in *Our History in Psychotherapy*.

85. Malone, interview (first and fourth quotations); Cox, interview (second quotation); participant in *Our History in Psychotherapy* (third quotation). Cox and John Barnett, another later member of the clinic, were Thomas Malone's students. Chalmers, interview. Some new members approached the group through more or less extended personal counseling or therapy, accenting emotional bonds. For example, Cox consulted Felder to resolve the question of becoming a psychiatrist (Cox, interview), and Phillips, sometimes along with his wife, saw Malone over a period of seven or eight years for therapy sessions before becoming connected with the clinic (*Our History in Psychotherapy*).

86. Carl Rogers to John [Warkentin], May 10, 1949 (first quotation); Carl Rogers to Carl Whitaker, Nov. 6, 1949 (second quotation), both in box 32, folder 2, Carl R. Rogers Papers, LC. Warkentin explained their earlier relationship in a letter to Rogers, May 11, 1949, box 32, folder 2, Rogers Papers.

87. In light of the connection between Rogers and the Atlanta group, it is intriguing that positions at Wisconsin were offered to Whitaker and Malone just after Rogers left the same university, as if the two men would replace him. On Rogers, see Howard Kirschenbaum, *On Becoming Carl Rogers* (New York: Delacorte Press, 1979), and Carl R. Rogers, *On Becoming a Person: A Therapist's View of Psychotherapy* (Boston: Houghton Mifflin, 1961).

88. Phillips recalled the group's professional influence on local therapists in *Our History in Psychotherapy*. A later generation of therapists associated with the clinic have connected the original perspective with recent medical trends. See, e.g., Craig G. Johnson, "Therapeutic Agendas: Patients, Therapists, Psychiatrists and their Problems" (typescript, Jan. 1995), in the author's possession. Thomas Malone's children similarly explore their father's viewpoint. Consider, e.g., Kareen Ror Malone, David Michael Malone, Patrick Thomas Malone, and Thomas Patrick Malone, "Psychotherapy as Non-Experience" (typescript, n.d.), in the author's possession. For Dai's comments, see Felder and Weiss, *Experiential Psychotherapy*, xxix–xxxi.

89. Felder, interview. Whitaker listed "Methodist church" under the category "religious affiliations" in his Emory "Personnel Record" (1946), folder "Carl Whitaker," Biographical Files. Between 1942 and 1944, he was also a lecturer at the Baptist and Presbyterian seminaries in Louisville. "Personnel Record." Although Malone was a non-practicing Catholic, he became involved in the founding of Galloway School, an Episcopalian institution, in Atlanta. Cox remembered that ministers referred congregants to the clinic, and Felder recalled that the group was consulted when Columbia (Presbyterian) Seminary in Atlanta developed a pastoral counseling program. Cox, interview; Felder, interview. William Phillips is an ordained Methodist minister. *Our History in Psychotherapy*.

90. L. J. Bass, "Your Right to Healing," *Shield of Faith*, Mar.–Apr. 1963, 13 (first and second quotations); George Ozdinec, "The End of the World," *Shield of Faith*, Mar.–Apr. 1963, 10 (third quotation). The periodical was published by the United Christian Ministerial Association. Copies of all Pentecostal periodicals cited are located in the Holy Spirit Research Center, Oral Roberts University, Tulsa, Okla. The leading study of the postwar Pentecostal healing revival is David Edwin Harrell Jr., *All Things Are Possible: The Healing and Charismatic Revivals in Modern America* (Bloomington: Indiana University Press, 1975). See also Grant Wacker, "The Pentecostal Tradition," in *Caring and Curing: Health and Medicine in the Western Religious Tradition*, ed. Ronald L. Numbers and Darrel W. Amundsen (New York: Macmillan, 1986), chap. 19; Anthea D. Butler, "Observing the Lives of the Saints: Sanctification as Practice in the Church of God in Christ," in *Practicing Protestants: Histories of Christian Life in America, 1630–1965*, ed. Laurie F. Maffley-Kipp, Leigh E. Schmidt, and Mark Valeri (Baltimore: Johns Hopkins University Press, 2006), esp. 161–63; and Stephens, *Fire Spreads*, esp. 174–76. On the racial inclusiveness of the postwar Pentecostal healing movement, Harrell comments only in passing. The Oral Roberts collection contains evidence that African Americans belonged to Pentecostal denominations affected by spiritual healing in the postwar South (see n. 116). Anthea D. Butler analyzes African American Pentecostalism in

Women in the Church of God in Christ: Making a Sanctified World (Chapel Hill: University of North Carolina Press, 2007). Further background information on Pentecostalism is in Grant Wacker, *Heaven Below: Early Pentecostals and American Culture* (Cambridge, Mass.: Harvard University Press, 2001), and Harvey Cox, *Fire from Heaven: The Rise of Pentecostal Spirituality and the Reshaping of Religion in the Twenty-First Century* (Reading, Mass.: Addison-Wesley, 1995). On pastoral counseling among liberal Christians, see esp. Holifield, *History of Pastoral Care in America*, chap. 7, and Myers-Shirk, *Helping the Good Shepherd*.

91. Frankie V. Adams to Rev. Mr. [Martin Luther] King [Sr.], July 11, 1933, box 4, folder 19, Frankie V. Adams Papers, AUC. Horace Bushnell's classic is *Christian Nurture* (1847; New Haven, Conn.: Yale University Press, 1967).

92. "Interview: JD [Jackson Davis], Sept. 25, 1943, Scarritt College, Nashville, Tennessee" (first quotation); "Interviews: RDC [Robert D. Calkins]," interoffice memorandum about a meeting with Hugh C. Stuntz (president, Scarritt College, New York), Jan. 11, 1952 (second quotation), both in box 155, folder 1436, series 1.1, GEB Archives. References to Scarritt's progressive curriculum appear in the latter memo. On the student exchange, see also J. L. Cuninggim (president, Scarritt College), "Rural Training for Christian Workers," proposal prepared for interview by Arthur R. Mann, "Interviews: ARM," interoffice memorandum, Jan. 22, 1942, box 154, folder 1435, series 1.1, GEB Archives. On the reunification of the regional Methodist churches, see John M. Moore, *The Long Road to Methodist Union* (Nashville: Methodist, 1943).

93. Wayne E. Oates, *Pastoral Counseling in Social Problems: Extremism, Race, Sex, Divorce* (Philadelphia: Westminster Press, 1966), 64. Biographical information is in "Dr. Wayne E. Oates: A Living Legacy," ⟨http://oates.org/cos/legacy/weo_history.html⟩ (June 14, 2008). On pastoral counseling during this period, see Holifield, *History of Pastoral Care in America*, esp. chap. 7. On Baptist views of healing, see Timothy P. Weber, "The Baptist Tradition," in Numbers and Amundsen, *Caring and Curing*, chap. 10.

94. Wayne E. Oates, *Anxiety in Christian Experience* (Philadelphia: Westminster Press, 1955), 88 (first quotation); Oates, *Pastoral Counseling in Social Problems*, 15 (second quotation).

95. Oates, *Pastoral Counseling in Social Problems*, 14 (first quotation), 19 (second quotation), 107 (third quotation), 63 (subsequent quotations).

96. Oates, *Anxiety in Christian Experience*, 77 (first quotation), 93 (second and third quotations). On Luther's trials, see Roland Bainton, *Here I Stand: A Life of Martin Luther* (New York: New American Library, 1950), esp. 33–34, 40–50. Oates linked neurotic concern for sin with Freud's ideas about compulsive rituals in *Anxiety in Christian Experience*, 90. He conveyed his supernatural focus when he explained the goal of counseling as enabling a person to become "a responsible person before God" in *Anxiety in Christian Experience*, 63.

97. Oates, *Anxiety in Christian Experience*, 125 (first quotation), 92 (second quotation). Oates advised parishioners and pastors about what to expect from secular psychology in *The Religious Dimensions of Personality* (New York: Association Press, 1957), ix, 298.

98. Oates mentioned his work as a chaplain at a state mental hospital in *Religious Dimensions of Personality*, 207.

99. By His Stripes, *White Wing Messenger*, Jan. 15, 1955, 14. The physical ills were mentioned in By His Stripes, *White Wing Messenger*, Jan. 1, 1955, 12.

100. A. A. Allen, *The Curse of Madness* (Miracle Valley, Ariz.: Allen, n.d.), 55. An advertisement for Grant's *Freedom from Evil Spirits* appeared with his column, Grant's Faith Clinic, *Voice of Healing*, June 1955, 10. *Voice of Healing* began as "An Inter-Evangelical Publication of the [William] Branham Healing Campaigns," Shreveport, La., 1948.

101. Louise Nankivell, "Dip Seven Times," *Voice of Healing*, July 1955, 8 (first and second quotations). On the relationship between atonement and healing, see also Charles S. Price, "Is Healing in the Atonement?" *Golden Grain*, Nov. 1928, 5–7, and Bass, "Your Right to Healing," 13–14. *Golden Grain* was described on the masthead of vol. 3, the oldest extant volume, as "A Magazine of Full Gospel Evangelism." Price was its editor; he began publication in Seattle and later moved to Pasadena, California.

102. Reg. G. Hanson, "How to Secure Anointed Handkerchiefs," *Healing Waters*, June 1948, 9 (first quotation); Mrs. Ilar Henry, Tenn., letter, By His Stripes, *White Wing Messenger*, Jan. 15, 1955, 14 (second and third quotations); "The Secret of Fasting and Prayer: How Fasting Saved an Insane Woman," *Voice of Healing*, July 1955, 18 (fourth quotation). *Healing Waters* was the first of several magazines published by Oral Roberts; its subtitle was *The Magazine of Bible Deliverance*. The divine gift of healing is not mentioned specifically in the biblical passage on which Pentecostals base their expectation that God's presence among humankind may be manifested in unusual forms, Acts 2.1–21. Healing miracles were nonetheless interpreted as signs of the outpouring of God's spirit; Jesus' work as a healer throughout the Gospels was the basis for faith in healing in the present age.

103. Charles S. Price, "The Dictator of the World," *Golden Grain*, May 1935, 7. For another expression of Pentecostal premillennialism, the belief that the world will be destroyed prior to the thousand-year reign of Jesus prophesied in the book of Revelation, see Ozdinec, "End of the World."

104. *Healing Waters*, Nov.–Dec. 1947, 1. Although most *Golden Grain* illustrations were like "Jesus in Gethsemane" (Mar. 1928, 17) or, more fancifully, a winged "Angel of Peace" (May 1928, cover), a photograph of Price with the caption, "Your Editor at the Grave of His Old Friend Williams Jennings Bryan, Arlington National Cemetery, Virginia," interestingly provided a cover in August 1928. In contrast to this respectful pose, a photo display illustrating every step in Roberts's charismatic cure of a woman suffering from depression was melodramatic and made Roberts the centerpiece. "Only God Knows the Agony I Suffered before He Healed Me," *America's Healing Magazine*, Jan. 1955, 6–7, 10.

105. "Requests for Prayer," *Golden Grain*, Mar. 1928, 17 (first and second quotations); "The Ministry of Casting Out Demons," *Healing Waters*, Aug. 1948, 8 (subsequent quotations). For a sample of postwar letters, see By His Stripes, *White Wing Messenger*, Jan. 1, 1955, 12, 14. It seems significant that correspondents in the 1920s requested prayers for healing from fellow readers, whereas those of the postwar era reported healing

miracles. The later communications convey both confidence in successful healing and erosion of a feeling of prayerful community.

106. Dan T. Muse, "The Great Pentecostal Revival," *Pentecostal Holiness Advocate*, May 19, 1949, 4. Tent advertisements, all in the *Voice of Healing*, include "For Sale" (Columbia, S.C.), Jan. 1956, 19; "For Sale Gospel Tents" (Valdosta, Ga.), Apr. 1960, 15; and "Gospel Tents Sold" (Elba, Ala.), Aug. 1960, 15.

107. The *Voice of Healing* gave extensive coverage to the Durham revival held in a tent on the Hillsboro road, June 3–27, 1948. See untitled front-page report, June 1948, 1; "Over 1,000 Saved in Durham Campaign," July 1948, 1, 11–12; and "3,342 Come for Salvation during Roberts Healing Campaign in Durham, N.C.," Aug. 1948, 1, 9–10. Harrell provides excellent biographical information on the postwar healers in *All Things Are Possible*, chaps. 3–4. Birthplaces of major figures include William Branham, Kentucky; Oral Roberts, Oklahoma; Jack Coe, Oklahoma; A. A. Allen, Arkansas; W. V. Grant, Arkansas; William Freeman, Missouri; and Gordon Lindsay, Illinois. See also autobiographical statements in Gordon Lindsay, ed., *Men Who Heard from Heaven: Sketches from the Life Stories of Evangelists Whose Ministries Are Reaching Millions, as Told by Themselves* (n.p.: Voice of Healing, 1953). "Salvation-Healing Campaign Schedules of the Voice of Healing Evangelists," a regular feature of the *Voice of Healing*, identified the home bases of the approximately fifty individuals on the circuit in the 1950s. See, e.g., the list provided in the Apr. 1955 issue, 22–23, which showed that the largest cluster of evangelists (eleven total) lived in Texas. For an account of the 1906 Azusa Street revival in Los Angeles, see Cox, *Fire from Heaven*, chap. 2.

108. J. M. Woodward, "Facts about Whiskey and Beer," *Pentecostal Holiness Advocate*, Jan. 5, 1933, 5; advertisements in *Bridal Call Crusader*, Nov. 7, 1934, 21.

109. "In the News: No. 2 of a Series, Anniston, Alabama," *White Wing Messenger*, Feb. 5, 1955, 4. On the difference in leadership, a carefully posed picture of the general overseer of the Church of God of Prophecy (headquarters, Cleveland, Tenn.) and his family stands in contrast to the cultivated stage presence of Oral Roberts. See Lillie Duggar, "Meet the General Overseer," *White Wing Messenger*, Jan. 1, 1955, 8–9.

110. *Healing Waters*, June 1948, 6 (first quotation); anonymous letter to Oral Roberts, "Medical Doctors Interested in Bro. Roberts [sic] Work," *Healing Waters*, May 1948 (second quotation); "Getting Medical Proof That God Heals," *Voice of Healing*, Jan. 1961, 13 (third quotation).

111. "Testimonies from the Oscar F. Capers Campaigns," *Voice of Healing*, May 1955, 16. For other instances of surgeries avoided, see Mrs. Alta M. Carrell, "Operation for Tumor Not Necessary," *Voice of Healing*, Aug. 1948, 4, and "Couldn't Afford Operation, the Lord Healed Her," under "Miracles of Healing," *Voice of Healing*, Nov. 1948, 9. For cancer, an alternative cure was "passing those cancers" out of the body, as Mrs. John Wood explained happened to her eleven-year-old son over a period of seventeen days in "The Prayer of Faith Shall Save the Sick," *America's Healing Magazine*, Nov. 1955, 11.

112. "A Sister in Christ" to "Prayer List," *White Wing Messenger*, Jan. 22, 1955, 13 (first and second quotations); "Patients of the Great Physician," *White Wing Messenger*, July 16, 1960, 10 (third quotation); "In Memoriam," *Pentecostal Holiness Advocate*, Dec. 1,

1949, 14 (fourth quotation); Promoted to Heaven, *White Wing Messenger*, Jan. 2, 1960, 13 (fifth quotation). On traditional southern attitudes toward doctors, death, and hoodoo, see chapter 1.

113. William Branham, "How the Gift Came to Me," *Voice of Healing*, Apr. 1948, 7. The evangelists did not seem to worry about the similarity between divine gifts of visions, voices, and glossolalia (speaking in tongues) and mental conditions considered by medicine as pathological. In their view spiritual gifts came from God, and mental illness, from Satan. Charles S. Price treated supernatural visitations as normal in "Visions," *Golden Grain*, Apr. 1935, 15–21, and "Seeing Visions and Dreaming Dreams," *Golden Grain*, Nov. 1944, 7–18. Even Wayne Oates, who was far from being a Pentecostal, took speaking in tongues seriously, in "A Socio-Psychological Study of Glossolalia" in *Glossolalia: Tongue Speaking in Biblical, Historical, and Psychological Perspective*, ed. Frank Stagg, E. Glenn Hinson, and Wayne E. Oates (Nashville: Abingdon Press, 1967), 76–99.

114. "Brother Branham Takes Extended Rest," *Voice of Healing*, July 1948, 1 (first and second quotations); "A Letter from Oral Roberts," *Voice of Healing*, Aug. 1948, 6 (third quotation). On Allen and Coe, see Harrell, *All Things Are Possible*, 70, 63.

115. "Frenzy of Faith in a Man's Touch," *Life*, Aug. 3, 1962, 12.

116. "Over 1,000 Saved in Durham Campaign," 11. Harrell notes the racial openness of the healing movement in *All Things Are Possible*, 98. Still, the magazines explained unconventional practices not only quietly but in a way that highlighted respect for local mores. During Roberts's South Africa campaign in 1955, for example, pictures and captions commented on race without textual elaboration. In "Great Moments on the Last Great Day of the Campaign," *America's Healing Magazine*, South Africa supplement (between Feb. and Apr. 1955 issues), 16, a caption read, "The color line is sharply drawn in South Africa, but Oral Roberts ministered to both black and white (in separate services) and was received with open arms by both races." Another photo caption from the same trip read, "The Indian congregation in Bethsham Tabernacle. Note the white folks in attendance." George E. Fisher, "South African Indian Report," *America's Healing Magazine*, Nov. 1955, 16. For additional discussion, see David Edwin Harrell Jr., *White Sects and Black Men in the Recent South* (Nashville: Vanderbilt University Press, 1971).

117. John A. Stubbs, "Overseers Give Instructions for Greater Progress in '55," *White Wing Messenger*, Jan. 29, 1955 (quotation). For the photograph, see "Annual Thanksgiving Service Blessed of God," *White Wing Messenger*, Dec. 10, 1955, cover. Similarly, the same magazine ran a wedding announcement for a black couple (pictured), who were church members, without comment. "Deadrick-Finlayson," *White Wing Messenger*, Jan. 22, 1955, 9.

118. Gordon Lindsay and Harry Hampel, "Shall We Have a Catholic President?" *Voice of Healing*, Sept. 1960, 4–5, 10. Anti-Catholicism was an ongoing theme, and Hampel was an established voice as the author of *My Deliverance from the Heresies of Rome*, advertised in *Voice of Healing*, June 1955, 23. On the state of Israel, see Charles S. Price, "Thunder over Palestine," *Golden Grain*, Apr. 1944, 3–32, and "Israel on the March:

100,000 Messianic Booklets Being Distributed from Village to Village," *Voice of Healing*, Apr. 1960, 6.

119. Allen, *Curse of Madness*, 3 (quotation). The book advertisements appeared with Lindsay and Hampel, "Shall We Have a Catholic President?"

120. "Salvation-Healing Campaign Schedules," *Voice of Healing*, Apr. 1955, 22–23. The information on the Roberts campaign is in "Summary of Brother Roberts' Ministry for Year 1954," *America's Healing Magazine*, Jan. 1955, 10.

121. Quoted in "Religious Quackery," *Time*, Feb. 9, 1962, 42. On the Coe trial, see *Tried . . . but Freed! The True Story of the Arrest and of the Case against Jack Coe in Miami, Florida* (n.p.: Herald of Healing, 1956). The feature on Roberts was "Frenzy of Faith in a Man's Touch."

122. "Religious Quackery," 42.

123. Martin Luther King Jr., "Letter from the Birmingham Jail," excerpted in *God's New Israel: Religious Interpretations of American Destiny*, ed. Conrad Cherry (Englewood Cliffs, N.J.: Prentice-Hall, 1971), 351 (first quotation), 352 (second and third quotations). King repeated that segregation robs the individual of a sense of personal worth in, for example, *Why We Can't Wait* (New York: Harper and Row, 1963), 85. The tradition of theological "personalism" that King absorbed during his graduate training in theology at Boston University began as a commentary on science. Devised by Borden Parker Bowne (1847–1910) and developed by Bowne's successors at Boston University, personalism was in many ways the humanistic equivalent of the social sciences' personality theory. Bowne presented himself as both psychologist and theologian in, respectively, *Introduction to Psychological Theory* (New York: Harper, 1886) and *Personalism* (Boston: Houghton Mifflin, 1908). By the 1920s personalist thinkers, perhaps reacting to professional specialization, wrote more narrowly about theology. See, e.g., Albert C. Knudson, *The Philosophy of Personalism: A Study in the Metaphysics of Personalism* (New York: Abingdon Press, 1927). The theological phraseology of personalism was even more pronounced when King studied with Edgar Brightman and his colleagues in the early 1950s. See John J. Ansbro, *Martin Luther King, Jr.: The Making of a Mind* (Maryknoll, N.Y.: Orbis Books, 1982), chap. 3; Paul Deats and Carol Robb, eds., *The Boston Personalist Tradition in Philosophy, Social Ethics, and Theology* (Macon, Ga.: Mercer University Press, 1986), esp. 4–5; and Gary Dorrien, *The Making of American Liberal Theology: Crisis, Irony, and Postmodernity, 1950–2005* (Louisville, Ky.: Westminster John Knox Press, 2006), 143–61. Although David Chappell emphasizes King's intellectual debt to Reinhold Niebuhr rather than the Boston personalist theologians, King's strong focus on the moral value of the individual person set him apart from Niebuhr's grander style of historical theorizing. See Chappell, *Stone of Hope*, esp. 45–53.

Chapter 5

1. Lillian Smith to Frank Smith, June 14, 1965, box 89, folder 13, Lillian E. Smith Papers, collection 1283, UGA (first and second quotations); Lillian Smith, *Killers of the*

Dream (New York: Norton, 1949), 238 (third quotation), 213 (fourth and fifth quotations).

2. Audrey M. Shuey, *The Testing of Negro Intelligence*, 2d ed. (New York: Social Science Press, 1966), 521 (first quotation); Henry E. Garrett, foreword to Shuey, *Testing of Negro Intelligence*, vii (second quotation); Audrey M. Shuey, introduction to *Testing of Negro Intelligence*, 4 (third quotation). The first edition was published by J. P. Bell (Lynchburg, Va., 1958). The second edition strengthened the conclusion by removing the word "some" before "native differences" and adding the phrase "inevitably point to" before Shuey's concluding words. Compare pp. 318 (1st ed.) and 521 (2d ed.). Shuey earned an A.B. degree at the University of Illinois (*Catalog of Randolph-Macon Woman's College, Session 1943–1944, Announcements, 1944–1945*, 11) and was a founding member of an Illinois Daughters of the American Revolution chapter in 1921 ("Daughters of the American Revolution, Sally Lincoln Chapter, Charleston, Coles County, Illinois," ⟨http://genealogytrails.com/ill/coles/darcharleston.html⟩ [June 14, 2008]). She received an A.M. degree from Wellesley College and subsequently taught at Northern Illinois State Teachers College. Edward Bradford Titchener to Audrey Shuey, Jan. 15, 1926, box 7, folder Jan. 14, 1926–Jan. 29, 1926, Edward Bradford Titchener Papers, collection 14-23-545, Division of Rare and Manuscript Collections, Cornell University Library, Ithaca, N.Y. Henry E. Garrett was her doctoral adviser at Columbia University, where she completed a 1931 dissertation titled "The Limits of Learning Ability in Kittens; from the Animal Laboratory of the Department of Psychology, Columbia University."

3. On connections between psychology and racial legislation, see esp. Kenneth B. Clark, *Prejudice and Your Child*, 2d ed. (Boston: Beacon Press, 1963); Daryl Michael Scott, *Contempt and Pity: Social Policy and the Image of the Damaged Black Psyche, 1880–1996* (Chapel Hill: University of North Carolina Press, 1997); John P. Jackson Jr., *Social Scientists for Social Justice: Making the Case against Segregation* (New York: New York University Press, 2001); Walter A. Jackson, *Gunnar Myrdal and America's Conscience: Social Engineering and Racial Liberalism, 1938–1987* (Chapel Hill: University of North Carolina Press, 1990); Andrew S. Winston, "Science in the Service of the Far Right: Henry E. Garrett, the IAAEE, and the Liberty Lobby," *Journal of Social Issues* 54 (1998): 179–210; William H. Tucker, *The Funding of Scientific Racism: Wickliffe Draper and the Pioneer Fund* (Urbana: University of Illinois Press, 2002); Lewis M. Killian, "Working for the Segregationist Establishment," *Journal of Applied Behavioral Science* 25 (1989): 487–98; and the essays in Andrew S. Winston, ed., *Defining Difference: Race and Racism in the History of Psychology* (Washington, D.C.: American Psychological Association, 2004).

4. Robert Coles, *Children of Crisis*, vol. 1, *A Study of Courage and Fear* (Boston: Little, Brown, 1964), 85 (first quotation), 353 (second quotation). The shifting relationship between the South and the rest of the nation during the civil rights era stirred debate about the region's distinctiveness that did not abate until the 1980s. See, e.g., Harry S. Ashmore, *An Epitaph for Dixie* (New York: Norton, 1957); Francis Butler Simkins, *The Everlasting South* (Baton Rouge: Louisiana State University Press, 1963); Grady Mc-

Whiney, *Southerners and Other Americans* (New York: Basic Books, 1973); John Egerton, *The Americanization of Dixie: The Southernization of America* (New York: Harper and Row, 1974); Carl N. Degler, *Place over Time: The Continuity of Southern Distinctiveness* (Baton Rouge: Louisiana State University Press, 1977); and Richard N. Current, *Northernizing the South* (Athens: University of Georgia Press, 1983).

5. Carleton Putnam, *Race and Reason: A Yankee View* (Washington, D.C.: Public Affairs Press, 1961), 55 (first quotation); Benjamin Muse, *Ten Years of Prelude: The Story of Integration since the Supreme Court's 1954 Decision* (New York: Viking, 1964), 276 (second quotation); Egerton, *Americanization of Dixie*, 75–103.

6. Kenneth B. Clark, *Dark Ghetto: Dilemmas of Social Power* (New York: Harper and Row, 1965), 22.

7. Coles, *Children of Crisis*, 1:134 (first and second quotations), 118 (third and fourth quotations). On the anger of one segregationist, John, and the fear of a black child, Ruby, see ibid., 298–315, 78–82.

8. Ibid., 150 (first, second, and third quotations), 167 (fourth quotation).

9. Muse, *Ten Years of Prelude*, 38 (first, second, and third quotations), 40 (fourth quotation), 44 (fifth quotation). Muse praised but also noted the limited power of moderates in ibid., 48–49, and characteristically condemned one itinerant rabble-rouser, Frederick John Kasper, in ibid., 94–104.

10. Putnam, *Race and Reason*, 44 (first and second quotations), 49 (third quotation). For Putnam's views on miscegenation, see ibid., 59, 94, and on Jews, ibid., 47, 56. Classic European and American statements of the same opinions include Arthur de Gobineau, *The Inequality of Human Races* (ca. 1853), trans. Adrian Collins (New York: Fertig, 1967), esp. chap. 4, and Madison Grant, *The Passing of the Great Race; or, The Racial Basis of European History* (New York: Scribner, 1916), esp. 15, 19.

11. On Overholser's interaction with the VA, see Charles Prudhomme and David F. Musto, "Historical Perspectives on Mental Health and Racism in the United States," in *Racism and Mental Health: Essays*, ed. Charles V. Willie, Bernard M. Kramer, and Bertram S. Brown (Pittsburgh: University of Pittsburgh Press, 1973), 47. His lectures appeared in Winfred Overholser, *The Psychiatrist and the Law* (New York: Harcourt, Brace, 1953).

12. Prudhomme and Musto, "Historical Perspectives on Mental Health and Racism," 44. As late as 1965, when 85 percent of St. Elizabeth's 1,600 "nursing assistants" were black, only one psychiatrist was an African American. Joseph H. Douglass, "Racial Integration in the Psychiatric Field," *JNMA* 57 (1965): 3. Overholser's argument that segregation enhanced the recovery of patients is less excusable in light of the currency of the counterargument—that "intergroup tension and prejudice represent a disturbance in the sphere of mental health." This was the opinion expressed in Rutherford B. Stevens, "Interracial Practices in Mental Hospitals," *Mental Hygiene* 36 (1952): 65.

13. [Frederick Payne Watts], "Journey from the Farm: The Life and Times of an Early Black Psychologist, as told by Frederick Payne Watts to Gabrael St. Clair during the Year 1996 in Washington, D.C.," transcribed by Gabrael St. Clair (typescript, 1997), 91 (first and second quotations), 90 (third and fourth quotations), box 1, Frederick Payne Watts

Papers, Howard. Although Watts remembered Mamie Clark as a "brilliant woman" (ibid., 36), she found him dull and unambitious when she was a student, a difference perhaps reflecting their diverging career paths. Mamie Clark to Kenneth Clark, "Sat. night" and "Sun. morning" (1938–40), box 3, folder 8, Kenneth Bancroft Clark Papers, LC.

14. Abram Kardiner and Lionel Ovesey, *The Mark of Oppression: Explorations in the Personality of the American Negro*, 2d ed. (Cleveland, Ohio: World, 1962), xvi (first quotation), 86 (second quotation), 134 (third quotation), xvi (fourth quotation), 187 (fifth quotation). Some examples of discussions of sexual issues are on the following pages in ibid.: impotence, 91, 112; frigidity, 145, 159, 229–30; and homosexuality, 137–38, 200. This study was not the only one to propose that the social cohesion of the black community was jeopardized by psychological damage. See Arnold M. Rose, *The Negro's Morale* (Minneapolis: University of Minnesota Press, 1949). Kardiner and Ovesey discussed their book's mixed reception in the preface to the second edition, *Mark of Oppression*, ix.

15. Coles, *Children of Crisis*, 1:261 (first quotation); *Louisiana Weekly*, Sept. 1, 1956, quoted in Dietrich C. Reitzes, *Negroes and Medicine* (Cambridge, Mass.: Harvard University Press, 1958), 299 (second quotation).

16. Quoted in Reitzes, *Negroes and Medicine*, 289. The number of black board-certified specialists is in ibid., xxvi. An earlier survey that similarly underscored the difficulties facing black doctors is Paul B. Cornely, "The Economics of Medical Practice and the Negro Physician," *JNMA* 43 (1951): 84–92. An argument emerged after the war that the general shortage of psychiatrists in the country could be remedied by training African Americans as an "untapped reservoir of personnel." Stevens, "Interracial Practices in Mental Hospitals," 63–64. See also Chester M. Pierce, "Manpower: The Need for Negro Psychiatrists," *JNMA* 60 (1968): 30.

17. Coles, *Children of Crisis*, 1:13.

18. Ibid., 3. Coles described the incident at the beach in ibid., 4–5. He described his other early encounters with southern racial issues in a telephone interview by the author, July 27, 2005.

19. Robert Coles, "Southern Children under Desegregation," also titled "Report for the APA, May 6, 1963" (typescript), 44 (first quotation), 45 (second quotation), box 474, folder 5045, series 1.3, GEB Archives. Additional materials in the GEB Archives help explain Coles's southern work in the context of his career: "*Grant in Aid* to the Southern Regional Council toward the Costs of a Study of the Adjustment Problems of Negro and White Students in Integrated Schools" (Apr. 13, 1962); "Curriculum Vitae" (n.d.); and "Curriculum Vitae, for: Dr. M. Robert Coles" (n.d.), all typescripts in box 474, folder 5045, series 1.3, GEB Archives. Coles explained his personal background in the telephone interview.

20. Coles, *Children of Crisis*, 1:120 (first quotation), 225 (second quotation), 339 (third and fourth quotations). For a collection of his writings on the South that appeared in popular magazines, see Robert Coles, *Farewell to the South* (Boston: Little, Brown, 1972).

21. Coles, telephone interview (quotation and personal details). Coles's contemporaneous scholarly articles include "Observation or Participation: The Problem of Psychiatric Research on Social Issues," *Journal of Nervous and Mental Disease* 141 (1965): 274–84; "The Lives of Migrant Farmers," *American Journal of Psychiatry* 122 (1965): 271–85; and "Racial Problems in Psychotherapy" in *Current Psychiatric Therapies*, ed. Jules H. Masserman (New York: Grune and Stratton, 1966), 6:110–13.

22. Alvin F. Poussaint and Joyce Ladner, "'Black Power': A Failure of Racial Integration within the Civil Rights Movement," *Archives of General Psychiatry* 18 (1968): 386.

23. On Poussaint's background, see Deborah Gillan Straub, ed., *Voices of Multicultural America: Notable Speeches Delivered by African, Asian, Hispanic, and Native Americans, 1790–1995* (New York: Gale Research, 1996), 983–84. Coles repeated Clark's opinion in his telephone interview.

24. Poussaint and Ladner, "'Black Power,'" 391 (first quotation); Alvin F. Poussaint, "The Stresses of the White Female Worker in the Civil Rights Movement in the South," *American Journal of Psychiatry* 123 (1968): 403 (second quotation); Poussaint and Ladner, "'Black Power,'" 391 (third and fourth quotations). Poussaint's most widely read essay connected with his civil rights activism, published in the *New York Times Magazine* in 1967, focused on the cultural roots of black self-hatred, not the South in particular. It was reprinted as Alvin F. Poussaint, "A Negro Psychiatrist Explains the Negro Psyche," in *Being Black: Psychological and Sociological Dilemmas*, comp. Robert V. Guthrie (San Francisco: Canfield Press, 1970), 15–25.

25. Coles, *Farewell to the South*, 16 (first quotation), 11 (second quotation). Poussaint drew on his experience as a dean at Harvard Medical School for "The Black Administrator in the White University," *Black Scholar* 6 (1974): 8–14. In 1975, along with co-author James P. Comer, he issued *Black Child Care*, reprinted as *Raising Black Children: Two Leading Psychiatrists Confront the Educational, Social, and Emotional Problems Facing Black Children* (New York: Plume, 1992).

26. Tilman C. Cothran, "Sociologists as Second-Class Citizens," in *A Decade of Sociological Challenges, Reflected in the Presidential Addresses of the Georgia Sociological and Anthropological Association, 1965–1974*, ed. Fred Roberts Crawford (Atlanta: Center for Research in Social Change, Emory University, 1975), 9–10 (first quotation), 10 (second quotation), 9 (third and fourth quotations).

27. Raymond Payne, "Sociology and Urbanism" (1967), in Crawford, *Decade of Sociological Challenges*, 13–18; Homer C. Cooper, "A Sociologist Looks at the Campus" (1970), in ibid., 37; Barbara Pittard Payne, "Women, Sociology and Macrosociety" (1971), in ibid., 39–48; Eugene G. Sherman Jr., "Urbanization, Communication and Education: A Precarious Search for Balance" (1973), in ibid., 57–60; Drenan Kelley, "The Dialectics of the Educational Process as Related to the Production and Transmission of Knowledge" (1974), in ibid., 61–68.

28. Lloyd C. Elam, "Development of the Department of Psychiatry at Meharry Medical College," in *Black Psychiatrists and American Psychiatry*, ed. Jeanne Spurlock (Washington, D.C.: American Psychiatric Association, 1999), 69. Elam was one of the first prominent black scholars who chose to live in the South. He repeated his view that

the South was hospitable to family life and discussed black migration to the region in an undated lecture, "Problems and Opportunities" (typescript), 6, Lloyd Charles Elam Papers, MMC. For biographical information, see William Greenburg, "New Meharry Head Has Many-Sided Outlook," *Nashville Tennessean*, Dec. 3, 1967, clipping; *Modern Medicine*, Jan. 15, 1975, 57, clipping; and Virginia Keathley, "Links Benefit at Barn Marks Clara's Birthday," *Nashville Tennessean*, Nov. 2, 1972, clipping, all in Elam Papers.

29. "Anti-Poverty Programs and the Psychiatrist" (typescript, n.d.), 2 (first quotation); "Urbanization: Implication for Mental Health" (typescript, n.d.), 10 (second quotation), both in folder "File (October and November)," Elam Papers. Development of course offerings may be traced in *Bulletin of Meharry Medical College, School of Medicine* 54 (Dec. 1958): 53; 57 (Dec. 1961): 68–69; and [no vol.], June 1964, 73–75, all in MMC. The field study is Ralph H. Hines, *The Health Status of Negroes in a Mid-Southern Urban Community*, 2 vols. (Nashville: Meharry Medical College, Department of Psychiatry, 1967). Elam's accomplishments came in spite of obstacles, such as the discontinuation of the nursing school by the time he arrived and insecure funding for new faculty positions. See Elam, "Development of the Department of Psychiatry," 70, 73–74.

30. Hines found that 91.6 percent of the neighborhood Meharry served was black. Hines, *Health Status of Negroes*, 1:20. Meharry underwent an internal racial transition during the 1960s. In the late 1950s, the entire student population was black (Reitzes, *Negroes and Medicine*, 6); by 1975, 20 percent of the students were white (*Modern Medicine*, Jan. 15, 1975, 57).

31. Lloyd C. Elam, "Psychological Aspects of Civil Rights Activity by Physicians" (typescript), with handwritten note stating, "Paper delivered to Med Committee against War at Oxford Univ. 7/10/66 by Dr. Elam," 4 (first, second, and third quotations), 2 (fourth quotation), Elam Papers. Elam was still a department chair when he delivered this talk; he became interim dean of the college in October 1966.

32. Frank Luton to Lloyd Elam, Oct. 23, 1968, folder "File (October and November)," Elam Papers.

33. [Frank H. Luton], "The Responsibility of the Psychiatrist in Desegregation" (typescript, n.d.), 9, box 3, folder 72, Frank H. Luton Papers, VUMC.

34. Ibid., 1 (first quotation), 2 (second and third quotations), 3 (fourth quotation), 5 (fifth quotation), 2 (sixth quotation), 7 (seventh quotation), 9 (eighth and ninth quotations). On Nashville school desegregation, see Muse, *Ten Years of Prelude*, 115–21. On medicine in Nashville, see Reitzes, *Negroes and Medicine*, 316–28.

35. [Wesley Critz George], "Using Schools to Promote Extremism," draft of letter to the *Durham (N.C.) Herald*, June 20, 1965 (first quotation); Jesse Helms to Wesley Critz George, June 16, 1965 (second quotation); Wesley Critz George to Robert Fant, July 6, 1965 (third quotation), all in box 11, folder 86, subseries 1.4, Wesley Critz George Papers, collection 3822, UNC.

36. As late as 1940, the year George became chair of the Department of Anatomy, he seemed an ordinary academic who specialized in tunicates and mollusks. See, e.g., Carl L. Hubbs to Wesley Critz George, Aug. 7, 1930, and Wesley Critz George to George [last name?], Nov. 19, 1940, both in box 1, folder 4, subseries 1.1, George

Papers. Samples of his correspondence with the psychologists include F. C. J. McGurk to Wesley Critz George, July 31, 1959, box 7, folder 44; Wesley Critz George to F. C. J. McGurk, Aug. 4, 1959, box 7, folder 44; Audrey M. Shuey to Wesley Critz George, Feb. 5, 1959, box 7, folder 42; Henry E. Garrett to Wesley Critz George, Jan. 2, 1962, box 9, folder 60; and Carleton Putnam to Wesley Critz George, Jan. 15, 1962, box 9, folder 60, all in subseries 1.4, George Papers. The bulk of his correspondence with this group of psychologists was with Henry Garrett. On the group, see Winston, "Science in the Service of the Far Right."

37. Wesley Critz George to Frank Graham, Sept. 30, 1933 (first three quotations); [Wesley Critz George] to Rev. Charles M. Jones, Mar. 23, 1944 (fourth quotation); Howard W. Odum to Wesley Critz George, May 26, 1944 (fifth quotation), all in box 1, folder 5, subseries 1.2, George Papers. George's initial letter to Odum, May 24, 1944, is also in box 1, folder 5, subseries 1.2, George Papers.

38. Wesley Critz George to Emmet Gribbin, Aug. 7, 1944, box 1, folder 5, subseries 1.2, George Papers (first and second quotations); George to McGurk, Aug. 4, 1959 (third quotation).

39. The typed copy of a letter to Mary Critz George from Roan Critz of New Jersey, a former slave of the family of Wesley Critz George, was dated Mar. 22, 1908, box 1, folder 1, subseries 1.1, George Papers. One instance of a letter to a politician is Wesley Critz George to Gov. Dan K. Moore, May 31, 1965, box 11, folder 86, subseries 1.4, George Papers. George seemed to write even more frequently to clergy. See Wesley Critz George to [Episcopal] Bishop Edwin Penick, June 19, 1946, and Bishop Edwin Penick to Wesley Critz George, June 20, 1946, both in box 1, folder 5, subseries 1.2, George Papers. He bought quantities of his own publications to distribute. On the marketing of *Race, Heredity and Civilization*, see Wesley Critz George to Archibald Roosevelt, Jan. 31, 1962, box 9, folder 60, subseries 1.4, George Papers. He was a leading figure in the Patriots of North Carolina Inc. and North Carolina Defenders of States' Rights Inc. in the middle and late 1950s. For a sample of the organizations' views, see "By-Laws" of the North Carolina Defenders of States' Rights (typescript, n.d.), box 7, folder 49, subseries 1.4, George Papers.

40. Jack Temple Kirby estimates that 9 million southerners left the region by 1960 in *Rural Worlds Lost: The American South, 1920–1960* (Baton Rouge: Louisiana State University Press, 1987), xv. For discussions of the social consequences of the exodus, see also Robert A. Margo, *Race and Schooling in the South, 1880–1950* (Chicago: University of Chicago Press, 1990), chap. 7; William M. Tuttle Jr., *Race Riot: Chicago and the Red Summer of 1919* (Urbana: University of Illinois Press, 1970), chap. "Going into Canaan"; and James N. Gregory, *American Exodus: The Dust Bowl Migration and Okie Culture in California* (New York: Oxford University Press, 1989), chap. 1. On black migration in particular, see Daniel M. Johnson and Rex R. Campbell, *Black Migration in America: A Social Demographic History* (Durham, N.C.: Duke University Press, 1981), esp. chaps. 5–10. Since the 1970s there has been significant migration of both black and white Americans to the South, resulting in growth of the southern population. See Curtis C. Roseman, "Migration Patterns," and John P. Marcum and Max W. Williams, "Popula-

tion," in *Encyclopedia of Southern Culture*, ed. Charles Reagan Wilson and William Ferris (Chapel Hill: University of North Carolina Press, 1989), 552, 556; James Grossman, "Migration, Black," in *The New Encyclopedia of Southern Culture*, ed. Charles Reagan Wilson (Chapel Hill: University of North Carolina Press, 2006), 2:107; and John Beck, "Migration and the Twentieth Century South: An Overview," AHA Teaching and Learning in the Digital Age, ⟨http://www.historians.org/Tl/LessonPlans/nc/Beck/Overview .htm⟩ (September 25, 2008).

41. Kardiner and Ovesey, *Mark of Oppression*, 84 (first quotation), xv (second quotation).

42. Clark, *Dark Ghetto*, 11. For Kardiner and Ovesey's upwardly mobile subjects, see *Mark of Oppression*, chap. 6.

43. On Clark's attitude toward the South, see chapter 3, as well as his recollections of his year at Hampton Institute in Virginia in Kenneth B. Clark, "Racial Progress and Retreat: A Personal Memoir" (1993), in *Toward Humanity and Justice: The Writings of Kenneth B. Clark, Scholar of the 1954* Brown v. Board of Education *Decision*, ed. Woody Klein (Westport, Conn.: Praeger, 2004), 188–89. Clark recalled his invitation to build up the psychology department at Hampton as an opportunity. But his support by a Rosenwald Fellowship during his one year at Hampton (1940–41) makes one wonder whether he ever made a long-term commitment, and the birth of his first child, Kate, in 1940, just as Mamie began the doctoral program in psychology at Columbia, must have pressured him to accept any job. On his family circumstances, see Mamie Clark to Kenneth Clark, "Wed. night," [1941?], box 3, folder 8, Clark Papers.

44. Clark, *Dark Ghetto*, xxiii (first quotation), xxiii–xxiv (second quotation). He acknowledged the origin of "ghetto" as a word denoting a Jewish quarter in ibid., 11, and he cited as his models Bruno Bettelheim and Viktor Frankl, Jewish scholars who suffered under Nazism and later used their psychological expertise to analyze dehumanizing experiences, in ibid., xvii.

45. Ibid., xxii (first quotation); Charles S. Johnson, *Growing Up in the Black Belt: Negro Youth in the Rural South* (1941; repr., New York: Schocken Books, 1967), 53 (second quotation), xxi (third and fourth quotations), 122 (fifth quotation); Clark, *Dark Ghetto*, 63 (sixth quotation), 111 (seventh quotation), 147 (eighth quotation).

46. Coles, "Lives of Migrant Farmers," 284 (first quotation), 273 (second quotation). On Frazier and Thomas, see chapter 3.

47. Johnson, *Growing Up in the Black Belt*, 257. He explained the teenagers' association of light skin color with superiority in ibid., 258–59. "Color and Status" is chap. 10 of ibid.

48. W. Lloyd Warner, Buford H. Junker, and Walter A. Adams, *Color and Human Nature: Negro Personality Development in a Northern City* (Washington, D.C.: American Council on Education, 1941), 290.

49. Ibid., 295 (first and second quotations).

50. Kardiner and Ovesey, *Mark of Oppression*, 129 (first quotation), 214 (second quotation), 190 (third quotation), 194 (fourth quotation).

51. Henry E. Garrett, "Klineberg's Chapter on Race and Psychology: A Review,"

Mankind Quarterly 1 (1960): 21. The deliberate understatement of possible causes of differences in test scores between the races by these psychologists (discussed below) means that they did not often clearly state the presumably natural basis of inferiority. Carleton Putnam, who had no professional training in psychology, most freely used words like "blood" and "genes" (e.g., *Race and Reason*, 93, 92). The favorite phrase of Travis Osborne, who was a psychologist at the University of Georgia, was "hereditary factors." See R. Travis Osborne, A. James Gregor, and Frank Miele, "Heritability of Numerical Facility," *Perceptual and Motor Skills* 24 (1967): 659, 660, 664, and R. T. Osborne and Frank Miele, "Racial Differences in Environmental Influences on Numerical Ability as Determined by Heritability Estimates," *Perceptual and Motor Skills* 28 (1969): 538.

52. Lawrence S. Kubie, "The Ontology of Racial Prejudice," *Journal of Nervous-Mental Disease* 141 (1965): 268. Following Freud, Kubie interpreted childhood responses to bodily wastes as universal reactions (ibid., 269), but he also acknowledged the role of culture in forming attitudes to color (ibid., 272). Kubie explained his efforts to gain admission for black students to Johns Hopkins's medical school, extending from 1956 to 1963, in a series of letters to Lillian Smith, box 15, folder 58, Smith Papers. See esp. Lawrence Kubie to Lillian Smith, Mar. 18, 1958, and Jan. 7, 1963.

53. Judith S. Schachter and Hugh F. Butts, "Transference and Countertransference in Interracial Analysis," *Journal of the American Psychoanalytic Association* 16 (1968): 792–808; Poussaint, "Stresses of the White Female Worker in the Civil Rights Movement." Coles confirmed that white southerners did not patronize black therapists in "Racial Problems in Psychotherapy," 110. Charles Prudhomme, the first African American certified as a psychoanalyst, explained that Adams and other black psychiatrists in Chicago were all but forced to practice in a segregated hospital in Prudhomme and Musto, "Historical Perspectives on Mental Health and Racism," 44. There was little dissent on the problems involved in treating black patients. See Douglass, "Racial Integration in the Psychiatric Field," esp. 5; Pierce, "Manpower"; Clark, *Dark Ghetto*, 82–84; and Carl E. Drake Sr., "Survey of Patient Visits in a Psychiatric Office," *JNMA* 60 (1968): 10–12.

54. Walter A. Adams, "The Negro Patient in Psychiatric Treatment," *American Journal of Orthopsychiatry* 20 (1950): 306 (first quotation), 305 (second quotation).

55. Janet A. Kennedy, "Problems Posed in the Analysis of Negro Patients," *Psychiatry* 15 (1952): 327 (first and second quotations), 326 (third quotation).

56. Coles, "Racial Problems in Psychotherapy," 113 (first quotation), 111 (subsequent quotations).

57. Clark, *Dark Ghetto*, 98. Clark's proposal for a cultural solution was in part a matter of necessity; at that time there were only four clinics in Harlem serving fewer than a thousand young people, and he estimated that twelve times the number being treated needed help. Ibid., 84.

58. Drake, "Survey of Patient Visits," 10 (first and second quotations); Douglass, "Racial Integration in the Psychiatric Field," 5 (third quotation). Douglass noted that blacks did not have access to early treatment from, for example, a family doctor, and so

ended up with more serious and costly problems. Douglass, "Racial Integration in the Psychiatric Field," 5.

59. William H. Grier and Price M. Cobbs, *Black Rage* (New York: Basic Books, 1968), 83 (first quotation), 84 (second quotation), 200 (third quotation), 208 (fourth quotation), 213 (fifth quotation). On the motive of self-protection in black childrearing, see ibid., 84, 171. Cobbs was born in Los Angeles, the child of a black doctor. His parents were born in the South, and he received a medical degree from Meharry Medical College in 1958. His autobiography shows clearly that southern racial customs were one reason that he did not choose to settle in the South, although *Black Rage* as a text did not reflect his regional awareness. Price M. Cobbs, *My American Life: From Rage to Entitlement* (New York: Atria Books, 2005), esp. chaps. 8, 9. Cobbs met Grier in California; Grier earned an M.D. degree at the University of Michigan. Cobbs, *My American Life*, 199. I have found little biographical information, but Grier does not appear to be a native southerner. See "William H. Grier," *Fellows and Members of the American Psychiatric Association, Biographical Directory, as of January, 1989* (Washington, D.C.: American Psychiatric Press, 1989), 606.

60. Grier and Cobbs, *Black Rage*, 186. The authors' focus on slavery was consistent to an extent with contemporaneous rediscovery of slavery in scholarly and policy circles. The Moynihan Report, for example, traced black problems to slavery, although its analysis also considered later phases of black history. Daniel Patrick Moynihan, *The Negro Family: The Case for National Action* (1965), in *The Moynihan Report and the Politics of Controversy*, ed. Lee Rainwater and William L. Yancey (Cambridge, Mass.: MIT Press, 1967), 61–62.

61. Abram Kardiner and Edward Preble, *They Studied Man* (Cleveland: World, 1961); Carl N. Degler, *In Search of Human Nature: The Decline and Revival of Darwinism in American Social Thought* (New York: Oxford University Press, 1991), 213. "Remembering Darwin" is the title of section 3. Kardiner claimed credit for the idea behind *They Studied Man*, but he acknowledged that Preble did much of the writing. Preface to *They Studied Man*, 9. Andrew Winston, Bethany Butzer, and Mark Ferris examined psychology texts and concluded that although cultural influence became a dominant explanation, natural endowment never disappeared from mainstream psychology as an explanatory factor. Andrew S. Winston, Bethany Butzer, and Mark D. Ferris, "Constructing Difference: Heredity, Intelligence, and Race in Textbooks, 1930–1970," in Winston, *Defining Difference*, 199–229.

62. Earl Warren writing for the Court, "Text of the Supreme Court Opinions, May 17, 1954," in Clark, *Prejudice and Your Child*, 159. Daryl Michael Scott's excellent analysis of the long-term consequences of the "damage" argument offers essential background to the interaction of psychology, race, and constitutional rights. Daryl Michael Scott, *Contempt and Pity*, chaps. 7–10.

63. Coles's existential perspective persisted in many of his later writings, including "The Varieties of Religious Experience" in *The Mind's Fate: Ways of Seeing Psychiatry and Psychoanalysis* (Boston: Little, Brown, 1975), 149–56, and *The Secular Mind* (Princeton, N.J.: Princeton University Press, 1999).

64. Clark, *Prejudice and Your Child*, 17 (first quotation), 23 (second quotation); Grier and Cobbs, *Black Rage*, 154; Comer and Poussaint, *Raising Black Children* (originally titled *Black Child Care*), 15.

65. Frank C. J. McGurk, "Comparative Test Scores of Negro and White School Children in Richmond, VA," *Journal of Educational Psychology* 34 (1943): 481 (first and second quotations); "Report Card," *Time*, Oct. 29, 1956, 81 (third and fourth quotations). Scant biographical information on McGurk includes a note in *Mankind Quarterly* 1 (1960): 134; a biographical entry in the *Directory of the American Psychological Association* (Washington, D.C.: American Psychological Association, 1981), 735; and his letter to Wesley Critz George, July 31, 1959, in which he wrote about his difficulty finding a doctoral program in psychology willing to sponsor his racial views and his self-consciousness about being a Catholic. He completed his Ph.D. at Catholic University in 1951.

66. Audrey M. Shuey, "Personality Traits of Jewish and Non-Jewish Students," *Archives of Psychology*, ed. R. S. Woodworth, vol. 41, no. 290 (1944): 37.

67. Harold Orlansky, "Jewish Personality Traits: A Review of Studies on an Elusive Problem," *Commentary* 2 (1946): 380.

68. Ibid., 377.

69. McGurk, "Comparative Test Scores of Negro and White School Children," 473.

70. Shuey, *Testing of Negro Intelligence*, 520 (first quotation), 391 (second quotation), 505 (third and fourth quotations). The methods and standards of natural science were a persistent ideal for twentieth-century social scientists, and these psychologists appealed to commonly held values. Scholars argue about when social scientists favored pure, as opposed to policy-oriented, research, but the significance of this distinction seems questionable when members of this group, who purported to use rigorous experimentation, nonetheless had clear social goals. On scientism during these decades, see Jackson, *Gunnar Myrdal and America's Conscience*; Dorothy Ross, *The Origins of American Social Science* (Cambridge: Cambridge University Press, 1991); Ellen Herman, *The Romance of American Psychology: Political Culture in the Age of Experts* (Berkeley: University of California Press, 1995); Mark C. Smith, *Social Science in the Crucible: The American Debate over Objectivity and Purpose, 1918–1941* (Durham, N.C.: Duke University Press, 1994); and Anne C. Rose, "Putting the South on the Psychological Map: The Impact of Region and Race on the Human Sciences during the 1930s," *Journal of Southern History* 71 (2005): 321–56. Graham Richards makes a valuable argument that Americans were unusually fixated on measuring comparative racial intelligence in "'It's an American Thing': The 'Race' and Intelligence Controversy from a British Perspective," in Winston, *Defining Difference*, 135–69.

71. Winston argues for the decisive influence of the *Davis* case in "Science in the Service of the Far Right," 184.

72. Ina C. Brown, review of *The Testing of Negro Intelligence*, 1st ed., by Audrey M. Shuey, *American Anthropologist* 62 (1960): 544.

73. McGurk to George, July 31, 1959. How members of the group secured their southern jobs remains a matter of speculation. Henry Garrett was a native Virginian, and it

is possible that his local connections allowed him to place Shuey at Randolph-Macon Woman's College a decade after she completed her dissertation under his direction, as well as opened the way for his own position in the Department of Education at the University of Virginia after his retirement from Columbia. The University of Virginia's Department of Psychology refused him an appointment, however, suggesting his limited welcome at the university. Winston, "Science in the Service of the Far Right," 181–82. The governor of Alabama commissioned George to prepare a report on race and intelligence, *The Biology of the Race Problem* (1962), described in the finding aid for the George Papers, ⟨http://www.lib.unc.edu/mss/inv/g/George,W.C.html⟩, a project about which he consulted Garrett. Wesley Critz George to Henry Garrett, Feb. 18, 1961; Henry Garrett to Wesley Critz George, Mar. 1, 1961, both in box 8, folder 54, subseries 1.4, George Papers. Possibly George used his Alabama ties to find McGurk a position at Alabama College. Members of the circle more actively cultivated George around the time they moved south, which was concurrent with the establishment of their organizational vehicles, the International Association for the Advancement of Ethnology and Eugenics in 1959 and *Mankind Quarterly* in 1960. See, e.g., John Brockenbrough Fox to Wesley Critz George, Sept. 10, 1959, box 7, folder 44; Wesley Critz George to John Fox, Sept. 12, 1959, box 7, folder 44; Donald A. Swan to Wesley Critz George, Jan. 10, 1961, box 8, folder 54; Henry E. Garrett to Wesley Critz George, Jan. 1, 1961, box 8, folder 54, all in subseries 1.4, George Papers. Despite their warrior mentality and conspiratorial secretiveness, evidenced, for example, in letters marked "confidential," they were not a uniformly close-knit group. As a woman, Shuey accepted a self-effacing marginal role. Busy with a heavy teaching load at a small women's college, she left only one piece of evidence of her personal link with the others, an invitation to Ernest van den Haag, another of the northern group, to speak at her college. *Catalog of Randolph-Macon Woman's College, Session 1965–1966, Announcements, 1966–1967*, 11. The authoritative account of the activities of these scholars, most of whom received assistance from the Pioneer Fund, is Tucker, *Funding of Scientific Racism*. The impact of the psychologists on the southern academy seems tame next to the initiative of British-born anthropologist Roger Pearson at the University of Southern Mississippi, who for a time around 1970 took over the combined departments of anthropology, religious studies, and philosophy by firing ideological opponents and hiring his cronies. Tucker, *Funding of Scientific Racism*, 159–70.

74. Clark, *Prejudice and Your Child*, 71 (first quotation), 218 (second and third quotations). The latter quotations appeared originally in Clark's "The Role of the Social Sciences in Desegregation" (presidential address, Society for the Psychological Study of Social Issues, Sept. 1960).

75. Alvin F. Poussaint, speech at the University of Michigan School of Social Work (Oct. 29, 1987), in Straub, *Voices of Multicultural America*, 985 (first quotation), 987 (second and third quotations).

76. Frantz Fanon, *The Wretched of the Earth* (1961), trans. Constance Farrington (New York: Grove Press, 1963), 203 (first quotation); Poussaint, speech at the University of Michigan School of Social Work, 989 (second quotation). Whereas *Wretched of the*

Earth, Fanon's account of the Algerian revolution against French colonialism, gained him a cult following on the political left in developed countries during the 1960s, his book *Black Skin, White Masks* (1952), trans. Charles Lam Markmann (New York: Grove Press, 1967), was a more theoretical work that asked whether Western psychology, purporting to be universal, was applicable to non-Western peoples.

77. Elam, "Psychological Aspects of Civil Rights Activity by Physicians," 8.

78. [Lloyd C. Elam], "Behavioral Blocks to Learning" (manuscript, n.d.), 1 (first quotation), 2 (second quotation), 3 (third and fourth quotations), Elam Papers.

79. Mihaly Bartalos, "Medical Genetics and Modern Medicine: An Overview," *JNMA* 60 (1968): 21–27.

80. John T. Doby, *Introduction to Social Psychology* (New York: Appleton-Century-Crofts, 1966), 84 (first quotation), 90 (second and third quotations). Discussion of the twins appears in ibid., 88. Doby's prominence in southern social science may be measured by his presidency of the Southern Sociological Society. His presidential address, published as "Man the Species and the Individual: A Sociological Perspective," *Social Forces* 49 (1970): 1–15, emphasized evolutionary theory and the unity of science. The speech was sufficiently representative of the return of the nature argument to social science to be cited in that context as one of the few southern sources in Degler, *In Search of Human Nature,* 225. I infer that Doby was not born in the South because he was an undergraduate at the University of Wisconsin and a graduate student at Columbia. Doby, *Introduction to Social Psychology,* x–xi.

81. Doby, *Introduction to Social Psychology,* 55. The text contains no mention of racial genetics; the index has an entry for "racial prejudice," with two page references, but no other mention of race. Like Lloyd Elam, Doby let class serve as a substitute for race. For example: "It would be easier to resocialize an able child from an underdeveloped country such as one of the new nations of Africa than to resocialize an equally able American child born into a fourth generation family of poverty." Ibid., 272–73. His point was that the American child, presumably black in light of the reference to Africa, was handicapped by prejudice; still, this discussion of racism was all but buried under the section heading "Influence of Small Groups on the Individual." Ibid., 272. I interpret Doby's style as a combination of scientism, on the one hand, and academic, and particularly southern, understatement, on the other. Doby later coauthored a paper on racial differences with one of his students that treated race so narrowly as a variable that the study's social importance, despite its suggestive title, is muted. Lala Carr Steelman and John T. Doby, "Family Size and Birth Order as Factors on the IQ Performance of Black and White Children," *Sociology of Education* 56 (1983): 101–9. The combined effect of Doby's overall emphasis on natural evolution and deemphasis of race, however, seemed to favor the social status quo.

82. Roger Brown, *Social Psychology* (New York: Free Press, 1965), 49. Brown's attention to what makes human beings different from animals appears in chapter 8, "The Acquisition of Morality"; part 3, "The Socialization of the Child"; and part 4, "Personality and Society."

83. Doby, *Introduction to Social Psychology,* xiii (parts of section headings). The sec-

tion heading covering Brown's single animal behavior chapter, "The Social Behavior of Animals" (chap. 1), is "A Comparative Baseline," a phrase serving to set humans off from the animal world. Brown, *Social Psychology*, xi.

84. Brown, *Social Psychology*, 176 (first and second quotations); Doby, *Introduction to Social Psychology*, 154 (third and fourth quotations).

85. R. Travis Osborne and Frank C. J. McGurk, eds., *The Testing of Negro Intelligence*, vol. 2 (Athens, Ga.: Foundation for Human Understanding, 1982). Instances of Osborne's statistical analyses include Osborne, Gregor, and Miele, "Heritability of Numerical Facility," and Osborne and Miele, "Racial Differences in Environmental Influences on Numerical Ability." Twins have been a favorite subject of researchers who focus on heredity, and Osborne produced one twin study, *Twins: Black and White* (Athens, Ga.: Foundation for Human Understanding, 1980). For biographical information on Osborne, see *Directory of the American Psychological Association* (1981), 834; Tucker, *Funding of Scientific Racism*, 115, 156–58; "R. Travis Osborne," *Wikipedia*, ⟨http://en.wikipedia.org/wiki/R._Travis_Osborne⟩ (June 14, 2008); and "Grantees," Pioneer Fund Inc., ⟨http://www.pioneerfund.org/Grantees.html⟩ (June 14, 2008).

86. Garrett's forewords to the 1958 and 1966 editions of Shuey's book, *The Testing of Negro Intelligence*, appear in both cases on pp. vii–viii. It is noteworthy that polarization among psychologists was largely a product of the civil rights era. Garrett was respected in the academic mainstream through the 1940s. Best known for his work on statistics, as well as his *Great Experiments in Psychology* (1930), rev. ed. (New York: Appleton, 1941), he was president of the American Psychological Association in 1946 and friendly with liberal colleagues whom he later cast as enemies. Winston, "Science in the Service of the Far Right," 182. He imagined himself at war with them. Writing to Wesley Critz George, he said of one critic, "I hear he is a Communist," and advised, "Instead of parrying blows, I think we must hit these people hard. Ridicule is always a good weapon." Garrett to George, Jan. 2, 1962.

87. Putnam, *Race and Reason*, title page (first quotation), 37 (second quotation). On Putnam's background, see T. R. Waring, foreword to ibid., iii–iv. On the book's reception, see ibid., 4–14, and Tucker, *Funding of Scientific Racism*, 106. For autobiographical and biographical information on Putnam, see *Race and Reason*, 1–3, and "Memorials: Carleton Putnam '24," *Princeton Alumni Weekly*, ⟨http://webscript.princeton.edu/~paw/ memorials/memdisplay.php?id=4732⟩ (September 25, 2008).

88. Putnam, *Race and Reason*, 25 (Garrett), 25–26 (Shuey), 40–41 (McGurk); James Jackson Kilpatrick, *The Southern Case for School Segregation* (n.p.: Crowell-Collier Press, 1962), 58–59 (Putnam), 58–59, 74–83 (Shuey and McGurk), 69 (George), 74 (Garrett). At the same time, Kilpatrick attacked a by-then predictable array of opponents. Kilpatrick, *Southern Case for School Segregation*, 44 (Ashley Montagu), 46 (Otto Klineberg), 46, 57 (Kenneth Clark), 51, 57 (Franz Boas), 66–69 (Gunnar Myrdal).

89. Kilpatrick, *Southern Case for School Segregation*, 220; introduction to Putnam, *Race and Reason*, vii–viii. The introduction, drafted and circulated by Garrett, was also signed by George (who had not read the book), as well as R. Ruggles Gates and Robert

Gayre of Gayre, advocates of eugenics born in Canada and Scotland, respectively. See Garrett to George, Jan. 1, 1961, and Tucker, *Funding of Scientific Racism*, 74–75, 91–92.

90. Garrett, "Klineberg's Chapter on Race and Psychology." Winston identifies Corrado Gini as "Mussolini's eugenicist and scientific advisor" in "Science in the Service of the Far Right," 191. See also a sketch of Gini in *Mankind Quarterly* 1 (1961): 186. For a sample of his views, consider the conclusion of his review of Shuey's book: "A small group of persons of high intellectual capacity, directing a mass of persons of lesser ability, but given to work and conformity, could conceivably enjoy an advantage over a nation in which each member is gifted with superior intelligence and who, as a consequence, is little disposed to follow the orders of others without criticism or resistance." Henry E. Garrett, review of *The Testing of Negro Intelligence*, by Audrey M. Shuey, *Mankind Quarterly* 1 (1960): 125.

91. These three names appeared in Grace Lichtenstein, "Fund Backs Controversial Study of 'Racial Betterment,'" *New York Times*, Dec. 11, 1977, available at ⟨http://www.hartford-hwp.com/archives/45/022.html⟩ (June 16, 2008). Garrett was no longer alive when the article appeared. For a detailed account of this philanthropy, see Tucker, *Funding of Scientific Racism*, esp. chap. 3. McGurk, Putnam, and Shuey appear as authorities in Willie Martin, "Black and White," pt. 2, at one time posted on the website of the Christian Party, copy in the author's possession. Deborah E. Lipstadt includes the names of McGurk, Osborne, and Putnam among Holocaust deniers in *Denying the Holocaust: The Growing Assault on Truth and Memory* (New York: Plume, 1994), 152. The scientific style cultivated by both groups underlines their kinship.

92. Doby, "Man the Species and the Individual," 1.

Epilogue

1. On migration to the South, see Curtis C. Roseman, "Migration Patterns," and John P. Marcum and Max W. Williams, "Population," in *Encyclopedia of Southern Culture*, ed. Charles Reagan Wilson and William Ferris (Chapel Hill: University of North Carolina Press, 1989), 552, 556; James Grossman, "Migration, Black," in *The New Encyclopedia of Southern Culture*, ed. Charles Reagan Wilson (Chapel Hill: University of North Carolina Press, 2006), 2:107; and John Beck, "Migration and the Twentieth Century South: An Overview," AHA Teaching and Learning in the Digital Age, ⟨http://www.historians.org/Tl/LessonPlans/nc/Beck/Overview.htm⟩ (September 25, 2008). The former social character of the South is still statistically apparent behind recent trends, however. According to the U.S. Census Bureau, the South remained 31.4 percent rural in 1990, the most rural of four regions (the others being the Northeast, Midwest, and West) and above the national average of 24.8 percent. See "Urban and Rural Population: 1900 to 1990" (U.S. Census Bureau, Oct. 1995), ⟨http://www.census.gov/population/censusdata/urpop0090.txt⟩ (June 16, 2008). Despite the region's continuing distinction as most rural, it is now closer to the national norm than in 1900, when, at 82.0 percent rural, it deviated from the national average of 60.4 percent by nearly

22 points. In terms of the racial configuration of the southern population, according to the 2000 census, 54.8 percent of African Americans then lived in the South; African Americans (those who responded to the census that they were black only) constituted 12.3 percent of all Americans. Jesse McKinnon, "The Black Population: 2000," Census 2000 Brief 01-5 (U.S. Census Bureau, Aug. 2001), 2–3, ⟨http://www.census.gov/prod/2001pubs/c2kbr01-5.pdf⟩ (June 14, 2008).

2. Vivian W. Pinn-Wiggins, "Diversity in Medical Education and Health Care Access: After the '80s, What?" *JNMA* 82 (1990): 90.

3. Stephen F. Jencks, Timothy Cuerdon, Dale R. Burwen, Barbara Fleming, Peter M. Houck, Annette E. Kussmaul, David S. Nilasena, Diana L. Ordin, and David R. Arday, "Quality of Medical Care Delivered to Medicare Beneficiaries: A Profile at State and National Levels," *Journal of the American Medical Association* 284 (2000): 1674; Brian S. Armour and M. Melinda Pitts, "The Quality of Preventive and Diagnostic Medicare Care: Why Do Southern States Underperform?" *Economic Review* 90 (2005): 66 (quotation). Consider also general evidence as recent as 1980 showing that the South had higher mortality rates, lower life expectancy, and lower educational achievement than other American regions. Marcum and Williams, "Population," 556–57. Although many social scientific studies of American health care focus on variables such as race, income, and location (rural or urban) that do not register the South's particular problems, a few scholars highlight southern regionalism. See esp. Susan E. Keefe, ed., *Appalachian Mental Health* (Lexington: University Press of Kentucky, 1988), and Susan E. Keefe, ed., *Appalachian Cultural Competency: A Guide for Medical, Mental Health, and Social Service Professionals* (Knoxville: University of Tennessee Press, 2005).

4. Rosalynn Carter with Susan K. Golant, *Helping Someone with Mental Illness: A Compassionate Guide for Family, Friends, and Caregivers* (New York: Three Rivers Press, 1998), ix (first quotation), 101 (second quotation). Carter discusses her own interest in mental health advocacy, beginning during her husband's term as Georgia's governor, in ibid., 8–17.

5. Ibid., 55. The phrase is the title of chap. 3.

6. Walker Percy, *The Thanatos Syndrome* (New York: Picador, 1987), 13 (first quotation), 265 (second quotation), 303 (third quotation).

7. Ibid., 11. On Percy's perspective on psychiatry and spiritual health, see the excellent essays in Carl Elliott and John Lantos, eds., *The Last Physician: Walker Percy and the Moral Life of Medicine* (Durham, N.C.: Duke University Press, 1999), esp. Robert Coles, "Dr. Percy's Hold on Medicine," 9–15; Carl Elliott, "Prozac and the Existential Novel," 59–69; and Jay Tolson, "Walker Percy, Reluctant Physician," 150–59. Percy dedicated *The Thanatos Syndrome* to Robert Coles.

INDEX

Abington, E. H., 26, 27, 28

Abolitionists, 159

Adams, Frankie V., 65, 141–42

Adams, Walter, 169, 171

Adler, Alfred, 41

Adolescence, 2

Africa, 156, 179

African Americans: intellectuals who were, 4, 7, 88–89, 93, 103–4, 154, 157, 176, 179–80, 242–43 (n. 61); as soldiers in World War I, 17; racial character attributed to, 19, 27, 63, 89, 110, 114, 156, 165; intelligence compared with whites, 19, 65, 70, 74, 82, 84–85, 170, 176–77; and stereotype of primitivism, 24, 31, 63, 89, 93; traditional attitude toward doctors, 27–28; medical schools for, 69–70, 79, 186; psychiatric treatment of, 79, 171, 172–73; psychiatric training at Duke, 85, 232 (n. 118); need for caution by, 93–94, 154, 158–59, 162–63; living in the North, 157–58, 166, 179; opinions of skin color, 169. *See also* Segregation

Africans, 63

Agrarians. *See* Southern Agrarianism

Alabama, founding of Tuskegee VA hospital in, 17–19

Alabama College, 179

Alcohol, and mental illness, 26

Alexander, Florence, 61

Allen, A. A., 144, 148

Allport, Gordon, 126

American Anthropologist, 178

American Catholic Sociological Society, 127

American Council of Jewish Women, 135

An American Dilemma, 104

American Jewish Committee, 177

American Mercury, 35

American Missionary Association, 121

American Psychiatric Association, 77, 157, 159

American Psychoanalytic Association, 49

American Regionalism, 109

American Sociological Society, 107

American Youth Commission (AYC), 95, 100, 101, 102, 103, 104, 169

Angell, James Rowland, 46, 99–100, 240 (n. 43)

Anniston, Ala., 146

Anthropology, and psychiatry, 97

Antilynching legislation, 88, 92, 93, 94

Anxiety in Christian Experience, 143

Arkansas, 28, 146

The Art of Intimacy, 137

Asian philosophies, and psychology, 48, 118, 124

Associationism, as school of psychology, 31

Asylums. See Mental institutions

Atlanta, 26, 62; psychiatric practice in, before World War II, 80; psychiatric practice in, after World War II, 130–40; segregation of medical facilities in, 133, 158

Atlanta Chamber of Commerce, 138

Atlanta Constitution, 38, 135

Atlanta Psychiatric Clinic, 150; therapeutic philosophy of, 130–31, 133–38; founding, 131, 134; and tensions at Emory, 134; and Atlanta community, 134–35, 137–38; scientific orientation of, 135–36; family therapy at, 136–37; and Freudian ideas, 137, 264 (n. 76); racial attitudes of, 137–38; relationships among members, 138–39; charismatic authority at, 139; and Carl Rogers, 139–40; legacy of, 140; and religion, 141, 266 (n. 89)

Atlanta School of Social Work, 65, 141

Atlanta University, 7, 102

Atlantic Monthly, 160

Augusta State Hospital, 47

The Authoritarian Personality, American reactions to, 117–18, 249–50 (nn. 3, 4)

Back Roads and Bicarbonate, 28

Baldwin, James Mark, 7

Baltimore, 7; psychiatric care in, 34, 44

Baptists, 56, 142

Barnard College, 111

Bateson, Gregory, 137

Battle Creek Sanitarium, 45

Bean, Robert Bennett, 8; as author of *The Races of Man*, 63–65

Beers, Clifford, 6; and mental hygiene movement, 8

Behaviorism, 34, 100, 240 (n. 44), 245 (n. 74)

Benedict, Ruth, 111, 175

Berlin Psychoanalytic Institute, 98

Bible: and psychology, 1; and treatment of mental illness, 22, 141; and conjure, 23

Bible Belt, 8, 125

Bilbo, Theodore, 93

Biloxi, Miss., 159

Birmingham, Ala., 182

Black Bourgeoisie, 113

Black Child Care, 176

Black Mountain College, 47

Black Rage, 173, 176

Boas, Franz, 7, 111, 175; and racial conservatives, 156

Borinski, Ernst, 119, 150; criticism of segregation, 120, 126; as outsider in the South, 120, 126, 129–30; as Holocaust refugee, 121; employment at Tougaloo College, 121, 124; as Jew, 121–22, 123, 126; ethical orientation of, 126, 127; and Social Science Forum, 126, 127

Boston Psychoanalytic Society, 160

Botkin, B. (Benjamin) A., 110, 247 (n. 85)

Bowne, Borden Parker, 271 (n. 123)

Branche, George C., 18 (ill.)

Branham, William, 147, 148

Brown, Ina, 178, 226 (n. 79)

Brown, Roger, 91, 181

Brown v. Board of Education, 3, 28, 154, 156; psychological argument of, 4, 15, 104, 106, 128, 175–76; roots in educational reform, 66; as source of contention, 82, 152–54, 175; social scientists' statement and, 104, 128, 243 (n. 64); black criticism of, 111; and reemphasis of psychobiology of race, 152–53, 165, 175; moral argument of, 175, 176. *See also* Supreme Court

Buddhism, 125

Bureau of Human Betterment, 73

Bushnell, Horace, 141

But for the Grace of God, 7

Caldwell, Erskine, 22

Camp John Hope, 65

Canady, Herman, 178

Cantril, Hadley, 5, 90–91, 94

Carnegie, Andrew, 72

Carnegie Foundation: report on African American medical schools, 71, 79; sponsor of *An American Dilemma*, 104

Carter, Rosalynn, as mental health advocate, 186–87

Cartesian tradition, 31

Cash, Mary. *See* Maury, Mary Cash

Cash, W. J. (Wilbur Joseph), 43; on southern character, 13, 21; self-diagnosis of, 32; personality of, 33; attitude toward doctors of, 33–34; medical treatments of, 34; reading on psychology, 34–35; *The Mind of the South* as autobiography, 35; suicide of, 35–36

Cason, Clarence, 14; as author of *90 Degrees in the Shade*, 87–88

Caste and Class in a Southern Town, 98–99, 102

Catholicism, 37, 118, 127; and social science, 122, 123, 126–27; and psychology, 127; Walker Percy as convert to, 187

Catholic University, 179

Catholic Worker Movement, 159

Cattell, James McKeen, 214 (n. 9)

Central State Hospital (Tennessee): and Nashville community, 29; as site for

psychiatric training, 71–72, 74; treatment of children at, 78

Chalmers, Rives, 140; psychiatric training of, 132; southern background of, 132; civic involvement, 138

Charlottesville, Va., 182

Chesnutt, Charles W., as author of *The Conjure Woman*, 24

Chicago, 58, 103, 162, 169

Child guidance clinics, 7, 102–3

Children: psychological care of, 7, 20–21, 63, 66, 78, 102–3; nurture in segregated society, 11–12, 42, 95, 100; as catalyst of interest in psychology, 50, 51–52, 75, 86; as subjects of psychological study, 52, 54–55, 78, 95, 104, 105, 106, 155, 159, 160, 214 (n. 9); rising expectations for, 52, 66, 68; summer camps and psychology, 65–66; black youth studies, 95, 100–104; white personality development, 106; as catalyst of desegregation, 154–55; of migratory workers, 168. *See also* Education

Children of Bondage, 95; methodology of, 100, 101–2

Children of Crisis, 155, 176

China: Christian missions and southern psychiatry, 53, 73, 125; Bingham Dai and psychiatry in, 120, 125

Chivers, Walter, 93

Christian Impact, 127

Christianity: traditional approach to mental illness, 21–22; tensions with medicine, 22, 72–73, 143; and healing, 22, 141; and conjure, 23; and child psychology, 56; missions and psychiatry, 73; and southern culture, 117, 141; revivalism and psychology, 118–19; and post–World War II psychology, 141; liberalism and counseling, 141–43; denominational colleges and psychiatry, 142. *See also* Catholicism; Pentecostalism; Protestantism; Religion

Christian Nurture, 141–42

Christian Party, 183

Church of God, 146

Church of God of Prophecy, 144, 148–49

City College of New York, 105

Civilization and Its Discontents, 109, 113

Civil rights: psychology of, 161; effect on psychotherapy, 171. *See also* Desegregation

Civil War, 110

Clark, Kenneth B.: attitude toward the South, 104–5, 167; background and training, 105; on African American psychology, 114; on desegregation, 155, 160; and Frederick Watts, 157; attitude toward science, 167; on northern racial ghettos, 167–68; criticism of psychotherapy, 172; on nature and nurture, 176; on power and prejudice, 179

Clark, Mamie Phipps: as native southerner, 105, 243–44 (n. 65); and Frederick Watts, 157

Clark University, 9, 55

Cleveland, Tenn., 141

Cobbs, Price, 11, 173, 280 (n. 59)

Coca-Cola, 26

Coe, Jack, 148, 149

Cold Blue Moon, 110

Coles, Robert: as observer of southern psychology, 12, 80, 154, 155, 159–60, 165; background and training, 159; innovation in psychiatry, 160; migration study, 168; on interracial psychotherapy, 172; moral interests of, 176

Color and Human Nature, 95, 103; classification by skin color in, 169

Columbia University, 90, 170, 175, 179, 183, 214 (n. 9); training of southerners at, 56, 61; graduate training in psychology at, 105, 152

Columbia University Presbyterian Hospital, 74

Comer, James, 176

Communism, 165

Confucianism, 119, 125, 127

Congregationalists, 122

Conjure: medical opposition to, 22–23; African roots of, 23; and healing, 23–24; root doctors and medicine, 27; and Pentecostal healing, 147

The Conjure Woman, 24

Conservatism: academic defense of racial, 82–83, 152–54, 156, 175; reassertion of racial natures, 170, 176–78; as global campaign, 175, 176, 178–79, 183; premise about individual value, 178; and regionalism, 182; migration of proponents of, to the South, 182–83, 281–82 (n. 73)

Conspiracy theories, 156, 180

"The Contents of Children's Minds," 54–55

Cornell University, 41

Cox, Ross, 139

Crews, Harry, 12, 22, 27

Crick, Francis, 175

Crofford's Sanitarium, 30

The Crowd, 91

Culture, theories of, 95, 98, 181; under attack after *Brown*, 153, 175, 178; vague intellectual boundaries with psychobiology, 176–77; and power arrangements, 179

The Curse of Madness, 144

Dai, Bingham, 150; professional training and placement, 48, 252 (n. 8); in *Brown* appeal, 104, 128, 243 (n. 64); Chinese background of, 119, 120, 125; and origin of critique of segregation, 120; positions in the South, 120–21; interdisciplinary orientation, 123, 124; analyzed by Harry Stack Sullivan,

124; training analyses conducted, 124, 128; psychological ideas of, 124–25, 255–56 (n. 25); religious interests of, 125, 257 (n. 30); ethics of, 127; social marginality, 128–29; and experiential therapy, 140

Dark Ghetto, 167, 172

Darwin, Charles, 175

Darwinian theory. *See* Evolution

Davidson, Donald, 46, 99, 114

Davis, Allison, 95, 100, 101, 102, 103, 104, 241 (n. 51)

Davis, Jackson, and reform of southern education, 51–52, 60, 61, 68–69

Davis, M. O., 18 (ill.)

Davis v. County School Board, 178

Deep South, 9, 101, 168. *See also* South

Degler, Carl, 175

Democracy and Education, 59

Department of the Interior, 103

Depression. *See* Great Depression

Desegregation, 12, 15; and nature-nurture debate, 152–54, 184; as spur to racial conservatism in psychology, 153; of schools, 153, 154–55, 176; as emotional process, 155–56, 159–60, 164; and fears of miscegenation, 156; psychological liberation of, 156, 163, 164; and psychiatrists, 164; as legal process, 166; psychotherapy as aid to, 170–73; white resistance to, 175; and challenge to ideas of nurture, 175, 184; of medical schools, 186

Dewey, John, 7, 54, 124; on education, 59, 60

Divine healing: theology of, 144–45; and mental health, 145. *See also* Pentecostalism

DNA, discovery of, 175

Doby, John T., 180–81, 182, 183–84, 283 (n. 80)

Dollard, John, 95; as student of Robert Park, 97; as protégé of Edward Sapir,

98; psychoanalytic training of, 98, 239 (n. 37); interpretation of the South, 98–99; southern fieldwork of, 98–99, 101; southern criticisms of, 99–100; and black youth studies, 100, 101; as mentor of Bingham Dai, 120

Dreams, 98, 124

Du Bois, W. E. B., 7, 89, 99

Duke, James B., 83

Duke University: William McDougall at, 53, 82–85; graduate psychology teaching at, 85, 232 (n. 117); Thomas Malone at, 132

Duke University School of Medicine, 48, 104; department of neuropsychiatry, 85, 120–21, 123, 124, 128, 253 (n. 10)

Durham, N.C., 53, 81–82, 83, 120–21, 128, 146

Ebenezer Baptist Church, 141

Education: psychology teaching in the South, 6, 30–31, 53–54, 62–63, 67–68, 82, 85, 86, 122–24; northern training of southerners, 7, 45–46; northern training of international students of color, 48, 74; reform in the South, 49–50, 51–54, 57–65, 82, 102; child psychology and, 54–55, 61, 62; state governments and, 58; goal of literacy in, 61; southern health texts, 63–65; racial conservatism in, 63–65, 81–82; changing racial goals of, 66; rising expectations for, 66; of children and psychiatrists compared, 70, 81; desegregation of, 88, 153, 154–55, 176. *See also* Schools; Teachers

Edwards, Austin Southwick, as author of *The Fundamental Principles of Learning and Study*, 30–31

"The Effects of Segregation and the Consequences of Desegregation," 104, 243 (n. 64)

Egerton, John, 31

Ego psychology, 90–91, 124

Elam, Lloyd C., 165; decision to move south, 43, 162; and Meharry psychiatry department, 162; on racial problems, 162–63, 165; on psychiatry's social role, 162–63, 180

Elements of Folk Psychology, 108

Emerson, Ralph Waldo, 137

Emory University, 180

Emory University School of Medicine, 28, 80, 130–31, 132, 133–34, 139

Enlightenment: and interest in human nature, 1; and faith in reason, 92

Episcopalianism, and healing, 150

Erikson, Erik, 159

Ethics, communal, 119, 127

Ethnography, 23, 106

Eugenics: and sterilization, 29, 81, 133, 261–62 (n. 58); advocacy by William McDougall, 82, 84

Evangelicalism: and mental healing, 22; and child nurture, 56; individualism of, 127. *See also* Christianity

Evans-Pritchard, E. E., 23

Evolution: theory of, 2; and child development, 54; racial interpretations of, 63, 65, 85, 89, 108, 180; social interpretations of, 106, 112–13; and DNA, 175; resurgence as theory in the South, 180–82, 183–84

Existentialism, 118

Existential psychiatry, 130–31

Existential psychology: and civil rights activism, 120; tension between rationality and irrationality in, 143; kinship with Pentecostal healing, 149; and Martin Luther King Jr., 150–51

Experiential Psychotherapy, 140

Faith healing. *See* Divine healing; Pentecostalism

Families, and mental illness, 20–21, 24–27

Fanon, Frantz, 179

Fascism. *See* Holocaust; Nazism

Fatalism, as southern attitude, 21, 27, 147

Faulkner, William, 10, 31; Lillian Smith's criticism of, 40; treatment in Memphis, 45; on lynching, 92–93, 94–95

Felder, Richard, 138–39, 140; psychiatric training of, 132; southern background of, 132; psychotherapeutic ideas of, 133, 136; and Bingham Dai, 140; on religion and therapy, 141

Ferenczi, Sandor, 41

Few, William Preston, 83, 85

Fichter, Joseph, 119, 150; as southern Jesuit, 122; as social scientist, 122, 123, 124, 254 (n. 16); on sociology and Catholicism, 126; as author of *Southern Parish*, 126, 257 (n. 35); racial liberalism of, 126–27, 257–58 (n. 37); ethics of, 127; social marginality of, 130

Fisk University, 41, 48, 54, 71, 74, 78, 96, 113, 120, 124

Fletcher, John Gould, 32, 33, 43; opinions of his suicide, 25; use of alcohol, 26; psychiatric treatment of, 36, 37, 45, 204 (n. 66); view of mental illness, 36–37; reading of Freud, 37; suicide of, 37; religious views, 37–38

Folk culture: of the South, 27, 31–32, 106–7, 110, 113, 115–16, 173–74; and social science, 88, 107–8; black analysts of, 107, 111–15; and public policy, 114; of migratory workers, 168

Folk medicine, 27

Folk mind, 106–7; and psychological study, 108–14

Folkways, 108

Frank, Lawrence K., 72, 225 (n. 71)

Franklin Springs, Ga., 146

Frazier, E. Franklin, 104; as author of *Negro Youth at the Crossways*, 95, 102,

113; as student of Robert Park, 97, 100; criticism of John Dollard, 99; and Harry Stack Sullivan, 101; career of, 103; and folk psychology, 111–14; as author of *The Negro Family in the United States*, 113–14, 168, 173; and The Moynihan Report, 114

Freeman, Douglas Southall, 100

Freud, Anna, 46, 159

Freud, Sigmund, 25, 34, 37, 39, 41, 43, 98, 99, 109, 113, 142, 144, 175. *See also* Freudian psychology; Psychoanalysis

Freudian psychology, 46; popularity of, 30, 90; in the South, 80, 109, 142; in interpretation of the South, 98; and behaviorism, 100; and Bingham Dai, 124–25; and folk psychology, 109; and Atlanta Psychiatric Clinic, 137; and Christianity, 142; in interracial therapy, 171–72. *See also* Psychoanalysis

Friedman, Lawrence, 11, 89

Fromm, Erich, 144

Fromm-Reichmann, Frieda, 132

F scale, 117

Fuller, Solomon, 19, 197 (n. 4)

Gallup polls, 92

Game theory, 91

Garrett, Henry E., 170, 178, 179, 182, 183, 243–44 (n. 65), 284 (n. 86)

Gartly, George, 44–45

Gartly-Ramsey Hospital, 30, 45

General Education Board (GEB), 51, 66; support of education reform by, 57–58; founding of, 58; moderate goals of, 58, 67, 100; political methods of, 60–61; racial attitudes of, 60–61, 62; support of psychological research by, 61–62; attitude toward the South of, 66–67; and psychiatric reform, 79; and black youth studies, 95, 100–103

Genetics: and racial conservatism, 15,

165; discoveries in, 175; and black professionals, 180

George, Wesley Critz: and conservative psychologists, 164, 179; biological theory of race, 165

George Peabody College. *See* Peabody College for Teachers

Georgia, mental health reform in, 133

Georgia Association for Mental Health, 133

Georgia Federation of Women's Clubs, 133

Georgia Sociological and Anthropological Association, 162

Germany, as center of psychological study, 96, 202 (n. 47)

Gesell, Arnold, 62

Gestalt psychology, 62; and folk psychology, 109

Giddings, Franklin Henry, 245 (n. 73)

Government Hospital for the Insane. *See* St. Elizabeth's Hospital

Grant, Madison, 8

Grant, W. V., 144

Great Depression, 58; attention to the South during, 87, 98, 106

Great Society, 114

Green, E. M., 9, 23

Gregg, Alan, 72, 74, 135

Grier, William, 11, 173

The Group Mind, 84, 85

Growing Up in the Black Belt, 44, 78, 101, 167

Guggenheim Fellowship, 33

Hall, G. Stanley, 7, 62; as author of *Adolescence*, 2; as recipient of first American doctorate in psychology, 7, 54; as mentor of southern students, 9; on child development, 54–55, 60

Hampton Institute, 62, 105

Harding, Warren, 17

Harlem, 105, 160, 172

Harris, Trudier, 20–21

Harvard Medical School, 46, 161

Harvard University, 7, 54, 82, 91, 122, 154, 157, 181

Hawthorne, Julian, 60

Healing Waters, 144, 146, 148

Health: southern teaching about, 62–63; mental subjects in texts, 63

Helms, Jesse, 164

Helping Someone with Mental Illness, 186–87

Hernandez, Rafael: training of, 48; as first African American board-certified psychiatrist, 48, 74; career path of, 76, 77; teaching of, 77

Hinduism, 125

Hines, Frank T., 19

Hirsch, Sidney, 47

Hobson, Fred, 10

Holocaust, refugee intellectuals from, 44, 47, 117, 121, 126, 130, 159. *See also* Nazism

Holt, Edwin B., 240 (n. 44)

Honor, ethos of, 3, 25–26, 194 (n. 26)

Hoodoo. *See* Conjure

Horney, Karen, 125

Howard University, 103, 105, 113, 157, 180, 186

Howard University College of Medicine, 48, 71, 223 (n. 64)

Hubbard Hospital (Nashville), 79

Hurston, Zora Neale, 23; and folk concept, 111, 247 (n. 88)

I'll Take My Stand, 37, 72

Immigration, and social science, 106

Introduction to Social Psychology (Doby), 180–81

Introduction to Social Psychology (McDougall), 84

Intruder in the Dust, 93

IQ tests. *See* Testing

Is America Safe for Democracy?, 86

James, William, 2, 7, 43, 54, 124, 214 (n. 9)

Jeanes Fund, 58

Jeanes teachers, 58, 59–60, 68

Jesuits, 119

Jesus, 39, 127, 143, 144, 145, 146

Jews, 37, 47, 97, 119, 121–22, 126, 130, 149, 156, 164–65, 167, 177

Jim Crow. *See* Segregation

Job (book of Bible), 23

Johns Hopkins University, 8, 54

Johns Hopkins University Hospital, 34, 79

Johns Hopkins University School of Medicine, 46, 170

Johnson, Charles S., 96, 104, 112; on southern black character, 13, 95, 167; as parent, 41–43; and Harry Stack Sullivan, 42, 44, 101, 209 (n. 103); as author of *Growing Up in the Black Belt*, 44, 78, 95, 101, 167; on personality, 95, 111–12; as student of Robert Park, 96, 97, 100; as southern black intellectual, 103–4; in *Brown* appeal, 104; and folk concept, 111–12; analysis of psychology of skin color, 169

Johnson, Lyndon, 114

Johnson, Robert Burgette, 33; and relationship with family, 41–43

Journal of the National Medical Association, 172, 180

Judaism, 118, 127. *See also* Jews

Jung, Carl, 25, 41, 137

Kardiner, Abram, 157–58, 166, 169, 175

Kennedy, Janet, 171

Kennedy, John, 149

Kent College of Law, 77

Kierkegaard, Søren, 144

Killers of the Dream, 38, 39, 152

Kilpatrick, James Jackson, 183

King, Martin Luther, Jr., and psychology, 150–51, 271 (n. 123)

King, Martin Luther, Sr., 138, 141

Klein, Melanie, 137

Klineberg, Otto, 183, 243–44 (n. 65)

Kubie, Lawrence: racial liberalism of, 39; friendship with Lillian Smith, 39–41; as observer of psychiatric training at Emory, 134, 136, 138; on color and prejudice, 170

Kuklick, Bruce, 82

Ku Klux Klan, 17, 87, 90

Lamarck, Jean-Baptiste de, 231 (n. 114)

Lanier, Lyle, 65, 99

Lanterns on the Levee, 13, 25, 115

Laurel Falls Camp, 65–66

Le Bon, Gustave, as author of The Crowd, 91, 93

Lewis, Sinclair, 91

Liberalism: racial, 152, 170, 175; and nurture argument, 184

Life, 148, 149

Louisville, Ky., 103, 142

Loyola University (New Orleans), 122, 123, 255 (nn. 19, 21)

Luther, Martin, 143

Lutheran Church, 149

Luton, Frank, 133; reports on Tennessee mental hospitals, 29, 78–79; training of, 46; friendship with Merrill Moore, 46–47; psychiatry teaching of, 70, 72, 74, 76, 80–81; as therapist, 72–73, 76, 80–81; religious views of, 73; as advocate for psychiatry, 75, 76, 77; and rural mental health care, 76, 77–78; limited achievement of, 76–77, 78; on desegregation, 163–64, 165

Lyman, Richard S., 123; and psychiatry at Duke, 85, 121–22, 253 (n. 10); professional training of African Americans, 85, 122, 232 (n. 118); as mentor of Bingham Dai, 120, 252 (n. 8)

Lynching, 88, 159; and southern violence, 14, 90; and mentally ill, 26, 92; as symbol of white primitivism, 89–90, 92; southern white views of, 91–93; southern black views of, 92, 93–94. See also Mob psychology

"Lynchings, Fears, and Folkways," 107–8

Lynd, Helen, 31

Lynd, Robert, 31

MacDonald, Michael, 25

Malcolm X, 173

Malone, Patrick, 139, 140

Malone, Thomas, 139, 140; psychiatric ideas of, 28, 135; training in psychology, 132; as therapist, 135, 138; and Freudian language, 137; racial attitudes of, 138; as teacher, 139

Mankind Quarterly, 176, 183

Marett, R. R., 109

The Mark of Oppression, 157–58, 166, 175

Marks, Eli, 101

Marshall, Thurgood, as NAACP attorney, 93

Massachusetts Institute of Technology, 91

Maury, Mary Cash, 35

Mays, Benjamin, 11, 12, 51, 138

Mays, Hezekiah, 12

McDougall, William: racial views of, 82, 84, 85–86, 232–33 (n. 120); as advocate of science, 82, 84–85, 86, 230 (n. 110); as chair of Duke psychology department, 82, 85; attitude toward the South, 82–84; as Lamarckian, 83, 231 (n. 114); and parapsychology, 83–84; psychological ideas of, 83–86; as therapist, 85

McGill, Ralph, 38–37

McGurk, Frank, 176, 177, 178, 179, 182, 183

McLaurin, Melton, 9, 11, 20–21, 29

McPherson, Aimee Semple, 146

Mead, George Herbert, 124

Medical Association of Georgia, 135

Medical Committee against War, 163

Medicare, 173, 186

Medications. *See* Therapies

Medicine. *See* Physicians; South: suspicion of medicine in; Therapies

Meharry Medical College: as southern African American medical school, 26, 28, 163, 186, 223 (n. 64), 276 (n. 30); fieldwork conducted by, 26, 78; Lloyd C. Elam at, 43, 162–63; Rafael Hernandez at, 48, 74, 76, 77; financial need of, 53; philanthropic support for, 70–71, 75; psychiatric treatment at affiliated hospital, 71, 79; psychiatry teaching at, 73–74, 77, 162, 225–26 (n. 74)

Melville, Herman, 137

Memphis, Tenn., psychiatric practice in, 26, 30, 44–45, 80, 81

Mencius, 125

Mencken, H. L., 35

Mendel, Gregor, 231 (n. 114)

Menninger, Karl, 38, 41

Menninger, William, 75–76

Mental illness: traditional views of, 19, 20–21, 25, 29, 30, 31–32, 49; and culture, 20; religious views of, 20–21, 141–45; home remedies for, 26; and racial assumptions, 70. *See also* Psychotherapy; Therapies

Mental institutions, in the South, 7, 21, 28–30, 133, 224 (n. 67)

Mental sciences. *See* Psychiatry; Psychoanalysis; Psychology

Merton, Thomas, 38

Methodism, 40, 47, 142; and Nashville medical schools, 72, 73, 74

Meyer, Adolf, 7, 34, 46

"Middletown," 31

Migration: out of the South, 2, 58, 88–89, 103, 113, 158, 166, 173, 186; of southern scholars, 4, 7, 103–4; of psychological professionals and ideas

to the South, 43–49, 82, 119–20, 126, 130, 131–32, 145, 154, 175, 179, 180; studies of, 112–13, 168

Mill, John Stuart, 31

Milledgeville State Hospital (Georgia), 7, 9, 22, 23, 133

The Mind of the South, 13, 21, 33

A Mind That Found Itself, 6, 8

Miracles, of healing, 144, 147

Miscegenation, 10, 13, 98, 156, 159, 165

Mississippi: education in, 6, 57, 60–61; Indianola studied, 98

Mississippi Delta, 22, 25

Mob psychology, 88, 90, 94; and racial stereotypes, 94

Modernism, 37

Moore, Merrill: as Fugitive poet, 46; as psychiatrist of Robert Frost, 46; as friend of Frank Luton, 46–47; as friend of Hanns Sachs, 46–47

Morehouse College, 11, 51, 93, 138

Morgan, L. H. (Lewis Henry), 106

Morrison, Robert, 135

Moton, Robert Russa, 17–19

Moynihan, Daniel Patrick, 114

Moynihan Report, 114

Mullowney, John, 73, 74, 75

Muse, Benjamin, 156

Mussolini, Benito, 183

Myrdal, Gunnar, 104, 158

Nankivell, Louise, 144

Nashville, Tenn.: early psychiatrists from, 46; psychiatry reform in, 53, 70–79, 86, 162; as center of black medical training, 79

Nashville City Hospital, 71, 79

Natchez, 101, 103

Nation, 107

National Association for the Advancement of Colored People (NAACP), 18, 88, 90, 92

National Institutes of Health, 162, 173

National Medical Association, 18

Nature: psychological theories focused on, 8, 9, 82, 88, 153, 170, 175, 176–78, 180–81, 183; and racial assumptions, 15, 27, 55–56, 64–65, 82, 84, 89, 93, 97, 153, 156, 165, 170, 178; William McDougall and ideas of, 84–85; Howard Odum and ideas of, 109–10; scientific focus on human, 175, 176. *See also* Nurture

Nazism, 122, 187; comparison to lynch mobs, 90; and folk theory, 108. *See also* Holocaust, refugee intellectuals from

Negroes. *See* African Americans

The Negro Family: The Case for National Action. See Moynihan Report

The Negro Family in the United States: folk analysis in, 113–14, 168, 173; and public policy, 114

Negro Youth at the Crossways, 95, 102, 113

Neighborhood Union (Atlanta), 30

Newby, I. A., 3, 8

New Deal: and southern education, 58; and social science, 88, 114

Newman, Israel, 47

New Negro, 105

New Orleans, La., 80, 101, 122, 160, 182; school desegregation in, 155

New Orleans Psychoanalytic Society, 80

New Republic, 160

New York City, 8, 105, 142, 166, 167, 171

New Yorker, 160

New York University, 65

Nietzsche, Friedrich, 38

North: views of the South in, 5, 104–6, 153, 159, 182–83; educational opportunities in, 7, 45–46, 48, 55, 100, 122–23; racial patterns in, 9, 166–67; psychological fields in universities in, 140; equation of racial identity and skin color in, 169, 174; interracial psychotherapy in, 170–72

North Carolina, 11, 20, 29

North Carolina College for Negroes, 61

North Carolina State Asylum, 29

N scale, 118

Nuremberg Laws, 121

Nurture: theories of, 1, 51–53, 82, 84, 88, 170, 175, 179; tested as psychological idea by *Brown*, 15, 153, 175; and hopes for children, 51–53, 66, 68; egalitarian message of, 52–53, 67; and racial assumptions, 53, 55–56, 89, 97, 152–53, 158; and black youth studies, 95; and power arrangements, 179; in postwar southern academy, 183–84; and northern liberalism, 184. *See also* Nature

Oak Ridge, Tenn., 131

Oates, Wayne, 150; critic of revivalism, 142; dissertation on Freud and Christianity, 142; at Southern Baptist Theological Seminary, 142; counseling ideas of, 142–43, 144

Odum, Howard: on race, 11, 107, 109–10, 116, 246 (n. 82); as student of G. Stanley Hall, 55; doctorate at Columbia, 56; textbook proposal of, 66–67; regional theory of, 89, 106–7, 116, 182; on folk psychology, 89, 106–10, 112, 113, 115, 181; on lynching, 90, 107–8; and William Graham Sumner, 108, 109; and Wilhelm Wundt, 108–9; and Freud, 109; and Gestalt school, 109; and black analysts of folk culture, 112–13; and public policy, 114; criticized by Wesley Critz George, 165

Ohio State University, 140

On Becoming a Person, 140

Osborne, R. Travis, 182, 183

Overholser, Winfred, 157, 229 (n. 99)

Ovesey, Lionel, 157–58, 166, 169

Oxford University, 83, 163

Parapsychology, 82, 84, 85, 232 (n. 117)

Park, Robert Ezra, 7; and Booker T.

Washington, 96; sociological theory of, 96; as mentor of doctoral students with southern careers, 96, 104; retirement at Fisk, 96, 120; on race, 96–97; as mentor of black doctoral students, 97; as mentor of Bingham Dai, 120

The Passing of the Great Race, 8

Pastoral counseling, 141, 143; ideas of Wayne Oates on, 142–43

Paul (the apostle), 143

Peabody College for Teachers, 53, 70, 85

Peiping (Beijing) Union Medical College, 120

Pennsylvania State Hospital for the Insane, 9

Pentecostal Holiness Church, 146

Pentecostalism, 118; and popular healing, 22; postwar healing revival, 119, 141, 150; therapeutic methods of, 141, 144, 147, 148; healing theology of, 144–45, 147, 150; psychological focus of postwar healing, 145; and millennialism, 145, 146, 149; origins in southern borderlands, 145–46; regional tempers, 146, 149; affinity with southern attitude toward doctors, 146–47; and conjure, 147; healers in, 147–48, 269 (n. 107); and frank discussion of mental problems, 148; and racial issues, 148–49, 266–67 (n. 90), 270 (n. 116); and politics, 149; charges of fraud, 149–50

Percy, Camille, 44, 45

Percy, Le Roy (of Birmingham), 7, 25, 44

Percy, Mattie Sue Phinizy, 25

Percy, Walker, 186; on mental illness, region, and faith, 187–88

Percy, William Alexander: on southern manners, 13, 25; on black psychology, 115

Personality: theories of, 88, 98, 157–58, 157–58, 187; biracial authorship of black youth studies of, 95, 100–101;

concept in black youth studies, 95, 101–2, 104, 111; and theology of Martin Luther King Jr., 150–51; criticism of theories after *Brown*, 153, 158

Peterson, Joseph, 65

Philanthropy, 4; and southern education reform, 51–53, 57–61, 66–68, 81, 217–18 (n. 29); economic goals of, 58; and racial attitudes, 60, 62, 66–68; and southern medical education, 70–71, 75, 81, 85, 130–31, 224 (n. 67); and social science research, 88. *See also* General Education Board; Jeanes Fund; Rockefeller Foundation; Rosenwald Fund

Phillips, William, 139

Philosophy, roots of psychology in, 1, 7, 30, 118

Phinizy, Mattie Sue. *See* Percy, Mattie Sue Phinizy

Phipps Psychiatric Clinic, 7

Physicians: southern suspicion of, 27–28; in southern communities, 27–28, 43; and treatment of mental illness, 28, 130–31, 133–34; and desegregation, 158–59, 163; of African American background, 158–59, 186

Plessy v. Ferguson, 2, 3

Pioneer Fund, 183

The Polish Peasant in Europe and America, 112, 113

Populism, 142–43

Poussaint, Alvin: in the South, 160–61; on psychology of civil rights workers, 161, 165; as therapist, 171; on nature and nurture, 176; on institutional racism, 179

Poverty: and medicine, 43; effects on schools, 57, 59–60

Powdermaker, Hortense, 98, 101, 239 (n. 36)

Power, as social variable, 153, 175, 179

Pragmatism, philosophical, 54–55, 112

Prejudice. *See* Racism

Primitivism, 106, 110, 115

Princeton University, 5, 91

The Principles of Psychology, 2

Progressive movement, and education, 53, 56, 59–60, 65

Protestantism: Calvinist, 21, 56; and childrearing, 56; evangelical, 118; liberal, 118; dominance in the South, 118, 141. *See also* Christianity

Provident Hospital (Chicago), 171

Provincialism: as image of the South, 5–6; as outlook, 14–15

Prudhomme, Charles, as first African American certified psychoanalyst, 49

The Psychiatrist and the Law, 157

Psychiatry, 125

Psychiatry: treatment options, 7–8, 36, 78–80, 133–34, 138; teaching in the South, 53, 70–77, 85, 120–21, 232 (n. 118); teaching at African American medical schools, 53, 74, 77, 162, 229 (n. 99); obstacles in the South to, 70, 72–75, 81, 86; and religion, 72–73; as profession, 76; as career choice, 132, 139, 159; and desegregation, 157, 162, 164

Psychoanalysis, 9; seen as Jewish system, 37; Hanns Sachs and, 46–47; in New Orleans, 80; and interpretation of the South, 98–99; southern doubts about, 99; and behaviorism, 100, 240 (n. 44); and authoritarian personality, 117; and Atlanta Psychiatric Clinic, 137; and Robert Coles, 160. *See also* Freudian psychology

Psychology: as academic discipline, 2, 4, 5–6, 43, 140, 154; laboratories, 2, 6, 85; as component of southern teacher training, 6, 61, 62, 67; early practitioners of, 6–7; in southern colleges, 9, 30–31, 62, 85, 123–24, 183–84; and religion, 20, 56, 142, 216 (n. 21),

250–51 (n. 5); early transmission of ideas to the South, 43–43; nurture as theory of, 51–53, 88, 153, 175; egalitarian implications of, 52–53, 67; and Progressive education, 53–54, 57; and racial distinctions, 55–56, 63, 65, 152–53, 176–78; social conservatives and, 82–83, 152–54, 175, 176–79, 182–83, 281–82 (n. 73); and defense of segregation, 86, 152–53, 175; social theories of, 88, 180–82; and mob theory, 89–94; in black youth studies, 95, 100–102; modest southern influence on, 104, 153–54; and folk analysis, 108; existential, 118; challenged by desegregation, 152–55, 159, 165; spread of ideas in the South, 153, 185; reassertion of natural differences between races, 176–78. *See also* Selfhood; Testing

The Psychology of Social Movements, 90

Psychotherapy: for children, 7, 21–22, 66, 78, 102–3; and social class, 7–8, 44, 79–81; southern skepticism of, 32–33, 43; and medication, 78–79, 173; verbal forms of, 79, 80, 133–34, 136, 173; private practice of, 80, 81, 134, 137, 138, 229–30 (n. 101); involving nonwhite patients, 98, 99, 102–3, 124–25, 138, 173, 256 (n. 27); experiential, 131, 133, 136, 138, 140; experimentation during World War II, 131–32; clinical tradition and social justice, 156–57; interracial, 161, 170–73; and personal approach to color, 169

Puckett, Newbell N., 110, 247 (n. 85)

Putnam, Carleton, 156, 182, 183

Race: as analytical category, 3, 4, 5, 165–66, 166–67, 171; as scientific variable, 8–9, 19, 54, 95, 103, 104, 153, 156, 169; seen as personal trait, 153, 167, 168–

69, 174; seen as neurosis, 169, 170; re-definition as natural trait, 170, 184
Race and Reason, 156, 182–83
Races: interdependence of, 10–11; disruption of white authority in healing, 20, 27; symbiotic view of, 89–90
The Races of Man, 63
Racial attitudes: of northern philanthropists, 60; of conservative psychologists, 82, 152, 153, 154, 176–78; and liberalism, 107; and social science, 116; of Pentecostal healers, 148–49
Racial theories, of personality, 19, 95, 152–53, 157–58. *See also* African Americans: racial character attributed to
Racism: as international issue, 3; in professions, 4, 7, 48, 70, 74, 77, 103, 157, 160, 163; in medical care, 4, 70, 74; in white assessment of black capacity, 9, 19, 53, 62, 70, 73–74, 81, 93; and personality damage, 95, 104; black protest of, 105; and social research, 115, 184; and authoritarian personality, 118; in China missions, 125; as distinct from segregation, 157–58; and civil rights, 161; as national trait, 161, 166, 174; clinical responses to, 170–72; institutional, 179
Rainbow round My Shoulder, 11, 110
Ramsay, R. C., 44–45
Randolph-Macon Woman's College, 153, 179
Rank, Otto, 41
Ransom, John Crowe, 46
Raper, Arthur, 91–92, 93
Reconstruction, 115, 122
Redfield, Robert, 106
Regionalism: importance of place, 5; and neglect of the South, 5, 103, 119, 173–74, 182, 183–84; and social science, 89, 95, 106, 183–84; and folk psychology, 106; as component of racial

identity, 153, 171, 174; and decline of southern distinctiveness, 153, 186; in fiction of Walker Percy, 187–88
Reid, Ira, 102, 104
Religion: southern, 3, 117; and assumptions about mental illness, 21–22; and character formation in children, 65; and existential psychology, 117–19, 250–51 (n. 5); and science, 188. *See also* Christianity
"The Responsibility of the Psychiatrist in Desegregation," 164
Rhine, J. B., 84, 85
Richmond News Leader, 100, 183
Riverside Hospital (Tennessee), 79
Roberts, Oral: as healer, 144, 145, 148; ministry in the South, 146, 148; entrepreneurship of, 146, 148, 149
Rockefeller Foundation, 51; as sponsor of psychological professionals of color, 48; and reform of southern medical schools, 71–72, 79, 80, 85; and rural mental health, 78; and Yale University, 97–98; and psychiatry teaching at Emory, 130–31, 134, 135
Rogers, Carl, 118; and Atlanta Psychiatric Clinic, 139–40
Roman, Charles Victor, 28
Roosevelt, Franklin Delano, 74
The Roots of Psychotherapy, 28, 135, 135–36, 137
Rope and Faggot, 10, 90
Rosenwald Fund, 58, 60, 74
Rotary Club, 78, 135
Rural life: and education, 59, 77; and psychological care, 76, 77–78; and social workers, 142. *See also* Migration
Rural Negro Health, 78

Sachs, Hanns, 46–47, 98
St. Elizabeth's Hospital, 8, 22, 157, 229 (n. 99)

St. Johns University (Shanghai), 125

Sanitariums, in Memphis, 44–45, 80. *See also* Mental institutions, in the South

Sapir, Edward: at University of Chicago, 96, 97; cultural theory of, 97; Yale seminar on culture and personality, 97–98, 120, 125

Saul, Leon, 124, 125

Scarritt College for Christian Workers, 74; and social work education, 71, 142; and philanthropies, 72; and racial liberalism, 178, 225 (n. 70)

Schools: physical conditions of, 57, 60, 61, 68; in rural communities, 59–60; desegregation of, 153, 154–55, 159, 176. *See also* Education; Teachers

Science: objectivity as goal of, 4–5, 167, 185–86, 281 (n. 70); and race, 19, 55, 63, 156; and religion, 20, 72, 119, 125, 143, 149, 150, 188; and asylum reform, 29; and social reform, 70, 72, 82, 167, 178; seen as source of progress, 111; restrained by culture, 154; experimentation in, 167; as method of conservative psychologists, 177–78, 183–84

Segregation, 157, 173, 186; as social system, 2, 10; as psychological system, 2, 9–14, 154, 155, 174; as legal system, 2, 24, 152, 153, 154; as deterrent to psychological investigation, 3–4, 185; in colleges, 9, 43–44, 48, 101, 121–22, 127, 130, 167; and childrearing, 11–12, 42, 101; and emotion, 13–14; and southern identity, 14–15; and medical profession, 43–44, 77, 158, 163, 186, 229 (n. 99), 276 (n. 30); in hospitals, 44, 77, 79, 80, 133, 158, 163, 171, 273 (n. 12), 279 (n. 53); and school reform, 51–52, 61; and nature-nurture debate, 55–56, 153, 184; as deterrent to southern psychiatric reform, 69, 73–75, 81; and spatial separation, 74–75, 155, 194 (n. 24); defended by psychological theory, 86, 93, 152–53, 165; and psychology of black youth, 88, 95, 100, 101, 104; dangers of discussing, 89, 93–94, 154, 158; Freudian interpretation of, 98–99; and theory of folkways, 106–7, 112–13; religious responses to, 119–20, 150–51; and racial classification, 121, 130; dismantling of, 152–54; socially replicated in the North, 166–67, 174

Selfhood: psychological theories of, 1, 6, 19, 24, 185; and segregation, 2, 9–14, 52–53, 95, 114–16, 154, 174, 184, 185; and southern education reform, 53, 86; as subject of intellectual conflict during desegregation, 153

Seventh-Day Adventists, 45

Sexuality: and treatment of mental illness, 73; in mob studies, 90; in interpretations of the South, 98, 113, 156; in interpretations of prejudice, 158

Shadow of the Plantation, 111–12

Shuey, Audrey, 164, 178, 182, 183; on racial psychology, 152–53, 177–78; on Jewish ethnicity, 177; method of, 177–78; move to the South, 179; as female conservative professional, 281–82 (n. 73)

Slavery, 9, 24, 113, 173–74

Smith, Ellison ("Cotton Ed"), 93, 115

Smith, Lillian, 21, 27, 32, 33, 43; on racial prejudice as psychological disorder, 38, 152–53; cancer of, 39; friendship with Lawrence Kubie, 39–41; view of mental disorders, 40–41; reading in psychology, 41, 66; as camp director, 65–66; on lynching, 90; self-reflections of, 152

Smith College, 21

Social class: and psychiatric treatment, 7–8, 44–45, 79–80; and race, 75; and elite support of psychiatry, 75–76, 81

Social Darwinism. *See* Evolution
Social and Mental Traits of the Negro, 110
Social Psychology, 91, 181
Social Science Forum, 126, 127, 257 (n. 33), 258 (n. 41)
Social sciences: as agent of reform, 86, 87, 98, 115, 167; popular subjects in, 88; racial division of labor in, 93; folk concept in, 115; and ethics, 119, 127, 130; adaptation of southern field methods, 167–68; rise of racial conservatism in, 176
Sociology: of lynching, 92; and psychoanalysis, 98–99; of black nurture, 101–2
The Sound and the Fury, 31
South: out-migration from, 2, 58, 88–89, 103–4, 113, 158, 166, 168, 173, 186; demography of, 2, 285–86 (n. 1); as subculture, 3; as haven for racially conservative psychologists, 4, 9, 82–83, 154, 178–79, 182–83; as symbol of American problems, 5, 87, 90, 105, 153, 154, 162, 174; provincialism of, 5–6, 106; mental institutions in, 7, 21, 28–30, 133; literary memoirs in, 10; evasiveness in, 12–13, 88–89, 93–94, 115–16, 150, 154, 162, 165, 184, 188; definition of, 14; violence in, 14, 88, 90, 98–99, 156; traditionalism of, 20, 31, 106–7; religion and illness in, 21–24; suspicion of medicine in, 27, 32, 70, 81, 146; physicians in, 27–28, 43, 158–59; public schools in, 51–53; poverty in, 57; in-migration to, 82–83, 86, 119–20, 130, 131–32, 186, 285–86 (n. 1); northern studies of, 95, 98, 105–6, 110–11, 161–62; inattention to, 103, 104, 153–54, 166; folk ideal and, 106–7, 115–16; piety of, 117–18; religious minorities in, 119, 121–22; psychological professionalism in, 140;

decline of regional distinctiveness, 153, 161, 186; desegregation in, 154–56; as state of mind, 166–67; praised for white racial dominance, 182–83
South Carolina, 12, 25; physicians in, 43; education in, 56, 57, 59–60, 67–68
South Carolina Lunatic Asylum, 29
Southern Agrarianism, 37, 72, 99
Southern Baptist Theological Seminary, 142
The Southern Case for School Segregation, 183
Southern Commission on the Study of Lynching, 91
Southern Education Board (SEB), 58
Southern Medical Association, 70
Southern Parish, 126, 130
Southern Regional Council, 156
Southern Society for Philosophy and Psychology, 7
Southern Sociological Society, 183–84, 283 (n. 80)
Spelman College, child development program at, 62
Starr, Milton, 47
Stein, Gertrude, 95
Sterilization. *See* Eugenics
A Study of Courage and Fear. See Children of Crisis
Suicide, southern attitudes toward, 25
Sullivan, Harry Stack: acquaintance with Charles S. Johnson, 42, 209 (n. 103); acquaintance with Percy family, 44; and black youth studies, 44, 101; friend of Edward Sapir, 96, 97; interpersonal theory of, 97; mentor of Bingham Dai, 120, 124; teacher of Rives Chalmers, 132
Summer camps, and psychology, 65–66
Sumner, Francis C.: as student of G. Stanley Hall, 9, 55; and Kenneth and Mamie Clark, 243–44 (n. 65)

Sumner, William Graham, 106, 108, 181

Supreme Court, 104, 153, 156. See also *Brown v. Board of Education*

Sutherland, Robert L., 97, 102, 103

Tannenbaum, Frank, 90, 91, 94

Tate, Allen, 72

Teachers: exposure to psychology, 55, 61, 62, 67, 180; professionalism of, 61, 67–68; and desegregation, 155

Teachers College (Columbia University), 52

Tennessee, and public support of mental health, 76, 133

Tennessee Agricultural and Industrial College, 70, 74, 77

Ten Years of Prelude, 156

Testing: of intelligence, 19, 65, 85–86, 152, 170, 176, 177–78; of personality, 105; and personal approach to color, 169; and race, 170, 152, 176, 221 (n. 51)

The Testing of Negro Intelligence, 152, 177–78, 182

The Thanatos Syndrome, 187–88

Thayer veterans' hospital (Tennessee), 79

Therapeutic culture, 67

Therapies: eugenic ideas in, 29, 81; electric shock, 36, 79; medications in, 36, 79, 172–73; of Seventh-Day Adventists, 45; Asian, 48; verbal, 79, 80, 133–34, 136; faith-based, 141–51. *See also* Psychotherapy

They Studied Man, 175

Thomas, W. I. (William Isaac), 7, 106; on peasant character, 112–13, 168

Thorndike, Edward, 214 (n. 9)

Tildon, Toussaint, 18 (ill.), 49

Tillich, Paul, 40, 118, 144

Time, 92, 93, 105, 150, 177

Titchener, Edward Bradford, 202 (n. 47)

Totalitarianism, 98, 108. *See also* Nazism

Tougaloo College, 6, 121, 122; religious tradition at, 123–24; psychology teaching at, 123–24, 255 (n. 21); Social Science Forum, 126, 127

The Tragedy of Lynching, 91–92, 93

Trinity College (North Carolina), 83

Tulane University, 79

Tuskegee Institute, 17, 96, 101

Tuskegee Veterans Administration Hospital: controversy surrounding, 17–19, 196 (n. 1); first African American psychiatrists at, 17–19, 197 (n. 4); syphilis experiment at, 49

Twain, Mark, 31

Tylor, E. B., 106

U.S. Air Force, 159

U.S. Army, 77, 121, 132

U.S. Congress, 92–93

U.S. Navy, 132

U.S. News and World Report, 179

U.S. Public Health Service, 49

University of Alabama, 87, 88

University of Arkansas, 67

University of Chicago, 34, 41, 46, 100, 103, 120, 121, 139; culture and personality theories at, 95–97; folk concept at, 112

University of Georgia, psychological study at, 9, 30–31, 182

University of Jena, 121

University of Louisville School of Medicine, 143

University of Minnesota, 105

University of Mississippi, 19, 57

University of North Carolina, 92, 122; Howard Odum at, 106, 114; Wesley Critz George at, 164–65

University of North Carolina Press, 87–88

University of North Carolina Woman's College, 61

University of Tennessee College of Medicine, 45, 80
University of Virginia, 8–9, 63, 179
University of Wisconsin, 131, 140

Vance, Rupert, 114
Vanderbilt University, 72, 99
Vanderbilt University School of Medicine, 29, 46, 163; philanthropic support for, 70–71, 72, 75, 79; treatment provided by, 71, 78–79; psychiatry teaching at, 72, 76; judged as hub for southern medicine, 79
Veterans Administration (VA), 17; and desegregation of hospitals, 77, 157
Veterans Administration Hospital no. 91. *See* Tuskegee Veterans Administration Hospital
Victorian science, 19, 156. *See also* Evolution; Science
Villanova University, 179
Virginia: as site of first southern state mental institution, 28; literacy in, 61; education in, 67, 68, 178
Voice of Healing, 149

Wallace (Alcoholic) Sanitarium, 26
Ward, Joseph H., 17
Warkentin, John, 131–32, 133, 134, 135, 138, 139–40
Warner, W. Lloyd, 95, 103, 169, 241 (n. 51)
Warren, Robert Penn, 46
Washington, Booker T., 17
Washington, D.C., 8; psychiatric treatment in, 22, 157; study of black youth in, 103, 105; psychiatric study in, 132
Watson, James, 175
Watson, John B., 7, 34, 46
Watts, Frederick, 157
Weiss, Avrum, 140
Western Behavioral Sciences Institute, 140

Western culture: psychology of self in, 1, 9, 124; attitude toward race in, 3, 55–56; distrust of solitude in, 24–25; mind-body dualism in, 108; folk customs in, 115
Whitaker, Carl, 140; and psychiatric training of doctors, 28, 134; therapeutic ideas of, 130, 131, 132, 133, 135–36, 138; training and career of, 131–32, 136; scientific orientation of, 135; as therapist, 135, 138; and Freudian ideas, 137; as administrator, 139; as churchgoer, 141
White, Walter, 10; on lynching, 90, 91, 93; as proponent of national anti-lynching law, 92–94; denounced in Senate, 93
White, William Alanson, 7, 229 (n. 99)
White Citizens' Councils, 156
White race: as subject of lynching studies, 89, 94; seen as guardians of civilization, 89–90, 182; image of primitivism of, 89–93; young people of, 106; social science neglect of, 115
White Wing Messenger, 144, 147, 149
Whitman, Walt, 137
Williams, Ernest Y., 48
Williamsburg, Va., 28
Williamson County, Tenn., 78
Wings on My Feet, 110
Witchcraft. *See* Conjure
Witmer, Helen, 21–22
Woodworth, Robert, 214 (n. 9)
Work, Monroe, 101
World War I, 27, 30; African American soldiers in, 17; mentally disabled veterans of, 17–19; army IQ testing during, 19; as catalyst of social violence, 90
World War II, 47, 51, 90; and refugee intellectuals, 46–47, 117, 119, 120, 121, 130; and racial liberalism, 107,

152; and existential psychology, 118; and experimental therapies, 120–21, 131–32; and rise of racial conservatism, 176

The Wretched of the Earth, 179

Wundt, Wilhelm, 31, 43, 202 (n. 47); folk psychology of, 108

Xavier University (New Orleans), 126

Yale University, 99–100; infant behavior laboratory, 62; culture and personality seminar, 97–98, 120, 125

Yeats, William Butler, 137

Yerkes, Robert M., 221 (n. 51)

Znaniecki, Florian, 112